The Cambridge Companion to Elgar

Edward Elgar occupies a pivotal place in the British cultural
imagination. His music has been heard as emblematic of Empire and
the English landscape but is also the product of a private, introverted
sensibility. The recent success of Anthony Payne's elaboration of the
sketches for Elgar's Third Symphony has prompted a critical
revaluation of his music. This Companion provides an accessible and
vivid account of Elgar's work in its historical and cultural context.
Established authorities on British music and scholars new in the field
examine Elgar's music from a range of critical perspectives, including
nationalism, post-colonialism, decadence, reception, and musical
influences. There are also chapters on interpretation, including his
own (Elgar was the first major composer to commit a representative
quantity of his own work to record), and on Elgar's relationships
with the BBC and with his publishers. The book includes much new
material, drawing on original research, as well as providing a
comprehensive introduction to Elgar's major musical achievements.

The Cambridge Companion to

ELGAR

....

EDITED BY
Daniel M. Grimley and Julian Rushton

CAMBRIDGE
UNIVERSITY PRESS

PUBLISHED BY THE PRESS SYNDICATE OF THE UNIVERSITY OF CAMBRIDGE
The Pitt Building, Trumpington Street, Cambridge, United Kingdom

CAMBRIDGE UNIVERSITY PRESS
The Edinburgh Building, Cambridge CB2 2RU, UK
40 West 20th Street, New York, NY 10011–4211, USA
477 Williamstown Road, Port Melbourne, VIC 3207, Australia
Ruiz de Alarcón 13, 28014 Madrid, Spain
Dock House, The Waterfront, Cape Town 8001, South Africa

http://www.cambridge.org

First published 2004

Printed in the United Kingdom at the University Press, Cambridge

Typeface Minion 10.75/14 pt.   *System* LaTeX 2$_\varepsilon$ [TB]

A catalogue record for this book is available from the British Library

Library of Congress Cataloguing in Publication data
The Cambridge companion to Elgar / edited by Daniel M. Grimley and Julian Rushton.
    p.   cm.
Includes bibliographical references and index.
ISBN 0 521 82623 3 (hb) – ISBN 0 521 53363 5 (pb)
1. Elgar, Edward, 1857–1934 – Criticism and interpretation.   I. Grimley, Daniel M.   II. Rushton,
Julian.
ML410.E41C36   2004
780′.92 – dc22
[B]   2004047286

ISBN 0 521 82623 3 hardback
ISBN 0 521 53363 5 paperback

Contents

Notes on the contributors

Byron Adams is Professor of Music at the University of California, Riverside. He received his doctoral degree from Cornell University, and was awarded the first Ralph Vaughan Williams Research Fellowship in 1985. He has published widely on the subject of twentieth-century English music in journals such as *19th-Century Music, Music and Letters, Current Musicology*, and *Musical Quarterly*, as well as contributing essays to *Vaughan Williams Studies, Walt Whitman and Modern Music* and *Queer Episodes in Music and Modern Identity*. He was co-editor of *Vaughan Williams Essays* (Ashgate, 2003). Prof. Adams wrote four entries in the revised edition of the *New Grove Dictionary of Music and Musicians*, including those on Husa and Walton. In 2000, he was awarded the Philip Brett Award by the American Musicological Society for two essays that dealt with nationalism and homoeroticism in twentieth-century English music.

Robert Anderson was born in India and educated at Harrow and Cambridge. Director of Music at Gordonstoun School, he was also an associate editor of the *Musical Times* and has broadcast frequently. A professional Egyptologist, he has written the Elgar volume for the *Master Musicians* series (Dent, 1993); his *Elgar in Manuscript* was published in 1990 by the British Library, and his *Elgar and Chivalry* in 2002 by the Elgar Edition. He has also contributed to *Edward Elgar: Music and Literature* (Scolar, 1993), and was coordinating editor of the Elgar Complete Edition and Elgar Society Edition until 2004.

John Butt is Gardiner Professor of Music at the University of Glasgow, having previously held positions at the University of Cambridge and the University of California, Berkeley. He has published widely as a musicologist, particularly in the fields of Bach, the German Baroque, and the culture of historical performance. He is also active as a performer and has recorded the complete organ works of Elgar for Harmonia Mundi (France). He was the recipient of the 2003 Dent Medal of the Royal Musical Association.

Timothy Day is a music curator in the Sound Archive of the British Library. His publications include *A Century of Recorded Music: Listening to Musical History* (Yale, 2000) and a chapter on 'English cathedral music in the twentieth century' in *The Cambridge Companion to Singing* (2000). In 1999 he established the British Library's Saul Seminar series, *Studies in Recorded Music*, and in the same year inaugurated the Edison Fellowship scheme, to assist scholars who wish to carry out intensive work on the Library's collections of recordings of western art music.

Jeremy Dibble is Professor of Music at the University of Durham. His specialist interests in the Victorian, Edwardian, and Georgian eras are reflected in the two major books he has published on Hubert Parry and Charles Villiers Stanford and in his recent volume of Parry's violin sonatas for the Musica Britannica Trust. He has written on a wide range of topics including historiography, opera, and church music in Britain, and he has a keen interest in the work of Edward Dannreuther, Vaughan Williams, and Frederick Delius. He is currently working on a study of the life and music of John Stainer and a volume of Parry's piano trios for Musica Britannica.

Jenny Doctor's extensive work on the history of BBC music broadcasting has contributed to two books: *The BBC and Ultra-Modern Music, 1922–36: Shaping a Nation's Tastes* (Cambridge, 1999) and Humphrey Carpenter's *The Envy of the World: Fifty Years of the BBC Third Programme and Radio 3* (1996). She is currently working with the BBC Proms office on the preparation of a comprehensive database of works performed at the London Promenade Concerts for more than a century, and is a Research Fellow at Trinity College of Music.

Daniel M. Grimley wrote his doctoral dissertation on the music of Carl Nielsen at King's College, Cambridge (1998). After a research fellowship at Selwyn College, he taught at the University of Surrey before being appointed to a Lectureship in Music at the University of Nottingham in 2002. A specialist in Nordic music, he has recently edited *The Cambridge Companion to Sibelius*. Current projects include books on Grieg and on Landscape in Nordic Music, 1890–1930. He convened an Elgar conference with Christopher Mark at the University of Surrey in April 2002.

J. P. E. Harper-Scott completed a D.Phil. thesis on Elgar, Heidegger, Schenker, and meaning in music at Magdalen College, Oxford, under the supervision of Nicholas Marston and Suzannah Clark. Along with a special interest in the music of Elgar and Walton, his research focuses on musical analysis and hermeneutics.

Robin Holloway is a composer whose distinguished output over many years has gained him a firm place in the recent development of British music. His works include the opera *Clarissa*, three Concertos for Orchestra, a symphony commissioned for the Promenade Concerts in 2000, the dramatic ballad *Brand*, and a choral work based on *Peer Gynt*. His extensive writings on music include the influential study *Debussy and Wagner* (1978), contributions to Cambridge Studies on Haydn and Janáček, and a large selection of shorter pieces published in 2003, *Robin Holloway on Music: Essays and Diversions* (Claridge Press).

Christopher Kent, antiquarian, author, teacher, organist, and organ adviser, was born in 1949. He completed a Ph.D. on Elgar's sketches at King's College, London and subsequently joined the Department of Music at the University of Reading where he established an influential postgraduate course in Organ Historiography. He retired from this post in 2002 to devote more time to research, writing, and organ playing. He has published widely in relation to his interests in Elgar (*A Guide to Research*, 1993) and organography. A founder member of the editorial committee of the Elgar Complete Edition, he has also served as secretary of the British Institute of Organ Studies.

Charles Edward McGuire is Assistant Professor of Musicology at the Oberlin College Conservatory of Music, and has contributed articles to *19th-Century Music, Vaughan Williams Studies, The New Grove Dictionary of Music and Musicians* (second edition) and *The Elgar Society Journal*. He is the author of *Elgar's Oratorios: The Creation of an Epic Narrative* (2002). Besides Elgar and the oratorio, his research interests include the music of Ralph Vaughan Williams, film music, and nineteenth-century music festivals. Currently, he is completing a book on the intersection of nineteenth-century sight-singing methods, rational recreation, and Victorian moral philanthropy.

Diana McVeagh, an independent writer on music, published *Edward Elgar: his Life and Music* in 1955 and has since contributed to *Elgar Studies* (1990) and *Edward Elgar: Music and Literature* (1993). She wrote the entries on Elgar and Finzi for the *New Grove Dictionary of Music and Musicians* (1980, 2001) and on Delius for the forthcoming *New Dictionary of National Biography*. She has written for *The Times*, the *Musical Times*, and the *Times Literary Supplement*.

Christopher Mark is senior lecturer in music at the University of Surrey and co-founder and editor-in-chief of the journal *Twentieth-Century Music* (Cambridge). His research has centred on twentieth-century English composers, especially Britten, Tippett, and Roger Smalley. He is currently planning a large-scale study of melancholy in English music from Elgar to Birtwistle.

Julian Rushton retired as West Riding Professor of Music at the University of Leeds in 2002. Previously he taught at the University of East Anglia and the University of Cambridge. He is the author of *The Musical Language of Berlioz, Classical Music: A Concise History*, and Cambridge Handbooks on Mozart (*Don Giovanni* and *Idomeneo*), Berlioz: *Roméo et Juliette*, and Elgar: *Enigma Variations*. His *The Music of Berlioz* was published by Oxford University Press in 2001. He has edited four volumes of The New Berlioz Edition including *La Damnation de Faust*, and for *Musica Britannica*, Cipriani Potter's Symphony in G minor (2001). He has written several articles and chapters on Gluck, Haydn, Mozart, Berlioz, and Elgar, and contributed to the *New Grove*, the *New Grove Dictionary of Opera*, and other works of reference. He was President of the Royal Musical Association, 1994–9, and is Chairman of the Editorial Committee of *Musica Britannica* and a trustee of the Elgar Society Edition.

Aidan Thomson was appointed Lecturer in Music at Queen's University, Belfast in 2003, having previously taught at the Universities of Leeds and Oxford. In addition to Elgar, his current research interests include the Internationale Musikgesellschaft before 1914, and the idea of the urban in early twentieth-century orchestral music.

Acknowledgements

The editors wish to thank all their contributors, including each other, for their work in this volume. Our thanks are also due to the Elgar Birthplace and the British Library for permission to consult their collections of Elgar manuscripts; to Robert Montgomery of the Elgar Will Trust, for his kind and prompt assistance with the cover illustration; to Charles McGuire; and to J. P. E. Harper-Scott for preparing the index. The Elgar Conference at the University of Surrey in April 2002, organised by Daniel M. Grimley and Christopher Mark, brought the editors into direct contact with several contributors. To Penny Souster of Cambridge University Press, for her kindly encouragement throughout the preparation of this volume, our especial thanks and best wishes in her retirement.

Daniel M. Grimley
University of Nottingham

Julian Rushton
University of Leeds
October 2003

Bibliographical abbreviations

Elgar's works and writings	
ECE	Elgar Complete Edition, London: Novello (1981–); continued as Elgar Society Edition, London: Elgar Society (2002–)
Future	Elgar (ed. Percy M. Young), *A Future for English Music* (1968)
Lifetime	Moore, J. N. (ed.), *Edward Elgar: Letters of a Lifetime* (1990)
Publishers	Moore, J. N. (ed.), *Elgar and his Publishers: Letters of a Creative Life*. 2 vols. (through-paginated) (1987)
Windflower	Moore, J. N. (ed.), *Elgar: The Windflower Letters* (1989)
Kennedy, *Portrait*	Kennedy, M., *Portrait of Elgar*. Page references unless otherwise specified are to the first/third editions (1968/1987)
Monk, *Literature*	Monk, R. (ed.), *Edward Elgar, Music and Literature* (1993)
Monk, *Studies*	Monk, R. (ed.), *Elgar Studies* (1990)
Moore, *Elgar*	Moore, J. N., *Edward Elgar, a Creative Life* (1984)
MT	*The Musical Times*
Anderson, *Elgar*	Anderson, R., *Elgar* (The Master Musicians) (1993)
Anderson, *Manuscript*	Anderson, R., *Elgar in Manuscript* (1990)
Kent, *Guide*	Kent, C., *Elgar: A Guide to Research* (1993)
Redwood, *Companion*	Redwood, C. (ed.), *An Elgar Companion* (1982)
Young, *Elgar*	Young, P. M., *Elgar OM* (1955)

Chronology[1]

Note: if a place and/or date is given, then a performance is alluded to; when a work is mentioned without these details, it refers to the period of composition. Premieres without an ascribed conductor were conducted by Elgar. London: CP, Crystal Palace; SJH, St James's Hall; QH, Queen's Hall.

Year	Elgar's life	Contemporary events
1857	Edward William Elgar born Broadheath (2 June). Baptised 11 June in St George's (RC), Worcester.	Wagner begins *Tristan und Isolde* (perf. 1865); Berlioz working on *Les Troyens* (perf. 1863)
1859	Family removes to Worcester.	Spohr dies. Darwin publishes *Origin of Species*.
1864–9	School; begins piano lessons (1864); first datable compositions (1867); begins violin lessons and studies composition theory (1869).	1866, Smetana *The Bartered Bride*. Verdi *Don Carlos*. 1868, Rossini dies, Brahms Requiem, Wagner *Die Meistersinger*; 1869, Berlioz dies.
1870–2	1872, plays organ at Mass in St George's. Apprentice to a solicitor (to 1873).	1870, Franco-Prussian War; fall of Napoleon III; Papal infallibility. 1871, Paris Commune; Verdi, *Aida*.
1873–5	1873, Credo on Beethoven symphony themes.	1874, Musorgsky *Boris Godunov*. Verdi Requiem. 1875 Bizet *Carmen*.
1876	Teaches violin; composing Latin church music.	Brahms First Symphony. Tchaikovsky *Swan Lake*. First Bayreuth Festival: complete *Ring* performances. Invention of phonograph by Edison.
1877	Violin lessons with Pollitzer. Learns bassoon to play wind quintets.	Brahms Second Symphony. Bruckner Fifth Symphony. Dvořák *Symphonic Variations*, Tchaikovsky *Eugene Onegin*.
1878	'Shed' music for wind. Attends Crystal Palace concerts. Mozart G minor symphony imitation.	Tchaikovsky Fourth Symphony, Violin Concerto.

[1] Fuller chronologies, including many details of works in which Elgar played, and many details of unfinished works, are in Stewart R. Craggs, *Edward Elgar, a Source Book*, and Anderson, *Elgar*.

1879–81	Directs and writes music for Powick Lunatic Asylum. Composes church music.	Brahms Violin Concerto.
1882	March *Pas redoublé* perf. (Worcester). Meets Charles Buck; holiday in Settle. Visits Leipzig (Dec.) to see Helen Weaver.	Wagner *Parsifal* (Bayreuth). Royal College of Music founded in London.
1883	Hears *Tannhäuser*. Returns to England; hears other Wagner, Berlioz Requiem. *Intermezzo moresque* perf. (Worcester, Birmingham). Engagement to Helen.	Wagner dies (Venice, Feb.). Brahms Third Symphony.
1884	*Sevillana* perf. (Worcester, London/CP). Engagement broken (July). In orchestra, Three Choirs Festival (Worcester): Dvořák conducts (*Stabat Mater*, Sixth Symphony). Resigns from Powick. Op. 1 (Romance in e, vn, pf.) pub. Schott.	.
1885	*Sevillana* perf. (Birmingham). Organist at St George's.	General Gordon dies in Khartoum. Brahms Fourth Symphony.
1886–7	1886, teaches Alice Roberts; 1887, ladies' orchestral classes.	1886, Liszt dies (Bayreuth, July). 1887, Verdi *Otello* (Milan).
1888	Suite in D perf. (Birmingham); Suite for strings perf. (Worcester), cond. Elgar. Composes *Salut d'amour* (July); pub. 1889 (Schott). Engagement to Alice Roberts (Sept.).	Franck Symphony in D minor. Parry *Judith*. Tchaikovsky Fifth Symphony. Wilhelm II Emperor of Germany.
1889	Married (8 May); sees *Die Meistersinger* in London. Begins sketching *The Black Knight*. *Salut d'amour* (cond. Manns, London/CP). Moves to London (Oct.).	Mahler First Symphony. Strauss *Don Juan*.
1890	Carice Elgar born (14 Aug.). First part-song pub. Novello. Suite perf. (London/CP); *Froissart* perf. Worcester (10 Sept.), cond. Elgar; pub. Novello.	Cardinal Newman dies (Aug.).

1891	*Froissart* perf. (Birmingham, Feb.). Removes to Malvern (Forli). Teaches at Rosa Burley's Mount School.	
1892	*Serenade for Strings*; *The Black Knight* (pub. Novello). Bayreuth, hears *Parsifal*	
1893	*The Black Knight* perf. (18 April, Worcester Choral Society).	Gounod dies (Oct.). Tchaikovsky Sixth Symphony; dies (Nov.). Dvořák Ninth Symphony. Verdi *Falstaff*.
1894	Begins *King Olaf*. Alice received into RC church. Bavarian holiday; Wagner performances.	Debussy *Prélude à l'après-midi d'un faune*. Nicholas II Emperor of Russia.
1895	*Scenes from the Bavarian Highlands*. Organ Sonata (8 July, Blair, Worcester). Bavarian holiday.	
1896	*Bavarian Highlands* perf. (21 April, Worcester Festival Chorus). Completes *King Olaf* (perf. 30 Oct., N. Staffordshire Festival, Hanley) and composes *The Light of Life* (perf. 8 Sept., Worcester: Three Choirs Festival).	Bruckner dies (Oct.); Strauss *Also sprach Zarathustra*.
1897	Composes *The Banner of St George*, *Imperial March* (both perf. April–May, London) and *Te Deum and Benedictus* for Hereford. Foundation of Worcestershire Philharmonic.	Queen Victoria's Diamond Jubilee. Brahms dies (April).
1898	*Caractacus* (perf. 5 Oct., Leeds Festival). Begins *Variations on an Original Theme*.	Strauss *Don Quixote*. Parry Symphonic Variations.
1899	*Variations* (cond. Richter, 21 June, London); *The Light of Life* revived (Sept., Worcester). *Sea Pictures* (5 Oct., Norwich Festival).	Second Boer War. Strauss *Ein Heldenleben*. Schoenberg *Verklärte Nacht*. Sibelius First Symphony.
1900	*The Dream of Gerontius* (cond. Richter, 5 Oct., Birmingham Festival). First Hon. Mus.D. (Cambridge, 22 Nov.).[2]	Sullivan dies (22 Nov.). Puccini *Tosca*.

[2] Elgar later collected honorary doctorates from Durham (1904), Oxford (1905), Yale (1905), Aberdeen (1906).

1901	*Cockaigne* (12 March, London/QH). Welsh holiday. *Pomp and Circumstance* Nos. 1 and 2 (19 Oct., Liverpool). *Grania and Diarmid* (21 Oct., Dublin). *Concert Allegro* (2 Dec., London/SJH). *Gerontius* perf. Düsseldorf (19 Dec., cond. Buths).	Queen Victoria dies (Jan.). Verdi dies (Jan.). Mahler Fourth Symphony.
1902	Composes *Dream Children*, *Coronation Ode* (perf. Oct., Sheffield). *Gerontius* perf. Düsseldorf to acclamation by Richard Strauss (May). Elgar's mother dies (Sept.); *Gerontius* perf. Worcester (Sept.). Meets Stuart-Wortleys.	Illness of Edward VII leads to postponement of coronation and Elgar's Ode which is given before Royalty only in June 1903 (it includes 'Land of Hope and Glory').
1903	*Gerontius* perf. London (June). *The Apostles* comp., perf. (14 Oct., Birmingham Festival) although apparently incomplete. Death of Alfred Rodewald (Nov.); holiday in Italy (Alassio, Nov.–Jan.).	
1904	*In the South* first perf. at Elgar Festival (London, Covent Garden, 14–16 March). Knighthood (June). Elgars move to Hereford (Plas Gwyn). Holiday in Europe with Frank Schuster.	Puccini *Madama Butterfly*. Mahler Fifth Symphony. *Entente cordiale*, alliance of Britain and France. Dvořák dies. Henry Wood's Queen's Hall Orchestra becomes London Symphony Orchestra. Strauss *Salome*. Russo-Japanese war and failed revolution in Russia.
1905	Hon. Mus.D. Oxford (Feb.). *Introduction and Allegro*, *Pomp and Circumstance* No. 3 (perf. 8 March, London/QH). Take up Peyton Chair in Music and gives first Birmingham lectures (16 March). Visits USA (June). Freedom of the City of Worcester. Mediterranean holiday including Turkey; lectures in Birmingham.	
1906	*The Kingdom* comp., reduced from original plan, which is eventually abandoned. 2nd visit to USA. *Kingdom* perf. (3 Oct., Birmingham Festival). Lectures in Birmingham. Holiday in Naples (Dec.–Feb.).	Delius *Sea Drift*. Mahler Sixth Symphony.

1907	3rd visit to USA. *Pomp and Circumstance* No. 4; *Wand of Youth* suites. String quartet and symphony sketches.	Grieg dies (Sept.).
1908	Visits Rome (May). Completes First Symphony (cond. Richter, 3 Dec., Manchester; 7 Dec., London/QH). Resigns Birmingham chair (Aug.).	Mahler Seventh Symphony.
1909	Visits Florence (April). Death of August Jaeger (May). Presidency of Musical League of Composers (Sept.).	Strauss *Elektra*. Delius *A Mass of Life*. Schoenberg composes *Five Orchestral Pieces, Erwartung*.
1910	Violin Concerto, Romance for Bassoon. Moves to London (58 Cavendish St., March), then holiday in Cornwall with Schuster. Concerto perf. Kreisler (10 November, QH).	Edward VII dies (May). Stravinsky *The Firebird* (Paris). Vaughan Williams *A Sea Symphony*.
1911	4th visit to USA (March). Second Symphony (24 May, London/QH). Appointed to Order of Merit (June).	Mahler dies. Stravinsky *Petrushka*. The Indian capital transferred from Calcutta to Delhi. Sibelius Fourth Symphony.
1912	Removal to Severn House, Hampstead. *The Crown of India* (from 11 March, London/Coliseum). *The Music Makers* (1 Oct., Birmingham Festival).	Parry Fifth Symphony. Schoenberg *Five Orchestral Pieces* first performed under Henry Wood (London/QH).
1913	Visits Naples (Jan.). Death of Julia Worthington (June). *Falstaff* (1 Oct., Leeds Festival).	Stravinsky *Rite of Spring*. Schoenberg *Pierrot lunaire*. Shaw *Pygmalion*.
1914	Jan., first recording for The Gramophone Company (*Carissima*). *Carillon* (7 Dec.).	4 August, war declared.
1915	*For the Fallen, Polonia*. Cumbrian holiday. *The Starlight Express* (first perf. 29 Dec./Kingsway Theatre).	Sibelius Fifth Symphony (first version). Strauss *Alpine Symphony*.
1916	*Une voix dans le désert* perf. (29 Jan.). Recordings of *Starlight Express*. Perf. *For the Fallen, To Women* (3 May). Cumbrian holiday.	Battle of the Somme. Hans Richter dies (May).

1917	*The Sanguine Fan* (20 March); *Le drapeau belge* (14 April); *The Fringes of the Fleet* (11 June); *The Spirit of England* (24 Nov.).	USA enters the war. Battle of Passchendaele. Russian revolution; Lenin withdraws Russia from the war.
1918	Moves to Brinkwells, Sussex. Chamber music; completes Violin Sonata (Sept.) and String Quartet (Dec.).	Debussy dies (March); Parry dies (Oct.). Puccini *Il trittico*. Armistice: end of war with Austria and Germany (Nov.).
1919	Completes Piano Quintet (Feb.); chamber music perf. (21 May); Cello Concerto (perf. Felix Salmond, 27 Oct./QH; recorded with Beatrice Harrison).	Treaty of Versailles; founding of League of Nations. Delius Violin Concerto. Holst *The Planets*. Strauss *Die Frau ohne Schatten*.
1920	Death of Alice Elgar (7 April).	Holst *Hymn of Jesus*. Ravel *La valse*. Stravinsky *Pulcinella*.
1921	Orchestrates Bach Fugue in C min. (perf. 27 Oct./QH, cond. Goossens). Removal to 37 St James's Place, London.	
1922	Carice marries Samuel Blake (Jan.). Bach Fantasia and Fugue perf. (7 Sept., Gloucester).	First music radio broadcasts. Vaughan Willams Third Symphony (*Pastoral*). Bliss *A Colour Symphony*. Bax First Symphony. Walton *Façade*. Nielsen Fifth Symphony. Stravinsky *Les noces*.
1923	Music for *Arthur* (Binyon, perf. 12 March). Move to Kempsey (Napleton Grange), south of Worcester. Orchestration of Handel Overture in D minor (2 Sept., Worcester). Cruise to the Amazon (Nov.–Dec.).	
1924	Master of the King's Music. *Empire March* and songs for *Pageant of Empire* (21 July).	Deaths of Busoni, Fauré, Puccini, Stanford. Sibelius Seventh Symphony. Shaw *St Joan*. Hitler imprisoned, writing *Mein Kampf*.
1925		Berg *Wozzeck* perf. Holst *Choral Symphony*.
1926		Shostakovich First Symphony. Puccini *Turandot* (posthumously perf.). General Strike in Britain.
1927	*Gerontius* recording. *A Civic Fanfare* (4 Sept., Hereford). Frank Schuster dies (27 Dec.).	Busoni *Doktor Faustus* (posthumously perf.). Stravinsky *Oedipus Rex*.
1928	KCVO. Removes to Tiddington House, Stratford-upon-Avon. Music for *Beau Brummel* (5 Nov.).	Janáček dies. Schoenberg Orchestral Variations. Stravinsky *Apollo*.

1929	Removes to Marl Bank, Worcester. Improvisations recorded (6 Nov.).	Vaughan Williams *Sir John in Love*. Walton Viola Concerto. Bax Third Symphony.
1930	*Severn Suite* (perf. 27 Sept., brass bands); *Pomp and Circumstance* No. 5; *Nursery Suite*.	Stravinsky *Symphony of Psalms*. Vaughan Williams *Job*.
1931	Created first Baronet of Broadheath.	Nielsen dies. Walton *Belshazzar's Feast*. Bax Fourth Symphony.
1932	Orchestration of Chopin, Funeral March. *Severn Suite* orchestrated. Violin concerto recorded with Menuhin (July); intimations of Third Symphony and opera, *The Spanish Lady*, neither of which he completed.	Delius *Songs of Farewell*. Bax Fifth Symphony. Ravel Piano Concerto.
1933	Flies to France, visits Delius (May). Work on Third Symphony. Falls seriously ill with cancer (Oct.).	Hitler comes to power.
1934	Recordings monitored by telephone (Jan.–Feb.). Dies 23 Feb.; funeral 26 Feb., Little Malvern RC Church.	Deaths of Holst (May), Delius (June). Vaughan Williams Fourth Symphony. Bax Sixth Symphony.

The Elgar Complete Edition (Elgar Society Edition)

A date signifies that the volume had appeared by the end of 2003. All were published in the Elgar Complete Edition (Novello) except Vols. 18 (*The Crown of India*) and 25 (*Wand of Youth*, *Dream Children*), which are published by its continuation, the Elgar Society Edition (ESE).

Series I: Choral works
Vol. 1. *Spanish Serenade*; *The Black Knight*; *From the Bavarian Highlands*
Vol. 2. *The Banner of St George*; *The Snow*; *Fly, Singing Bird*; *Pageant of Empire*
Vol. 3. *The Light of Life* (*Lux Christi*) (1989)
Vol. 4. *Scenes from the Saga of King Olaf*
Vol. 5. *Caractacus* (1985)
Vol. 6. *The Dream of Gerontius* (1982)
Vol. 7. God Save the King (arrangement); *Coronation Ode*
Vol. 8. *The Apostles* (1983)
Vol. 9. *The Kingdom* (1984)
Vol. 10. *The Music Makers*; *The Spirit of England* (1986)
Vol. 11. Sacred music, with orchestra
Vol. 12. Sacred music, unaccompanied or with organ
Vol. 13. Secular part-songs and unison songs

Series II: Solo vocal works
Vol. 14. Solo songs, with orchestra
Vol. 15. Solo songs, with piano (1)
Vol. 16. Solo songs, with piano (2)

Series III: Dramatic works
Vol. 17. *Grania and Diarmid*; *Arthur*
Vol. 18. *The Crown of India* (2004)
Vol. 19. *The Starlight Express*
Vol. 20. *Carillon*; *Une voix dans le désert*; *Le drapeau belge*; *The Fringes of the Fleet*
Vol. 21. *The Sanguine Fan*; *Beau Brummel*

Series IV: Orchestral works
Vol. 22. Short orchestral works
Vol. 23. Short orchestral works
Vol. 24. Music for string orchestra
Vol. 25. *Dream Children*; *The Wand of Youth* (2001)
Vol. 26. *Severn Suite*; *Nursery Suite*
Vol. 27. *Variations on an Original Theme* ('Enigma') (1986)
Vol. 28. Overtures
Vol. 29. Marches

1 Introduction

DANIEL M. GRIMLEY AND JULIAN RUSHTON

International interest in Elgar's music has enjoyed a general revival following the performance and recordings of his Third Symphony, properly entitled 'the sketches for Symphony No. 3 elaborated by Anthony Payne'. When permission was granted by the family for Payne to make his work public, understanding and perception of Elgar was permanently altered. Hitherto it was assumed that the death of Alice Elgar in 1920 had suppressed his creative urge, a view supported by the relatively small-scale works of his last decade, and their dependence on earlier sketches. It appears, however, that he was sufficiently restored not only to contemplate an opera (*The Spanish Lady*) and a new symphony, but to reach a stage in composing the latter from which a complete score could be elaborated – obviously not identical to what Elgar would have written, but rich in ideas and deeply moving in performance.[1] And if both symphony and opera depended in part on earlier sketches, research into Elgar's compositional methods shows that to be true of many, if not all, his greatest works (see chapters 4 and 5).

In fact the level of interest in Elgar among musicians, including musical scholars, was already high. Elgar has never been long out of public view, at least in Britain, where his music is a fixture at the Last Night of the Proms. The Jacqueline du Pré phenomenon, in which a young artist working with a senior conductor (Sir John Barbirolli) presented the cello concerto unforgettably, seemed to recreate the history of Elgar recording his violin concerto with the young Yehudi Menuhin; but we should not forget that the concerto was in the repertoire of senior cellists such as Paul Tortelier. One of the most encouraging features of recent years has been the interest taken in Elgar by conductors, scholars, and audiences from, for example, Russia, Germany, Japan, and the United States. The idea of Elgar as a composer culturally confined to Britain has taken a hard knock, and the question now often discussed is whether there is anything intrinsically English about his music at all (on this see below, and chapters 8 and 15).

This book is not a biography, but a Companion. Its role is not to reiterate facts and views in memorials of Elgar by those who knew him.[2] Nor is it a replacement for the scholarly biographies and life-and-work studies by, among others, Diana McVeagh, Percy M. Young, Michael Kennedy, Jerrold Northrop Moore, and Robert Anderson.[3] Probably the best way to get to know the composer, after listening to his music, is to read personal documents, and we are fortunate in having newly edited editions of a large selection of letters.[4] Nevertheless, besides offering a concise chronology, a Companion should offer a framework within which the chapters by independent scholars with individual viewpoints, can, independently, be read (and if, for instance, letters are cited more than once, it is because the chapters need not be read consecutively). This introduction therefore offers a review of essential aspects of Elgar's personality, life, and music and reflects on some of the principal themes in his historical reception.

Notes on a life

> I have worked hard for forty years & at the last, Providence denies me a
> decent hearing of my work: so I submit – I always said God was against art
> and I still believe it. Anything obscene or trivial is blessed in this world and
> has a reward – I ask for no reward – only to live & to hear my work. I still
> hear it in my heart and in my head so I must be content. Still it is curious to
> be treated by the old-fashioned people as a criminal because my thoughts
> and ways are beyond them.[5]

Elgar's revelations of his personal feelings need not be distrusted merely because they cannot be taken literally (forty years? the above was written when he was forty-three). Such outrageous assertions, like the later 'as a child and as a young man and as a mature man no single person was ever kind to me', come from very specific causes of bitterness and are too often taken out of context.[6] The 'work' mentioned in the first quotation is not his entire oeuvre, but *The Dream of Gerontius*, following its inept premiere in 1900. Providence had not denied him decent hearings of other pieces, notably, during the previous year, the 'Enigma' Variations and *Sea Pictures*. The second complaint was made in 1921 when he had not long lost his wife and helpmeet, and was feeling unable to continue his life's work. Both come from private letters; they are not considered statements. And the second contains, typically, an Elgarian contrast, for it comes after something no less quotable: 'I am still at heart the dreamy child who used to be found in the reeds by Severn side with a sheet of paper trying to fix the sounds and longing for something very great.'

Here is a richly suggestive inconsistency, and, in all probability, its share of nostalgic distortion. Yet however much one may unpick such confessions, they contain essential truths about Elgar, whose music is so suggestive precisely of longing, of aspiration, mingled, perhaps, with a sense of not quite being able to attain a goal: of hope more than confidence. It seems right, in a way, that his projected oratorio trilogy remained incomplete, with his heroes, the apostles, not yet having encountered the hardest paths and bitterest frustrations (see chapter 7). Several commentators, including some contributors to this *Companion*, consider the upsurge of energy that ends such magnificent works as the First Symphony, the violin and cello concertos, as well as the chamber music, to be an expression more of will than of confidence (see chapters 9, 10, and 11). Other works end quietly, in a state of suspense: in purgatory (*Gerontius*), or with a sunset glow (Second Symphony). Nowadays the concept of Elgar as an uncomplicated imperialist, a kind of musical Colonel Blimp or, worse, a Cecil Rhodes, is no longer tenable, if it ever was (see below, and chapter 16). Of course this cultured man, who loved to spend his holidays in Europe, also played his part in hymning England, Britain, and Empire; fraught with sentiment about the past, he was also a man of his time and a prominent public figure who was proposed for Mayor of Hereford, who eventually became Master of the King's Music when that title still meant, if not much, then something, and who was not only knighted, and made a baronet, but appointed to the Order of Merit, which has no more than twenty-four living members.[7]

Where did this man come from, and what was he up against? Elgar lived most of his life in the period which Bertrand Russell ironically christened that of 'Freedom and Organization'.[8] In mid-career, national and international events had a profound effect upon him and his musical output; they included wars, European and imperial, and changes of government; his life extended from the 'Indian Mutiny' to Hitler's rise to power. Rapid industrial and technological developments, which in his lifetime included electricity, the telephone, sound recording and broadcasting, cycling, the motor car, and air travel, affected him in all his professional activity. His last visit to France, when he visited Delius, was made by plane, and he continued active in supervising recordings of his music almost to the end.

'... as a child'

Edward William Elgar was born into a social stratum which it seems fair to identify as 'lower middle class'. Although his father ran a business (Worcester's music shop) he was also an artisan, a church employee who also tuned pianos, entering the grander houses by the rear entrance. Elgar never forgot, as he moved among the artists of the metropolis, and into wealthy, even aristocratic, circles, that he emerged from 'trade' (see also chapters 3 and 5). His aspirations extended to London's premier club, the House of Lords; in the event he had to be content with a baronetcy. It was no small achievement, and if Elgar was unsatisfied it is an indication of his restless temperament and socially unsettled character.

Still more than his class, Elgar's Roman Catholicism made him an outsider. His faith was the outcome not of centuries of resistance to the Protestant establishment, but of William Henry Elgar's expedient conversion in order to become organist of St George's Catholic Church in Worcester in 1846. The family (or at least, one infers, Ann Elgar) converted a few years later. The first two children, born in 1848 and 1852, were baptised as Anglicans; from 1854 they were baptised Catholic, including Edward in 1857. Although his faith progressively weakened, even ended, Elgar did not take the natural step for one aiming at social preferment by joining the Established Anglican church. The effects of Roman Catholicism are discussed below (see especially chapters 7 and 8).

'. . . as a young man'

A third cause of Elgar's sensitivity was his provincial origin. In fact, birth and upbringing in Worcester were less of a drawback than might be assumed, and not only because, in the age of the train, London was quite easily reached. But Elgar never formally enrolled as a music student, and his achievement in matching, and eventually providing a role model for, the products of the Royal Colleges of Music must have been sweet to him. Nevertheless some products of those schools were helpful (even kind) to him (see chapter 2). If he felt snubbed, an inbuilt tendency to paranoia was probably to blame. As a child of nineteenth-century Worcester, he was no more deprived of opportunities for self-education than a child of Shakespeare's Stratford. Contrary to what has sometimes been maintained, Elgar did not lack general culture, and his education, however much it may have been through precept and in the home (notably from his mother), was sufficient basis to develop his later passions for exploration, in literature and in chemistry.

In music, he studied excellent models. The current edition of the standard German music dictionary urges that the priority in Elgar studies should no longer be the man, or the national composer, but the music in its widest context, including continental influences.[9] In fact commentary on Elgar has always tended to emphasise the German influences so current in British musical life, notably, in Elgar's case, Wagner, Brahms, and his own younger contemporary Richard Strauss. But for Elgar, of course, the canonical status of composers was by no means as fixed as it now seems, and he learned from musical figures not now considered prominent; Basil Maine, in a biography published when Elgar was still alive, mentions composers already obscure by 1930, if not 1870, such as C. P. E. Bach, Schobert and Kozeluch.[10] In a searching discussion of Elgar's style, Diana McVeagh mentions Mendelssohn, Spohr, and Gounod among early formative influences.[11] He also learned from his English inheritance, mainly of sacred music (see chapters 2 and 8), and from overseas composers of marked national, but not Germanic, character, such as Dvořák and Bizet. According to Maine, Elgar also learned from treatises, benefiting from the publishing zeal of Novello, which offered English translations of Catel's harmony treatise, Cherubini on counterpoint,

Berlioz on orchestration, and the spurious 'Mozart' thoroughbass treatise, whose authenticity Elgar seems not to have doubted.[12] Elgar also learned by setting himself compositional exercises, many of which survive; sacred works based on Beethoven symphonies, a fragment of a symphony based on Mozart's in G minor, and so forth. Although he lacked the direct example of experienced composers as teachers, no music college would have provided a better education.

Another chip on Elgar's shoulder emerges from his frequent insistence on his own poverty and the poor rewards of composition, other than popular work such as *The Crown of India*. In common with other composers, such as Schumann and Sibelius, Elgar had aspired to become a virtuoso. He was surely aware of the greater financial rewards this pathway would have offered, but because of his late start with violin lessons, his aspiration was foredoomed. It was only when aged twenty that he sought out Adolf Pollitzer for advanced lessons in London. These had long-term benefits: mastery of an instrument contributed to mastery of the orchestra, and he came into contact with what was then the central, largely German, tradition of European music, anticipating later contact with Hans Richter and Strauss.[13] Pollitzer urged Elgar to move to London to further his career as both composer and violinist, and provided an introduction to August Manns, conductor of the Crystal Palace concerts, an influential early supporter of Elgar's music. As a result, Elgar the provincial was not only an artist with an explosive imagination, but also a consummate professional musician with the means to realise his conceptions to fullest effect.

Given his inspired handling of stringed and other orchestral instruments, it is perhaps surprising that Elgar's 'first' instrument was in fact the piano. He took to the piano from an early age, and gained local fame for his ability to extemporise on it. But the piano quickly became a working instrument, on which he learned to realise baroque figured bass, a practical skill that developed his sense of harmonic syntax. He rarely seems to have associated the instrument with an aesthetic sense of tone colour. In the first of his Birmingham lectures, for example, he suggested:

> Now the rigid piano is capable of only two *qualities of tone simultaneously in the hands of a moderate player* – and most players are that. Better performers are able to produce further effects by allowing one part (one voice) to predominate in each hand, giving us four distinct weights of tone. Beyond this the piano cannot go.[14]

Elgar's apparently utilitarian attitude to the piano is not supported by his own solo piano works such as the *Concert Allegro* (1901), written for Fanny Davies, or the atmospheric miniature *In Smyrna* (1905), nor by his writing for the instrument in the Violin Sonata and Piano Quintet.

The organ and violin were central to much of Elgar's music-making, not least through his membership of the Glee Club, a circle of amateur and semi-professional musicians who met in the Crown Hotel in Worcester to rehearse and perform informal concerts. Programmes for the Glee Club reveal that its repertoire was broad-ranging and eclectic, from Haydn symphony movements (performed with reduced forces), to chamber music by Beethoven and Schubert, operatic overtures and arias, music by Mendelssohn and arrangements of popular songs and dances. The existence of such groups in England was widespread and their significance has not always received due recognition. The Glee Club not only provided Elgar with his first practical experience of working within an instrumental ensemble, but also introduced him to a wide range of music from the Classical and early Romantic periods that had a powerful impact on his subsequent development as a composer. The majority of Elgar's early works were pieces of chamber music intended for himself and members of the Glee Club to play. The Club's repertoire provided good models of musical style and form, and Elgar's sketchbooks include various attempts to compose music for string quartet, violin and piano, and piano trio. Other works include seven large-scale suites for wind quintet, 'Harmony Music' (translating the German 'Harmoniemusik') christened 'Sheds' by Elgar after the space at the back of his father's shop where the group rehearsed.

Elgar was well qualified to teach the violin, and he wrote a number of pedagogical pieces in addition to a range of lyrical miniatures, light music intended for domestic use, a genre that he cultivated successfully throughout his career. As a professional fiddler, he played for Stockley in Birmingham and at the Three Choirs Festival, sometimes under important musicians, such as Dvořák. He organised music at the Powick lunatic asylum, and taught violin in schools, necessitating tedious and tiring travel. Competent on keyboards and the bassoon, he was able to take advantage of a varied musical culture that allowed him to work with amateur groups, small and large, as well as professionals, and he embarked on his conducting career with the Worcestershire Philharmonic. Amateur as well as professional musicians are included among the 'Friends Pictured Within' the 'Enigma' Variations, including some friends he acquired through his wife (see chapter 10); among the benefits of this peripatetic way of life were his encounter with Caroline Alice Roberts, to whom he taught piano accompaniment.

They were married in 1889. For several years teaching and playing were his chief sources of income. Mrs Elgar came from a higher social stratum but had only a modest inheritance; he was obliged to work hard to maintain a household in the comfortable middle-class style to which she was accustomed, with a small core of domestic servants. Their frequent changes of address reflect changing economic fortunes. In a first flush of optimism, they removed to London where their only child, Carice (the name compresses her mother's) was born in August 1890. During this time Elgar was more exposed to first-rate music-making, but he failed to make an impact on the capital.

Before his marriage to an older woman, who undoubtedly was kind to him, he had fallen in love with another violinist, Helen Jessie ('Nelly') Weaver. Recent investigations of this short-lived romance, which got as far as an engagement in 1883, have considerably changed our view of Elgar, and not only of his early years.[15] His letter to Charles Buck declining an invitation to his wedding, and informing him of the end of his own engagement, nearly explodes with suppressed emotion:

> You ask me to let you know 'soon' whether I can visit you & also be at the marriage feast: With many thanks & many regrets I must say 'nay' to both.
>
> I will not sorry you with particulars but must tell you that things have not prospered with me this year at all, my prospects are worse than ever & to crown my miseries my engagement is broken off & I am lonely.
>
> Perhaps at some future time I may come out of my shell again but at present I remain here; I have not the heart to speak to anyone.[16]

No doubt many Victorian engagements ended through religious and economic differences between the parties, and Elgar was perhaps fortunate that Helen's health, forcing her emigration to New Zealand, made a clean break. Throughout his life he remained dependent on the sympathy of women, of whom Alice was only, as she surely understood, the chief; Rosa Burley, Lady Mary Lygon, Julia Worthington, and Alice Stuart-Wortley (the 'Windflower'), whatever the precise nature of his relationship with them, were women who, like Alice, had a professional or social confidence Elgar lacked. His literary-minded mother, it appears, was closer to him than his musically professional father.

'. . . as a mature man'

Nevertheless, it was partly through marrying another literary woman, whose belief in her husband was absolute, that Elgar was eventually able to break out of the debilitating grind of the local musical professional.[17] When commissions came, they were for provincial festivals of national standing, notably the Three Choirs, for which living in Worcester became an advantage; the festival commissioned *Froissart* (1890) and *The Light of Life* (1896). *The Black Knight* was also first performed in Worcester, and with it (1893) Elgar was taken up by the principal British publisher of choral music (see chapter 3). Novello recognised Elgar comparatively early, and initially as a contributor to enduring traditions of cantata, oratorio, and part-song, rather than as someone revolutionary, and possibly subversive, within them (see chapters 6 and 7), still less as a composer of large-scale instrumental music. Then came festival commissions from Hanley (1896, *King Olaf*), Leeds (1898, *Caractacus*), Norwich (1899, *Sea Pictures*) and Birmingham (1900, *Gerontius*), by which time Elgar was a major national figure. These were years of exceptional activity, of which numerous letters to publishers in the 1890s and 1900s form an extraordinary record.[18] Elgar's relationship to Novello's editor August Jaeger ripened into a bantering friendship. Despite its later history as a kind of funeral ode, the variation devoted to Jaeger, 'Nimrod', is a testimony to a creative dialogue based on mutual respect, and fruitful in that Jaeger's advice was sound and his encouragement, as well as discriminating praise, could have a healing effect on the mortally sensitive composer. (Elgar's dependence on Jaeger need not, however, be exaggerated; his productivity remained at its highest level for a decade after Jaeger's death in 1909.)

Before *Gerontius*, the orchestral Variations ('Enigma') had been performed in London; and these two works formed the basis of Elgar's international reputation and consequent professional visits to Germany and America. The former, in particular, produced some fascinating reception literature (see chapter 15). Yet in the following decade, at the height of his powers and success, Elgar continued to experience exasperation and depression in the intervals between creative outbursts of extraordinary energy. His health was never considered robust, but his problems lay in the mind; he would not forget the *Gerontius* premiere just because *The Apostles* was better performed (under his own direction) and greeted with acclaim.

His huge oratorio project was never completed, despite its long prior gestation (see chapter 7). A curiosity of the reception of *The Apostles* is the dissenting voice of Ernest Newman; far from resenting this, and his harsh verdict on *The Kingdom*, not to mention Newman's critique of Elgar's Birmingham lectures, the composer channelled his creative energies in directions suggested by Newman, and advocated for British composers a decade earlier by the oratorio-despising Bernard Shaw.[19] Over ten years Elgar produced two symphonies, two concertos (of which the Violin Concerto is as long as a symphony), a masterpiece of programme music, *Falstaff*, three large-scale chamber works (see chapters 9, 10, and 11), and much else, notably the introspective cantata, *The Music Makers* (see chapter 5) and the wartime choral, patriotic and theatre music (see chapters 12 and 16). The major orchestral works tend to dominate recent Elgar performance and reception alongside the earlier overtures, Variations, and *Introduction and Allegro*. For practical reasons and as a result of changing tastes, the oratorio as a genre declined in Britain, with Elgar its greatest climax, while symphonic and related genres developed with startling rapidity (see chapters 9, 10, and 11). The excitement created by the revelation of Elgar's 'Third Symphony' was testimony to the continuing interest in a genre in which twentieth-century British composers were probably more prolific than those of any other nation, partly as a result of Elgar's example.[20]

Nearly every commentator on Elgar has nevertheless noticed a difference in nature between the works composed in the years before the First World War, notably the symphonies, the Violin Concerto, and *Falstaff*, and those composed at the end of the war, the Cello Concerto and chamber music. Elgar sensed, however, that he was going out of date in his own lifetime. He sometimes encouraged younger colleagues, and gained three of them commissions at the 1922 Three Choirs Festival, possibly not expecting to like the outcome (see chapter 2); at least he was showing the kind of support which, not quite honestly, he claimed never to have received.

A study of Elgar's prime, the twenty years from 1899, reveals a major, rather than an overwhelming, presence in concert programmes and in critical assessments. He survived better than his immediate seniors and contemporaries, and his influence may be felt even in students of Stanford; his importance was openly acknowledged by Vaughan Williams (who wrote of finding with astonishment 'how much I cribbed from him, probably when I thought I was being most original') and Holst (who dated the 'modern Renaissance' to the Variations: 'here was music the like of which had not appeared in this country since Purcell's death').[21] Elgarian gestures appear in composers as aesthetically remote as Finzi, while Walton, whose bright-young-thing image of the 1920s was alien to Elgar, became his natural heir in oratorio, string concertos, symphonies, and coronation marches. Elgar's legacy extends to lighter music, for example the pleasingly evocative tone-pictures, not to mention the marches, of Eric Coates.

Reaction to the works of 1917–18, and particularly the elegiac Cello Concerto (see chapter 11), suggests that Elgar had almost predicted the crushing blow that came with the death of Alice in 1920. Yet the silence of his last years was only relative, and some works (the Bach transcriptions, *Pomp and Circumstance* No. 5, the *Severn* and *Nursery* Suites) are substantial. But his activity was directed more towards reproduction than new creativity. He had recorded before the war, but his intense involvement with recording in his last years left a larger recorded legacy than any composer of his generation (see chapter 13). He was also interested in broadcasting, and thoroughly merited the BBC commission that the indefatigable Shaw eventually negotiated, for the Third Symphony (see chapter 14). Suffering cancer, he was ill for much of 1933 but was able to return home and resume work, some of it by telephone to the recording studio. He died on 23 February 1934 – reluctantly, one feels; the evidence of W. H. Reed, who was often by his side, suggests that he was still deeply concerned for the fate of his music, including unfinished pieces.[22]

Modernism/Empire/landscape

If, as Jeremy Crump has suggested, 'it requires an effort of some historical imagination to come to terms with the frequent contemporary comments on the startling modernity of Elgar's music', Elgar's work can nevertheless be understood as part of a broader modernist musical practice. Crump concludes that 'the emphasis placed on Elgar's modernity served to locate him within the European mainstream'.[23] James Hepokoski lists Elgar as a senior member of a 'generational wave' of European modernists born around 1860, including Mahler, Strauss, Sibelius, Nielsen, and Debussy, whose work reveals similar preoccupations with issues of colour, large-scale form, timbre, subjectivity (nature-mysticism and spirituality), and extended diatonicism, despite the diversity of their completed work.[24] Various commentators in this volume agree that Elgar's work draws freely and willingly upon continental musical models. The parallels with Strauss are well known: the opening of the overture *In the South*, for example, with its spirit of youthfulness and enthusiasm (lusty whooping horns) recalling *Don Juan* and *Till Eulenspiegel* (see Ex. 10.1), a mood recaptured from the (revised) ending of the 'Enigma' Variations. It is possible to find points of correspondence with other composers' music as well: Fauré and Franck, for example, in the chamber works. But Elgar's work particularly invites comparison with that of his modernist contemporaries, notably Strauss and Mahler, through its use of allusion, musical borrowing and self-quotation.[25] As in Mahler's music, these quotations and borrowings take several different forms, depending on their context. Elgar is especially fond of reminiscences of past musical styles such as the antique style of the first Dream Interlude in *Falstaff*, 'Jack Falstaff, now Sir John, a boy, and page to Thomas Mowbray, Duke of Norfolk' (fig. 76), or the use of neo-Baroque textures in the *Introduction and Allegro*, discussed in chapter 9. Other works are characterised by allusions to musical styles not normally associated with the concert hall, such as popular songs: the Italian 'canto popolare' from *In the South* is one such example, as is the distant sound of a brass band that marches through *Cockaigne*. Tunes whose direct simplicity of outline and harmonic syntax seem intended to appeal to a large popular audience are an integral part of Elgar's musical style: the most famous example is the trio from the *Pomp and Circumstance* March No. 1. Here, as in the Kipling songs, *Fringes of the Fleet*, the music's popular idiom cannot be regarded as a form of allusion. But elsewhere Elgar clearly seeks to frame such references so that they appear outside the boundaries of the musical work. The 'Welsh tune' in the *Introduction and Allegro* is a good example, where the allusion to a popular melody also serves to heighten the music's sense of distance and retrospection.

Compared with Mahler, Elgar's use of allusion and borrowing often sounds nostalgic or wistful rather than bitter or ironic. Elgar's use of self-quotation belongs in a separate category. Specific points of reference to other works, such as the foreshadowing of the First Symphony's opening melody at the close of the 'Enigma' Variations, for example, are coincidental (see Ex. 10.3). Elgar's working methods, as Christopher Kent observes in chapter 4, often followed a collage- or mosaic-like procedure in which compositions were assembled from various scraps of pre-composed material. Hence, some interconnection between individual finished works was inevitable. But in other instances, the use of self-quotation is more deliberate: *The Music Makers*, Elgar's problematic setting of O'Shaughnessy's Ode, discussed by Diana McVeagh (chapter 5), is a special example. The elision of 'Nimrod' and the close of the Second Symphony at the words 'wrought flame in another man's heart' (fig. 53), is particularly powerful, but it would surely be a mistake to reflect their appearance in the later work back upon their original musical contexts. There is also a tendency for the abundance of references to pre-composed music in *The Music Makers* to obscure the work's individual qualities: the brooding chromatic opening, the bold use of a whole-tone scale at fig. 25, and the virtuosic brass writing at fig. 82. Elgar's attempt to 'write himself' into his own music, by using reference to his own works to weave an autobiographical thread through his music, is partly a Romantic device that can be traced back to Schumann, a composer who had a formative influence on Elgar's early career. But it is also a more modernist trait: the artist as hero is a familiar image from the work of Strauss and Mahler, both of whom sought to portray aspects of their own creative experience in large-scale symphonic works.

For all its continental modernist characteristics, Elgar's music nevertheless remains closely linked with ideas of Englishness, Empire and the English landscape. The nature of Elgar's imperialism is addressed in chapter 16 by Charles McGuire in the context of his wartime works, the period when Elgar's status as 'National Composer' was perhaps at its highest. But it is also significant that Elgar grew up in a period when Englishness was being culturally and politically redefined by specific patterns of historical change. As Eric Hobsbawm has observed, between 1876 and 1915, Britain increased its dependent territories by approximately four million square miles.[26] Imperialism as a concept first entered political discourse in Britain in the 1870s, and became widespread by the 1890s when it became associated with military and economic expansion and defence, fuelled by the growth of global trade. This process coincided with the completion of large-scale academic projects such as the *New English Dictionary* (1884–1928) and the *Dictionary of National Biography* (1885–1900), which took part in a broader discourse on political, cultural and economic identity,[27] as well as the foundation of national musical institutions such as the Associated Board of the Royal Schools of Music (1880) and the Royal College of Music (1882). Elgar, of course, emerged from outside either academic or official musical institutions, and in many senses he remained an 'outsider', despite his later success. But his music supported the institutionalisation of an imperialist culture through a series of works written for ceremonial occasions that celebrated the idea of empire. As David Cannadine has argued, works such as the *Imperial March* (1897) or the *Coronation Ode* (1902) were an integral part of the attempt to legitimise a particular social and economic order: the democratic acceptance of the principle of hereditary monarchy which underpinned the British Empire.[28] Elgar was thus closely linked with the spectacle of Empire, large-scale public events or displays whose apotheosis was arguably reached in his music for the *Crown of India* masque performed at the London Coliseum in 1911. Though subsequent writers have often looked down on Elgar's ceremonial music as occasional work, of lesser intrinsic value than his 'abstract' symphonies or concertos, it nevertheless forms a substantial part of his output. Furthermore, Elgar's background, as a provincial musician who gained official recognition in spite of his lower middle-class origins, and his long-held Conservative monarchist views, suggest that he embraced this project with genuine commitment and enthusiasm even before the time of national crisis engendered by the First World War.

In his sustained discussion of Elgar's imperialism, Jeffrey Richards has argued that Elgar's vision of Empire, as articulated in both his ceremonial pieces and other musical works, was subject to two radical reinterpretations in the 1960s.[29] One was a melancholy reappraisal of the second half of his career from the Second Symphony through the chamber music to the Cello Concerto, an interpretation that paralleled the supposed climax of imperialism in the First World War and its subsequent decline, and created a strong sense of teleology in Elgar's work towards the supposed creative silence after his wife's death in 1920. The second was a shift from 'imperial pomp to rural domesticity', an interpretation that sought to elevate Elgar's nature mysticism over other more supposedly jingoistic aspects of his musical character. Both readings, Richards suggests, are largely unsustainable on the basis of a balanced examination of the historical evidence. But the link between Empire and landscape remains a particularly close one. Elgar's relationship with the English countryside, and the role that landscape played in the formation of Elgar reception in the twentieth century, deserves far more extended discussion than can be afforded here.[30] It needs to be emphasised, however, that landscape and nature are never neutral metaphors: they are as ideologically constructed as any other form of cultural practice. Hence, the image of landscape to which Elgar responded, and which his own works in some senses perpetuated, is itself a reflection of the same historical context that supported patriotic works such as the *Pomp and Circumstance* marches or *The Spirit of England*.

For the metropolitan press in particular, Elgar's regionalism was perceived as both a weakness and a strength of his musical achievement. Though it occasionally underlined his lack of official academic training, and hence his class background, Elgar's Worcestershire origins were more often seen as a sign of his music's authentic Englishness, as evidence of an autochthonous relationship with nature and the English soil. In the popular imagination Elgar's Worcestershire embodied a rural ideal, an image that was somewhat removed from the largely urban surroundings of Elgar's own childhood, and that is reinforced by the location of the Birthplace Museum in a village setting at Broadheath outside Worcester, where he had lived for barely a year. At the turn of the century, such images were especially powerful, as regionalism began to be associated with national identity and certain forms of cultural or racial purity. By the 1930s, Crump argues, the perspective had changed again, in that 'the retreat to rural values was consonant with the view of "sunset splendour" in the Edwardian Elgar, and coincided with a cultural conservatism, marked in music by the decline in the fashion for superficially experimental works such as Walton's *Façade* (1921)'.[31] This conservative reinterpretation, of Elgar's music as a nostalgic return to a lost rural Golden Age, is perhaps as much the cause of the subsequent decline in the reception of his work in the 1950s as the more obviously patriotic aspects of his music, yet it is a trope that remains strong in Elgar appreciation even today.

Recent writers such as Jerrold Northrop Moore have heard the topographical characteristics of the English countryside morphologically represented in elements of Elgar's musical syntax. Moore, for example, suggests that Elgar's sequential melodic writing 'resembles and suggests the patterns of nature in the countryside round Broadheath: gentle undulations of field and hedgerow, copse and dell – fruit trees planted in rows to make an orchard – the linked chain of the Malvern hills rising up suddenly out of the Severn valley – and flowing through all that landscape, the curving and recurving river'.[32] Similarly, Moore later maintains, 'as the sequences in Edward's melody could give back the repeating shapes of his own countryside, so the subtly changing orchestral variety gave soft atmosphere and muted colours'.[33] This is a reading that Elgar on many occasions sought to encourage himself. His diary entries and correspondence make frequent mention of specific locations in the area between Worcester and Hereford such as Longdon Marsh, the Ankerdine hills or Birchwood (where he composed *Gerontius* and the Variations). Many of the associations gathered around the chamber works composed in Sussex suggest a similarly intense awareness of local detail. Elgar's dying wish, for his ashes to be scattered at the confluence of the Rivers Teme and Severn just south of Worcester, in one sense evokes an archetypal mythic account of the origin of music born from natural sounds such as the rustling of reed beds by the river bank, as Matthew Riley has observed, and in another sense literally grounds Elgar's creativity in a specific geographical location.[34]

In his inaugural professorial lecture at Birmingham, entitled 'A Future for English Music', Elgar argued: 'there are many possible futures. But the one I want to see coming into being is something that shall grow out of our own soil, something broad, noble, chivalrous, healthy and above all, an out-of-door sort of spirit'.[35] Though Elgar's comments were undoubtedly affected by the context and venue of his lecture, it is striking how often and compulsively he sought to portray himself as a man of the countryside, of rural interests and pursuits whether as rambler, woodsman or cyclist, as opposed to the urban professional classes to which he belonged. This strategy was intended to serve several purposes: to align Elgar with the landed gentry, towards whose company he initially aspired, and simultaneously to mark his difference from the community of urban professional musicians from whom he felt increasingly alienated.

Many of the assumptions and associations that underpin Elgar's music and landscape seem opposed to the image of Elgar as continental European modernist. But such contradictory readings vividly reflect the richness and complexity of Elgar's musical works, and it is the interpretative problems that they pose that have ensured the continued appeal of Elgar's music. Perhaps it was these images that were at the back of Ernest Newman's mind when he described the closing pages of the Second Symphony in the *Musical Times*, as 'a winding and broken river that at last gathers all its waters together and rolls out into the sea'.[36] Certainly, the image of a musical course constantly turning back on itself whilst simultaneously moving inexorably forwards is as apt a metaphor for the trajectory of Elgar's creative career as any. In that sense alone, landscape remains at the heart of Elgar's musical output.

2 Elgar and his British contemporaries

JEREMY DIBBLE

Central to a popular understanding of Elgar's solitary, autodidactic world –
one that accentuated his isolation from Britain's musical establishment –
has been a narrative that heightened the significance of his roots in 'trade',
his Roman Catholicism, his lack of a university education, his struggle for
recognition (when others of lesser ability were apparently enjoying greater
attention), and his own pejorative and often bitter remarks about the music
of his native colleagues. Matters have not been assisted by the prejudicial
assumptions of Shaw in 1920 who, through his hostility towards academia,
chose to venerate Elgar at the expense of the 'little clique of musicians, who,
with the late Hubert Parry as its centre, stood for British music thirty-five
years ago'. It was a statement refuted with some vigour by Elgar himself who
clearly retained an admiration for Parry.[1] Such polarised and entrenched
views had taken root some time earlier. Ernest Walker, a descendant of the
'Oxford School' of criticism (which included Parry and Hadow), devoted an
equal amount of space in his *A History of English Music* of 1907 to 'the trio
of composers [Parry, Stanford, Elgar] who stand by common consent at the
head of modern English music', and quietly denounced Elgar's 'hot-house
type of emotionalism', his 'forced pseudo-impressiveness', and a tendency
to allow colour to hide content.[2] This was a view endorsed by Edward
J. Dent, Professor of Music at Cambridge and a one-time Stanford pupil,
whose cursory treatment of Elgar (in favour of Parry and Stanford) in his
essay 'Engländer' for Guido Adler's *Handbuch der Musikgeschichte* in 1930
epitomised an academic scorn for Elgar's music. To defend Elgar's position
there were Ernest Newman and C. W. Orr (in particular his article in the
Musical Times, 'Elgar and the Public', of 1931), the angry rejoinder to Dent's
chapter in the form of a letter to the national newspapers in Britain and
Germany signed by the younger generation of composers including Philip
Heseltine, E. J. Moeran, John Ireland, and William Walton (as well as the
anti-academic Shaw), and Basil Maine's fulsome *Elgar: His Life and Works*,
published in May 1933. The cumulative weight of these and other writings
by Tovey, Foss, Vaughan Williams, and Howes,[3] and W. H. Reed's *Elgar
as I Knew Him* (1936), established Elgar's public profile and his role as a
national icon. Yet there were those who felt that the new wave of Elgar
literature still provided a distorted picture, as is evident from the appeal of
another Stanford pupil, Thomas Dunhill: 'Several of those who have written

in praise of Elgar have to a large extent defeated their own ends by viewing his works through a telescope, and then reversing the telescope to look at those of his contemporaries through the wrong end.'[4]

As one might expect, such polarised positions only served to obscure a more complex image of Elgar's interaction with his native colleagues. Moreover, Elgar's own experiences of and comments about his contemporaries, notably those of a more negative nature, require a fuller and more thorough contextualisation. We know, for example, that his early disappointment at the Covent Garden Theatre in 1884, when a rehearsal of his music was promised, and his despondent return to Worcester after Sullivan used up all the rehearsal time on a selection from one of his operas, was, as Elgar himself admitted, not the result of malice or aloofness on Sullivan's part. In 1898, at Leeds, when *Caractacus* was to be premiered, the two men met for the first time. Sullivan, according to Elgar, was astonished: '"But, my dear boy, I hadn't the slightest idea of it," he exclaimed, in his enthusiastic manner. "Why on earth didn't you come and tell me? I'd have rehearsed it myself for you." They were no idle words. He would have done it, just as he said.'[5] More importantly Elgar gained some assistance from Frederic Cowen, who had not only established his reputation as a composer of opera, choral works, and symphonies but was also a well-respected conductor of the Philharmonic Society. Cowen perused Elgar's early compositions and it has been suggested that he also provided Elgar with introductions to various London publishers. Such help was acknowledged by Elgar many years later at a banquet in Cowen's honour given by the Music Club on 14 May 1925.

Cowen's growing national reputation as a composer and executant during the early 1880s (not least with his 'Scandinavian' Symphony which attracted attention from all over Europe, including Brussels, Paris, Berlin, and Prague) was almost certainly the principal reason why Elgar had approached him.[6] However, Cowen's music was only part of a much larger tide of new talent that was emerging in London and the provinces. That Elgar recognised this change is implicit in his comments for his inaugural (and somewhat controversial) lecture, 'A Future for English Music', as Peyton Professor at Birmingham University on 16 March 1905.

> *In looking for* a practical starting point for anything that may be usefully considered in relation to present day music, I think it unnecessary to go back farther than 1880. I do not say definitely that that is the best starting point, but it is sufficient for the purpose. The history of music from the time of Purcell onwards is well known, and it would be merely a tiresome repetition of the *ordinary commercial lecture* to go over the two centuries *preceding 1880. Some of us who in that year* were young and taking an active part in music – a really active part such as playing in orchestras – felt that something at last was going to be done in the way of composition by the

English school. A large number of compositions during the twenty years following, were brought before us, and the whole atmosphere of English music was changed, owing to the spread of musical education, which was out of proportion to the natural growth of the population; or, to put it plainly, that musical taste has increased. *An interest* hitherto unknown was taken in the work of our native composers.[7]

Elgar's allusion to 1880 may have been simply a convenient 'round number', but he could have been referring to the premiere of Parry's *Prometheus Unbound*, given at Gloucester that same year, and a work which, owing to its unbridled Wagnerian influences, had a disturbing effect on some of the press. Whether Elgar was at Gloucester to hear Parry's new work is not known, but, as the words of his first Birmingham lecture stress, Elgar was experiencing and assimilating all that was going on in British music from the perspective of a *practical* musician. As an orchestral violinist Elgar participated in many of the amateur and semi-professional orchestras in the Midlands at a time when such bodies were enjoying an extraordinary revitalisation of interest and enthusiasm. He played first for the Worcester Three Choirs Festival in 1878 and last in 1893. In 1881 he began playing in Stockley's orchestra for the series of Birmingham Popular Concerts. There were other less prestigious but no less active societies which included the Hereford Philharmonic Society (which he led from April 1891) and the Worcester Festival Choral Society (whose orchestra he also led after 1891), and after he gave up playing, there were institutions such as the Worcestershire Philharmonic which exercised his energies as a conductor. Add to this his friendships with George Robertson Sinclair (who came to Hereford in 1889), Hugh Blair (organist of Worcester from 1895 to 1897), Ivor Atkins (who succeeded Blair in 1897), the two Gloucester organists, Charles Lee Williams and his successor, Herbert Brewer, and Charles Swinnerton Heap (organist, composer, and one of the most prominent choral conductors in the Birmingham conurbation), and Elgar was able to enjoy both a familiarity with the entire choral network of the region and (even as a Catholic 'outsider') the world of Anglican cathedral music.[8]

At Worcester in 1878 Elgar played in Stainer's cantata, *The Daughter of Jairus*, a work of post-Mendelssohnian proportions, though by no means without bold progressions, as can be seen in the striking overture. Other pieces by Armes and Ouseley belonged to an earlier generation whose works Elgar, hungry for the sound of modern European music, already found wearisome: he later recalled that 'they lacked that feeling for orchestral effect and elasticity in instrumentation so obvious in the works of French, Italian, and German composers'.[9] The colour of Parry's *Prometheus* – a streak of modernity the composer would jettison in later works – would have certainly fired Elgar's orchestral imagination in 1880, but the following year, when Alexander Mackenzie's cantata *The Bride* came to Worcester, Elgar immediately identified both with the composer's flair for instrumentation and the fact that Mackenzie had cut his teeth as an orchestral violinist:[10]

> The coming of Mackenzie then was a real event. Here was a man fully equipped in every department of musical knowledge, who had been a violinist in orchestras in Germany. It gave orchestral players a real lift and widened the outlook of the old-fashioned professor considerably. *The Bride* was a fine example of choral and orchestral writing . . .
> I had the honour to meet the composer the following morning and actually shook hands with him at Sansome Lodge.[11]

Dvořák's music, including his Sixth Symphony, held Elgar's attention at the Worcester Festival in 1884, but on 8 October 1885 he would be introduced for the first time, through his employment as a violinist in Stockley's Birmingham orchestra, to one of Stanford's major choral works, *The Three Holy Children*. Performed at the 1885 Birmingham Festival, for which it was commissioned, Stanford's oratorio provided Elgar with a vibrant example of choral and orchestral integration together with an insight into inventive choral forms. Further formative experiences were to follow in Cowen's *Ruth* at Worcester in 1887 and a clutch of Parry's works between 1887 and 1893 – *Blest Pair of Sirens*, the oratorios *Judith* and *Job*, the *Ode to St Cecilia* and the *Overture to an Unwritten Tragedy*, in which Elgar played under Parry's baton.[12]

To a large extent the more negative perspective of Elgar's relationship with his Victorian contemporaries stems from the important yet dispiriting years of 1889 and 1891 when Elgar, newly married, removed with his wife to London. Though this period constituted Elgar's 'university' experience, in that he learned much from concert-going, visiting the opera, and making himself known to London publishers, he was nevertheless personally disappointed with the lack of progress he was able to make with his career outside the Midlands. Added to which, his first major orchestral work, *Froissart*, written in Kensington between April and July 1890 and on which the composer undoubtedly rested his hopes, made no headway initially after its Worcester premiere later that year, as Manns, to whom Elgar showed the score, was in no hurry to programme it at the Crystal Palace. Back in Malvern, Elgar was forced to resume his teaching practice and to return, reluctantly, to playing his violin in regional orchestras. 'I played 1st violin for the sake of the fee as I cd. obtain no recognition as a composer' were the words he wrote somewhat despairingly on his festival programme at Worcester in 1893.[13] Kennedy has proffered an interpretation of these comments, suggesting that the premiere of Parry's *Job* prompted Elgar to compare his poor fortune (if poor fortune it was) with the burgeoning success of his contemporaries. This may be true, but if Elgar felt resentment, he had little reason to feel bitterness towards his colleagues, for in the early 1890s, as Kennedy has also submitted, he had little to offer the public.[14] Brief exposure occurred with the publication of *Froissart* by Novello and by circulation of the part-song 'My Love Dwelt in a Northern Land' in the *Musical Times* after its publication by Novello in 1890; but there was nothing substantial to raise Elgar's national profile nor was there anything to bring his name before his more nationally renowned peers. It was only in 1896, with the advent of *The Light of Life* at Worcester and *Scenes from the Saga of King Olaf* at the North Staffordshire Music Festival, that Elgar's name truly came before the public for the first time. This rise to fame was aided by Jaeger's assertive policy with Novello, the avid promotion of *King Olaf* in *The Musical Times*, and the first London performances of extracts from *Scenes from the Bavarian Highlands* and *King Olaf* at the Crystal Palace under Manns the following year. It was at exactly this time that Jaeger brought Elgar to the attention of Parry:

> Look out for Elgar's 'King Olaf'. Though unequal & in places open to criticism I think there is some *fine* stuff in this. The young man has imagination, beauty, strength, 'go'. He is exceptionally gifted & will 'take the shine out of' some of the gentlemen at the top of the profession (Excuse the slang!) I believe in him: and oh! he has **MELODY**!! Melody that touches one. He is not yet very *deep*, but he will grow, I feel sure. 'The Light of Life' I do *not* care for, *nor does he*! He spoke of it as a 'written to order' effort. 'Olaf' is very different stuff. Whether he will do anything *great*, the future will prove.[15]

After hearing Elgar's *Caractacus* rehearsed at St James's Hall for the Leeds Festival in 1898, Parry first met Elgar at the premiere on 5 October. Shortly after hearing *Caractacus* in London, Parry witnessed the premiere under Richter of the 'Enigma' Variations at St James's Hall on 19 June 1899 and enthusiastically recorded in his diary 'Elgar's Variations first rate. Quite brilliantly clever; and genuine orchestral music.' Of Elgar's subsequent works, Parry greatly admired *Cockaigne*, parts of *The Apostles*, the *Introduction and Allegro*, the Violin Concerto ('after my own heart') and *Falstaff*, but he was unconvinced by the over-tessellated leitmotivic scheme of *The Kingdom* in which, he noted, 'the mosaic-like juxtaposition of thematic bits jars and bewilders',[16] and he thoroughly disliked the sentiment of *The Music Makers* and *The Spirit of England*. As for the symphonies, he began by being deeply impressed by the First, the London premiere of which he attended (along with most of the capital's distinguished musical society) on 7 December 1908 at Queen's Hall. 'Place packed. Work received with enthusiasm. Very interesting, personal, new, magnetic. A lofty standard', was his first response.[17]

But repeated performances emphasised an emotional abandon (and one suspects a thematic over-concentration) uncongenial to Parry's classical inclinations, and, though he admired the orchestral technique of the Second Symphony, he was to find this work 'blatant and vulgar'.[18]

The surviving documentary evidence confirms that Elgar returned Parry's admiration. With the publication of *Grove's Dictionary of Music and Musicians* between 1879 and 1889 Elgar learned much from Parry's articles.[19] We know too that, besides his practical experience of Parry's music as a violinist, he also keenly followed Parry's progress as a composer, making a special note of hearing the premiere of Parry's Fourth Symphony under Richter on 1 July 1889, only weeks after settling in Kensington with his new wife. After Elgar's rise to fame at the end of the 1890s, he continued to be a student of Parry's music. 'CHHP *Job*' appears below a discarded sketch in Part One of *Gerontius* (the Litany),[20] and a letter to Parry of 27 May 1903, while Elgar was working on *The Apostles*, exhibits Elgar's dependence on Parry's knowledge of word-setting. Further gestures of approbation were shown in Elgar's performances of Parry's *The Lotus-Eaters* and the *Ode to Music* with the Worcestershire Philharmonic and, in 1904, in gratitude 'for an act of friendly intervention on Parry's part', Elgar offered to take on any tasks of drudgery for his friend, 'anything in fact that an ordinary copyist could or could not quite do, I would take the greatest pride and pleasure in doing it for you'.[21] After Parry had successfully agitated for Elgar's honorary D. Mus. at Oxford, Elgar was particularly delighted by the university's invitation, because, as he expounded in a letter to Parry in January 1905, 'it permits me, in some slight way, to become associated with your name for one glorified moment . . . I only wrote this to thank you and to say that the degree would come as a doubly pleasant thing now, in view of my taking up the Peyton Professorship at Birmingham.'[22] When Elgar appeared for the first time in his official capacity at Birmingham, he used the opportunity of his inaugural lecture to heap praise upon his older contemporary with the accolade 'the head of our art in this country.'[23]

Elgar's lecture may have been flattering to Parry, but its criticisms of British music and the British composer angered both Stanford and Mackenzie. Indeed, in Stanford's case, the Birmingham lectures were to prove a decisive watershed in his professional association with Elgar. It was with the publication of *King Olaf* that Stanford became aware of Elgar's gifts, and his enthusiasm for the younger man's music was quickly passed on to Mackenzie.[24] As a regular visitor to Malvern, Stanford took the opportunity to be better acquainted with Elgar during the RCM vacations. Stanford played Elgar the whole of his new Requiem for the 1897 Birmingham Festival; and Elgar heard Stanford's *Shamus O'Brien* when it was touring in Worcester. Stanford directed performances of *King Olaf*, the 'Enigma' Variations, the

Sea Pictures, and *Cockaigne* at the RCM and Leeds,[25] and besides other generous personal gestures, such as his role (and Parry's) in Elgar's successful election to the Athenaeum Club on 12 April 1904, he agitated vigorously for Elgar's honorary doctorate at Cambridge University in 1900 as 'the most prominent and the most brilliant of the younger generation',[26] and lobbied Elgar on more than one occasion for new works.[27] Yet, the letters between Elgar and Jaeger overwhelmingly reveal that Elgar liked neither Stanford nor his music. He mistrusted the Irishman's overt ambition and political conniving (especially on behalf of his own pupils), and there was always the lingering sense of inferiority, he the non-intellectual and Stanford the university professor. Elgar's ill-judged comments in his first two Birmingham lectures (rightly described by Kennedy as an 'insensitive blunder'),[28] which Stanford clearly believed were aimed at him, were an unpardonable insult. An estrangement ensued until 1922 when Granville Bantock effected a reconciliation between the two men; Elgar, however, always claimed ignorance of the reason for their estrangement.

With *Caractacus*, the Variations, and *Gerontius* Elgar eclipsed the achievements of his senior contemporaries. Moreover, Parry, Stanford and Mackenzie were only too well aware of the neglect of their own music by Britain's chief conductors (especially Richter, Henry Wood, and Cowen) as Elgar came to the fore. Richard Strauss's eulogy of Elgar, as the 'first English progressivist', also placed him in the vanguard of modern British music and gave him an almost iconic status in the eyes of the younger generation, notably Holst and Vaughan Williams.[29] Of these Elgar took a particular interest in the music of William Hurlstone (whose *Variations on a Swedish Air* he greatly admired), and Samuel Coleridge-Taylor, who had received Jaeger's ringing endorsement.[30] Elgar's encouragement of Coleridge-Taylor took the form of a recommendation to the 1898 Gloucester Festival for a new orchestral work – the Ballade in A minor. This, along with *Hiawatha's Wedding Feast*, premiered at the RCM under Stanford on 11 November the same year, and which Elgar attended, were instrumental in forging Coleridge-Taylor's meteoric rise to fame. With the success of *Hiawatha* and the Ballade, Taylor rapidly began to attract commissions, at which point Elgar appears to have abandoned his initial enthusiasm for bitter criticism. By 1901, Taylor's cantata *The Blind Girl of Castèl-Cuillé*, written for Leeds, was dismissed as 'cheap' and 'flung off to degrade the choral singing of the country',[31] while *The Atonement*, composed for Hereford in 1903, was condemned as 'a disgrace to any civilised country' which rudely exposed Taylor's 'utter want of education'.[32] Some have attributed this volte-face as a sign of Elgar's insecurity and aversion to competition.

Others that Elgar chose to support, particularly those with a predilection for Richard Strauss, were Granville Bantock (who was considered by many critics to be more progressive than Elgar), Percy Pitt, W. H. Bell, Cyril Scott, and Josef Holbrooke. As a self-styled rebel and radical, Bantock professed himself the foe of academia (a stance which chimed with Elgar's own). He pursued his radicalism (with the help of William Wallace) as conductor of the municipal orchestra at New Brighton, using the venue to promote concerts of new British music. A programme of Elgar took place there on 16 July 1899 and sparked a lifelong friendship between the two men. Elgar promoted Bantock's own music (including such works as the *Russian Scenes* and *Dante and Beatrice*) and used his influence to secure Bantock's appointment as Principal of the Birmingham and Midland Institute in 1901 (in spite of Bantock's antipathy to academia). In turn Bantock appointed Elgar as official Visitor to the Institute and succeeded him as Peyton Professor at Birmingham University in 1908.

The perception of Elgar as the leader of a new musical 'modernism' in Britain was forged by his appointment as president of the Musical League, an organisation spearheaded by Delius and Bantock (with the support of Henry Wood, Percy Grainger, Norman O'Neill, Arnold Bax, Havergal Brian, and Pitt) to promote the music of less well-known British composers.[33] Delius's contact with Elgar was no more than intermittent. They had briefly worked together as adjudicators for the Norwich Festival in 1907 and had met in London the same year while ideas for the Musical League were being discussed. Elgar's music, however, was never congenial to Delius, who, as an iconoclast, atheist, republican, and socialist, was diametrically and temperamentally opposite to Elgar's politically conservative disposition. Delius reserved some appreciation for the *Introduction and Allegro* and *Falstaff*, but he was intrinsically antipathetic to Elgar's oratorios and symphonies, and disliked his 'thick' orchestration.

As has often been noted, the end of the First World War, which coincided with the death of Parry, signalled a sea-change in British musical reception. A rejection of the country's Victorian and Edwardian musical legacy did not immediately lead to the neglect of Elgar's music (as it did of Parry's, Stanford's and Mackenzie's), but Elgar himself was undoubtedly aware that public attention had shifted elsewhere. In January 1922, Elgar entertained Richard Strauss to lunch in order to meet a group of younger English composers, among them, Ireland, Bax, Bliss, Goossens, and Rutland Boughton, and, through the offices of Ethel Smyth, he lent support to the knighthood of Dan Godfrey, conductor of the Bournemouth Municipal Orchestra. Yet, Elgar was wary of Britain's post-war musical development. He disliked the music of Vaughan Williams and Holst, and was openly hostile towards the works of Bliss and Goossens at the Three Choirs Festival in 1922,[34] though he did express some enthusiasm for Constant Lambert's *Rio Grande* and the work of Bax.[35] In 1924 there was a debate in court circles as to who would succeed Sir Walter Parratt as Master of the King's Music. In a nationalist environment where Vaughan Williams's assimilation of folk song was considered more representative, Elgar's 'German methods' were clearly thought to be a negative factor; but in the end Elgar's fame and achievement (and, ironically, Hugh Allen's recommendation from the Royal College of Music), were crucial to his eventual appointment.[36]

In the last years of Elgar's life, which witnessed a degree of rejuvenation in his composing activities, not least with the commissions of the *Nursery Suite*, the *Pomp and Circumstance* March No. 5 and the Third Symphony, as well as the public interest in his music generated by the newly emerging recording industry, Elgar's association with the younger generation appears to have been replaced by a retreat into nostalgia and a solidarity with his older contemporaries. He is known to have admonished Vaughan Williams for his criticism of Parry's orchestration of the Symphonic Variations;[37] he paid tribute to Mackenzie in an article for a Worcester publication, the *Three Pears Magazine*; and was instrumental in recommending Bantock's knighthood in 1930. He also appears to have drawn much comfort from his correspondence with Cowen, on whose advice he had relied early on in his career. Elgar lamented that the present generation undervalued Cowen's contribution as a conductor,[38] and, at an after-dinner speech on Cowen's eightieth birthday in 1932, he described Cowen as 'a dominating factor in the musical life of this country since 1875'.[39] More fully documented, however, was Elgar's visit to Delius on 30 May 1933, which arose as an interlude between the rehearsals and the French premiere of Elgar's Violin Concerto with the young Yehudi Menuhin. It was a curiously providential meeting (which Elgar reported in the *Daily Telegraph* and Fenby summarised in *Delius as I Knew Him*), for the following year the deaths of both men (which flanked the premature deaths of Holst and O'Neill) would signal the end of an era, though it would be with the deaths of Mackenzie and Cowen in 1935 that links with a past age would finally dissolve.

3 Elgar and his publishers

ROBERT ANDERSON

'Elgar Brothers', the music shop at 10 High Street, Worcester, became a mounting embarrassment to Elgar as his composing confidence increased and he aspired to a higher social position. Retail trade might have been acceptable as background to his Helen Weaver engagement. But there were rumours also of a connection with Sarah-Anne Wilkinson Newholme made while staying with Dr Charles Buck in Yorkshire, then of an attempted engagement to Gertrude Walker, musical daughter of the rector and squire at Abbots Norton, with whom Elgar shared many a concert platform, and who went on to breed dogs and become local secretary of the British Shakespeare Society. Above all there was Alice Roberts, a major-general's daughter born in India, whose social concerns in her early writings became rather, after her marriage to Elgar on 8 May 1889, a determination to raise her composer husband out of the sphere he was born in. Occasionally Elgar's mother might visit the home of the couple; occasionally the father would be summoned to tend a piano; but there is no record of the parents being invited together. To anticipate the *Gerontius* premiere, F. G. Edwards of the *Musical Times* planned a major article on Elgar. Alice Elgar, in a letter to Edwards of 18 September 1900, put her foot down firmly on certain matters, and notably the 'shop'; 'Then as E. has *nothing* to do with the business in Worcester would you please leave out details which do not affect him & with which he has nothing to do – His interests being quite unconnected with business.'[1]

Yet the 'shop' was of considerable use to the young Elgar. Music orders familiarised him with publishers likely to take on certain types of composition. His connections with St George's Church gave him informed access to possible Catholic publishers. Then there were the great German houses, such as Breitkopf & Härtel or Schott, each with a tradition of magazine publication and support of the most eminent composers, and each with a London office. Worcester, as cathedral city and triennial home to the Three Choirs Festival, was a ready outlet for Novello publications. When Parry's *Judith* appeared under the Novello imprint in 1888, some three years after Elgar's first known publishing agreement, the back of the vocal score was packed with advertisements for a seemingly interminable list among 'Novello's Original Octavo Editions' of 'Oratorios, Cantatas, Odes, Masses, &c.', followed by 'Violin & Pianoforte Albums', including *Thirty Melodies* by Berthold Tours, an important Novello personality in Elgar's early dealings with the firm. After a series of 'Vocal Albums' and 'Vocal Duets' came 'Pianoforte Albums' edited by Berthold Tours; 'Music Primers' edited by Sir John Stainer, some of which had provided Elgar with essential props to his musical self-education; and finally a selection from the 'Oratorios, Cantatas, Masses, &c.', all priced at one shilling. Of great significance to Elgar's future was the fact that August Johannes Jaeger (1860–1909), who joined the firm in 1890, sang in the Novello Choir that gave the first London performances of *Judith* in December 1888.

Elgar had been to the London office of Schott in Regent Street for violin music when studying with Pollitzer. Charles G. J. Volkert (1854–1929) joined the staff in 1873 and became the manager fourteen years later. In 1885 he signed the acceptance for Elgar's 'Romance' for violin and piano in E minor, Op. 1; his major coup was securing the copyright of *Salut d'amour* for two guineas. Later he paid Elgar a royalty, and further acknowledged his gratitude with a wedding present to the composer's daughter. Other violin pieces, the *Allegretto on G-E-D-G-E, Idylle, Pastourelle,* and *Virelai,* plus the song 'As I Laye A-thynkynge', went to John Beare (1847–1928), violin dealer, friend of the family, and brother-in-law of Dr Buck. *Through the Long Days* was taken up by Stanley Lucas, *Sevillana* by G. Metzler, Catholic choral works by Alphonse Cary, 'Queen Mary's Song' (a Tennyson setting), the violin and piano pieces *Bizarrerie* and *Mot d'amour,* and the *Vesper Voluntaries* for organ by Orsborn and Tuckwood. Charles Tuckwood also published a further batch of songs.

It was at the beginning of 1890 that Elgar first approached Novello with a pair of part-songs. Again the 'shop' had smoothed the way, since Elgar's father was inevitably a regular customer. The commercial success of the firm dates from 1829, when J. Alfred Novello (1810–96) realised the possibilities in cheap editions of the choral classics. He published *Novello's Choral Handbook* and Joseph Mainzer's *Singing for the Million.* In 1844 first appeared *The Musical Times and Singing Class Circular,* a periodical eventually home to many articles on Elgar. Percy Scholes has a wry comment on its origin: '*The Musical Times* was born of a mania – a most extraordinary mania which, largely promoted by a foreign immigrant, suddenly overspread our country.'[2] This was a mania for sight-singing, foundation of England's choral tradition. It was inspired by the tireless activity of Mainzer, lapsed priest from Trier who had conducted massed singing classes in the Roman Colosseum and taken refuge in England because of revolutionary sympathies. The Novello 'octavo format' derived from the shape of the *Musical Times.*

Elgar initiated his Novello correspondence with a letter that resulted in the acceptance of 'My Love Dwelt in a Northern Land'. Already he had a

Worcester Three Choirs commission for a short orchestral work. This was to be the concert overture *Froissart*. He approached Novello about publication on 27 July 1890: 'I have written for the Worcester Festival an overture for Full Orchestra & should be glad to know if I might submit the Full-score for your inspection.'[3] Novello concurred, but the agreement implied only the engraving of string parts, the copying of wind, and no full score. Elgar was later to lament constantly his absence of full scores to show prospective conductors. Two years on, a fundamental question arose. Elgar submitted the String Serenade, Op. 20 to Novello. It was turned down: 'We find however that this class of music is practically unsaleable, & we therefore regret to say that we do not see our way to make you an offer for it.'[4] Was Novello the right publisher for Elgar's instrumental music? The fact that Breitkopf & Härtel, with an office in Great Marlborough Street, printed the Serenade the following year and *La Capricieuse* for violin and piano suggests possibly not, an impression reinforced when Novello took fright in 1895 at the difficulty of the Organ Sonata and proposed issuing the work in four separate sections. Again Breitkopf & Härtel undertook the task.

Meanwhile Elgar produced a series of choral works for Novello, starting with the 'Spanish Serenade', a Longfellow setting. Elgar orchestrated the work, but the original accompaniment was for piano. Though professing himself no pianist, Elgar always devised for his choral works an idiomatic keyboard accompaniment that was in a sense the original of which the later scoring was an arrangement. In this case Novello, probably in the person of Berthold Tours, was critical: 'We shall have much pleasure in accepting the above for publication, but we find that the Piano accompaniment is rather difficult.' It was the same with *The Black Knight* in October 1892, also Longfellow, as Elgar explained in a letter of the 16th: 'Since my interview with Mr. Tours on Wednesday last I have most carefully gone through the P. F. accompaniment of the above-named Cantata & have removed all the difficulties which he was so kind as to point out.'[5]

In 1895 Elgar was possessed by two major works: *Lux Christi*, a short oratorio to a somewhat limp libretto by Edward Capel-Cure for the 1896 Worcester Festival, and more Longfellow as tamed by H. A. Acworth out of 'The Saga of King Olaf' from *Tales of a Wayside Inn* for the North Stafford-shire Festival. Novello, with its eye on a Protestant cathedral, preferred *The Light of Life* to the original title, and Berthold Tours was again out for simplification. An Elgar letter of 6 April 1896 implies that he had to shorten the Worcester work and eliminate some passages in eight parts.[6] Cuts had also to be made in *King Olaf*, and it may be that the work emerged more sectional than Elgar originally planned. The success of *Olaf* was nevertheless sufficient for Novello to require of Elgar two compositions to celebrate in 1897 Queen Victoria's Diamond Jubilee, the *Imperial March* and *The*

Banner of St George. Even so, there was carping about the March sketch in December 1896; it might be adversely criticised on account of the fact that 'it contains so many short phrases of two bars & even one bar'. The suggestion was for 'phrases say sometimes of eight bars'.[7]

It can only have come as a major relief to Elgar when his Novello contact turned into Jaeger, who travelled from Huddersfield to London via Hereford so as to hear the Te Deum and Benedictus, Op. 34 in September 1897. His generous praise in a letter of 15 September showed Novello in a new light:

> I hunted for you high & low during the Service (awfully long!) & afterwards, but you were not to be seen. Never mind, I spent a most enjoyable 22 Hours in the delightful cathedral Town & I *have* heard your finest, most spontaneous & most deeply felt & most effective work & I was *very* happy.[8]

The tribute was in this case perhaps over-generous, but Jaeger now became an essential prop to Elgar's creative life, supplement to the continuous support watchfully provided by Alice Elgar. The correspondence between the two men formed a mostly high-spirited commentary on work in hand (Jaeger could also manage Elgar's black depressions). The depth of Elgar's appreciation is enshrined even in his first masterpiece, the 'Enigma' Variations, where Jaeger is translated into 'Nimrod', the mighty hunter of Genesis (10:9). Elgar played innumerable variations on his name, producing such version s as 'Jaerodnimger', 'Jägerer', 'Corporal Nym', 'Jägerissimus', 'Jay' (with drawing of the appropriate bird), 'Demon (?)', 'Grosvenor', 'Jaggs', 'Jaybird', 'Moss-head', 'Pig', 'Augustus darling', 'Lieber Augustin', 'Shylock', 'Jagpot', 'Jaggernaut', 'Glorious Moss', 'Jag', 'Skittles', 'Jaguar', 'Jagbird', 'Heart Friend', 'Nim', 'Minrod'.

Elgar owed to Jaeger and his persistence a revised and extended conclusion to the Variations, exuberant enough to gather into the orchestra an effulgent organ part. Jaeger also suggested the mighty climax near the end of *The Dream of Gerontius* where, 'for one moment', every instrument exerts its fullest force, as a result of which the order of the subsequent sections had to be changed. There were passages in *The Apostles* to which Jaeger felt he could never be reconciled; he described one progression as 'crude', referring to it repeatedly with spellings almost as varied as the changes Elgar was playing on his name. Jaeger's inspiration continued as fundamental stimulus as far as the *Introduction and Allegro* of 1905. When the newly formed London Symphony Orchestra wanted something from Elgar, Jaeger was ready with a suggestion on 28 October 1904: 'Why not a *brilliant* quick *String* Scherzo, or something for those fine strings *only*? a real bring down the House *torrent* of a thing such as Bach could write.'[9] Jaeger had in mind Brandenburg Concerto No. 3, which they had heard together in Cologne. Jaeger's championing of Elgar extended not only to many articles and reviews in the *Musical Times* but also to detailed analyses of *The Dream of Gerontius*, *The Apostles*, and *The Kingdom*. Undertaken in the spirit of the Wagner commentaries by Wolzogen, they became over-fussy in the labelling of motifs and drew gentle remonstrance from Elgar when Jaeger complained, for instance, that a motif did not appear when the text seemed to demand it.[10]

Novello did not print a major Elgar full score until the very end of 1899, when the 'Enigma' Variations had clearly made its mark. On 24 January 1901 Elgar suggested to Jaeger the foundation of 'an Elgar society for the furtherance of the master's works', enclosing the words 'master's works' in an oblong attempt at a 'halo' so imprecise Elgar had to explain it did not represent a 'bug'.[11] Such a society was not formed for fifty years. Full scores of *Gerontius* and *The Apostles* appeared in due course, but Elgar's position in the eyes of Novello was finally secured by the three-day festival of his music at Covent Garden in March 1904, graced by the King and Queen, and the knighthood of the following June. The question of an exclusive publishing contract had been broached near the beginning of the year, and Elgar finally agreed to the proposal on 7 June, with the proviso that certain works should be reserved for Messrs Boosey, such as any future *Pomp and Circumstance* marches, and a short list of compositions never undertaken: 'the pendant to Cockaigne'; 'the Cycle for Mr. Plunkett Greene'; 'an Opera *if* Mr. A C Benson finds the libretto'; 'a possible addition to a Song they have for Soprano making it a portion of a cycle'.[12]

On 24 September 1904 Jaeger announced that full scores of the earlier choral works would be undertaken: *The Light of Life* and *The Banner of St George* would be printed in house, while *The Black Knight*, *King Olaf* and *Caractacus* would be engraved by the Leipzig firm of Geidel. Jaeger, well aware of what Breitkopf & Härtel had achieved since launching a superb series of complete editions with the Bach Gesellschaft project of 1850 (it had taken fifty years) now postulated a similar Elgar venture: '"The Complete works of The Master" will soon be an accomplished FACK!'[13] In the event, the first volume of an Elgar Complete Edition had to wait until 1981, when copyright in his music had only three years to run.

Despite the tireless activity of Jaeger and a dedicated Novello team working on Elgar's behalf, there were many moments of distrust between Elgar and the firm. The first occurred over the Variations, when Novello demanded what Elgar considered an unreasonable fee for an extra orchestral rehearsal at the time of the first performance. He expressed his 'disgust'. The disagreement was compounded by Elgar's disappointment over the royalty to be paid for the piano version of the work. The immediate result was that *Sea Pictures* was published by Boosey. They secured also, to the dismay of Jaeger, the *Cockaigne* overture, and the *Pomp and Circumstance* Marches Nos. 1 and 2. For *Sursum corda* Elgar turned again to Schott (1901). He reverted to

Novello for the magisterial series of orchestral works beginning with *In the South* (1904), including the symphonies and Violin Concerto, and ending with *Falstaff* (1913). By then he had become increasingly disillusioned over his royalties and therefore dubious about the value of the exclusive contract with Novello. He wrote on 27 June 1911, expressing sadness but with decision made: 'I must as soon as possible make some other plans: with very much regret I must ask you to accept this as notice to terminate the agreement existing between us as to publishing; – I believe twelve months' notice is required . . .'[14] The question of notice arose when Elgar received a surprise commission for music to the *Crown of India* Masque, planned as part of a music-hall event at the Coliseum in March 1912. Under the quixotic impression that there might even be subsequent foreign performances of music supporting a very jingoistic text, Elgar entered into publication agreements with Enoch and Hawkes. Novello cited the terms of their contract, but then generously withdrew.

The least attractive Novello letter about Elgar was sent on 6 February 1914 by one of the directors, Augustus Littleton, to Henry Clayton, the company secretary, concerning the five choral songs, Opp. 71, 72 and 73:

> The price is high amounting to extortion, but the point is that plenty of other houses would jump at the stuff at the price . . . I don't want any more Elgar symphonies or concertos, but am ready to take as many partsongs as he can produce even at extortionate rates.[15]

When Elgar offered the Cello Concerto to Novello, it was accepted and produced in cello and piano score a month after the October 1919 premiere. The full score did not follow until February 1921, after the concerto had been recorded by Elgar with Beatrice Harrison.[16] The miniature score came out in 1937.

Yet even Elgar part-songs were to be questioned by Novello. In July 1923 he submitted two for male voices, 'The Wanderer' to words from a 1661 anthology, *Wit and Drollery*, and 'Zut! Zut! Zut!' to his own text under the pseudonym Richard Mardon. John West was to assess them. The first was acceptable, if only for its brevity:

> This is smooth & singable – if at times rather *ordinary* in character; but it is not what I shd. of [*sic*] thought the composer *could* have done with the poem. There were opportunities of *contrast* & more independence of part-writing.

The marching song was summarily dismissed: 'I am sorry to say this is rather *cheap* for Elgar – *cheap* without being sufficiently *interesting*.'[17] The result was an exchange of letters that included an Elgar request to 'tear up the M.S.S. – or return them to me & I can do so'. Clayton replied that

Neither I nor anyone else here would wantonly destroy an Elgar MS., so if
that is to be the fate of your two partsongs for men's voices, you must apply
the finishing touch yourself.[18]

In the end Novello agreed to fifty guineas, half what Elgar had wanted.

Novello continued sporadic Elgar publication, but in May 1930 he was
negotiating a comparatively lucrative contract with Keith Prowse. He would
receive an annual payment of £250, royalties, and a proportion of radio and
gramophone rights. In return he should submit three works a year, which
might be 'songs or pieces'. Keith Prowse wanted an exclusive contract, but
as in 1904 Elgar insisted on exceptions: Boosey must have any further *Pomp
and Circumstance* marches and choral music might still go to Novello.[19] The
most important works to come Keith Prowse's way were the *Nursery Suite* of
1930 and the orchestral version of the *Severn Suite*. There seemed, however,
a good chance that 'So Many True Princesses', the Masefield setting Elgar
made for the unveiling of a memorial statue to Queen Alexandra, might
also be published by Keith Prowse, should the Poet Laureate be persuaded
to write alternative words. Despite requests from composer and publisher,
Masefield did not oblige.

There then came a still greater possibility. In London about the time
of his seventy-fifth birthday for a performance of the *Memorial Ode* on
8 June 1932, Elgar took the opportunity of calling on Wayne Daley at Keith
Prowse to discuss the project of a third symphony. This had been repeatedly
urged on Elgar by him and Shaw, and on 10 June Elgar wrote to Daley from
Worcester: 'I was very glad to see you again & to have your views about the
third Symphony.'[20] Three months later Daley wondered if he might discuss
the symphony idea with Basil Maine, then engaged on a life-and-works
account of the composer. Elgar replied that he would keep Maine informed.
When the commissioning of the symphony by the BBC was announced,
Harold Brooke of Novello expressed profound chagrin that the work was
not to join its fellows at Novello. Daley's request for 'a few particulars to
pass on, such as the key, opus, movements etc.' was greeted with silence.
The symphony, as finally realised by Anthony Payne, was published in 1998
by Boosey & Hawkes.

Novello, nevertheless, held the main key to Elgar's posthumous reputation. With a steady increase in performances between the centenary of
Elgar's birth in 1957 and the fiftieth anniversary of his death in 1984, when
copyright would expire, it seemed commercial sense and Elgar's due that
Jaeger's prophecy of 1904 should be fulfilled and the complete works of the
master at last become 'an accomplished FACK!' Symphony No. 1 appeared
in 1981, first among forty-three volumes that might perhaps be published
by 2007, a celebratory terminal date. It was not to be. Novello was subject to

takeovers, by Granada in 1970 and by Filmtrax in 1988. The Elgar Complete Edition survived both of them, and also an attempt by Granada to sell some Elgar material then on permanent loan to the British Library, and now part of its collection.

The arrival of Music Sales in 1993 proved another matter. The Complete Edition was axed, and there have since been two auctions, in 1997 and 2002, of the Novello archive so crucial to the edition. No longer is it possible, for instance, to enjoy Elgar's affectionate letter in Italian to the Novello staff who had overseen the printing of *The Apostles*, addressed as 'Signiori l'Occidente, Cacciatore, Cane da Fermo e Ruscello' (West, Jaeger, Pointer, Brooke), or to relish the unseemly scramble by various orchestral managements for the first performance of the Violin Concerto that came Novello's way as Elgar's concert agent. Countless treasures that should be in the public domain have been irrevocably dispersed for a few thousand pounds. Elgar has now gone back into copyright until the end of 2004 as the result of European Union legislation of more than usual lunacy, and Jaeger's dream now depends on the vision and good governance for many years to come of the Elgar Society, which courageously relaunched the edition in October 2001.

4 Magic by mosaic: some aspects of Elgar's compositional methods

CHRISTOPHER KENT

If a stranger had asked Elgar 'How do you compose?' they would be very lucky to have received a reasoned answer. More likely, they might have been met with a curt rebuff or a tirade of banter. Yet Elgar might have responded more seriously to the question if he felt that the person was genuinely sympathetic to his own personality as well as to his music. Fortunately, we do not have to rely on anecdotes to answer this question. Instead, we have a plethora of documentary manuscript materials: sketchbooks, working sketches, short scores, full scores and sets of corrected proofs from which we can follow the creative habits of his entire life and gain invaluable perspectives on his stylistic growth from juvenilia to maturity. However, there have been some losses, as his daughter Carice noted when he moved from Severn House, Hampstead in July 1921, just over a year after the death of Lady Elgar: 'Very busy day – turning out stationery cupboard – Father went through all his sketches MSS etc. sad work. Destroyed much & got it all in order. He spent a second day at the task.'[1]

Elgar's manuscripts are not the only answer to our initial question: he was not alone among the composers of his age, nor since, who are conveniently labelled 'Romantic' on account of their sincere indebtedness to the stimuli they received from environments and literature. It was to Robert J. Buckley that Elgar revealed the early importance of environment:

> The composer once related an incident to his first biographer . . . when
> he was nine or ten years old Edward Elgar was discovered sitting on a bank
> by the river with pencil and a piece of paper whereon were ruled five
> parallel lines. He was trying, he said, to write down what the reeds were
> singing.[2]

This cannot be passed over as an isolated incident of his childhood: during a visit to Elgar at Hereford in 1909 Oscar Wilde's son Vyvyan Holland gave an account of Elgar humming to himself and jotting themes on small sheets of music paper as they walked along the bank of the River Wye. The same author also recounted that Elgar 'had musical day dreams in the same way that other people had dreams of heroism and adventure, and that he could express almost any thought that came into his head in terms of music'.[3] Elgar wrote similarly to Sydney Colvin in 1921: 'I am still at heart the dreamy child

Example 4.1 'Overture', sketch (*c*.1882)

who used to be found in the reeds by the Severn side with a sheet of paper trying to fix the sounds and longing for something great. I am still looking for this.'[4] It was probably from his father that Elgar acquired the habit of jotting down passing inspirations out of doors in sketchbooks. In later years Edward recalled how when he and his father were forced to shelter from the rain under a tree the latter brought out his manuscript book to note some passing inspiration.[5]

In 1882, during a visit to Northern England, his friend Dr Charles Buck described the effect on Elgar of his first sight of Lake Windermere as 'extraordinary . . . Not a word could be got out of him, and suddenly he began to write furiously. When he had finished he said he had never known the same sensation before, and that he was simply obliged to write.'[6] It is possible that the unidentified fragments entitled 'Overture' from the manuscript collection of some of Elgar's music for St George's Church, Worcester (now in the Jesuit Archive, London) may have stemmed from this experience (Ex. 4.1).[7]

A further unpublished instance of Elgar's spontaneous jottings from the same visit to Charles Buck at Giggleswick can be seen on the verso of the ink fair copy of the cello part of an incomplete Piano Trio which Elgar played with his host. These pencil jottings (Ex. 4.2), which are missing from the published edition of this manuscript, illustrate aspects of Elgar's creative thinking which show three familiar elements of his mature style and working habits:[8] a) a melodic contour featuring rising sixths and sevenths, b) an incipit of a contrapuntal countermelody, and c) Elgar thinking directly in terms of the orchestra. It may not be inappropriate to relate Exx. 4.1 and 4.2 to his unfinished 'Lakes Overture'.

Elgar continued to express his indebtedness to environmental stimulation throughout his life. A typical example is in correspondence with Jaeger in 1898; beneath a quotation from the 'Woodland Interlude' from *Caractacus* (Ex. 4.3), he wrote: '. . . This is what I hear all day – the trees are singing my music – or have I sung theirs? It is too beautiful here.'[9] Elgar's communion with nature not only gave rise to ideas, but also aided the planning of larger structures. According to W. H. Reed an area of wetland overhung by willow trees became associated with the closing scene of *The Apostles*:

Example 4.2 'Overture', sketch (*c*.1882)

Example 4.3 *Caractacus*, 'Woodland Interlude', sketch (1898)

> Here he used to sit and dream. A great deal of *The Apostles* took shape in his mind here. He told me ... he had to go there more than once to think out those climaxes in 'The Ascension', for they had to be so built up each time, that they never reached a pitch of intensity as at the last and greatest climax, or he would have felt that the architecture of this movement was imperfect.[10]

It is significant that few of Elgar's mature works from *Caractacus* onwards are without an associated place name for which there is some creative association: Birchwood Lodge, a summer retreat near Malvern for *Caractacus* and *The Dream of Gerontius*, Longdon Marsh for *The Apostles*, Rome and Hereford for Symphony No. 1, Venice and Tintagel for Symphony

No. 2. But literature was an equally strong creative stimulant to Elgar: few
scores of major orchestral works are without quotations. The extent to which
literature stirred Elgar's inventiveness can be gauged from a memoir of the
actress Nancy Price:

> Many delightful hours I spent with Elgar in his studio. He liked me to read
> poetry while he improvised music to accompany it. I often wish some of
> that music had been preserved . . . He was able to improvise on the instant
> of the spoken word.[11]

This also shows that as well as his environment, poetry and literature, the
keyboard was an equally important element of Elgar's creative processes. It
was in order to underline the significance of this that in 1929 Elgar recorded
at his own request a set of six keyboard improvisations. He also noted for
posterity on the soundboard of the Broadwood square piano that he used
at Birchwood Lodge the names of the works for which it had been used:
'Caractacus & c [18]98/ Sea Pictures [18]99/ Gerontius 1900/ Carice and
Edward Elgar pianoforte repairers &c/ August 1901'. It has been noted that
Elgar may have been attracted by 'the more orchestral tonalities' that the
earlier square pianos possess.[12]

   This aspect of his creative process remained consistent throughout his
life; on the threshold of his maturity he declared to Buckley, his first biographer, that 'there is music in the air, music around us, the world is full of it
and (here his hands made a rapid gesture of capture) and you simply – simply take as much as you require'.[13] During 1919 Elgar was present at a lunch
party given by Lalla Vandervelde, at which the interior decorator Roger Fry
and George Bernard Shaw were among the guests. A glib remark by Fry, who
suggested that 'After all there is only one art: all the arts are the same', drew a
trenchant response from Elgar which Shaw recorded inimitably: 'My attention was taken by a growl from the other side of the table. It was Elgar, with
his fangs bared and all his hackles bristling in an appalling rage. "Music", he
spluttered, "is written on the skies for you to note down. And you compare
that to a DAMNED imitation."'[14]

   The last words on the matter of how he composed are best left to the
composer himself: 'I can only write when the spirit moves me. I cannot write
to order.'[15] However, he did take care to explain to Basil Maine that he saw a
distinction between music that took shape poetically from his imagination
and music that he wrote down mechanically:

> I take no credit for the inspiration that people may discover in my music, I
> cannot tell you how it comes to me. Of course, I could write out a piece of
> music here and now as you would write a letter, mechanically that is to say.
> But before the real stuff will come I must be quiet and apart.[16]

Attractive as these various anecdotal accounts of Elgar's initial creative activities may seem, there remained the labour of preparing the score for the publisher. The recollections of Troyte Griffith shed some further light on this:

> He planned his work and on the whole, adhered to his plan rigorously. He sketched his music at various times – more often than not in the open air – but from 9–1 daily he made it a rule to write down his fugitive thoughts in permanent form. When he began writing he sat at his upright piano, trying themes and making notes on music paper, and later he sat at a table and got up from time to time to try a few bars on the piano. Orchestration was a carefully organised business. Lady Elgar prepared the paper for the full score, and he worked methodically doing ten to twelve pages a day. When the [orchestral?] parts came from the printer, he played through every part on the piano with Mr [John] Austin playing the violin or viola, ruthlessly stopping in the middle of a bar, never wasting a second. They played the Violin Concerto on a Sunday at Hereford from 10 o'clock in the morning to 11 o'clock at night, only stopping for meals, Elgar objurgating Novello's when he found a mistake. But when he finished work he was off duty.[17]

Elgar worked rapidly at every aspect of composition: 'the outer surroundings did not exist for him when he got down to the donkey work, writing the music first in short and then in full score. He worked at great speed, oblivious of anything but the sounds he was carrying in his head . . .'[18]

He avoided writer's cramp by using a dip pen rather than a fountain pen, which required him to lean forward to the inkwell and clean his pen by plunging it into a potato. The artefacts displayed on Elgar's writing table at the Birthplace Museum relate to what is seen widely in his mature manuscripts: the use of dip pens, five-nibbed pens for ruling staves, pencils and coloured crayons, date stamps, letter and number stamps for rehearsal figures. The short score of the theme of the 'Variations on an Original Theme', Op. 36 (Ex. 4.4) is a clear instance of Elgar's *basso continuo* thinking where in the first six bars the melody and bass are in black ink, and the 'realised' harmonies in between are in pencil.[19] Then the short score working sketch for Variation I (C.A.E.) gives a good example of his evolution of stratified textures (Ex. 4.5). Again, this initial thinking is in two parts with the outer parts in black ink, the syncopated counter-figurations of the strings added in red crayon, and finally the horn parts below in pencil on a fourth stave. Other revisions in pencil on the stave suggest that Elgar was uncharacteristically evolving an orchestral texture from a piano score, although in the case of Op. 36 this is a confirmation of the anecdotal evidence that the work began as a series of piano improvisations.[20]

But for deeper insight into Elgar's working methods we must examine the equally vital and tangible evidence that exists in his sketchbooks,

Example **4.4** *Variations on an Original Theme*, 'Enigma', Op. 36, Theme: short score

draft and fair-copy manuscripts, and corrected proofs. From the beginning Elgar was punctilious in his working methods. It has been suggested that he acquired these during the short time spent as a clerk in the offices of the Worcester solicitor William Allen.[21] Elgar used three sets of sketchbooks during his career. He was consistently methodical in his referencing system, using Roman numerals for each volume and Arabic numerals for their page numbers. The earliest set comprises five softbound volumes, commonly known as the 'Shed Books' since they contain pieces composed for a wind quintet (in which he was the bassoonist) that rehearsed in a shed at the back of the Elgars' music shop.[22] These oblong books may have been made with manuscript paper from his father's shop stitched together in gatherings with flimsy covers made from 'butcher's paper'. The quality of the materials they contain is diverse, ranging from faint fragmentary pencil sketches to fair copies made with a fine-nibbed pen in black ink. Although much of the material in the 'Shed Books' relates to the music for his wind quintet, the remainder reflects the diversity of his other activities as a composer, whether for the band of the Worcester City and County Lunatic Asylum, the Choir of St George's Catholic Church, or his aspiration to become a concert violinist. Equally significant are the varied transcriptions and arrangements contained in these and other early sketch materials.

He frequently made several copies of the same material, often only with a few minor alterations. He used figured bass throughout his life not only as a convenient means of harmonic shorthand, but also because it suited his method of building up textures by layers and through the interleaving and interplay of countermelodies and motifs. A fragment of a movement for violin and piano serves as an example not only of the use of figured bass but also of the emerging of a potential countermelody from the quaver motif of the three-part texture (Ex. 4.6).[23]

Example 4.5 *Variations on an Original Theme*, 'Enigma', Op. 36, Variation 1: sketch

N.B. small note heads are in red crayon in Elgar's sketch

Example 4.6 Movement for violin and piano, fragment

From these sketchbooks it is clear that recycling and revising materials became a lifelong habit. The Menuet of the Trio for Violin, Cello and Pianoforte, referred to above, was first sketched in one of the 'Shed' manuscripts and revised at Giggleswick on 4 September 1882, when the Trio was added.[24] Work was resumed in 1886, but it was not completed. However, some of the materials were used in *Caractacus* (1898), and in 1915 the melody of the Trio became the main theme of *Rosemary*. Further examples of recycling music from the 1890s can be found in the unfulfilled plans for two suites for strings. Although they were undeveloped in this form, most of the incipits were developed in other locations (Ex. 4.7).[25] The first movement ('Praelud[iu]m') to Suite [I] was used for the 'Woodland Interlude' in *Caractacus*, and the second movement ('Mau[re]sque') became the main theme of the *Sérénade Mauresque* from the *Three Characteristic Pieces* (Op. 10, No. 2). Then the theme for cellos of a movement entitled 'Träumerei' from the Second Suite became the main theme of the third movement of the Organ Sonata, Op. 28.

As his style matured this relocation of materials became more sophisticated. As well as themes, smaller motifs became the subjects of a technique that was likened to a mosaic method of construction by Diana McVeagh.[26] One of the many other examples of this method that have already been discussed in recent Elgar literature is the Second Symphony, where the introduction to the Larghetto was at various times considered for the scene 'At the Beautiful Gate' (*The Kingdom*), and for an unpublished part-song setting of Edgar Allan Poe's poem 'Israfel'[27] (Ex. 4.8). Not surprisingly, it is in the Symphonic Study *Falstaff*, the work that stands at the apex of Elgar's mature orchestral output, that we see this fluent relocation of themes and motifs not just between one project and another but with degrees of unerring deftness within the work itself (Ex. 4.9).[28] Such relocations of materials might also entail changes in tempo or in details of rhythmic notation, as when a theme migrated from the Violin Concerto to the Second Symphony Rondo (Ex. 4.10).[29]

Another remarkable redeployment was the third movement of some incomplete ballet music, dated 21 July 1879, which was held in reserve until

Example 4.7 Sketches for String suites, recycled ideas

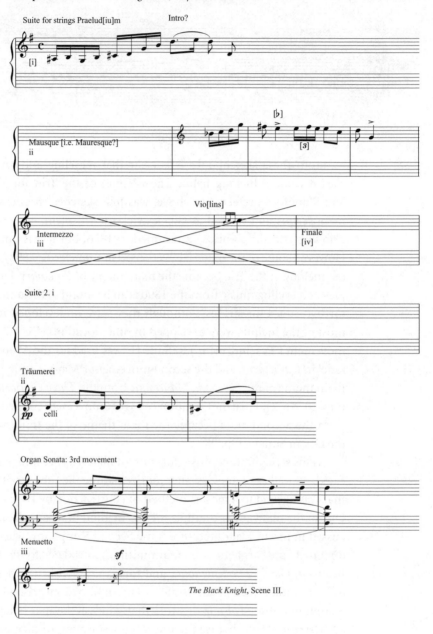

1907–8 when it was rescored with a new second theme as the final movement of *The Wand of Youth* (Second Suite), 'The Wild Bears'. In the light of these examples, his attempts to draw together materials destined for *The Last Judgement, King Arthur* and *Callicles* for his unfinished Third Symphony is entirely characteristic.

Example 4.8 Israfel [(E. A. Poe)] '8pts./6pts.?' [9 pts!]

Example 4.9 BL. Add. MS. 63154 f. 10 Sketch Book II, p. 3 [*Falstaff*]

From Elgar's second set of sketchbooks, which probably covered the period from *c.*1887–1901, only fragments and referenced copies of materials have survived. Their loss is most unfortunate in that they cover a number of works from the most significant period of Elgar's stylistic development. How many volumes were there? There are numerous references to three of them (I–III) in the working sketches for *The Dream of Gerontius* from which he drew extensively for materials for the choruses.[30] This may mean he began his setting of Newman's poem with the choruses, and that he also recycled materials from earlier projects. Their significance is illustrated in materials relating to the Chorus of Angelicals, particularly in relation to the evolution of Elgar's techniques of assembling structures from motivic fragments in a mosaic-like manner. The top half of a sketch for the chorus 'Praise to the Holiest in the Height' begins with an intended ink fair copy of the main theme as introduced by the semi-chorus of Angelicals, the overwritten K

Example 4.10 Violin Concerto sketch, recycled in Second Symphony

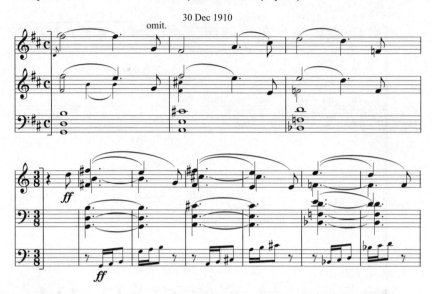

indicating that it had been 'Koppid' on to a further version. Above the first phrase in pencil is the text of Verse X, 'Glory to him . . .' sung by the tenors and basses of the chorus. Also feathered in pencil is an *aide-mémoire* of the later monotone interjection, 'Hark to those sounds. . . .' of the Angel. The lower half of the sketch comprises three paste-on fragments. The first of these is of particular interest in that it has three references to the sketchbook locations of the materials: 6a III, 15 III, and 19a III. Between the staves of this descending pan-diatonic sequence is the deleted note: 'work in Alleluia theme' (Ex. 4.11). The second sketch (Ex. 4.12) focuses on the descending sequence of whole-tone thirds which become a leitmotif associated with the Judgement of the Soul. The first sketch of this material is not amongst the majority of the *Gerontius* sketches, but it is with some manuscripts and proofs that Elgar gave to Ernest Newman which are still in private possession. Originally this material was 'from 25 II' (i.e. copied from p. 25 of Sketchbook II), and comprised a threefold sequence in ascending minor thirds. Above the third statement Elgar has written the text 'I go before my Judge', but in the final version (fig. 114) only the second and third statements are used. Of equal significance in this sketch are the two incipits to which this threefold sequence might have led. Both of them are to themes in E major: there is a curving line at the end of the third system which leads to the 'Fear' theme from Part I of *Gerontius*, but the theme at the head of the third system is a theme unrelated to the work which was eventually to become Mary Magdalene's 'Forgiveness' theme in *The Apostles* (fig. 78, bar 8).

Example 4.11 *The Dream of Gerontius*, Chorus of Angelicals, sketch

Example 4.12 *The Dream of Gerontius*, The Judgement of the Soul, sketch

The origins of Elgar's third and main set of sketchbooks, which he used from late 1901 until the end of his life, are documented in this famous letter from the composer to Jaeger:

> My sketchbooks are rotten – I know the sketches are and so are you . . . I want some new ones: do get for me 12 quires of *oblong* paper (B[oosey & H[awkes] No. 23, 6, 7, 9, sizes which see [. . .] 3 quires of each), and have each 3 quires bound in buckram or art linen or some decent coloured cloth (*all different colours*) . . .[31]

Elgar used each of these volumes in a seemingly random way, sometimes working from both ends simultaneously. The materials can range from pencil incipits, working sketches where countermelodies might be superimposed pencil on an inked melody and bass, to passages of full or vocal score. There are also planning sketches. A number of these have already become familiar through previous publications, including the conclusion to Part One of *The Dream of Gerontius* and the metamorphosis from the Scherzo to the Adagio of the First Symphony.[32] The first two volumes are extensively taken up with the oratorio trilogy. One of these is among the earliest planning sketches for the Judas scene of *The Apostles*.[33] Although

Example 4.13 Sketches for *The Apostles*

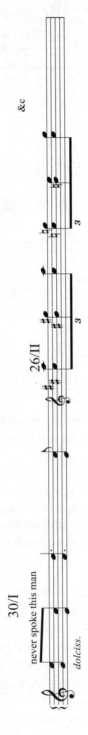

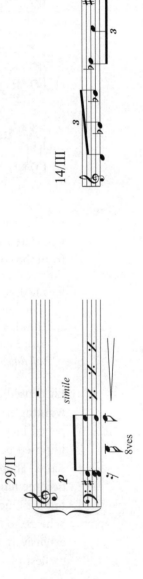

Example 4.14 *Variations on an Original Theme*, 'Enigma', Op. 36, Theme: sketch

not all of the materials drawn from Sketchbooks I and II were used for the piece, this sketch shows a remarkable example of Elgar's transformation of a rejected fragment to fit a later context in a technically flawless and dramatically appropriate manner (Ex. 4.13). The fragment noted '?Christ being mocked' was eventually to re-emerge in the mock battle scene of *Falstaff* (q.v. Ex. 4.9 above).

It is rare to find in Elgar's sketches substantial changes to the essential features of the music. If these do occur they are not infrequently accompanied by exclamations that reveal his ruthless self-criticism, particularly when he would cross through any material that seemed commonplace with exclamations such as 'bad' or 'rot'. Conversely, if something pleased him he would deem it 'Good', as in the sequence dated 'Jany 23 [19]03' which he considered as material suitable for either the Mary Magdalene or the Golgotha sections of *The Apostles*.

The fairly rare melodic adjustments in Elgar's sketches can be most subtle and telling. One such alteration was made to the viola and cello counter-motif at the end of the theme of the 'Variations on an Original Theme' ('Enigma'), Op. 36 (Ex. 4.14). However, a most rarefied change was made to the semiquaver motif within the melodic contour in bar 2 of the second theme of the Adagio of the First Symphony (Ex. 4.15); then in two bars after fig. 95 he made further adjustments, replacing a repetition of the ('X bad . . .') semiquaver figuration with a more fluent syncopation.

Harmonic changes are similarly uncommon. More often than not they were made to avoid a 'commonplace' progression. One such example can be found in the early sketches for the development section of the first movement of the First Symphony (Ex. 4.16). The materials at *x* (worked 'cadentially' from rehearsal figure 24) and those at *y* provide the foundation of the progression at fig. 44. Although each is marked 'good', the original intention to follow the Neapolitan B♭ first-inversion triad in the key of A minor with its diminished seventh is deleted. This was replaced by the diatonic dissonance of the ♮ 4/3 on the submediant F.

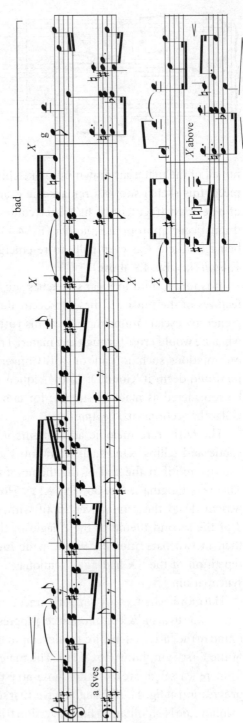

Example 4.15 First Symphony, Adagio, sketch

Example 4.16 First Symphony, Allegro (first movement), sketch

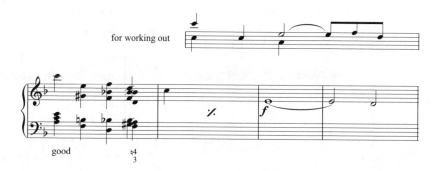

Example 4.17 *Cockaigne*, sketch

Elgar's fluent sequential structures can be easily taken for granted. Yet there are more sophisticated contexts in which he has dovetailed two sequences to create a much less simple structure. An outstanding instance of this occurs in the sketches for the development of the first movement of the Second Symphony.[34]

Elgar's gift for inventing spontaneous melodic counterpoint frequently grew directly from his innately orchestral thinking as he evolved his textures in the stratified manner illustrated in Ex. 4.5 above. There is a most striking (albeit humorous) example of this facility to be found among sketches for the overture *Cockaigne,* where Elgar's theme associated with courting couples strolling in the park fits flawlessly with the main theme of the 'Wedding March' from Mendelssohn's incidental music to *A Midsummer Night's Dream.* Moreover as Ex. 4.17 shows, Elgar's bass line is entirely grammatical harmonically.

Example 4.18 *The Dream of Gerontius*, fig. 24, sketches

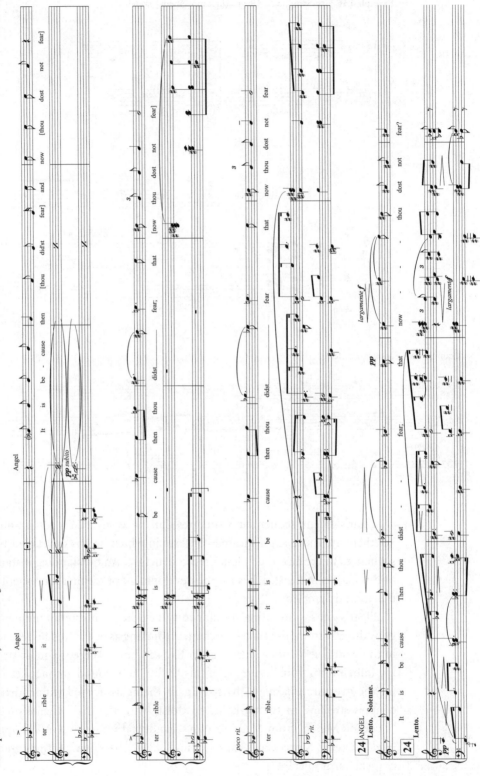

Example 4.19 *Variations on an Original Theme, 'Enigma', Op. 36, Finale: sketch*

Over the task of word-setting, Elgar's sketches often show him to be less assured and fluent, to the extent that several attempts were often needed before he was satisfied. The sketches for *The Dream of Gerontius* make very interesting reading in this respect. Ex. 4.18 collates Elgar's four attempts at the phrase of the Angel: 'It is because then thou didst fear, that now thou dost not fear.' At the conclusion of the extended second ending of the Variations Elgar added the quotation 'Great is the art of beginning, but greater the art of ending.'[35] Although the extended coda of the finale (E.D.U.) owes its existence largely to the constructive criticism of August Jaeger, the sketches of the original ending are not without evidence of uncertainty (Ex. 4.19).[36] But this was not to be the last time that Elgar experienced uncertainty over concluding cadences: among several other notable examples are the close of Part I of *The Apostles*[37] and the first and fourth movements of the Second Symphony.[38]

In conclusion, it is important to stress that given the scope of the present study it has only been possible to consider Elgar's compositional methods from a limited number of perspectives. There are many opportunities for scholars to continue to broaden this field of research activity.

5 Elgar's musical language: the shorter instrumental works

Elgar never received a composition lesson in his life. That may be looked at in two ways. The fact that his father kept a music *shop* has more often than not been seen as a social disadvantage: being born into trade contributed to the chip on his shoulder, and it certainly bothered his wife. But should not the emphasis rightly be on *music* shop? For what better environment could the penurious young composer have had than the music, books, and instruments all around him: the shop formed his private library, his laboratory. He learned by listening and doing.

His earliest notated piece, which he wrote down in 1867, is a single line in the bass clef, later used in 'Fairies and Giants' in *The Wand of Youth* Suite No. 1. Already present are two abiding elements of his style: loping compound rhythm, and sequences – of five repetitions in bars 2–4. In the answering phrase the first sequential repeat is modified by an accidental, A♯ in G major. In 1919 Elgar completed his Cello Concerto. The main theme of the first movement is a single line of three two-bar sequences played by the violas; in the soloist's answering phrase the second repeat is modified by an accidental, C♯ in E minor. The distance between the ten-year-old and the sixty-two-year-old composer at that moment seems touchingly short.

Elgar's early compositions were naturally modelled on other men's music. The 1872 song 'The Language of Flowers' is, alas, absolutely of its period, its only distinction biographical, in its dedication to his sister Lucy. The more substantial *Chantant* for piano of the same year is Schumannesque, the tiny *Griffinesque* of 1884 is Chopinesque. Also perhaps influenced by Schumann is the violin and piano *Allegretto on G-E-D-G-E*; like Schumann's ABEGG theme, it encodes a lady's surname, in Elgar's case two ladies, sisters.

In 1876 Elgar began teaching the violin, and in March 1877 he composed his first surviving violin piece, the fluent but undistinguished *Reminiscences*. He then took violin lessons himself in London with Adolf Pollitzer, and produced the fiendishly difficult five *Etudes caractéristiques* for solo violin, almost certainly prompted by Paganini's *Caprices* (and not to be confused with the Six Easy Pieces published in 1892, like the piano Sonatina composed for his young niece May). Modern violinists reckon that the *Etudes* were too difficult for Elgar himself to play (though he was competent enough to perform all the Beethoven violin sonatas in public in 1892). Technical exercises they may have been, but composing the *Etudes* expanded his range. His violin and piano *Romance* of 1878 foreshadows the mysterious Introduction of *King Olaf*, its melody tensed or suppled by the appoggiaturas which became so significant a part of his expressive style; and the *fioritura* looks forward to the Violin Concerto. The violin and piano *Pastourelle* again looks forward to *King Olaf*, to the lilting Thyri music. *Gavotte* (1885) is a showy compendium of double stopping glissandi, harmonics, spiccato.

In 1878 Elgar joined the Three Choirs Festival orchestra, playing in, among other things, Mozart's G minor symphony, No. 40. As a discipline he began a movement modelled on it, no doubt realising that freely composing on such a broad scale demanded more than he could yet command. He also formed a wind quintet. He had taught himself the bassoon, and among his friends he had two competent flutes and an oboe, and a weak clarinet. For such an unorthodox combination there was no repertory, so he provided it. The Intermezzos, which he later affectionately called 'mine own children', are high-spirited epigrammatic vignettes. The Dances and Promenades, which sometimes have piquant inner parts, are shortish, usually in ternary form. The Evesham Variations – strikingly unlike the later 'Enigma' – are purely decorative, not motivic.

However, in what Elgar called the Harmony Music (after the German *Harmoniemusik* wind ensembles) he began to teach himself how to extend his material. There are movements of a length (ten to twelve minutes) that demands organisation. In these he explores the basic elements of classical design, of key structure, of strong simple modulations, of development and recapitulation. Lessons from Mozart had been well learnt. Harmony Music No. 2 and No. 4, both lasting over ten minutes with their repeats, are full-scale sonata movements, with resourceful developments; Harmony Music No. 5 is in four movements, lasting altogether twenty minutes. Never less than engaging, these wind pieces hardly ever sound like Elgar, except perhaps in their transparent instrumentation. The final bars of Promenade No. 4 and Variation IV of the Evesham Andante are not so very far from the first nine bars of R.B.T. (Variation III) in 'Enigma' or the six bars after fig. 13 in W.M.B. (Variation IV), or the textures of 'Ysobel' or 'Dorabella'. For the most part, however, the wind music is classically orthodox, diatonic but with some wit. Its emotional simplicity, contrasted with the symphonies of 1908 and 1911, show how long and arduous was Elgar's journey of self-discovery.

Between 1879 and 1884 Elgar was director of the Powick Asylum Band. This consisted at most of a piano, some strings, two cornets, a euphonium, piccolo, flute, and clarinet (did he think of this awkward combination with a chuckle when he composed Falstaff's 'scarecrow' march?). For this scratch band he wrote quadrilles in the traditional five sections (no odder this than Fauré's quadrilles on themes by Wagner), polkas, and lancers. Some are based on popular tunes, all are formulaic, but most are catchy and fun to dance to. In later life he used this early unpublished music as a quarry. Ideas from the wind quintets (the Menuetto from Harmony Music No. 5, and the Promenade No. 5) went into the *Severn Suite* of 1930. The Andante arioso in Harmony No. 6 of 1879 became the *Cantique* of 1912. He was all the time composing string chamber music, too, some incomplete, some absorbed by the wind music. An Intermezzo composed for a D minor quartet of *c.*1888 became No. 3 of the organ Vesper Voluntaries. In old age he intended using an early Sarabande in *The Spanish Lady*. Part of an 1882 piano trio was recast as *Douce pensée* for solo piano in the same year, and in 1914 it became *Rosemary* for small orchestra; Elgar's 1929 recording of this, with seductive portamento, is a perfect period piece.

All Elgar's 'liftings' show the transforming power of his orchestration. The fifth section of the quadrille *L'assommoir*, already borrowed from a proposed Elgar children's play, later became 'The Wild Bears' in the second *Wand of Youth* suite. A series of seven chords from the polka 'Helcia' opens 'Sabbath Morning at Sea', the third of the *Sea Pictures*: jolly 'Helcia', given a pedal point, wind backed by divided low-register strings, added horns and a timpani roll at the climax, gains a 'solemn face' and contributes to the song's elevated ending. The opposite happens to the bears: in 1879 they are heavily grounded by a booming pedal bass; in 1907 the 'pedal' is given to mid-register wind, while the lower strings' light staccato allows a dancing Presto. These quotations have no emotional significance; they merely show a prudent creator using up old ideas.

From the age of fifteen Elgar occasionally deputised for his father as organist of St George's Roman Catholic Church, and in 1885 he became the organist; so he composed music for the choir. Mostly this is conventional, even sentimental, with sweetly moving parts. He quotes a hymn tune of 1878 in the Aubade of *The Nursery Suite* (1931). He also absorbed as much music as he could in the cathedral down the road; *Gerontius* sounds its best in a cathedral acoustic.

So it was a hands-on apprenticeship. He played in wind quintets, conducted the quadrilles, coached the choir. His compositions were tailor-made for his resources. He knew what would sound good, not because any teacher, but because his own ear, told him. He knew what worked on the fiddle because he performed on it and taught it. He knew what came off in an orchestra because he played for the Three Choirs from 1878 and in Stockley's orchestra at Birmingham (1882–9); he also conducted an amateur orchestra in Worcester (from 1882). This is not to decry academic training; but few would-be composers working on their own are as industrious, receptive, or discriminating as Elgar. When he was Master of the King's Music, he drew up on his official writing paper a bill for his complete education: it came to £56.10s.

All his compositions so far were for domestic and local use. Then in 1882 he spent three weeks on holiday in Leipzig, attending concerts of Brahms and Schumann (his 'ideal'), whose influences can be heard in the broad melodies of the violin and piano *Virelai* and *Idylle*. He also attended performances there of Wagner's *Tannhäuser* and *Lohengrin*, and heard the Prelude to *Parsifal*. He was ready for Wagner: in his early St George's days he had played the overture to *Tannhäuser* on the organ, telling a friend 'it was by a man who is not yet understood. You will hear more of him one day.' In 1876 he had arranged *The Flying Dutchman* overture for the local Glee Club ensemble (whatever can it have sounded like?). Home from Leipzig he composed his own *Intermezzo moresque* (later called *Sérénade Mauresque*). The following year he went to London for the Wagner memorial concert, hearing the *Siegfried Idyll* and excerpts from *Tristan und Isolde* and *Götterdämmerung*. Perhaps that exposure spurred him to compose the substantial orchestral piece *Sevillana* (1884), rumbustious, but with an enchanting middle section worthy of *The Sanguine Fan* and *The Starlight Express*. *Sevillana* and the *Sérénade mauresque* are the earliest examples of Elgar's 'Spanish' idioms (found later in *The Black Knight* and the Piano Quintet).

The *Sérénade* and a Mazurka of the same period foretell important characteristics. In both, Elgar enriches repeats with embellishments or countertunes, so fertile is his imagination. This he had already done in the wind quintet piece *Mrs Winslow's Soothing Syrup* (1878), and it was to become a feature of the 'Enigma' Variations. In the *Sérénade* the wistful middle section is comparable with the 'Moglio' passage (fig. 10) of *In the South*, prompted by the name of a village near where the overture was composed; and at one bar after L a timpani roll under muted and tremolo strings adds to the mystery much as in the celebrated Romanza (Variation XIII, or '***') in 'Enigma'.

In 1888 Elgar composed *Salut d'amour*, one of his most popular pieces, and also *Mot d'amour*. Both – aptly for tender declarations of love – show the withdrawal into private territory, often by a single chord, that became so vital a part of his musical personality. *Mot d'amour* begins shyly, not reaching a settled tonic of D major till the tenth bar, but attains a sweeping Largamente which unexpectedly withdraws on to a first-inversion dominant of F♯. Such 'out-of-key' chords are always pianissimo, usually under a fermata. This is far more than a harmonic resource, more of an emotional confession. Possibly Elgar gave a clue to the meaning it held for him in *For the Fallen*, when the syllable 'mem' in 'we will remember them' (two bars before fig. 22) escapes on to a second inversion of F major among the prevailing sharps.

Pieces such as *Salut* and *Mot d'amour* invite a melting rubato. One that would hardly work at all without rubato is, appropriately for such a teasing title, the violin and piano *La Capricieuse* (1891), beloved of Kreisler and Heifetz. Many of these early pieces are hard to date precisely and exist in several arrangements made to suit their publishers, who extracted the best commercial results from their purchases, and found that foreign titles sold best.

On Elgar's marriage in 1889, his wife's tiny income spurred them to adventure to London, to make his name and fortune. He made neither, and their retreat to provincial Malvern in 1891 seemed like a defeat. But those months could more profitably be seen as his university year, his professors being Weber, Brahms, Liszt, and Wagner, for day after day he attended the Crystal Palace concerts where August Manns was performing the most recent continental as well as British music. Elgar had made exhausting day visits there ever since Pollitzer had introduced him to Manns in 1878, but his immersion now was complete. For instance, in July 1889 he attended three performances of *Die Meistersinger* at Covent Garden.

One thing Elgar learnt in this wider sound-world was the importance of texture. The little choral song 'Spanish Serenade' (1892) is a ravishing concoction of sustained against moving sound. The String Serenade in E minor, possibly based on a suite performed in 1888, found its final form in 1892. Often in its opening five-strand *Allegro* Elgar thins the texture to one, two, or three strands, or thickens it with divisi, enjoying the effect of the differing registers, in sophisticated sonic shading. So much characteristic Elgar is here: the upward sweep first to a seventh, then to an octave, then in the reprise to a ninth, with the climax (cue H) formed by a threefold sequence. After the airy Allegro, how rich and full is the Larghetto particularly at the divisi reprise (cue L), where the first cellos reinforce the crescendo, then slip away during the diminuendo. He rehearsed the Serenade with the Ladies' Orchestral Class; he was 'always writing these things and trying them out on us'.[1] Maybe that is where he learned to give such detailed expression marks in his scores. His salon music is no less scrupulously marked than his major works.

During the 1890s the formative influence on the expansion of Elgar's style was Wagner. The overture *Froissart* (1890) shares with Weber a romantic atmosphere, and with Mendelssohn certain developmental procedures. Many of its themes, however, include a three-note cell possibly derived from the opening of Walther's Prize Song (E, B, C: a drop of a fourth followed by a semitone rise): that is motivic matching for thematic unity, rather than true motivic development. During his London year Elgar had ambitiously outlined a medieval choral work, touchingly signing the sketch with his wife's name as well as his own. In 1892 he resumed work on this, *The*

Black Knight. When the sable Knight rides in to the fight, the King's castle begins to rock to a sequence of chromatic chords (four bars before K) markedly similar to the version of 'magic sleep' which destroys Valhalla in the final orchestral bars of *Götterdämmerung*. Later in 1892 Elgar had the chance of a visit to Bayreuth, where he heard *Tristan, Die Meistersinger,* and (twice) *Parsifal.* In *The Light of Life* (1896) the orchestral interlude three bars after C, over which Elgar wrote the unsung words 'And he worshipped Him', is harmonically close to *Parsifal* Act 3 scene 2, where Kundry washes the Redeemer's feet. The phrase became loaded with emotional significance for Elgar. Such similarities – and there are others – are almost certainly subconscious. His admiration for the *Meistersinger* quintet must have encouraged his arching melodies with their triplets tied over strong beats, their appoggiaturas, and sinuous inner parts. To observe the difference even such tiny details can make, compare the piano Sonatina of 1889 with its revision in 1931.

Elgar's first major work after hearing the complete *Ring* at Bayreuth in 1893 was *King Olaf* (1896). Though as a whole *Olaf* is uneven, it shows a new mastery. Elgar has now fully learned the emotive power of chromaticism. He has also learned how to use sequences as harmonic propulsion, not as an automatic, even lazy, way of lengthening melodic phrases, as in the early *Reminiscences.* In the Introduction, the sequences build up, not just by step, to the word 'begin', with the modulation dramatically placed there for emphasis. No longer does Wagner's influence show itself in particular passages patched into Elgar's earlier style: it is the difference between imitation and absorbing the principles. Elgar has assimilated Wagner's methods, has learned, partly by using open-ended phrases to avoid perfect cadences, how to achieve continuity and length. Also his leitmotifs are now not just referential but structural, in linear and contrapuntal combinations. 'King Olaf's Return' has real symphonic development, and the vocal line has a Verdian thrust and scope (Elgar had played in the Requiem in 1887). For the first time melody, harmony, and orchestration are integrated in the service of drama. This achievement was not consistently maintained: there are passages which seem to run on auto-pilot in the *Te Deum and Benedictus* and in the Vesper Voluntaries for organ. But it was to reach its culmination in *The Dream of Gerontius,* in which many of the motifs modulate sequentially within their own length and end on chords which could lead off in any one of several directions. This rapid succession of keys incompletely established allows the music to be fluid, mobile, and lyrical.

One of the strengths of this self-taught composer is how well he was guided by intuition to fill his own needs. During the 1890s he had taught himself to achieve continuity. Now he needed to concentrate his style. So far he had composed mostly for the market, either knowing what would sell or working to commission. He was 'possessed' by the idea of composing a symphony celebrating General Gordon, but was not certain enough of himself to work at it without the bait of performance. Also, after years of depending on texts, he was hesitant about facing the challenge of a symphony. Variations, on the other hand, each brief but derived from the same idea, were not only within his powers but a perfect exercise in extending them. So came about his Op. 36, the 'Enigma' Variations.

The identity of the people behind the initials was soon revealed, and the solution to the 'enigma' itself can hardly now be confirmed. But the Variations are made of notes, not riddles. The theme itself is compelling: six bars in G minor with blank first beats in the melody suggest something unfulfilled, waiting for completion; and the paired quaver–crotchet rhythm is teasingly reversed. Elgar himself described the theme as 'Nothing – but something might be made of it.' Its form appears to be simple: a ternary ABA^1. B has four bars of a rising repeated figure beginning in turn on the notes B, D, F♯, and back to B; but over it, for flute and oboe, are four descending scale notes from F♯, sounding like nothing more than surface harmonic filling-in. That is deceptive, for these four notes are thematic material, used extensively in the variations.

Also A^1, though the melody is identical, sounds radically different. The bass is sustained, the melody enriched with sixths and octaves. But there is also a heart-stopping tenor countermelody, which is an eloquent synthesis of A and B. Its first two notes are from bar 2 of A; the next two are the last two of A's bar 3, inverted; the next four are in shape the 'insignificant' descending notes of B. So the repeat is itself a variation, and far from being as simple as it may sound to a casual listener, the 'enigma' theme is already multi-layered and fertile, perfect material from which to draw thirteen variations. Adding countermelodies is a trait that goes back to Elgar's early wind music. There it was decorative; here – and strikingly in the symphonies – it fortifies or adds new emotional weight to the music.

The Variations are not at all Wagnerian. If German, they are Brahmsian in their motivic resourcefulness, but they are really more French. Frederick Ashton proved what delectable ballet music they can be. It is tempting to describe them as Elgar's salon pieces raised to their highest plane. But that does them less than justice. Take 'W.N.' (Variation VIII, the lady with the laugh) which lasts only one minute forty-five seconds. Bars 1–4 are melodically derived from B, but with the sequence extending upwards, not falling back, and with each rhythmic pattern reversing the one before (as in A). Bars 5–8 repeat bars 1–4, but chromatically inflected and with the rhythmic pattern doubly reversed. Bars 9 and 10 are derived from B, but with a chuckling pendant; bar 15 is bar 11 but a semitone higher, and with the sequence extended by two bars. Bars 23 and 24 repeat bars 5 and 6, but enriched with the trills and the even semiquavers from bars 9 and 10. This sweetest, sunniest Allegretto would charm the birds if standing on its own, with no relationship to the theme. But compared with, say, the open melody, regular sequences, and light chordal accompaniment of *Chanson de matin*, blithe though that piece is, the variation is compressed, ingenious, and superbly integrated. It is Elgar wittily at play.

To celebrate Queen Victoria's Diamond Jubilee Elgar composed his *Imperial March*. It caught the public's attention and launched him in London. It was not the first march he had composed – there are march-like passages in the 1890s choral works – but it was his first detached ceremonial piece, predating the five *Pomp and Circumstance* marches. Usually in his marches the quick sections have sharp peremptory rhythms, often broken by rests or triplets, sometimes hammered on staccato repeated notes. The music then moves from jagged to smooth: the central Trios are sustained, their melodies a skilful mixture of steps and leaps. The famous trio tune of *Pomp and Circumstance* No. 1 is supported throughout its 16+16+8 bars by a single repeated harmony to each bar, except in bar 32 when on the second crotchet an F♯ changes to F natural to swing it round. No wonder a tune of such stability has come to represent continuity and tradition! It is far more comfortable than the great opening of the First Symphony, the apotheosis of all Elgar's marches. On paper, even played on the piano, that may seem confident. Actually heard, the introductory drum rolls, the tune's syncopation and uneven 7+10+6-bar phrases and shifting staccato bass, the third bass crotchet, D flat, contradicting the C in the melody – all with the veiled hollow sound of woodwind doubled by divided violas – make it more tentative than confident.

It is absorbing to trace the growing complexity of Elgar's noble slow tunes. In 1888 came an indication of his grand processional manner, in the *Ecce sacerdos magnus*, composed for his own church. The previous year he had sketched a melody which in 1894 became *Sursum corda*, hastily revived for his first royal occasion, the visit of the future George V to Worcester Cathedral. Though the opening of its aspiring melody is over-regular, the second strain shows one of his mature characteristics: he repeats the rhythm of a couple of bars exactly but expands the intervals inside the basic shape. He uses the same device in the Larghetto of the string Serenade, when bars 5 and 6, spanning an octave, are repeated but spanning a ninth; in this tune too he propels the melody forward by dissonance on a strong beat, and balances the sixteen-bar tune by repeating the opening bars to close it. (Similarly he 'balances' the twenty-bar tune of the Second Symphony's Larghetto, with greater sophistication, at a differing pitch level.) In 'Softly and Gently' he enriches the song by contrapuntal imitations and increasing chromatic inflections. His most complex, intricate structure is the Adagio of the First Symphony, sketched in 1907 for a string quartet. Here the melody's syncopations and elaborate decoration create a Tristanesque melodic–harmonic tension in which delayed resolutions accumulate force to build a sustained and sublime paragraph. This is all the more extraordinary since the theme was metamorphosed from equal flying semiquavers over simple stable tonality in the previous movement.

In 1902 Elgar worked up two orchestral idylls from old sketches and called them *Dream Children*. The title is that of an essay by Charles Lamb, in which an old bachelor dreams of children round his knee. Elgar headed the pieces with a quotation from the essay, which reads in part 'and while I stood gazing, both the children gradually grew fainter: . . . "we are not of Alice, nor of thee, nor are we children at all. We are nothing; less than nothing, and dreams. We are only what might have been."' It was a period that idealised childhood: Kenneth Grahame's *Dream Days* was published in 1898, and Barrie's *Peter Pan* in 1904. In human terms, it is sad that Elgar should have composed this piece seemingly ignoring his own little daughter, but musically the image met a need of his. How close this sentiment is, too, to the first interlude in his *Falstaff*, which in his essay on the work he calls 'a dream picture', and – again – 'what might have been'. *Dream Children* could easily have begun life as piano improvisations; they are almost entirely composed of sequences, modified just enough to sustain attention. The sorrowful Andante runs in parallel thirds, like the B section of the 'Enigma' theme and like 'Fairy Pipers' to come; and like the cross-over thirds in the second *Falstaff* interlude at fig. 103: all are beguiling. The Andante opens innocently, then deepens in feeling, becoming richer, more passionate, and that richer sound-world is sustained over the reprise. The innocence is shadowed, as it were, by the subsequent experience. It parallels how Elgar's adult life coloured his memories of childhood. That is not confined to these pieces: these modified recapitulations were an integral part of his technique. In his symphonic works the repetitions are weighted emotionally and thematically by what happens as they are developed.

Memories soon provided another stimulus, this time of his own childhood at Broadheath. Composers have always found the suite a congenial form for a collection of character pieces, and an expedient way to bring theatre music to the concert hall. Mendelssohn's *A Midsummer Night's Dream* and Grieg's *Peer Gynt* suites are early examples, Britten's *Gloriana* a more recent one. Elgar's *Wand of Youth* suites are unique in that the 'production' was a private affair, the composer only a boy. By the time he was fifty in 1907 Elgar had behind him brilliant orchestral works and three great oratorios. However, as yet there was no symphony. As a birthday present his brother in Worcester sent him an old sea chest that had belonged to the Dover Elgar family. Maybe that set him to think of recapturing his boyhood. Many of the numbers of the two *Wand of Youth* suites exist in part or in outline in his early sketchbooks; these he revised and rescored for full orchestra. His own programme note dates some of them back to the Elgar children's play, planned but never performed, when he was twelve or fourteen (how many men of fifty can remember precise dates from their childhood?). The play was to have been an allegory, a moral tale, in which the rebellious Elgar children lured their 'despotic' parents to cross a brook from the everyday world to a transfiguring fairyland. But the sketches show that some of the pieces were originally composed for chamber music, or wind quintet or Powick combinations, so possibly Elgar's associating them with the play was retrospective, part of a nostalgic reinvention of his past.

As well as the movements already detailed above, the waltz of the 'Sun Dance' and 'Moths and Butterflies' date from 1878; the opening of the March was sketched in 1879, its central section in 1880; and the Minuet 'à la Handel' in 1881. Into new sketchbooks of 1900 and 1901 Elgar had copied old worthwhile ideas which he now developed as the Overture and the 'Tame Bears'. He made the fifteen pieces into two suites, calling them Op. 1, 'Music to a Child's Play'. In that they are separate, brief, and captivating, they might be compared with 'Enigma'; but unlike the Variations they have no common source. Elgar however seemed to enjoy setting himself limitations. Whether or not 'Slumber Scene' was composed over a three-note ground bass for a child to play, as Elgar stated, his harmonic shifts over it are a tour de force, the soporific rhythm soothing, never monotonous. The 'Fountain Dance' spurts and falls, 'Wild Bears' scurry, over pedal basses. Many of the numbers – 'Moths and Butterflies', for instance – have a 'Dorabella' lightness. Occasionally the sunshine is clouded over: in 'Serenade' (fig. 13) and 'Sun Dance' (fig. 37) a timpani roll over a pedal note brings a sudden dark reminder of the 'Romanza' in the 'Enigma' Variations. The pathos of the tame bear's awkward gait demonstrates Elgar's sympathy with the 'poor bear – captive, made to dance', as his wife recorded. Some of the music found a later provenance: He quoted parts of 'Little Bells' (fig. 21) and 'Fairy Pipers' (fig. 34) in *The Starlight Express*, both passages of the utmost tenderness drawn from simple but eloquent harmonies, as though for sheer affection he could not let them go.

Wherever did he find such an evocative title? The double implication – of a magic rod and of a conductor's baton – is brilliant. The work begun in May 1907 still had no title in September. In early October he met Walford Davies whose 'Holiday Tunes' for children had recently been performed. On 6 October Elgar had his title; might something Davies said have suggested it?

By no means all the *Wand of Youth* music, in its final form, is emotionally simple. Often there is a melancholy undertow. But in general these pieces from the earliest stirrings of his imagination define and single out some of the feelings shortly to be combined in the symphonies. Elgar's nostalgia, his obsession with youth and dreams, is understandable in one whose later years were so far removed from his childhood: for a sensitive man, ambitions must be achieved at some cost to continuity: memory, not actuality, becomes life's link. But to make too much of that belittles Elgar. He was not the only man of his time to move from cottage to court: so did Barrie and Hardy. Elgar's great works date from his forties and fifties, the products of a mature technique and imagination.

Soon after completing *The Wand of Youth* Elgar sought copyright permission for the Ode *The Music Makers*. The *Daily News* had announced in 1904 that he was engaged in setting the poem, just after the great three-day survey of his music, the Elgar Festival at Covent Garden attended by royalty: that had set the seal on himself as the music maker. But it was not until 1912 that he began serious work. O'Shaughnessy's poem, published in 1873, has been dismissed as Swinburne and water. Some line-endings are limply contrived: 'Gleams/it seems'; 'As they may/yesterday'; 'Deathless ditties/great cities'. But Elgar had an unerring instinct for the sentiment that would release his creativity. How could he fail to respond to 'Our souls with high music ringing'? The poem has memorable lines: 'Sitting by desolate streams'; 'Each age is a dream that is dying'; 'A singer who sings no more'. Alliteration, cadences, and imagery are deeply evocative.

O'Shaughnessy's contention is that artists, by their inspiration, are the 'movers and shakers' of the world, the true makers of history. Elgar wrote before the first performance of the artist's 'tremendous responsibility' and of the 'unending influence of his creation'; and acknowledged that 'the main-spring of O'Shaughnessy's Ode is the sense of progress, of never-ending change'. Yet the pervasive motto of his music, the 'artist' theme, is the gentle, withdrawn choral opening 'We are the music makers/And we are the dreamers of dreams.' He set the poem as an unbroken span, with no cuts; but he repeats the 'artist' theme six times as a refrain. It is almost as if he undermines the poet, who with brave optimism greets the dazzling unknown, the glorious future, which will renew the world *in spite* 'of a dreamer who slumbers, And a singer who sings no more'. That conclusion will not do for Elgar, and his work ends as it began with 'We are the music makers . . .', 'ma più lento'. For all the grand, forceful passages of music, the impression that remains is of the artist's apartness: music can influence only the inner life of the individual, not politics, nor empires, nor the building of great cities.

That is emphasised by Elgar's quotation from his own 'Enigma' Variations at the words 'sitting by desolate streams'. He revealed that the 'enigma' theme expressed his sense of the loneliness of the artist in 1898, and that the adaptation from Tasso he wrote on the Variations score might with equal truth be written at the end of this: 'Bramo assai, poco spero, nulla chieggio', 'I essay much, I hope little, I ask nothing', in Elgar's translation. Surely in linking these two works Elgar gives the strongest possible hint that the 'enigma' is himself. His phrase, 'A man's attitude to life', is often quoted about his Cello Concerto of 1919. But he had described his First Symphony as 'a composer's outlook on life' in the programme note for its first London performance in 1908. About *The Music Makers* he wrote 'art must be the man'; in that work, the Violin Concerto and the Second Symphony he confessed he had 'shewn' himself.

The 'enigma' theme is the first of Elgar's many self-quotations in *The Music Makers*. The idea may have been prompted by the 'works of peace' section in Strauss's *Ein Heldenleben* in which he quotes his own music: Elgar heard the work in 1902. Here he quotes his own great published works, among them the two symphonies and the Violin Concerto (detailed complete lists are given in Kennedy's *Portrait of Elgar*, appendix II and in the Elgar Complete Edition vol. X). He did make use of ideas discarded from earlier published works: some from *Gerontius*, some from *The Apostles*. He also used ideas from projected but unfinished works: the 1907 string quartet, a setting of a *Callicles* song by Matthew Arnold. But these were all from his maturity. In *The Wand of Youth* his early unpublished sketches, though acknowledged, were a private matter for the professional composer. Now he went public. But the curious thing is, *The Music Makers* seems even more private, more confessional. Elgar's music often suggests some intimate coded message. Here, when he parades his own works, the effect is personal and introspective. O'Shaughnessy's poem is about music's possible influence on grand affairs. Elgar seems to tell us more about the introspective process of creation than about its effects. At 'an empire's glory' he quotes snatches of 'Rule Britannia' and the 'Marseillaise', not his own music.

All the quotations are placed for their 'propriety and appositeness' to the words. So 'dreams' brings the opening of *The Dream of Gerontius* in the orchestra (four bars after fig. 10); 'sea-breakers' brings two bars from *Sea Pictures*. That these and the 'enigma' theme can follow seamlessly within the opening twelve choral bars indicates how homogeneous was Elgar's style. Elgar begged for not too much insistence 'on the *extent* of the quotations which after all form a very small portion of the work'. Indeed, it may take longer to read about than to listen to them. But they are important. Often the newly composed music is less distinguished by comparison, sometimes even strained or facile. The most 'advanced' passage, which might well have been inspired by its words – 'the dazzling unknown shore' – was adapted from a 1907 sketch. (Harmonically Elgar's most daring piece, the piano miniature *Skizze*, lasting just over one minute, was composed in 1901.) The most striking quotation is of 'Nimrod', in tribute to Jaeger who had recently died, a passage so achingly intense that formally it overbalances the whole. The final heart-rending allusion is to the death of Gerontius – 'Novissima hora est' – but it might well disclose Elgar's awareness of his own mortality, or more widely of the short human span of all artists. Taken together the quotations turn this music from being a setting of O'Shaughnessy's Ode into what amounts to Elgar's musical and spiritual autobiography. The theme is surely inspiration, a heady mixture of aspiration and anguish. At fig. 39, as the 'yearning' theme reaches its highest note, the orchestra falls silent and the chorus breathes the word 'inspiration'; the phrase is almost exactly the one under the words 'and he worshipped Him' (in *The Light of Life*: see above) and will recur in the Cello Concerto at the *con passione* climax at fig. 69. Elgar's own music is sometimes the best interpreter of his language.

Neither Elgar's life nor his music is simple. In both there are many layers and contradictions. It was his good fortune that with his complicated nature he was born at a time when harmonic resources enabled him to express such ambiguities. The great achievement of his music is how he integrated the uncertainties within it.

6 The early choral works

ROBIN HOLLOWAY

Hard to bear is the poignancy of loss induced by so many once living kinds of music separated by time and change, imprisoned in obsolete genres or superseded beliefs and practices. Manifestly important music, sometimes supremely great, is cut off from roots deep-nourished in a context of social, civic, or religious usage, to be preserved in artificial surroundings, most notably the technically flawless CD. Somewhere along this shadow-line of defunctive music lie the pre-*Gerontius* choral works with orchestra by Elgar. A quick glance at the lists on the back of old Novello vocal scores of their hard-core staples (mainly Handel) suffices to reveal the extended wasteland, once teeming with life, of the Victorian oratorio. Elgar's compositional growth is firmly grounded in this copious provincial choral culture. His earlier cantatas make a determined bid to join it, his later to raise and enhance it; taken together they cover almost his entire composing life, which coincides with English choral culture at its apogee.

While the two last oratorios have never quite gained the safe mainstream, *Gerontius* is unbudgeable. And in more general terms his reputation has never stood higher in all the years since its first peak in the twentieth century's first decade. But the pre-*Gerontius* pieces, for the most part clear milestones on a great composer's path to prime-of-life powers, none utterly negligible, some patently inspired, are largely neglected. That they have all been recorded goes to endorse my opening remarks: this is exhumation, not living repertory, available anywhere but in the concert hall where it belongs. Perhaps these pieces are killed by the downside of the once vigorous culture that produced them: the provincial philistinism memorably lambasted in Shaw's concert notices of the 1880s and 90s. Plots are stilted and ludicrous (goes the consensus), texts fustian, the genre in general old-fangled and unworkable. These charges can't be denied but they can be sidestepped. Despite the tendency in recent musicology to 'privilege' verbal text, on a par with or even above its setting, the fact is that, ever since the relinquishment of biblical and liturgical words, vocal music in all its genres is far more often a transcendence of doggerel, triteness, insipidity, than it is a meet-and-match of true minds.

These remarks emphatically include the sacred or secular oratorio in English all the way from its roots in Purcell via Handel to Elgar and beyond. and in this great tradition of pure awfulness, Elgar stands firm and square.

Take for a start the imperishable *Gerontius*. How Newman's poem, second in its day for popularity only to *In Memoriam*, nowadays groans, creaks and embarrasses when divorced from its setting, and sometimes also as set. Nobody turns a hair, and many are on their knees. Yet this seemingly robust tastelessness jibs at the Rev. Edward Capel-Cure, Shapcott Wensley and H. A. Acworth, CIE (Companion of the Order of the Indian Empire). I don't perceive any marked qualitative distinction between their texts, nor the more 'professional' trash of Longfellow – in his own right or translating Uhland – and the sainted Cardinal; nor, when Elgar hits top form, in the music. The vital thing is the conviction and intensity of the composer's response: when authentically charged up they sweep grotty words before them. In *Gerontius* what matters is the passionate identification with which the composer inhabits the situations, becoming the dying Everyman on his deathbed of pain, or the newborn soul skimming weightless and sin-free; his awed fearfulness before the judgement; his cry of unworthiness; his long, achingly nostalgic withdrawal. Outside its protagonist, rendered with such unforgettable inwardness, *Gerontius* is a very uneven work; far more so than *King Olaf* and *Caractacus*.

This is contentious: what seems to me certain is the earlier works' superior freshness and freedom of idiom and of manner. They are not yet self-conscious; they are, within the bounds of their genre and culture, wonderfully exuberant, unaffectedly heartfelt, skilful without ostentation, ardently and generously musical – a vital emanation from a composer stretching his wings in an environment spacious enough, surprisingly, to give him room.

All this is magnificently manifest in *The Black Knight* (Op. 25). The young(ish) composer's ambition is shown by his later calling the work 'a sort of Symphony in four divisions' (conventionalised by Novello's 'Cantata').[1] Uhland's ballad (1806), itself drawing on a seventeenth-century reworking of a weird putative happening in early Scottish history, came to Elgar via Longfellow: the source is *Hyperion: A Romance* (1839).

The first movement of the 'Symphony' combines a fluent euphonious chivalric idiom out of Weber and Mendelssohn with touches of early Wagner and a muscular Brahmsian warmth, with easy mastery unobtrusively all-permeating rather than ostentatiously displayed – as when the swinging 3/4 yields momentarily to flowing 12/8 with pastoral mordents for 'luxuriant spring'. Then fanfares and vigorous semiquaver motion evoke the jousting play. The story is told entirely by the chorus even when direct speech is involved, which adds to the sense, paradoxically, of a quasi-instrumental continuity. Everything is shapely, neat, exact, *à la* Mendelssohn – a clear ancestor being *Die erste Walpurgisnacht* – but with a capacity to expand its lungs that transcends its source, most particularly in the passage towards the 'sonata' return, then the greatly more energetic 'recapitulation' whose greater scope necessitates many verbal repetitions in the closing return of the opening two lines.

It links into a 'second movement', a foursquare scherzo-cum-toy-march out of *Jeux d'enfants* and *Nutcracker*. The first sign of something untoward is Tchaikovskian too – a sinister gesture *à la* Carabosse as the stranger replies to the demand for his 'name and scutcheon'. The continuation of his reply – 'I am a Prince of mighty sway' – is pure Tchaikovsky ballet entrance/preparation music: the final setting of these words arrives at one of two moments only to show evidence of mature Wagner, but still wholly within the earlier idiom, regulated and 'grammarised' to effect a return to the home key, now in the minor mode. The march now loses its dinkiness and grows feverish, yet 'the castle 'gan to rock' is set with relish – a scale of descending major thirds *fff* against rising chromatic trombones. These lines have to be repeated to achieve the purely musical size, and this too adds to the sense of ghoulish enjoyment. Then the rhyming 'shock' from which the prince can scarcely rise is softened by the absence of obvious onomatopoeia: rather the whole scene recedes poetically into the distance, a characteristic Elgarian strategy.

The third movement joins on after a long-sustained link-note. At first it perpetuates the sense of unreal safety by an Allegretto dance motion in Elgar's wistful 'dream children' mode, commencing fragile, turning beefier at the almost *Merrie England* strain that follows. 'Pipe and viol', though, is a Sullivan-style madrigal, surpassing the model in all respects, not least by underlying this pretty music with four inconspicuous but perceptible periods of 13/4. There's a tabor too! In this modest beginning lie the seeds of the achingly evocative pastoral interludes in *Falstaff* thirty years on. Again, the first couplet has to be continually reset to allow the musical design full scope. Only once does this become a trifle absurd – the shadowy intruder's invitation to the dance ('with manner bland/Doth ask the maiden's hand') doesn't bear repetition. But this momentary miscalculation within what we by now recognise as the composer's chosen treatment of his dark tale is dispersed by the mysterious four-chord progression introducing the dance's second phase. 'A measure weird and dark' – a sort of Kardomah Café oriental number crossed with the Dvořák of the more melancholy Slavonic Dances, and as innocent of depravity or evil. Because of the work's chosen manner, the naive kitschiness is more rather than less sinister, while eschewing cheap attempts, anyway ineffective, to 'make your flesh creep'. The return of the main melody under a descant of fluttery semiquavers manages this without appearing to try. Prettiness in music, like cheapness, can be a strangely potent resource. And the passage where the flowers fall from the blighted girl's breast and hair is exquisitely pretty – a mixture of the *Liebeslieder* waltz ('How lovely is thy dwelling-place') in Brahms's Requiem with some favourite strains from Humperdinck's *Hänsel und Gretel* – *The Black Knight*'s exact contemporary (1890–3), so it is a matter of two purely musical musicians drawing from the same sources, rather than one influencing the other.

The finale begins in lovely unrolling curves of stately ceremonial music: the work is still unthreatened, it seems, by the story it sets itself to tell. Even the king's 'distraught' mood is rendered in a dainty twostep, gradually paling as his gaze registers his children's unnatural pallor. Unnatural calm and sweetness long drawn out pervade the children's courteous reply: it leads into an a cappella part-song of magical simplicity, as their father embraces his fading offspring. Their death is equally underplayed: horror is narrated with euphony – poignant and wistful, avoiding lament, let alone expressionism. The king's outburst is less convincing. It essays melodramatics, to arrive at the grand tutti return in E♭ of the work's opening (there in G) – six bars of full-fat pomp and circumstance; then another none-too-compelling outburst of woe and longing – 'take me too, the joyless father!' – and a rapid *rit. e dim.* to reintroduce the dark stranger in preparation for his closing one-liner (subtle, that this introduction adapts the music of the first line he spoke, back in scene ii). Its 'hollow, cavernous' unison on the dominant of the home key yields to warm harmony as, in resumption of part-song texture, the first word ('Roses') reaches with classical firmness the home key of G which began and will close the entire 'symphony'. Thus the 'tonal recap' controverts the 'thematic [and tempo and mood] recap' with simple poetic justice, suggestive wide beyond its craftsmanly facture. Elgar's E minor interruption soon burns out into the gentle ghost of the confident momentum of the work's opening, gradually entwined with chromatic triplets, before the chorus softly evokes the season, still 'luxuriant Spring', though its blooms are blasted and Pentecostal gladness long forgot: and so to the deeply gentle, almost traumatised fade-out end.

A comparison that runs all the way would be with Mahler's youthful cantata *Das klagende Lied*, surely unknown to Elgar. This also grew out of early German Romantic subject-matter and its musical treatment, with *Euryanthe* and *Lohengrin* clear ancestors and only a few stabs of late Wagner. Both works tell, in a dreamy hybrid of opera, song-cycle, ballad, a tale of dark destruction, setting proud castle and knightly carouse against a glowing evocation of the natural world. *Das klagende Lied* involves sibling jealousy, lust, murder, and supernatural retribution wherein everyone and everything is annihilated. Its idiom is folkloric, martial, *singvereinisch*, together with an extraordinary vein of near-hysteria that gets the tale's latent morbidity out into the open. Whereas in *The Black Knight* no one has erred: the dark stain is both external and inexplicable, the style is warm, full, sweet; and yet the ending is equally bleak. Does Elgar's treatment too much soften, indeed prettify, its sable content, or is it the work's genius that the events are told *en rose*, with such decorum both expressive and technical as paradoxically to enhance the sinister effect? Both are works of uncanny, disturbing power.

We need not long be detained by *From the Bavarian Highlands*: six choral songs Op. 27 to words by Alice Elgar, after South German folk songs, written with piano accompaniment in 1895 and orchestrated the next year. They come from the salon side of Elgar's copious gift, with Dvořák the audibly presiding influence. The first, in tripping 3/8, only just avoids banality by its five-phrases in the middle section; the second is pure Dvořák *Ländler* (compare Op. 46, No. 4 in the same key); while the third is positively obsessed by the famous *Humoresque*. The fourth ('Aspiration') is prayerful; the fifth a dainty valse. The sixth and last is the most ambitious, a Dvořák symphonic scherzo with a hint of the bucolic Brahms (D major Serenade, fifth movement). Its longer phrases give Elgar's innate tendency to expansion its only opportunity in this work. A hushed one-in-a-bar trio section is followed by a fugato on scherzo material expertly swivelled round to return in triumph to the home key and the repeat of the trio as climax.

The Light of Life digs deeper, establishing prophetic idioms for religious strains to come.[2] This 'short oratorio' Op. 29 builds upon the episode of Jesus healing the blind man (St John's Gospel, chapter 9), versified by Capel-Cure. The verse is certainly fustian, but the trajectory is sure, and the message profound. The immediately striking advance is an enrichment of harmonic range, orchestral elaboration, and wide-spreading continuity of the sixteen numbers; most of the score is continuous, with a free flow of motives working in and out and across the divisions. Later, leitmotivic Wagner has made its mark, though not much in actual idiom, upon Elgar's most ambitious work to date. The central miracle is resourcefully expanded into a sequence of scenes and meditations in which the soloists are cast sometimes as characters (tenor the blind man, soprano his mother, baritone Jesus), sometimes as commentators.[3] The contralto narrates, and joins the mother in a duet. The pity of individual blindness is linked in an image-cluster of some penetration to the God who made night and day, to Jesus as Light of the World, sent to comprehend and ameliorate mankind's inner spiritual darkness and the night of sin; by the closing chorus in praise of illumination and spiritual perfecting it has accumulated considerable weight of resonance.

The new note in the music is apparent from its opening 'Meditation' for orchestra alone, a sort of proto-*Gerontius* prelude, mingling painful (if not yet anguished) with elevating and pastoral and inward-looking. Loosely yet skilfully worked together, it ends with the dangerously luscious passage of warm uplift (connoting religiosity *à la* Liszt, with a touch of pure Broadway in its fifth bar, yet as texture – three-part writing with the vagrant flowing chromatic inner voice doubled in octaves – highly prophetic of *The Apostles* and *The Kingdom*) just about rescued by a fine sequential chromatic descent over a dominant pedal into the first chorus. All this material will recur and grow throughout the work and receive its apotheosis in the closing chorus.

As the story proceeds, the main generality is the music's size and easy flow. For instance, the first stanza of the blind man's first solo (in praise of light) and the second (lamenting that God hides from him) punctuates a quasi-recapitulation and coda of the first chorus to make a larger shape, after the example of *The Black Knight*'s 'symphonism'. Thus the first narrative weaves a self-contained miniature ternary structure which opens out into the mother's first appearance, an entire aria – this time *not* interrupted – asking God not to judge parent or child (grateful, euphonious, somewhat faceless, with a fulsome/sentimental climax on 'Lighten, O lighten mine eyes, O Lord' that would not sit amiss in a Boosey ballad). Jesus's tripartite reply is that he has not sinned, nor his parents, but that God's power might be manifest through him: 'I must do my Father's work for the night cometh when no man can work', boldly conflated by Capel-Cure with 'I am the Light of the World, and who follows me shall not walk in darkness' – set to material from the 'Meditation', retrospectively extending its meaning into this new context after the manner of Wagner's act-preludes.

Which in turn closes into the opening of a vigorous chorus, effectively vital after a tendency so far to droop somewhat, but vitiated by false, strained word-repetition to cover the exigencies of phrase-extension and to fit around pre-made themes (the first sign of a fault difficult to take in *Gerontius* and almost unbearable in its successors whether sacred or secular). Dvořák in blithest Slavonic style incongruously appears in both 'middle eights' (women in parallel thirds lilting and swishing their folkloric skirts to hymn Christ's sufferings and sacrifice to come). Yet even these lapses are partially redeemed by the same music's soft return at the close which also makes the first real stopping-point in the work as a whole. But not really, for the next scene follows in key, mood, and *tinta*.

There follows the delectable duet (the two female soloists, or all the women of the chorus): Elgar of the salon at his perfect best, maybe not quite appropriate to the awful words ('Night comes in: the soul is dark; All joy is dead, All gladness fled, And life has missed its mark') but quite transcending them in quality. Tender sweetness does in the end suit and illuminate the episode's close: Jesus can touch and make whole. Without break into the next scene. The narrator tells of the successful cure, the neighbours wonder, over a bass of sixths bristling with mordents that could come out of *Falstaff*, and a bustle of semiquavers straight out of Variation XI of Op. 36, or the First Symphony's scherzo. Several grand choral moments also prefigure the composer of the future: a splendid blast of bombast on 'Since the world began was it not heard that any man opened the eyes of one that was blind'; then its curtailed return; then after an archaising fugato to show the supersession of previous received wisdom. Its inward-gazing complement, 'and the eyes of the blind shall see', is a cappella *pp* to *ff* crowned by the re-entry of the whole orchestra, *fff*, followed by superb re-descent into softness. The larger-than-life methods of Verdi's contemporary Te Deum make an exact parallel.

The tenor's reply begins wistfully pretty, gathering intensity when gradually infiltrated by the closing theme, then other material, from the 'Meditation', to end with a seraphic recollection of Brahms's seventh 'Haydn' variation, enhanced with Elgar's textural signature, the internal voice in octaves. The Pharisees object to the miracle; its beneficiary testifies; the contralto steps out of her narrator's role for a developed aria; the Jews still don't believe until the man's mother is questioned, testifies in turn, and bounces the ball back to her son. All this is somewhat routine after the high levels earlier, with stilted verbal manipulation abounding. The aggravated Pharisees for a moment prefigure the demons in *Gerontius* as they anathematise the heresy, releasing a number for the mother and full women's voices, indifferent in itself save for one moment exactly replicating a well-loved turn in 'Softly and gently' from the Angel's farewell.

But routine has set in, together with a marked tendency towards the pious lethargy that will prove fatal to the post-*Gerontius* oratorios. Inspiration returns for the healed man's confession of faith and his healer's haloed setting of 'I am the good shepherd', successfully etherealising the rustic Slavonic strains so incongruous earlier. Between these comes a purely orchestral rendition of words printed above but not set ('and he worshipped Him' – John 9:38), wherein the shimmering mystic chromaticism of Elgar's eventual religious idiom is fully formed for eight rather queasy bars. Another familiar trait is consolidated here from its invention in *The Black Knight*: Jesus's last solo passage in grand full-front *nobilmente* (and E♭ major), which Elgar was to make for good and ill so much his own. But the verbal 'fixing' is at its clumsiest around here: with relief we reach the *Schlusschor*, frequently extracted as an anthem, 'Light of the world, we know thy praise'. It swings infectiously along as a 3/4 march with stirring syncopations over a sturdy crotchet bass: the style is *Blest Pair of Sirens* with wider wings and deeper lungs. A more pathetic strain follows with contrapuntal entries piling up on 'Thou dids't not disdain to take/Our low estate', in a way that could on a clear day show the second subject of the Second Symphony's finale in the far distance. For the moment, however, all this is good solid provincial *Kappellmeisterei*, brimming over with confidence and competence. As the softer paragraph broadens towards its end the nascent symphonist flexes his muscles: the sequential treatment of the not-quite-awful theme from near the end of the 'Meditation' really takes off for a few thrilling pages.

Even the laborious home-key return at 'Thy word is now our sov'reign law' (with its desperate repeat of 'sov'reign') ends in genuine magnificence. The chromatic detumescence on the penultimate page may not suit all tastes. It was of course implicit in the passage that closes the 'Meditation', whose memorable cadence into the first chorus is now redeployed to bring the last to a dying fall which suddenly changes its mind to burn up into a loud commercial ending, with fanfares, for the blaze of noon.

The Banner of St George had been performed in an earlier version the year before *The Light of Life* was completed, and might have been sketched earlier still. The absurd and wordy text by one Shapcott Wensley, thick with exclamation marks, presents the tale in two scenes: (1) a fearsome dragon ravages the local maidens, but the king's daughter is willing to sacrifice herself for the community; (2) the red-cross knight arrives and dispatches the dragon, stopping for no reward. In an Epilogue his mission is compared to England's Imperial role ('Great race, whose empire of splendour/Has dazzled a wondering world!'). This sad stuff perhaps surprisingly didn't kindle Elgar's innate feeling for such sentiments. The by-now-expected easy euphony can't disguise a lack of urgency. Scene 1 flows uneventfully on; scene 2 unwisely continues a similar placid 3/4 motion; the advent of George livens things up a little, but the momentum remains three-square and all too amiable. The dragon is hopelessly tame; George's farewell is hopelessly demure. The Epilogue at last changes to a solid 4/4 march in the uplifting patriotic vein which Elgar is often accused, unjustly, of cheapening. Here though the result *is* discreditable. The trio/middle eight ('O ne'er may the flag beloved [the composer abjures the archaism demanded by his poet's metre] Unfurl in a strife unblest!') and the march's return *fff largamente e grandioso*, are flagrant flatulent bombast, though it goes without saying that Elgar gets up a resplendent ceremonial sonority just perfect for the English who 'don't like music but love the noise it makes'.

With *King Olaf* and *Caractacus* we are back on course: in these two as much as in the 'Enigma' Variations Elgar reaches maturity – stylistic, technical, expressive. *King Olaf* reverts to Longfellow, childhood favourite of the composer and his mother. The source this time is *Tales of a Wayside Inn* (first series, 1863), a neo-Chaucerian anthology of stories. Jerrold Northrop Moore points out how this tale was especially suited to appeal: it is the Musician's Tale of the heroic Norwegian who brought the Christian faith to his pagan lands before, like Siegfried, being undone by treachery from within and without through his relations with women; in the end, and beyond his death, only his mother remains faithful.[4] A Malvern neighbour, Acworth was called in to cut and reshape the overgenerous original, adding further explanations, often insufficient, to cover the elisions.

It doesn't break into parts; rather, there are eight named scenes, contained within a Prologue and Epilogue for chorus and orchestra. Nevertheless, three distinct areas can be discerned: it clearly pauses for breath after Olaf's defeat of the pagan Ironbeard, before moving on to his three women; and again before his own defeat and passing. Numbers are not *enchaînés* as in the earlier works; but they are longer, and more firmly defined and structured; thus overall continuity is greater than before, with a new sweep and exactness of aim. And the orchestration is more than confident, it is masterly; also so intrinsic to the musical invention that here and hereafter Elgar's vocal scores are forced to omit plentiful compositional detail in order to remain playable.

The Prologue opens superbly, on a broad all-pervading orchestral figure, distinctive and eloquent with melancholy and mystery, opening up the old book of sagas, formally invoked as source of the tale now to be told. In this first part the bass solo doubles as Skald (the bard) and Ironbeard; the tenor narrates Olaf's youth before representing the hero himself. The Skald summons up Thor, god of thunder and war; his words are placed in the chorus in a stark saraband–tattoo over a quaver bass powerful with repressed energy – a grandson of Siegfried's forging-song and hence cousin to the mighty obstinacy of Bruckner's late scherzos. The following tenor solo shows the length, diversity yet enhanced continuity, and the high quality of the ideas. Also their quantity: they tumble over each other in cornucopian generosity: warm arcs of lyricism for Olaf's sea-voyage to accept Thor's challenge; stirring chivalric heroics at the thought of father to be avenged and lost territories resumed; magical pianissimo skimming/shimmering 12/8 with mystic enharmony as the sea-foam dashes and the wind wails in the sails; the return of this metre now shapely and limber in the hero's own theme, with its construction almost entirely on rising and falling fifths. There is plentiful other thematic invention in this intoxicating and healthy music which seems to be exulting in the verdancy of its new-woken powers. It's notable too for its narrative speed and directedness: it gobbles up text virtually without repetitions, let alone the clumsy verbal long-circuiting often necessitated in previous works by the legitimate demands of the purely musical phrasing.

The Skald's invitation to tell what happened after Olaf's arrival is taken up by a broadly flowing chorus, supple and muscular beneath its golden surface, moving easily into a more martial 9/8 and back again to the initial 3/4 underpinned by the 9/8 on a drum tattoo, evincing in simple form the mastery of momentum-modulation so wonderfully fulfilled in the symphonies. Olaf rouses his race to challenge Ironbeard. Elgar, paramount at portraits in music alone, tends towards woodenness when attempting characters in action and diction; but the actual ideas remain top-drawer and the new sense of narrative energy still carries things forward. The newly uninhibited orchestration also helps, for instance at a hulking return of the saraband rhythm combined with swinging bravado in the violins' descant. Pagan image is smashed by Christian axe (though the text is as opaque as the music is direct). Ironbeard's angry and pathetic death is inspired, with some strikingly individual harmony and scoring (the most thrilling in both respects the tingling diminished seventh, on 'true to honour and truth'). Ironbeard's fierce spirit melts tenderly into the air, and the chorus continues its narration: the Cross of compassion is raised over the bloody sacrifice-stone, and the Skalds hymn Christ, not Odin. This dangerous moment is restrained, inward, deeply felt, sensitive (one senses) to Olaf's unconscious compunction at felling such a fine upstanding foe. Its solemn pall of orchestral sonority – bardic harps and two marvellous percussion rumbles, then the superb simple climax as 'the pow'r of Christ was felt' – is exalted and rich without fulsomeness. A closing alla breve hymn begins in block chords, joined by dripping harps as Olaf joins his people at prayer: the choral harmony breaks into lines, the orchestral soars aloft (with sequential arches of generous cantabile like the lyric episode in the finale of the first symphony: the circumstance of both is 'a *massive* hope for the future').[5] Yet the chorus doesn't end here. Instead Elgar repeats an epitome of the quatrain just set to a lyricised return of the saraband rhythm as if to indicate with touching conviction that Pagan and Christian can coexist in a peaceful present. The ending is grand and fervent – a double fortissimo climax, an allargando and diminuendo, then as the choir sinks out of sight on 'peace' the orchestra swells up again to end in confidence and strength. It ends the implicit 'Part I'; virtually flawless on a different plane from any of the composer's previous ventures into this genre.

'Part II' begins with No. 6, the story of Gudrun, narration yielding to scena in No. 7. Still seeking annealing reconciliation, Olaf foolishly weds his enemy's daughter. She steals into the bedchamber, dagger in hand (it's disconcerting to find that this section is Longfellow not Acworth). The music renders his disarming her with muted trumpet; and the chorus closes the scene in narrative obscurity – hunting motifs (and something more specific, the motif of Brünnhilde's betrayed vulnerability in *Siegfried* Act 3) are heard to seal the separation before the couple have even conjoined. Drama is so clearly not Elgar's forte that unconvincingness here doesn't surprise. Yet the score is still rich in good musical material: the lovely opening, reintroduced with some psychological subtlety as Gudrun is revealed in the moonshine with the dagger, and again as the scene closes. Next comes one of *King Olaf*'s triumphs, a choral ballad, 'The Wraith of Odin'. This is finer than the comparable ballad in *The Black Knight* (second movement): more mature, compact, aimed; a marvellous thing, driven by mercurial yet fierce semiquavers like the scherzo in the first symphony, similarly masterful in its ability to slow the rate without losing the momentum, to take up and develop the 'Saga-Dream of Olden Times' music that opens the whole work. Other ideas also recur and are developed – Ironbeard's dying salute to Thor and the conversion hymn that closed 'Part I' – Elgar the cyclic, synthesising symphonist at work.

Sigrid, the second lady in Olaf's love life, follows. The narrative, told again by a recitative (No. 10) introducing a ballad (No. 11), is far from lucid. The music, unlike most of Gudrun's melodrama, is delectable, Elgar's 'girlie' manner at its most winsome, in this 9/8 ballad for women's voices only. It encloses a duet for Olaf and Sigrid completely convincing as an expression of wary wooing without a sparkle of sexual desire, deftly and drolly emblematised in the wriggly formalistic turns in almost every bar of the orchestra when he, then she, exchange guarded compliments (Elgar the ironist, not a familiar face). Tactlessly, he tells her direct: 'thou has not beauty, thou has not youth'. Outraged, she rouses the old gods. He departs in a huff; there's an insult over a glove and a smack, told by the women in the brief return of the lilting 9/8: and Sigrid ends the episode on a note of menace – 'I am the one who can watch and wait.'

Now comes the last of the hero's disastrous adventures with women: Thyri, introduced in a brief recitative (No. 12) setting up her theme in *echt*-Elgar three-part texture before the tale is told in another choral ballad (No. 13) – an extra 'Song from the Bavarian Highlands', incongruously delectable, a waltz/*Scherzo capriccioso* of grace and charm with tremendous cumulative strength as it effortlessly unrolls while also forwarding the story (for all that the action is hardly clear: again, pure if muddy Longfellow). It is worthy of a symphony. Thyri's pretty solo is tinged with Grieg until she begins to wheedle in Kundry's potent seduction strains from *Parsifal* Act 2. Olaf's love song is the result. He bears her spring flowers as his tribute; but she wants more. The work's best duet ensues. The return of her material, his love song, and the ballad, all interwoven, goes with a will, to end with a promise of spring not to be fulfilled here; when it does come, at the close of the whole work, it will be very different in tone and meaning. Meanwhile the duet's latent untruth is brought involuntarily out in its flat conventional ending, an unaccompanied operatic flourish for the lovers, perfunctorily rounded off by the orchestra.

'Part III' begins (No. 15) in a choral recitative (misnomer for such melodious, richly wrought, fully thematic music) telling how Sigrid marries Svend, king of the Danes, and persuades him into vengeance. Another ballad (No. 16) describes the sea-battle in which the hero, valiant to the last, is outnumbered, defeated, 'and so perishes in the flood'. It is a first-rate number, with its manly vigour and skill in alternating and combining 4/4 with 12/8; Elgar knows exactly what will work for and appeal to his amateur forces to get them to yield their all. Symphonic development continues throughout, with elements of reminiscence looming larger, tending towards closing the work with its first-heard material: Olaf's limber 12/8 theme, then the broad 3/4 of his earliest ocean-journey; then, after a terrific overwhelming of his dragon-boat, comes a superb stroke, the return of the mystic enharmonic 12/8 music, transformed, extended, raised from its original shimmering *pp* to a coruscating *fff* before it rapidly diminishes. But not disappears: for the same skimming momentum continues in the orchestra as the choral harmony broadens, then sinks, to merge with the tolling bell of the hero's passing.

In the epilogue narrative vagueness is compounded. A hitherto unmentioned character, Astrid, Abbess of Drontheim (bass solo! – she turns out to be Olaf's mother), hears mysterious runic voices in the night while she prays. For these all three soloists join, returning to rhythm, material, and key (B♭ minor) of the saraband originally given to Thor, together after the first four bars with its chomping chromatic quaver bass. In its solemn setting the effect is genuinely uplifting, as the same saraband rhythm is taken up by all voices (soloists instructed to unite with the choir, always a sign of high seriousness), swelling in rich warm sequences advocating patient self-conquest, subsiding into the three solo voices alone, and declining into the work's penultimate section and spiritual heart, the once-celebrated 'As torrents in summer'. This apotheosis of the soppy sentimental Victorian part-song hardly differs from its models in idiom, though we note the latent power in the suspensions and the implicitly expressive weight in the detached triplets, with word-repetition for once reinforcing rather than diluting meaning; yet it turns out to be the inspired, exactly right apotheosis. The first two stanzas are a cappella in warm hymnic E♭. One bar of deft organ-loft modulation reintroduces the soloists for verse 3 in G, arching gratefully on new material in praise of truth and love against hatred and anger, crowned by the choral re-entry for verse 4, returning to the part-song's opening (but retaining G major) and making explicit, under a nimbus of flowing semiquavers, its rhythmic identity with the saraband. Remembering this motif's origin ('I am the god Thor'), this transformation must be called imaginatively handsome, a musical metaphor for forging weapons into ploughshares. The overall effect is of the closing chorus of *The Light of Life*, with greater mastery of more distinguished material and incomparably profounder feeling. The structure closes softly, only at the last minute modulating back, this time with high Elgarian art, via a hint of E♭ major, to the melancholy G minor music with which the whole work had begun. The saga is done, the storybook closed:

> A strain of music ends the tale,
> A low monotonous funeral wail,
> That with its cadence wild and sweet
> Makes the Saga more complete.

A curious end. Sad and withdrawn as Tennyson's *Passing of Arthur*, it under-cuts for sure any suspicion that the preceding uplift, with all its glowing conviction of the certainty of renewal, is complacent or bland. The very last two bars extend the ambiguity: they close on a *tierce de Picardie* for chorus and orchestra; then the voices diminuendo to nothing, then the major third is drained away from the instruments, leaving only a wide-spaced long-sustained bare fifth. Compare the withdrawal of well-upholstered comfort at the end of the funeral march in the Second Symphony, a far more sophis-ticated and complex instance of the same refusal to rest easy.

Invited in 1897 to produce a new work for Leeds the following year, Elgar offered a symphony, but the Festival Committee insisted upon a cantata, and the result was *Caractacus*, first performed in Leeds Town Hall in October 1898. Elgar turned again to Acworth, who this time had to start from scratch with no prototype to build upon, producing both scenario and versification for a libretto that has been widely regretted ever since, though it suffices as surely for setting as it is deficient in narrative clarity, character-depiction, and dramatic shapeliness.

Caractacus, king of Britain, his principal headquarters the Herefordshire Beacon on the Malvern Hills, defying and defeated by the Romans, pardoned in Rome itself: the appeal to Elgar is strong and manifold – the nostalgic sad-ness of a lost but noble cause, the beloved boyhood landscape, the impulse from romance-spinning with his mother, are irresistible.[6] Its music, like *King Olaf*, abounds in *echt*-Elgarian ideas of wide-ranging character – vigorous, spirited, virile; tender, delicate, refined: it commands still more extended spans, presented by a symphonically commentating and developing texture aware of but not directly beholden to Wagner's literalism: the orchestration with its many sources (Dvořák, French music, Tchaikovsky, Verdi, as well as German composers from Mendelssohn to Brahms) is still more sonorous or sparing as occasion requires, evincing endlessly unfailing technical resource and accuracy of imagination.[7] *Caractacus* is more ambitious perhaps, more patchy certainly, than its predecessor. In as much as it moves further away from the cantata medium towards semi-opera it is at an obvious disadvan-tage, and the story itself is possibly less appealing. At its best the work is as fine as anything he wrote: also as complex in substance, yet still fresh and springy, lacking as yet the later tendency to fuzz and fuss when in doubt.

Scene I. The British camp on the Malvern hills. Night. Caractacus and his army enter the camp. He invites his weary men to rest, in a beautiful aria of wistful response to nature in her balmy mood, before exhortations to exer-tion as he sees his peaceful reign threatened with its inevitable end. Enter his daughter Eigen, first of many windflowers, then Orbin her betrothed. She relates a mysterious prophecy heard near the sacred oak from the lips of a

Druid maiden. Overlapping solos develop into a trio – fluent, slightly shop-soiled sentimental ardour. It broadens into hymnic unison as the augury is interpreted for all three to portend Britain's glory; builds up in a stirring swell of patriotic E♭ major, declines *à la* 'Nimrod' into a gently cradling chorus urging the weary king to rest again. It kindles to inspire him and the men for the coming battle, then cradles down again, to close on the opposite injunction – the work's opening words, heard on and off subliminally throughout the scene, for the watchmen to remain wakeful and alert. All this is a continuous span of various tempi and character, so commandingly through-composed that it can bear some of the relatively uninspired stretches in its stride.

Scene II. The Sacred Oak by the Tomb of the Kings. The spooky dance-rounds of the Arch-Druid, his Druids and Druidesses and Bards, might invite smiling comparison with Gilbert below par ('Tread the mystic circle found,/Measure of the holy ground/Thro' the fire and thro' the smoke/Girdle slow the sacred oak', etc.), and in the music, Sullivan on Substances. Such comparison would fail to do justice to this cunningly wrought fabric with its exquisite light-music dance lilt, in a fragile, rhythmically subtle two- and three-part texture as the Druid maidens enter the rounds.[8] A stark and splendid unison invocation summons Taranis, 'Lord of dread and lord of pow'r'. A victim is sacrificed: Taranis emerges to tell the future in a fine combination of the new stark with the preceding wistful, now manifesting unexpected strength. Orbin (who, the 'Argument' at the start of the score tells us, but not the text, 'belongs to the half-priestly order of minstrels') is invited to read the runes, which indicate, with suitable ambiguity, defeat for the king, information the Arch-Druid decides to suppress so as to keep Caractacus in arms. The dainty dance-rounds resume in the background of his treacherous thoughts, gradually echoed by the male Druids as the maidens dance on, till their rounds are broken and Caractacus enters with his soldiers. He enquires his destiny and is treated to a grand exhortation: 'Go forth, O king, to conquer/And all the land shall know/When falls thy charmed sword-edge/In thunder on the foe' (rather cunningly worded by the not-so-hapless Acworth for legal loopholes). Its E♭ flatulence is taken up *grandioso* by the chorus. This duff music is, just maybe, intended as dramatic irony since the declaration is knowingly mendacious. This second scene, begun with such distinction, grows bitty until Orbin bids for the truth to be told. The Druids denounce him (with a hint of the demons in *Gerontius*). He rushes off and is duly cursed. Absurdity remains perilously near; in vain the cries to Taranis, in augmentation and *fff*, to doom the fleeing apostate: neither they nor the vehement orchestral ending raise a shudder, nor anything save the certain sense that Elgar cannot deal believably with melodramatics and rapid action when attached to an actual story.

Scene III. The Forest near the Severn. Morning. After the orchestral introduction of enchanting faery delicacy comes an extremely Sullivanesque choral madrigal over drones in the divided basses. Many epochs of British music meet here: the Victorian Arcadia all the way from the Savoy operas to Lionel Monckton; the Edwardian vision of *Merrie England*, only four years around the corner, with a pipe-and-tabor evocation of Tudorbethan (hence to Eric Coates and Ronald Binge): as well as its purported time-and-place, the pagan West Country of the first century AD: Ireland if not Britten, and *Midsummer Marriage* for sure, with *Silbury Air* on the remote horizon. Its bashful sweetness is slightly askewed by an odd chromatic progression that introduces the opening and its return towards the end. Straight into Eigen, flowing 12/8 and utterly characteristic – rising and falling sevenths, inner part doubled at the octave, tender harmonic coloration, chromaticism French rather than Bayreuth. Orbin's entry brings a further bout of unconvincing amateur dramatics, in quasi-operatic recitative fragmenting music from previous numbers. His closing wishes, that the gods grant him strength to protect her father and that their own lovers' parting will not be for ever, brings forth the Clara Butt/Albert Hall strain later to be so abused in Elgar's music, here still unknowing and surprised, before the madrigal steals back (again, prefaced by its mystery-progression) under their words. Its melting away is one of the loveliest moments in Elgar. It leads on into far and away his most successful duet, vernal and decorous, not erotic let alone sensual, maybe a tiny bit drawing-room-ish for its open-air setting, rapturous in its warmth and easy flow, touchingly vulnerable yet strong – even (frankly) a little coarse in the lovers' octave unison at the climax. Here – life-comradeship with the inspiring mother/sister/wife/muse – is surely where lies Elgar's Eros. Why, after this touching moment of intimate tenderness crowning the work's pastoral heart, the composer has chosen to close it with a sudden uprush-crescendo of the formerly gentle rustle-of-summer foliage followed by a curt Amen cadence, Taranis only knows.

Scene IV. The Malvern hills. Eigen awaits with her maidens the outcome of her father's decisive engagement with the Romans – Elgar's girlish side at its anxious fluttery best. She sings in her usual 12/8, the music gradually permeated then taken over completely by the prophecy she relayed in scene I. Caractacus enters with the disordered remnants of his army. They sing in a sort of cross between fast waltz and scherzo, con fuoco, a splendidly vital piece describing the din and bloodiness of battle. Then follows one of the score's manifest high points, the inspired lament for the king and his people, noble in defeat; it transforms the regular four-beat clunk of Acworth's text ('Oh, my warriors, tell me truly/O'er the red graves where ye lie,/That your monarch led you duly,/First to charge and last to fly') into a supple 7/4 $(3 + 2 + 2)$.[9] Elgar's effecting this by play of regular and irregular shows high rhetorical art, but what strikes one is how effortless and uneccentric the rhythm is: everything moves with natural eloquence, the very accents of dignified public elegy. If this suggests the 'Albert Hall' idiom, it is both richly transformed by unmissable deep feeling, and quite transcended, in the great span of its facture (like the great edifice itself), that can include a contrasting middle section from the king (who launches the piece, and leads throughout) all the way up to a superb climax and rapidly down to a dying fall: profundity, and heroic size, in a mere twenty-nine bars.

Scene V. The Severn. We are to understand from the Argument that 'Caractacus and his family, including Orbin, are soon after betrayed into the hands of the enemy'. This is not mentioned in the text of this brief muted pastoral, headed with a 'stage direction': 'British captives embarking on the Roman galleys'. This number is a lyric intermezzo, to cover a gap in the plot. A grand defeated chromatic descent in 3/4 (which never recurs) introduces a drooping lyric march of lament, beautiful and graceful, concluding with a fine orchestral epilogue, which suddenly dries its tears and gathers an upsurge of strength as upbeat to Scene VI. Rome. The Triumphal Procession. An operatic march, sturdy and a bit bombastic, its trio full-fat Eb major and songful rising sequences. That Elgar knows exactly what he's invoking is shown by marking the first choral entry (in the basses) *pomposamente*. A mournful counter-strain follows as Caractacus, his daughter, her betrothed, pass by barefoot and shamed. The orchestra now builds symphonically, with Elgar's sure instinct for ceremonial timing (compare in *Falstaff* the precise moment when the new-crowned Henry V appears in the coronation procession) to reach a mighty return of the march opening, now swung against a broad unison choral setting of the same opening lines, cut off by a sharp cry of 'hark!' and a new motion of fizzing energy, heralding the Emperor himself; grand, frankly pagan splendour, whose next emergence in English music will be *Belshazzar's Feast*. Claudius invites his royal slave, by pleading his cause, to avert his fate. Caractacus permits himself to plead, not for his own life but for those of 'my guileless daughter and the warrior bard,/Her lover, fled from priestly bonds at home'. The Emperor (though not the populace) is moved: La clemenza di Claudio introduces a lilting quartet for all this scene's principals, tending towards unction laced with saccharine, perhaps in unconscious embodiment of the conquered ones' further defeat by the vanquisher's gracious act. Its unaccompanied link is weak: then as the orchestra re-enters and assists the four soloists to a well-tailored operatic climax, comparative distinction is achieved, and a touching declining cadence.

Its dulcet C major prepares for the retrospective closure, but the perspective is now shifted right around. Catching the mood of Victoria's Diamond Jubilee (1897), Acworth/Elgar closed on a note of triumphalist time-travelling, wherein defeat at Roman hands is reversed in a prophetic vision of the British Empire that will outlast and outsize the Roman. 'England for the English is all I say', wrote Elgar to Jaeger when he dared voice a tasteful demur: 'hands off! There's nothing apologetic about me'.[10] *Caractacus* is dedicated 'by special permission' to Her Most Gracious Majesty and there is no reason whatsoever to suggest a scintilla of irony, reservation, insincerity in such homage or in the ambitions that underlie it. It is his Op. 35; the virtually antithetical ambition behind Op. 36 – to lovingly encapsulate within an unprecedented flowering of Elgar's light-music idiom a private world of family, friends, and himself – speaks volumes.

The soft staccato bass of the passing watchmen under their cries of 'Alert!' becomes now a powerful legato, swelling in mighty upward wrenches as the centuries roll away, the Roman Empire crumbles, the oak of erstwhile Druids spreads its branches wide over the whole globe, and – C minor to Eb major – 'Britons, alert!' becomes the watchword and rallying-call. Here the Eb triumph is temporary: C minor is quickly reasserted, and the real climax comes just after, in C major, thus subsuming ancient pagan Rome (including its identifying hammered-out quaver triples) within modern Britain. A salvo on solo side-drum signals the call to the watchmen to be transformed into a general summons to national loin-girding, swelling in ample imitative entries saved from banality by the curiously restive syncopations underlying the easy 4/4. This English recreation of the closing *Meistersinger* chorus, as yet without its *Preislied*, modulates ever-sharpward in praise of the Union Jack, guaranteeing that 'No slave shall be for subject/No trophy wet with tears'. Sharps turn ineluctably to flats, till Eb major swallows up Roman C once for all. The missing victory *Preislied* to 'hymn the praise of Britain' swings in grandioso in choral unison, then is stamped out in the bass as the upper parts fill out the harmony, and the work ends celebrating its land in a blaze of hope and glory, superb of its kind.

Changed ideologies and imperatives should not embarrass legitimate admiration for such music nor indeed for what it celebrates so fervently. Yet in fact the closing pages do give forth a certain uncertainty: cadences are undercut, evading or even avoiding the dominant; C minor remains strong, and the very close is a IV^6–I which can sound rather unfinal despite being placed over a mighty Eb pedal. So it could plausibly be claimed that this tonal ambiguity, for all the splendid 'noise it makes', echoes the implicit hollowness of aspirations that have proved unstable to say the least. This is surely our loss – our detached and 'correct' hindsight with its inhibition over taking these sentiments frankly and freely. Elgar's patriotic aim was ardent, deeply felt, in tune with the mood of the time and place, yet imaginatively rich, beyond 'the common man' whose fanfare he composes, inseparably bound up with his manhood, his compositional prowess, his artistic being.

It cannot be impugned as shallow, jingoistic, strident: and he's given it his all in this superbly composed close to *Caractacus*, absolutely right for its occasion and its culture. As always awful words and their 'unacceptable' message can be completely transcended by musical calibre. I look forward to this work's widespread and unashamed revival, based upon a just estimate of its musical worth. But the defeat without apotheosis of Olaf, the absence there of tub-thumping, the close of the Saga-book in a retreat down the ages of melancholy nostalgic retrospect, appeals to us more, and very likely resonates more profoundly with equally fervent and authentic places in their composer's complex personality.

7 Elgar's later oratorios: Roman Catholicism, decadence and the Wagnerian dialectic of shame and grace

BYRON ADAMS

To Philip Brett, in memoriam

Time clears up all errors: the untruth of today is driven out by the contrary untruth of tomorrow, and the many-coloured impressions of particular minds are all eventually absorbed into the consistent light of truth. JOHN HENRY NEWMAN, 1850

'That is the penalty of my English environment.' So Edward Elgar replied to Frederick Delius, who had just opined that he 'thought it was a great pity that [Elgar] had wasted so much time and energy in writing those long-winded oratorios'.[1] Elgar was visiting Delius at his home in Grez-sur-Loing on 30 May 1933, just before conducting the French premiere of his Violin Concerto. Delius, a fervent disciple of Nietzsche, despised any music associated with organised religion; he once remarked to his amanuensis Eric Fenby that Elgar 'might have been a great composer if he had thrown all that religious paraphernalia overboard. *Gerontius* is a nauseating work, and, of course, tremendously influenced by *Parsifal.*'[2]

Assuming that Delius, who was as a rule brutally frank, did report Elgar's reply accurately, a question arises immediately: why did Elgar thus casually dismiss *The Dream of Gerontius*,[3] *The Apostles,* and *The Kingdom* as penance imposed upon him by his environment? Even if offered in courtesy or in jest, Elgar's remark constitutes a shocking, almost Petrine, threefold denial. This appears to repudiate the oratorios, belittle the loyalty of the English listeners who supported his career, and leave Christian faith out of the question entirely. Even for such a tortured personality, riven by lacerating self-doubt and envy, Elgar's denial seems at first inexplicable. To understand the forces that motivated Elgar's renunciation of the three great oratorios and shaped their creation in the first place, one must first attend Elgar's deathbed. This chapter will place those oratorios within a cultural, historical and aesthetic perspective so as to illuminate not only their position within Elgar's oeuvre, but also the ambivalent attitudes of their creator towards religious belief, society and aesthetics.

The first part of *The Dream of Gerontius*, Op. 38, is surely the most poignant depiction of a death in the whole of English music, unrivalled until the final scene of Britten's *Death in Venice*. Elgar's eponymous protagonist faces and overcomes the terror and pain of death, and, supported by his Roman Catholic faith and the devoted attentions of a ministering priest, attendants and friends, passes from death into eternal life. Those surrounding Gerontius's deathbed demonstrate a deep respect for the dying man through their prayers and ministrations.

Compare, then, this noble vision with the composer's own demise. Instead of sympathetic attendants, busy minions of the Gramophone Company surrounded the stricken man. Evidently at Elgar's own bidding, ghoulish photographs were taken of the emaciated composer in bed gazing upon phonograph records with the rapt devotion of a believer *in extremis* looking upon a crucifix. In a stunt designed to publicise their latest technology, the Gramophone Company rigged up microphones in the composer's sickroom, and the dying man was cynically manoeuvred into supervising a recording session of excerpts from his *Caractacus* at the HMV Abbey Road Studios in London.[4]

Arthur Thomson, the Birmingham doctor who delivered the fatal diagnosis of cancer to the composer, reported that Elgar 'told me that he had no faith whatever in an afterlife: "I believe there is nothing but complete oblivion."'[5] Approaching his final dissolution, Elgar expressed in a lucid moment the perfectly rational desire to be cremated and have his ashes scattered at the confluence of the Severn and Teme rivers, a request in direct conflict with the doctrines of the Roman Catholic Church of which he was still a member.[6] Only when Elgar lapsed into unconsciousness due to heavy doses of morphine did his daughter summon a priest to administer the Viaticum. Disregarded entirely was the composer's insistence that the fragmentary sketches of his Third Symphony be burnt.[7] Betrayed by friends and family, manipulated by ruthless commercial interests and without consolation, Elgar died on 23 February 1934, and was buried next to his wife in the cemetery of St Wulstan's Roman Catholic Church in Little Malvern. No Severn and Teme, no faith or hope, and with the preserved fragments of the Third Symphony left ticking like a time bomb.

The reasons for the lack of respect shown to the composer around his protracted deathbed are several and obvious. Elgar's daughter Carice, who endured a lonely childhood overshadowed by the unnervingly volatile composer, had so internalised the strictures of her formidable and obsessively respectable mother that she could not imagine honouring the scandalous final wishes of her wayward father. Elgar's need for approbation, combined with his enduring naiveté, enabled his exploitation by the Gramophone Company. For the same reasons, he gave in to pressure from Carice and his friend W. H. Reed that the shards of the Third Symphony should be preserved as long as, in Reed's words, 'no one would ever tamper with it in any way'.[8] As Michael Kennedy observes, Elgar's 'final days were dreadful indeed'.[9] But the true bleakness of Elgar's death derives from the absence of disinterested and authentic spiritual consolation extended to the dying man; even the priest who administered the last rites may well have exaggerated his role at the great man's deathbed.[10] In part, both Elgar's gradual lapse into creative silence after 1919 and the tragic nature of his dying can be explained by the loss of his faith, a flickering light to be sure, but one that still that blazed up sufficiently to inspire some of the finest passages in *The Dream of Gerontius, The Apostles,* and *The Kingdom.* Ironically, the composition of these three musical frescoes, all created in a concentrated span between 1900 and 1906, may well have contributed to Elgar's spiritual and psychological corrosion. Nothing – plaudits, friendship, or love – could assuage the suppurating wound of Elgar's narcissistic longing. For this primal hurt, the composer blamed many others, including, at times, the entire British musical public.[11] But, more often than not, he vented his bitterness upon God, or, rather, his peculiarly conflicted and personal image of God. After the unhappy premiere of *The Dream of Gerontius,* he wrote to his friend August Jaeger that 'I always said that God was against art & I still believe it'.[12] Stung by disappointment, Elgar might have been excused this outburst, but it was hardly a unique instance of his pique towards the Almighty. In 1918, for example, Elgar declined to set a 'peace ode' by Laurence Binyon, declaring: 'I regret the appeal to the Heavenly Spirit which is cruelly obtuse to the individual sorrow and sacrifice – a cruelty that I resent bitterly & disappointedly.'[13]

Elgar's resentment at God's indifference to his personal agonies becomes a recurring refrain after the fraught composition of *The Kingdom* in 1906. The dark evolution of Elgar's disappointed theism is reflected in the composition of the three mature oratorios, for his disillusionment with God was exacerbated severely by the failure of the grand Wagnerian design of which *The Apostles* and *The Kingdom* represent only fragments. But Elgar's dismissal of his oratorios to Delius, and the implicit anger at the deity expressed by that remark, also resulted from the aesthetic premises and cultural interactions that attended the genesis of these works. In order to approach this subject, a visit to a sordid cell in Reading Gaol in 1895 can provide a helpful point of departure.

'Doth burn ere it transform': *The Dream of Gerontius*

> I was very much shocked at Oscar's appearance, though scarcely
> surprised . . . You can imagine how painful it was to meet him . . . he seemed
> quite broken-hearted and kept on describing his punishment as savage . . .
> He has been reading Pater and Newman lately, one book a week. I do not
> know what work he does.[14]

As this passage, taken from a letter written on 8 October 1895 by Arthur Clifton, attests, Oscar Wilde courageously continued his literary work amid the torments of Reading Gaol. That he was reading Walter Pater is unsurprising, for Pater had exercised a profound influence upon Wilde during the latter's matriculation at Oxford, but that Wilde was contemplating the work of Cardinal John Henry Newman may initially appear to be an anomalous choice. In fact, Wilde was fascinated with Newman's writings and personal history. Before Newman's conversion to Catholicism, he had been a Fellow of Oriel College and was well remembered at Oxford during Wilde's years there as an undergraduate. In 1875, Wilde sent a copy of his early poem 'Rome Unvisited' to Newman; the elderly cleric was delighted by its style and pro-Catholic sentiments.[15] Several of Wilde's early poems echo the imagery of Newman's epic *The Dream of Gerontius*, which was published in 1865, a decade before Wilde began his undergraduate flirtation with Roman Catholicism. Indeed, the following lines from Wilde's early poem 'San Miniato' are highly reminiscent of *The Dream of Gerontius*:

> O crowned by God with love and flame,
> O crowned by Christ the Holy One,
> O listen, ere the searching sun
> Show to the world my sin and shame.[16]

In his dialogue *The Critic as Artist*, Wilde later paid ambivalent homage to Newman: 'The mode of thought that Cardinal Newman represented – if that can be called a mode of thought which seeks to solve intellectual problems by a denial of the supremacy of the intellect – may not, cannot, I think survive. But the world will never weary of watching that troubled soul in its progress from darkness to darkness.'[17] Despite this ambiguous reflection, Wilde once awarded Newman a supreme accolade. At the conclusion of his essay 'Mr Pater's Last Volume', Wilde prophetically intertwined the names of the decadent Pater with the other-worldly Newman: 'But in Mr Pater, as in Cardinal Newman, we find the union of personality with perfection.'[18]

While Arthur Clifton did not 'know what work' Wilde was doing in Reading Gaol, or why he was reading Pater and Newman, it seems likely that Wilde was beginning to ponder his epistle to Lord Alfred Douglas, the *De Profundis*. Wilde may well have taken Newman's *Apologia pro Vita Sua* as a model, for the style and even aspects of the theology articulated by Wilde in his letter owe a debt to Newman's infinitely more abstemious spiritual autobiography. Viewed in this light, Wilde's juxtaposition of Pater with Newman can be understood as proof of the obsessive interest with Roman Catholicism evinced by artists whose work reflected the 'decadent' strain of aesthetics that briefly flourished in *fin de siècle* France and England. (The admittedly problematic term 'decadence' is used throughout this essay without pejorative intent as a convenient characterisation of a shared collection of aesthetic signifiers.)

In his volume *Decadence and Catholicism*, Ellis Hanson writes: 'In a literary context, the word *decadence* is wonderfully suggestive of the *fin de siècle* fascination with cultural degeneration, the persistent and highly influential myth that religion, sexuality, art, even language itself, had fallen at last into an inevitable decay.' Hanson continues by asserting: 'both stylistically and thematically, decadence is an aesthetic in which failure and decay are regarded as seductive, mystical or beautiful . . . in decadent writing, as in certain romantic poets, melancholy acquires a mystical significance that should be familiar to us from the rhetoric of the Church'. Hanson argues convincingly that 'Roman Catholicism is central to both the stylistic peculiarities and the thematic preoccupations of the decadents'.[19] Catholicism provided Wilde and other decadents with a nexus for exploring such diverse elements of their aesthetic as eroticism, shame, and suffering, both corporeal and spiritual. The elaborate ritual of late nineteenth-century Catholicism provided a burnished patina of institutionalised mysticism to the preoccupations of such decadent writers as Baudelaire, Verlaine, Pater, and Wilde.

The decadents were adept in transgressing the indistinct boundaries between eroticism and certain manifestations of Catholic mystical experience. As Hanson writes 'Eroticism, however "perverse" or "aberrant", is what renders the decadent discourse of Catholicism extraordinary, not shallow . . . no matter how much the Church might deny it, no matter how much good Christians might rebel against it, sexual pleasure is an important element of virtually every religious experience.' While Hanson's sweeping generalisation here is certainly extravagant, it is equally true that a persistent strain of mystical Catholicism has been expressed through highly charged and often erotic imagery. Such idiosyncratic constructions of Catholicism provided the decadent writers with an entrée into other arts, such as music. The exploitation of Catholic myth and mysticism in such music dramas as *Tannhäuser*, *Lohengrin* and, above all, *Parsifal* permitted decadents to swoon into the mystical and erotic realm of the composer they revered above all others: Richard Wagner. Hanson describes how the decadents 'discovered grace in the depths of shame' in Wagner's 'Catholic universe', as well as learning that under 'the cowl of monasticism was a cult of homoerotic community' such as the misogynist knights in *Parsifal*.[20]

In 1900, the year in which Wilde died in exile in France, Elgar composed his first mature oratorio, a work that, by a fortuitous combination of circumstances, contained several of the aesthetic signifiers of the then rapidly waning decadent movement. By choosing Newman's poem *The Dream of Gerontius* as the basis for a sacred choral work and by adorning the verse in a musical idiom profoundly influenced by Wagner, Elgar united a dazzling array of decadent signifiers in one spectacular and moving *Gesamtkunstwerk*.

Elgar understood that Newman's supernal vision could only be realised in musical terms by adapting compositional processes developed by Wagner. Steeped in Wagner's music dramas, Elgar cannily apprehended the similarities of tone between the hieratic atmosphere of the first and last acts of *Parsifal*, which he attended twice at Bayreuth in 1892,[21] and the liturgical mysticism of Newman's *The Dream of Gerontius*. This may explain why the composer overruled the misgivings of his publishers and braved the anti-Catholic prejudices endemic to Victorian society in order to set Newman's poem.

Elgar did not import Wagnerian allurements into the genre of the oratorio without brooking criticism from the more conservative members of the English musical establishment, who expressed ambivalence towards both Wagner's music and his notoriety. Hanson quotes once such commentator:

> Edmund Gurney, writing in England in 1883, can exclaim, 'It is a joy to remember as we follow the sublime story of *Parsifal*, that in one of his last published letters Wagner makes an earnest and unhesitating profession to allegiance to Christ'; but then he must also confess that, even in its finest moments, Wagner's music betrays 'a faint flower of disease, something overripe in its lusciousness and febrile passion'.[22]

The critic E. A. Baughan wrote that:

> Wagner especially is a composer for the sufferer from an abnormal nervous state; he just meets the needs of the modern decadent, and as this shattered specimen of humanity now exists in large numbers, it follows that the Bayreuth master is the popular composer of the day. This is the line that Nietsche [*sic*] took, judging music through the distorted glass of his own nerves . . . and Nordau, too, has cast his poisoned arrows not only at Wagner but at most of the great composers.[23]

Aidan Thomson has noted that the reactionary writer Charles Maclean castigated Elgar and other English composers who succumbed to 'Wagnerian temptations'. Thomson observes that 'the implication is that English composers who wrote in an unlyrical, Wagnerian manner were somehow unpatriotic, or given [Maclean's] reference to "temptation", immoral'.[24]

Elgar was nevertheless undeterred from choosing Wagner as an exemplar. Nor did he, obsessed with maintaining a façade of inviolable rectitude, shrink from absorbing elements of *Parsifal* into his own musical idiom. Robert Anderson has aptly noted that *The Dream of Gerontius* 'was unthinkable without Wagner, and indeed without *Parsifal*'.[25] Several early reviews of the oratorio invoke Wagner's music drama to describe Elgar's oratorio; after the notoriously dishevelled premiere of *The Dream of Gerontius* in Birmingham on 3 October 1900, Arthur Johnstone wrote in the *Manchester Guardian* that 'there is indeed much in the work that could not have been there but for *Parsifal*. But it is not allowable for a modern composer of religious music to be ignorant of *Parsifal*.' By 1939, Neville Cardus could wearily exclaim, 'the debt which Elgar owed to *Parsifal* has been commented upon often enough by the enthusiastic hunters-down of the obvious'.[26]

Thus Charles McGuire is surely correct when he asserts: '*Gerontius* remains arguably the most Wagnerian of any of Elgar's oratorios. While Elgar did not employ the same type of themes and thematic transformation that Wagner used, he borrowed the rough outlines: the idea that themes would dominate the structure of the work.'[27] But McGuire also insightfully identifies aspects of Elgar's practice that differ from Wagner's. Elgar retains traditional formal divisions such as arias and choruses; he eschews Wagner's constant thematic and harmonic elision, creating discrete melodies articulated by cadences; and his use of recurring themes to identify recurring concepts and situations is a highly idiosyncratic adaptation of the Wagnerian system.[28]

Why, then, aside from the obvious musical debt that Elgar owed to Wagner, do commentators so often cite *Parsifal* as the most potent influence upon *Gerontius*? Because there appears to be a shared perception among critics and scholars, quite apart from concerns of technique, that certain sections of Wagner's music drama and Elgar's oratorio share an unsettling aura of decadence. Elgar's contemporaries did not universally welcome the Wagnerian luxuriance of his style. In his review of the premiere, Joseph Bennett, the conservative critic of the *Daily Telegraph*, was disconcerted by the whiffs of decadence that wafted to him from across the concert hall: 'Those who know the composer of *Gerontius* are aware of a peculiar artistic temperament, in which, of course, extreme susceptibility, uplifting enthusiasms, and a tendency towards more or less mysticism have a place. Such a man when armed with technical skill, and able to put a healthy restraint upon himself, may go far and do much.'[29]

A generation or so later, W. J. Turner, commenting on one of Elgar's later oratorios, opined:

> Unlike *The Dream of Gerontius*, which is definitely Catholic, *The Kingdom*
> has no sectarian bias but is broadly Christian. Nevertheless, the music
> has the same definite flavour of what I hope I may call, without offence,
> erotic religiosity as *Gerontius*, though more temperately and discreetly
> expressed ... *The Kingdom*, like *Parsifal* – only, I repeat, [*The Kingdom*] is
> the work of a gentleman – is dim, rich, warm and enervating.

(Turner, who, one notes, draws a pejorative distinction between 'Catholic' and 'Christian', goes on to claim that, due to his submission to Wagner's influence, Elgar is not 'wholly and characteristically English'.)[30] Despite his stammering equivocations, Turner's use of the phrase 'erotic religiosity' is a particularly apt evocation of the rich enervated atmosphere shared by both *Parsifal* and *Gerontius*. Turner is not just uneasy with the Wagnerian provenance of Elgar's work, but he is also on the lookout for the seductive effeminising influence of the Roman Church. In his article, Turner displayed a reductive binary opposition between diatonic and chromatic that reflected the received opinion of many male British musicians and critics in the late nineteenth and early twentieth centuries. For Turner, a diatonic idiom was the only means to express a forthright and Protestant British manliness, the direct result of healthy and habitual self-restraint. Chromaticism, on the other hand, was redolent of the foreign, the effeminate, the hysterical, the morbid, the decadent and, through the pernicious influence of *Parsifal*, the erotic religiosity of Catholicism. Turner finds himself forced to put *Gerontius* in the latter dangerous company.

The high tension that informs Turner's diatribe is characteristic of the struggle that attended the self-conscious construction of an English national identity, especially in music. Such tensions were endemic to British musical culture from the late nineteenth century to the death of Benjamin Britten. Much of this reasoning is defensive. Turner and other male musicians were protecting themselves from the accepted Victorian and Edwardian stereotype of the male musician as effete, nervous, and neurasthenic.

This particularly pernicious strain of popular opinion intensified dramatically after the Wilde trials in 1895. A singularly unfortunate, even dire, effect of these trials was to foster a fallacious connection in the popular mind between effeminacy and homosexuality. This untenable assumption only hardened the social opprobrium towards musicians and led several generations of English composers – regardless of sexual orientation – to repudiate any stylistic elements such as chromaticism that might suggest either decadence or aestheticism. To retain their status as gentlemen, male composers had to expurgate any lingering aspects of decadence from their styles and banish the contagion of effeminacy from their public behaviour.

Elgar's contemporary Hubert Parry, a composer who camouflaged a thoughtful disposition with hair-raising displays of manly sportsmanship, had little use for either *Parsifal* or *Gerontius*. For Parry, both works were suspect on ethical grounds and both stank of decadence. Although he had been an enthusiastic supporter of Wagner's earlier work, Parry described the *Parsifal* Prelude to his pupil Ralph Vaughan Williams as 'mere scene painting'. Vaughan Williams commented further that Parry 'had an almost moral abhorrence of mere luscious sound'.[31] The sonic sumptuousness of

Elgar's oratorio, together with its ardent expression of Catholic dogma, revolted Parry, who commented in his diary that *Gerontius* 'reeks too much of the morbid and unnatural terrors and hysterics engendered by priestcraft to be congenial – vivid though it certainly is'. In a later entry, Parry reiterated his disgust at Newman's poem by calling it 'revolting. Debased and craven religion, hysteric and morbid'.[32]

Parry was scarcely alone in his reaction to the Catholicism of Elgar's oratorio; in 1909, E. A. Baughan wrote that the religious sentiment expressed in *Gerontius* 'is almost grovelling in its anguish of remorse, and it has the peculiar sentimentality that is characteristic of the later Roman Catholic Church'. Baughan further declared: 'No doubt [*Gerontius*] appeals to many, but I must confess that I prefer the human tenderness of Brahms, in his Requiem, the massive manliness of Handel at his best . . . In the works of these masters, Man expresses his reverence for his Maker, without losing his manliness. In Elgar's music I detect the hysterical prostration of the confessional. It is too much a repentance of nerves.'[33] The intemperate language shared by Parry and Baughan is highly reminiscent of the marginalising terminology used by the Victorian and Edwardian medical establishment to describe the psychology of women and effete men – such as decadent poets – who were prone to displays of uncontrolled emotion or erotic excess. Such fashionable medical hypotheses drew heavily on such words as 'morbid', 'sentimental', 'hysterical', and 'unnatural'. Notice that Parry lays the propagation of such horrors to the 'priestcraft', thereby not only betraying his personal bias against Catholicism, but parroting the lurking suspicions of most non-Catholic Englishmen about the supposed corruption and effeminacy of Rome's celibate priesthood. Dating from the time of the Anglican reformation, this prejudice only deepened during the Victorian era.[34] Charles Kingsley, who was Newman's great ideological adversary among the Anglican 'Broad Church' clergy, once wrote that 'in [Newman] and all that school, there is an element of foppery – even in dress and manner; a fastidious, maundering die-away effeminacy, which is taken for purity and refinement'.[35] It cannot be doubted that Newman's sensibility was the antithesis of the muscular Christianity expounded by Kingsley. Nor were Kingsley's suspicions wide of the mark, for, as Peter Gay has noted, 'John Henry Newman's affection for Froude, like the passionate male friendships that punctuated the lives of [Tractarians such as] Edward Pusey and John Keble, had little that was overtly carnal about them, but an erotic ingredient, half joyful and half desperate, is unmistakable.'[36] Passages of Newman's poetry and prose express a delicately sublimated homoeroticism as refracted through the doctrinal prism of his unwavering Catholicism; these homoerotic nuances may well have enabled Wilde to find in Newman a spiritual precursor of the decadents.

As Wilde was a reader of almost preternatural perception, one wonders how he parsed this moving paean at the end of the *Apologia pro Vita Sua*: 'Dear Ambrose St John; whom God gave me, when He took every one else away; who are the link between my old life and my new; who have now for twenty years been so devoted to me, so patient, so zealous, so tender; who have let me lean so hard upon you.'[37] Ambrose St John had been an Anglican clergyman who converted to Catholicism with Newman in 1845; the two clerics were inseparable companions until St John's death in 1875. In a touching letter written soon after St John's death, Newman eulogised his friend: 'from the first he loved me with an intensity of love, which was unaccountable. At Rome 28 years ago [in 1847] he was always so working for and relieving me of all trouble, that being young and Saxon-looking, the Romans called him my Angel Guardian.'[38] Newman clearly modelled the Guardian Angel in *Gerontius* after Ambrose St John.[39] Upon Cardinal Newman's own death in 1890, he was interred, not, as might have been expected of a prince of the Church, in the Catholic cathedral in Birmingham, but at Rednal with St John in the same grave.[40]

Aside from deriving inspiration from a male muse, certain passages in Newman's poem express a visionary strain that echoes the charged homo-erotic language of such saints as St John of the Cross. Homoeroticism, which the sociologist George L. Mosse defines as 'latently erotic aspects of personal relationships among men',[41] pervades the writings of certain of the more extravagantly ecstatic Catholic saints and seers. Thus Newman is following a hallowed tradition when his Guardian Angel expresses religious senti-ment through phrases that have associations with more earthly ecstasies. The Angel's veiled allusion to the reception of the Stigmata by St Francis of Assisi, who was one of the saints most favoured by decadent poets, is saturated with this language:

> . . . that sight of the Most Fair
> Will gladden thee, but it will pierce thee too . . .
> There was a mortal who is now above
> In the mid glory: he, when near to die,
> Was given communion with the Crucified; –
> Such, that the Master's very wounds were stamped
> Upon his flesh; and, from the agony
> Which thrilled through body and soul in that embrace
> Learn that the flame of Everlasting Love
> Doth burn ere it transform.

As the Angel dips the Soul of Gerontius into the lake of Purgatory, he soothes his precious charge with these words: 'Softly and gently, dearly ransomed soul,/In my most loving arms I now enfold thee . . . Be brave and patient on thy bed of sorrow;/Swiftly shall pass thy night of trial here,/And I will come and wake thee on the morrow.'

Elgar's intimate friendships with men such as August Jaeger, who is lovingly portrayed as 'Nimrod' in the 'Enigma' Variations, inspired much of his finest music. It is not surprising, then, that Elgar responded with alacrity to Newman's unconscious admixture of Catholicism and homoerotic sentiment by composing some of his most refulgent and, indeed, sensuous music. In his expert redaction of Newman's unwieldy poem, Elgar chose to retain two unambiguous references to the Angel's male gender as the Soul of Gerontius sings: 'I will address him. Mighty One, my Lord, My Guardian Spirit, all hail!' By choosing a mezzo-soprano for the Angel, Elgar created a figure as androgynous as those angels of indeterminate gender that appear in Pre-Raphaelite canvases. In the duet between the Angel and the Soul of Gerontius, the only such moment in the entire oratorio, Elgar intensifies the homoerotic overtones within an already ambiguous context by using an idiom that recalls Wagner less than it does the operatic love duets of Massenet and Puccini.[42]

Like the Knights of the Grail in *Parsifal*, the dramatis personae that populate Newman's *The Dream of Gerontius*, both terrestrial and celestial, exist within an environment as homosocial as that of the Birmingham Oratory. The priests and attendants praying at Gerontius's deathbed would hardly have included women, even nuns, in their ranks; in heaven, the Guardian Angel is male; God, as traditionally portrayed in Catholic theology, is male; and the hosts of heaven can be construed as either of indeterminate gender or, more likely in the case of an author as indifferent to women as Newman, male by default. The ethereal sonority that enfolds Elgar's guileless Angelicals is reminiscent of the chorus of boys at the end of *Parsifal*, thus unforgettably evoked by Verlaine: 'Ô ces voix d'enfants chantant dans la coupole!'[43]

In both Newman's poem and Elgar's oratorio, such sublimated homoeroticism coexists with – and is amplified by – another powerful signifier of decadent aesthetics, namely shame. As he comments on Nietzsche's scathing critique of Wagner's *Tannhäuser*, Hanson writes: 'For Wagner, as for many decadents from Baudelaire to Wilde, the Church was indispensable as the only institution that really appreciated the beauty and artistry of shame.'[44] Like Catholic theologians, the decadents understood the distinction between sin and shame: sin represents a defiant transgression against the laws of God, while shame results from the fallen nature of all humanity according to the doctrine of Original Sin. In other words, sin is an act; shame is a state of being.

The decadents relished the voluptuousness of shame, as well as the performative aspects of its physical expression, such as lowered eyes, tongues tied with embarrassment, and faces rouged with humiliation. The poetry of Wilde and Verlaine is imbued with the signifiers of shame; one of Lord Alfred Douglas's most notorious poems is entitled 'To Shame'. In *The Dream of Gerontius*, Newman simultaneously anticipated the decadents' obsession with shame – recall Wilde's poem 'San Miniato' quoted earlier – while corroborating the Catholic doctrine regarding the distinction between it and sin:

> O loving wisdom of our God!
> When all was sin and shame,
> A second Adam to the fight
> And to the rescue came.

Elgar, who excised many passages of celestial description and Catholic dogma as he redacted Newman's poem, retained these lines that allude to the fallen nature of mankind. The most spectacular expression of shame in *The Dream of Gerontius* occurs at the climax of the entire score. Before Gerontius loses his voice in the depths of Purgatory, he sings of his shame with an anguish like that of Amfortas in *Parsifal*: 'Take me away, and in the lowest deep/There let me be,/And there in hope the lone night-watches keep,/Told out for me.' In lines from Newman's poem that Elgar did not set, the Guardian Angel foreshadows the pain that his charge will experience in God's presence: 'The shame of self at the thought of seeing Him, – /Will be thy veriest, sharpest purgatory.'

Elgar had to be goaded into composing the searing music for Gerontius's climactic outburst of shame. August Jaeger, a perfect Wagnerite whose devotion to Elgar recalls the unaccountable love that Ambrose St John felt for Newman,[45] good-naturedly taunted the composer into recomposing this crucial passage: 'You may take it for Gospel that Wagner would have made this the climax of expression in the work . . . Wagner always revelled in seemingly "IMPOSSIBLE" situations & this one would have brought forth his most splendid powers.'[46]

That Elgar was reluctant to rise to this daunting challenge is understandable for a man whose 'tormented life'[47] was nearly stifled by shame: shame of his humble class origins; of his status as a Roman Catholic in an Anglican society; of his unfashionable profession as a musician; and, just perhaps, of the unsettling emotions that he felt for Jaeger and other male friends. In the throes of one of the depressions that haunted him, Elgar, whose habitual repression of his shame was a sacrifice on the altar of Victorian respectability, accused God as being 'against art'. To Elgar, mired in his own resentment and guilt, it must have seemed as if his magnificent propitiatory offerings to God – for all three mature oratorios are dedicated '*Ad Majorem Dei Gloriam*' – fell upon deaf ears.

Wilde once teasingly declared 'autobiography is irresistible', but the greatest of his autobiographical writings, *De Profundis*, was created in the genuinely shameful crucible of Reading Gaol. In response to the scandal of his conversion to Catholicism, Newman wrote his *Apologia* in a white heat of inspiration, and later, in a poem, envisioned a God that 'tears the soul from out its case/And burns away the stains'. Like the writings of Wilde and Newman, Elgar's music is essentially autobiographical; he once opined that 'after all art must be the man, & all true art is, to a great extent, egotism'.[48] To slough off the stifling inhibitions that threatened to cripple his creativity, however, Elgar often projected himself into the personality of another;[49] in this case he cast himself as an old man named Gerontius who suffers death and is transported by an angel through heaven. In his next oratorio, *The Apostles*, Elgar expanded this strategy of autobiographical projection by expressing himself through the personalities of three biblical characters.

'The soul in anguish': *The Apostles*

'Wherefore I say unto thee, her sins, which are many, are forgiven; for she loved much: but to whom little is forgiven, *the same* loveth little' (Luke 7:47). Christ speaks these words immediately after a woman – identified in the Gospel only as 'a sinner' – appears uninvited to a dinner party and, in a moving gesture of penance, anoints His feet with ointment, washes them with her tears and dries them with her hair. A persistent tradition identifies this sinner as Mary Magdalene, although there is no authority for such an assumption in the Gospels. Over the centuries, however, the very name 'Mary Magdalene' has become a signifier for a fallen woman who repents of her maculate transgressions. Sensuous but sanctified, Mary Magdalene is both a moral example and an enduring scandal, for her insistent and specifically feminine corporeality refuses to be effaced when shame is redeemed through grace.

The penitent Magdalene had an intense resonance for Wilde; as Hanson observes, 'Mary Magdalene as a beautiful sinner is a recurrent figure in Wilde's work from his earliest poems to his prison letters. His enthusiasm for her was no doubt enlivened by the final act of Wagner's *Parsifal*, in which the sinner Kundry, in the passionate throes of redemption, re-enacts the signature gesture of Mary Magdalene by laving her saviour's feet and drying them with the seductive tresses of her hair.'[50] Hanson further notes: 'In *De Profundis*, Wilde's elaborate and well-wrought letter to [Lord Alfred] Douglas, Mary Magdalene gives her finest performance. Wilde's description of her is to Saint Luke what his Salome was to Saint Matthew: a poetic elaboration that further aestheticises the stories of the Gospels.'[51] Wilde recasts the Gospel narrative so as to conjure up a veritable Pre-Raphaelite painting before the reader's ravished eyes: 'Mary Magdalene, when she sees Christ, breaks the rich vase of alabaster that one of her seven lovers had given her and spills the odorous spices over his tired dusty feet, and for that one moment's sake sits forever with Ruth and Beatrice in the tresses of the snow-white Rose of Paradise.'[52] Contemplating this passage, Hanson drolly exclaims: 'Humility is rarely this divine!'

Mary Magdalene gave an equally fine performance as one of the principal dramatis personae in *The Apostles*. Indeed, she is one of three characters that dominate the action of Elgar's oratorio, which takes as its putative subject the calling of the apostles. The others, Peter and Judas, were among the twelve, of course: all were male. In biblical times, a female apostle was out of the question. Indeed, the careers of both Peter and Judas are retailed in all of the four canonical Gospels, but, apostle or not, Mary Magdalene makes only a few brief verifiable appearances – most as a witness of the Resurrection. In an article from 1909 entitled '"The Apostles" and Elgar's Future', E. A. Baughan remarks with asperity, 'the repentance of Mary Magdalene, which really has nothing to do with the Apostles, is made the subject of a lengthy treatment. It is an unessential detail.'[53] Why, then, did Elgar lavish so much attention on Mary Magdalene in *The Apostles*? An investigation of this provocative question illuminates certain aspects of Elgar's creative process as well as the peculiar conditions under which both *The Apostles* and *The Kingdom* were created.

The growing popularity of *Gerontius* assured that Elgar would be asked to compose further oratorios to satiate the voracious appetite for such novelties evinced by British choral societies. In October 1901, Elgar was approached by the Birmingham Festival, which, anxious to remove the blot of the unhappy premiere of *Gerontius* from its escutcheon, commissioned Elgar to write a large choral work on a religious theme for the 1903 festival. Elgar proposed as his subject that of the calling of the apostles; this notion had engaged him from the moment in childhood when his schoolmaster had described the apostles as 'poor men, young men, at the time of their calling; perhaps before the descent of the Holy Ghost not cleverer than some of you here'.[54]

From such nonchalant beginnings, Elgar conceived a huge project: a trilogy of oratorios that would span the calling of the apostles through the founding of the early Church and then, in the third panel of this musical triptych, the Last Judgement. The grand design for this project emulated Wagner's *Der Ring des Nibelungen*.[55] As was evident from his pivotal role in effecting a revision of the climax of *Gerontius*, August Jaeger was forever goading Elgar to emulate Wagner's titanic – and daunting – achievement. Thus Elgar made a pilgrimage to Bayreuth in 1902 seeking inspiration for the composition of the first of the trilogy, *The Apostles*, Op. 49. There he heard the first three operas of the *Ring*, as well as *Parsifal*. By 1902, Elgar had attended no fewer than three performances of *Parsifal* at Bayreuth.[56] By 2 July 1902, Elgar wrote exultantly to Ivor Atkins, organist of Worcester Cathedral, 'I am now plotting GIGANTIC WORK.'[57]

Elgar's ambitions were Wagnerian in scope but not necessarily in detail. Indeed, as with *Gerontius*, Elgar frequently diverges from Wagnerian practice. In one crucial respect, however, Elgar rashly elected to follow Wagner's example: he decided to generate his own text for the trilogy. Elgar's literary impulses were encouraged further that year by a gift of Ellis's translation of the Wagner prose works, which included a draft of a scenario suggestively entitled *Jesus of Nazareth*.[58] (Elgar did not, however, emulate Wagner's prudent practice of finishing his libretti before composing the music; the English composer created both text and music more or less simultaneously.)

Lacking Wagner's literary expertise, Elgar wisely decided to construct a libretto by selecting episodes from the Gospels, rather as Wagner selected elements from Wolfram von Eschenbach and others to create the plot of *Parsifal*. Elgar then filled in this frame with verses excerpted from scripture. However, he was anxious to honour the deadline imposed by Birmingham; he badly misjudged the time it would take to complete such an extended design. In the end, only a fragment of the original plan was finished, resulting in two oratorios: *The Apostles* and its concise successor, *The Kingdom*. The final oratorio of the trilogy, provisionally entitled *The Last Judgement*, was barely sketched; only a few jottings of music for this score are extant. Assembling the libretto for *The Apostles*, Elgar behaved like a *bricoleur*, gathering shards of biblical narrative, wrenching verses out of their original contexts and combining them all into a succession of what Charles McGuire, drawing upon earlier discussions of the score, has aptly termed '*tableaux*'.[59] By using scripture, Elgar vitiated the principal criticism levelled by Anglican clergy and others at the Roman Catholicism of *The Dream of Gerontius*. In order to ensure the propriety of his text for *The Apostles*, the composer consulted two Anglican clergymen, Edward Capel-Cure and Charles Gorton. Elgar's caution paid off handsomely, for, unlike *Gerontius*, neither the premiere of *The Apostles* nor that of *The Kingdom* was marred by controversy over the text. After the first performance at Birmingham, *The Apostles* was quickly taken up by the Three Choirs Festival and performed in the vaulted cathedrals with a special solemnity that recalls the reverent atmosphere that enveloped productions of *Parsifal* at Bayreuth.[60] To encourage a comparison with Wagner at these performances, Jaeger provided, with the composer's active assistance, an elaborate essay about each, labelling the various leitmotivs and identifying their significance just as was done by Hans von Wolzogen for Wagner's music dramas.

Owing to the biblical provenance of the texts and their popularity at the Three Choirs Festival, a persistent strain in Elgar scholarship identifies both

The Apostles and *The Kingdom* as essentially Anglican oratorios; some writers even imply that Elgar capitulated to the prejudices of an overwhelmingly Protestant society. Concerning *The Apostles*, Vaughan Williams once opined: 'I always feel that [Elgar] was oppressed by the fact that he was writing for the Church of England and could not get rid of the bombazine and bonnets of the Anglican Sunday morning service.'[61] Such an opinion, while far from inaccurate, does not take into account fully the curious hybrid nature of the libretti of both works. Elgar's libretti, while careful not to expound overt Roman Catholicism, are hardly an orthodox expression of Broad Church Anglican piety as is found in oratorios by Ouseley, Stainer, and Stanford.[62] Poised between Elgar's ingrained Roman Catholicism and the Protestantism shared by many in his audience, *The Apostles* and *The Kingdom* are spiritually and aesthetically close to the High Church Anglicanism, also known as Anglo-Catholicism, first posited by Newman (before his conversion to Rome), Froude, Keble, and the other Tractarian founders of the Oxford Movement.

Prominent among the doctrinal anomalies that permeate both *The Apostles* and *The Kingdom* is Elgar's oddly hesitant treatment of the Saviour, who appears in the first of the two oratorios. While *The Apostles* is organised around specific incidents in the life of Christ, the narrative proceeds with a disconcerting obliquity: the Saviour is reduced to a mere bystander at the drama of the apostles unfolding around Him. Elgar is clearly more interested in the human sufferings and doubts of the apostles than in the supernal travails of their Master. Moreover, Elgar gave two apostles, Peter and Judas, special prominence, assigning brief roles to John and the Virgin Mary, and restricting the rest of Christ's followers to choral utterances. And in an ultimate inversion of importance, Elgar lavishes a degree of attention upon Mary Magdalene far out of proportion to her modest role in the Gospels.

Peter, Judas, and Mary Magdalene: Elgar's concentration on these three provides a key to a deeper understanding of both composer and creation. Despite his stated intention, Elgar uses the subject of the calling of the apostles as a pretext for continuing his exploration of the Wagnerian dialectic of shame and grace begun with *Gerontius*. Peter, leader of the apostles, thrice denies Christ and is shamed but is redeemed through his remorse. Judas literally dies of shame. Mary Magdalene, a woman shamed by remembrance of her sins, repents and is forgiven through a spectacular act of contrition.

Elgar would doubtless have been appalled to have his name linked with the likes of Baudelaire and Wilde. But several passages in the text of *The Apostles* reflect how deeply *fin de siècle* aestheticism pervaded Elgar's imagination, for, although he assembled the libretto from the Bible, he subverted, perhaps inadvertently, the original meaning of his biblical sources in order to realise his own artistic vision. While their scriptural provenance reassured Anglican audiences, the Bible verses in *The Apostles* are juxtaposed in ways that are at times curiously reminiscent of the outpourings of decadent authors.

The most highly coloured example of this procedure is found in the extended third tableau of the first part of *The Apostles*. Entitled 'In the Tower of Magdala', this passage commences with Mary Magdalene giving vent to her shame over the fleshly excesses of her former life. As there is no scriptural basis for this episode, Elgar expropriated aspects of Longfellow's portrait of Mary Magdalene found in the American poet's epic *The Divine Tragedy*. In place of Longfellow's rather bland verse, however, Elgar substitutes a powerful series of exclamations drawn from Baruch, Esther, Micah, Lamentations, and Ecclesiastes: 'O Lord Almighty, God of Israel, the soul in anguish, the troubled spirit crieth unto Thee . . . Help me, desolate woman, which have no helper but Thee: Hear and have pity.' Mary Magdalene's remorse does not preclude her from recalling scenes in detail from her earlier, shameful existence. At the first climax of this extended solo passage, she remembers, 'Whatsoever mine eyes desired I kept not from them, I withheld not my heart from any joy.' Elgar brilliantly contrasts her penitence with a vision of her former life as a chorus of revelling phantoms sings: 'Let us fill ourselves with costly wine and ointments, and let no flower of the spring pass by us. Let us crown ourselves with rosebuds before they be withered.' Elgar may have extracted the words for this fantasy sequence from the Apocryphal Book of Wisdom, but the sentiment is strikingly redolent of that poetic sigh of erotic regret, 'Cynara' by Ernest Dowson, who was both a decadent poet and fervent Roman Catholic. A few lines from 'Cynara' will suffice to suggest their uncanny resonance with Elgar's juxtaposition of biblical verses: 'thy breath was shed/Upon my soul between the kisses and the wine . . . I have forgot much, Cynara, gone with the wind,/Flung roses, roses riotously with the throng/Dancing to put thy pale lost lilies out of mind.'[63]

Elgar intensifies the vividness of his fantasy sequence with music modelled on Wagner's depiction in *Tannhäuser* of the Venusberg's earthly delights as well as on the teasingly sensuous music of the *Blumenmädchen* who flit across the second act of *Parsifal*. The unstable but alluring harmonic progressions, the transparent orchestration, even the use of the tambourine that plays throughout the bacchanal in the Venusberg: all of these distinctive sonorities employed by Wagner as signifiers of erotic abandon are also used by Elgar to portray Mary Magdalene's chequered past. Unconsciously following the same path as Wilde, Elgar embellishes and aestheticises the Gospel narratives, intensifying this process with musical signifiers for sensuality, thus producing a Wagnerian portrait of the penitent Magdalene.

These are hardly the only Wagnerian influences that can be uncovered in this oratorio, however. Indeed, it can be argued that *The Apostles*, while less overtly Wagnerian than *Gerontius*, owes as specific a debt to *Parsifal* as is apparent in the earlier score. Elgar even opens *The Apostles* in A♭ major, the key of the opening of *Parsifal*. A poignant Wagnerian reference is found in the section that Elgar labels 'In Capernaum'. In the course of Elgar's tableau, Mary Magdalene washes the feet of her Saviour, the sublimely self-abnegating gesture of penance that is recalled by the repentant Kundry in the last act of *Parsifal*. Unlike Kundry, however, Mary Magdalene does not forfeit her voice upon repentance, but joins the apostles to witness the Ascension at the conclusion of the oratorio.

But for Judas, driven to suicide by the enormity of his betrayal, there is no hope for grace – there is only betrayal, shame and despair. Elgar, influenced by the hypotheses of Archbishop Richard Whateley and others, envisioned a humanised and tragic Judas. Elgar viewed Judas as a Jewish zealot so impatient for the Messiah's coming that he hatches a disastrous plot to hasten the establishment of a purely political kingdom of Israel rid of the detested Romans.[64] From the beginning, however, the composer sympathised with Judas, who is portrayed as an anomaly within the band of apostles; as Jerrold Northrop Moore observes, '[Elgar's] plan was to show Judas as the outsider of outsiders.'[65] As a Roman Catholic, as a tradesman's son, as a musician, Elgar saw himself as an outsider to class-bound Victorian society. As McGuire notes, 'Feeling marginalised himself, Elgar identified readily with other outsider characters – ones who could, as Jerrold Northrop Moore has remarked, "open aspects of himself he wanted to explore".'[66]

But what if the character contained aspects of himself that Elgar might have preferred to avoid? In Judas, the 'outsider of outsiders' who betrays his Master, Elgar discovered his dark familiar. Beneath Elgar's carefully cul-tivated *nobilmente* manner lurked a shadowy fascination with all of the obsessions that corrupted Judas: earthly power and honour; resentment of the rich coupled with covetousness; and repeated attempts to force the Hand of God. Creating Judas's great scene in the second part of *The Apostles* must have been agony for the highly strung composer, and yet Elgar composes music for this passage that is some of the most compelling in the entire work.[67]

In Judas, Elgar may well have discerned a character through which he might express his own habitual despair.[68] During the composition of *The Apostles*, Elgar wrote to Canon Gorton: 'To my mind *Judas'* crime or sin was despair; not only the betrayal, which was done for a worldly purpose. In these days, when every "modern" person seems to think "suicide" is the natural way out of everything (Ibsen &c. &c.) my plan, if explained, may do some good.'[69] Compare this pious declaration with the harrowing testimony of the critic Ernest Newman, who recalled that Elgar 'gave me even then the impression of an exceptionally nervous, self-divided and secretly unhappy man . . . I remember a dinner . . . at which Mrs Elgar tactfully steered the conversation away from the topic of suicide that had suddenly arisen; she whispered to me that Edward was always talking of making an end of himself.'[70] Shortly after the miserable premiere of *Gerontius*, Elgar wrote to Jaeger, 'I really wish I were dead over & over again but I dare not, for the sake of my relatives, do the job myself.'[71]

And what of betrayal? In *The Apostles*, as in scripture, Judas, by the most famous of homoerotic gestures, betrays the Son of Man with a kiss. In Elgar's retelling, Judas loves his Master too much, and betrays himself into destroying Him. Elgar has Judas sing in shame and anguish, 'I have sinned in that I have betrayed the innocent blood' (Matthew 27:4) . . . 'Never man spake like this Man'; 'he satisfied the longing soul with goodness' (Psalm 107:9). What goodness did Elgar betray within himself to assuage partially his aggrieved sense of exclusion from the respectable masculine realms of British society? Why, after the traumatic first performance of *Gerontius*, did he seek to shut his heart against 'every religious feeling & every soft, gentle impulse *for ever*'?[72] Why did he wish to transform himself so utterly into that hard, manly and conspicuously unmusical denizen of Edwardian society known as the 'English gentleman'?[73] Why did he gradually distance himself from August Jaeger when that most loyal of friends entered the final stages of consumption?[74] Why did he renounce music itself on many occasions?[75] Why did he gradually throttle his work as a composer – the only portal to his inner life – after the death of his wife in 1920?

Although the repressed composer might seem to be the antithesis of the decadent author, both shared a predilection toward self-betrayal. Elgar, like Wilde (if not so flamboyant or fatal), was his own Judas. Through the music he composed for this benighted character, Elgar may have dimly, fitfully apprehended this cruel truth; Wilde, the more self-conscious of the two, knew it surely:

> All men kill the thing they love
> By all let this be heard,
> Some do it with a bitter look,
> Some with a flattering word,
> The coward does it with a kiss,
> The brave man with a sword![76]

'The road that leads to nowhere': *The Kingdom* and *The Last Judgement*

Though Judas is cast into outer darkness, Peter attains pardon for his three-fold denial of Christ through the grace extended to him by virtue of his faith. Peter's shame casts a fleeting shadow over the extended sermon he delivers during the third section of *The Kingdom*, Op. 51. Before beginning this grandiose exhortation, Peter quietly sings a few words spoken to him by Christ at the Last Supper: 'But I have prayed for thee, that thy faith fail not: and when thou art converted, strengthen thy brethren' (Luke 22: 32).[77] Peter has a poignant reason to recall those words, for moments after uttering them, Christ predicted his apostles' denial: 'I tell thee, Peter, the cock shall not crow this day, before that thou shalt thrice deny that thou knowest me' (Luke 22:34). Peter's sermon represents one of the more overtly dramatic events found in *The Kingdom*; such passages are rare in this most contemplative of Elgar's mature oratorios. Despite the eloquence of this sermon, Elgar's vision of Peter in *The Kingdom* often suggests an earnest Anglican parson from one of Trollope's 'Barchester' novels rather than an apostle enflamed through grace provided by the Holy Ghost.

The penitent Magdalene also reappears in *The Kingdom*, mainly as a companion for the Virgin Mary, now a subdued mezzo-soprano in attendance upon the Mother of God's higher register. As so often happens to repentant fallen women, Mary Magdalene's contrition has effaced her abject yet scandalous allure. In *The Kingdom*, Elgar has replaced the sumptuous Wildean sinner of *The Apostles* with a pallid 'Holy Woman'.

While it will be recalled that W. J. Turner described *The Kingdom* as 'rich, dim and enervated', he further identified it as the 'Christian' work of a 'gentleman'. Within the context of Turner's article, this half-hearted approbation has an ominous ring. Upon its premiere at the Birmingham Festival on 3 October 1906, *The Kingdom* met with a generally respectful response, especially from the more conservative critics such as Joseph Bennett, who, it will be remembered, had reservations about *Gerontius*. In his critique for the *Daily Telegraph*, Bennett wrote, 'I confess that had my opinion been asked of *Gerontius* or *The Apostles* before either was tested publicly, I should have declared that such music stood no chance of acceptance by our good English folk ... the attention given to the music, and the response elicited by every tour de force ... these things are not to be explained away by flippant tongues.'[78] One commentator went so far as to declare, 'I believe that in the history of art [*The Kingdom*] will rank definitely with the "Matthew Passion" of Bach.'[79] Finally, the critic of *The Times*, in a positive review, noted that 'those whose taste is offended by the "Fantasy", or the realistic jingling of the coins on the Temple floor in the earlier work [*The Apostles*], will be relieved to find nothing in the later which can be accused of bad taste'.[80]

Despite such encomiums, including a revealing comparison to that most Protestant of choral works, Bach's St Matthew Passion, there was at least one notable dissenting voice, that of Ernest Newman. Unlike most of his critical brethren, Newman, a loyal Wagnerite, harboured severe reservations concerning *The Apostles*,[81] and he detested *The Kingdom*: 'The general level of inspiration is, in my opinion, below that of *Gerontius* or *The Apostles*. Some of the choral portions are so obvious in sentiment that one can hardly believe that they came from the delicately spiritual brain that conceived *Gerontius*.' A year after the first performance of *The Kingdom*, Newman implored Elgar publicly to stop writing oratorios and concentrate on creating instrumental scores, for 'at present he is simply riding post-haste along the road that leads to nowhere'.[82]

Even so, certain distinguished admirers, such as Adrian Boult, have argued for the superiority of *The Kingdom* as the finest and most consistent of Elgar's oratorios. While Boult's preference represents a minority view, it is nevertheless an opinion shared by several influential musicians. Vaughan Williams, writing to Michael Kennedy, commented: 'On the whole I like *The Kingdom* better [than *The Apostles*], though of course there is nothing so bad in *The Apostles* as the Lord's prayer.'[83] The reasons why some listeners prefer *The Kingdom* to the other oratorios, and why others, such as Newman, disparage it, may well hold a key to Elgar's failure to complete his triptych as planned originally.

By the time he commenced work on *The Kingdom*, Elgar's enthusiasm for completing the trilogy had begun to fade, as had his faith. Paradoxically, the excursion into biblical exegesis that Elgar did during the creation of *The Apostles* and *The Kingdom* could have played a part in the unravelling of the composer's already frayed beliefs. Elgar possessed an intuitive intelligence but he was unversed in systematic theology: his training as a Catholic had been liturgical and doctrinal. For such a quick but undisciplined intellect, the contradictory speculations advanced by the various authors that Elgar consulted, including such sceptics as Ernest Renan, may have caused only distress.

Whatever the reason, Anderson is surely correct when he speculates: 'it seems likely that Elgar underwent a crisis of faith during this period, one of the factors that weighed against his completing the trilogy for the 1909 Birmingham festival'.[84] Such a crisis is consonant with the composer's erratic behaviour during the composition of his final oratorio. Lady Elgar's diaries for this fraught period are filled with the chronicles of her husband's psychosomatic illnesses as well as his bewilderingly rapid alternations of mood between exultation and black despair; her desperation is palpable. At one point, she began to intercept her husband's mail lest the post bring a letter from Jaeger containing criticism of the work-in-progress – or anything that would deflect him from completing the oratorio in time for the first performance.[85]

The reasons for Elgar's disaffection and unhappiness while he was composing *The Kingdom* are several. The gradual waning of his religious convictions may well have exacerbated a growing loss of confidence in his ability to complete a massive project that had been imprudently conceived from the start. Wagner, after all, required almost a quarter of a century to plan and fully execute *Der Ring des Nibelungen*; the English composer undertook a trilogy of oratorios, generating the text himself, in the space of nine years, all while pursuing a busy professional life.

Aside from the toll taken by overconfidence, by the time he came to compose *The Kingdom* Elgar may have discovered that following the careers of the apostles after Christ's Ascension failed to hold his attention. Recall that Elgar was attracted to the subject of the apostles in part as a pretext for exploring the motivations of Judas. Without Judas, and with Mary Magdalene a shadow of her former voluptuously contrite self, Elgar may have discovered that the resolute figure of Peter did not 'open aspects of himself he wanted to explore'. In a letter to Jaeger posted during the composition of *The Dream of Gerontius*, Elgar expounded upon the character of his protagonist: 'Look here: I imagined Gerontius to be a man like us, not a Priest or Saint, but a *sinner*, a repentant one of course but still no end of a *worldly man* in his life … I've not filled *his* part with Church tunes & rubbish but a good, healthy full-blooded romantic, remembered worldliness.'[86] Elgar could readily identify with sinners such as Gerontius, Mary Magdalene and Judas, expressing through them his own fallen state in music of romantic worldliness, but he found saints such as the Virgin Mary, John, and Peter much more difficult to inhabit.

Given his inherent lack of sympathy with most of its dramatis personae and under enormous pressure to compete the cycle of oratorios, Elgar composed *The Kingdom* through an act of sheer creative will-power. Furthermore, without the focal point provided by Christ and without an antagonist like Judas, Elgar must have found the libretto of *The Kingdom* difficult to organise: the result is a series of diffuse tableaux that, while containing some beautiful music, are often quite static.

As *The Times* remarked with approval, there is nothing in *The Kingdom* that can be 'accused of bad taste'. Elgar's espousal of British restraint, allied with the comforting appearance of Anglicanism, led certain admirers such as Boult to value the score above the other oratorios. For Ernest Newman and many other listeners, such decorum was purchased at the expense of liveliness. By way of praising *The Kingdom*, the reviewer for *The Times* cites two glaring instances of questionable artistic judgement in *The Apostles*: the first is the glittering orchestral sonority illustrating Judas casting his blood money upon the Temple floor, while the second is Mary Magdalene's veiled erotic reminiscences in the 'Fantasy'. In these enticing passages, Elgar paints two enthrallingly sinful characters in their most shamefully colourful aspects. The imaginative vivacity that enlivens the finest passages in *The*

Apostles – the exuberance that some listeners considered 'vulgar'[87] – burns very low in *The Kingdom*.

If, as McGuire asserts, *Gerontius* is the most Wagnerian of Elgar's mature oratorios, then *The Kingdom* is surely the least. Although a luxuriant poly-phonic tissue of leitmotivs is still much in evidence, the unremittingly pious tone of *The Kingdom* is far removed from the 'erotic religiosity' of *Parsifal*. Vaughan Williams's observation about the deleterious effect on Elgar of the 'bombazine and bonnets of the Anglican Sunday morning service' is nowhere more apposite than at the opening of *The Kingdom*. Here the stylis-tic inconsistencies found in the score are apparent immediately: a prelude of Wagnerian vigour is succeeded by the first choral entry, 'Seek ye first the Kingdom of God', which sounds disconcertingly like an anthem by Goss, Stainer, or Ouseley.[88]

By 1906, however, both Wagner and decadence were falling out of favour, so that the discomfited composer may have found it difficult to sustain his commitment to such an ambitious and protracted undertaking. After the Wilde trials of 1895, English poets, anxious to avoid being tarred with the same brush as their unfortunate colleague, rapidly abandoned the aesthetic premises that had informed the work of the decadents. No longer dandi-fied creatures lounging at the Café Royal, authors were found strenuously tramping about rural footpaths.[89]

Whether or not Elgar was affected consciously by this aesthetic revolution while composing his final oratorio, it is evident nevertheless that the scarlet and golden threads of *fin de siècle* aesthetics that glisten through the poly-phonic tapestries of *Gerontius* and *The Apostles* are rarely discerned in *The Kingdom*. Significantly, the most sustained lyric passage in *The Kingdom*, an extended solo for the Virgin Mary beginning 'The Sun goeth down', combines a lingering Catholic Mariolatry with a hint of the voluptuous melancholy with which decadent authors saluted the Mater Dolorosa.

A radical change of aesthetics was taking place in British music for much the same reasons that influenced the other arts. A new generation of com-posers rejected the enervated chromatic twilight of the decadent Wagner in favour of healthy, manly diatonic sunlight. Composers such as Vaughan Williams scoured the countryside for folk songs, revered Purcell, and studied the Tudor composers. Elgar's younger colleagues avidly followed modernist developments arising in France rather than looking to German models. In light of these new developments, Elgar may have considered that both the aesthetic premises and the musical idiom of *The Kingdom* were rapidly becoming out of date.

Despite the general acclaim accorded *The Kingdom*, and disregarding continuing pressure put upon him to finish the trilogy, Elgar took Ernest Newman's advice to heart and turned from the composition of the oratorio to pursue instrumental music. Elgar did not wholly abandon choral music, for he continued to supply lucrative part-songs and Anglican anthems to his publishers, but major choral works would be few and far between after 1906. While Moore and others have suggested that the troubled creation of *The Kingdom* was a necessary crucible that prepared him to compose the great orchestral works that appeared between 1906 and 1919, Elgar himself continued to be haunted by a sense of failure over his inability to complete the project as envisioned. The poet A. C. Benson, Elgar's collaborator for the *Coronation Ode*, recorded in his diary that the composer confided 'that it was no sort of pleasure to him to hear *The Kingdom*, because it was so far behind what he had dreamed of – it only caused him shame & sorrow . . . he petitioned for a seat close to the door [at a Cambridge performance], that he might rush out if overcome'.[90]

For the rest of his life, Elgar puttered about with his sketches for *The Last Judgement*, which was to be based largely upon The Book of Revelation and St Augustine's *Civitas Dei*.[91] Lady Elgar's death dashed any real chance that the final oratorio would be completed, although the composer's partisans continued to hope for a recrudescence of Elgar's creative faculties. The composer himself knew that this was not to be. After a 1926 performance of Vaughan Williams's apocalyptic short oratorio *Sancta Civitas*, Elgar informed his younger colleague that 'I once thought of setting those words, but I shall never do that now, and I am glad that I didn't because you have done it for me'.[92]

Despite the sonorous opportunities provided by such lurid creatures as the Whore of Babylon and the Anti-Christ, Elgar's lapsed faith made the final oratorio an untenable proposition. Just how far his religious convictions had decayed is illustrated by a proposal that Elgar made to Ivor Atkins, organist of Worcester Cathedral, in 1929. Elgar sought to compose a setting of *Adonais*, Shelley's notoriously atheistic and subtly homoerotic elegy for Keats; he further proposed that this choral and orchestral work be performed in the cathedral during a Three Choirs Festival. That ecclesiastical authority gently but firmly discouraged this extraordinary idea surely came as no surprise to the elderly composer; it is hard to imagine that he made the offer seriously.[93]

And yet these nihilistic lines from Shelley's poem must have evoked an empathetic response from the ageing composer: 'Life, like a dome of many-coloured glass,/Stains the white radiance of Eternity,/Until Death tramples it to fragments.'[94] Such sentiments are far from those enshrined by Cardinal Newman in *The Dream of Gerontius*, but entirely consonant with those of Judas in *The Apostles*: 'we shall be hereafter as though we had never been . . . and our life shall pass away as the trace of a cloud, and shall be dispersed as a mist, that is driven away with the beams of the sun' (Wisdom 2:3–4).

Elgar may have felt that God had condemned him, like Judas, to be an eternal 'outsider of outsiders'. Even the imprisoned Wilde believed that he had been granted grace; Elgar, however, locked in the prison of his wounded psyche, was so enmeshed in his self-loathing that he was unable to partake of such consolation. Lacking Wagner's heroic egotism, the chronically self-doubting Elgar may have felt there was no surcease for his frequent depressions, no balm to assuage his gnawing anxiety, and no grace to mitigate his shame. Instead he lashed out at both God and humanity, repudiating some of his most radiant music – the vessel that brought grace to repentant sinners like Gerontius – as a mere 'penalty' of his 'English environment'.

On his deathbed, Elgar's thoughts returned for a final time to the unfinished trilogy. He had drawn on his jottings for *The Last Judgement* to assemble sketches for the Third Symphony, and perhaps the two projects, both uncompleted, became conflated in his wandering mind. In a poignant gesture of farewell, he handed W. H. Reed a scrap of paper upon which he had scribbled a theme intended for *The Last Judgement* and, choking back tears, said simply, 'Billy, this is the end.'[95]

8 Roman Catholicism and being musically English: Elgar's church and organ music

JOHN BUTT

His Majesty is . . . inclined to appoint some eminent musician [as Master of the King's Music], but the question arises as to who this should be. Sir Edward Elgar has applied for the post and . . . it seems difficult to resist his claims. At the same time it is generally thought that Vaughan Williams is the most representative of British Music; Elgar having always adopted German methods.[1]
(SIR FREDRICK PONSONBY, 1924)

It might seem odd that, in the 1920s, some thought Elgar unrepresentative of British music; there is no doubt that he had been held as supremely British – or at least English – during the Edwardian era, and he was to become regarded thus again. But this exception does go some way to prove the rule that no music is essentially intrinsic to any nationality: certain traits may become associated with nationhood, as much by the composer as by the audience, but these associations are just as provisional as any other connotations music might hold. To Ponsonby's generation, Vaughan Williams and his generation had tapped the roots of Englishness by rediscovering the folk repertory and returning to the idioms of the Tudor and Elizabethan eras. Elgar's idiom lacked this purity, perhaps even representing the false imperial optimism that lay at the roots of the Great War; moreover, Elgar did not have the luxury of erasing his Germanic musical roots – as the royal family had managed to do with its dynastic title.

Another conception held of Elgar, at least during the latter part of his lifetime, was that he was essentially a sacred composer. This he mentioned caustically in his last letter to Delius, on Christmas Day 1933: 'It has been a matter of no small amusement to me that, as my name somewhat unfortunately is indissolubly connected with "sacred" music, some of your friends and mine have tried to make me believe that I am ill-disposed to the trend and sympathy of your [*Mass of Life*].'[2] While the cliché that Elgar progressively abandoned God for chemistry and dogs contains a grain of truth, there is no doubt that religion played a fundamental part in his compositional thought, and on several different levels. Nevertheless, there is an obvious contradiction between Elgar the archetypal Englishman and Elgar the Roman Catholic churchman. Although Catholic emancipation had been achieved in 1829, there was still a fundamental suspicion of Catholicism in establishment circles, not least because many believed it impossible to owe equal allegiance to the British monarch and to the Pope.

Elgar's Roman Catholic background

Elgar's Catholic upbringing tends to be underplayed in most writings on the composer, but it may nevertheless be one of the most significant sources of his compositional character. It also relates to the question of the status of the organ in his writing, since it was his father's decision to take the post of organist in St George's Catholic Church in Worcester that led to his mother's fervent conversion and hence to the Catholic ethos of the entire family. But if the organ was the very catalyst for Elgar's identity as a permanent outsider, it was also the instrument most central to the Anglican establishment, both ecclesiastical and academic. Any ambivalence on Elgar's part would thus be understandable.

He frequently assisted his father from 1872, and was organist himself from 1885–9.[3] St George's would have opened up a far wider range of continental music – based around Viennese masses – than Elgar might have enjoyed had he grown up within the Anglican tradition. Hubert Leicester's references to frequent performances of mass music by Mozart, Haydn, Beethoven, Hummel, and Weber are substantiated by surviving service orders from 1851–80 (in the Birthplace Museum), which also include works by Pergolesi, Handel and Spohr. According to Leicester, the church (at least during Elgar's father's tenure) had also enjoyed the frequent services of opera singers visiting Worcester, since these were invariably Catholic.[4] The church was, moreover, proud of its tradition of assembling an orchestra for major masses, a practice that drew listeners from miles around. While it might be an exaggeration to explain Elgar's avid interest in the Austro-German mainstream (and indeed the orchestra) entirely in terms of his confessional background, this latter must surely have given his early upbringing a richness that he would not necessarily have acquired in the Anglican church.

Even more interesting is the influence that Gregorian chant must have played in Elgar's upbringing and later in his career. He was apparently being chided as a child by his father for trying to write music on a four-line, rather than five-line, staff, suggesting that chant may have played a considerable and largely unconscious part in his early musical experiences; there is also a manuscript from *c.*1878 in which he penned the modal scales.[5] This aspect of his upbringing, and particularly the development in chant culture in the early years of the new century, has been ignored, if not denied, in much writing on the composer.[6] Nevertheless, it may be worth considering what the influence of chant and modal melodic and harmonic thinking might have been on a composer who assimilated so many things intuitively, with little formal training. He clearly had no difficulties in absorbing the indigenous English sentimental style, with its roots in the foreigners, Handel, and

Mendelssohn, and developed to a level of passable excellence by S. S. Wesley, Sullivan, and Parry. What rendered him outstanding was his mastery of the most advanced compositional technique of the Germanic tradition. If one were to imagine these two traditions tempered – almost unwittingly – by the tonal ambiguity generated by Gregorian chant, it is not entirely implausible to imagine a style that is traditionally English, technically excellent, and up-to-date, yet tinged with a melodic, tonal, and harmonic ambiguity, something that could be heard as nostalgic ineffability, an underlying uncertainty and melancholy. Modal elements were, of course, to become central to the rediscovered Englishness of Vaughan Williams and his contemporaries, but these were acquired through conscious study of the folk and Tudor repertory – a completely different route from Elgar's. In the light of this later style, Elgar's music may well sound in retrospect as 'authentically' English, as if the composer had somehow already intuited the old modal idioms that the younger generation actively sought. Perhaps, then, part of the very Englishness with which Elgar is so often yoked had its roots in that aspect of his background which was most 'foreign' at the time, namely his loyalty to the Pope and the heritage of St Gregory.

Direct evidence for the use of Gregorian chant at St George's is sparse, but not entirely absent, before the celebrated 'Motu Proprio' issued by the Pope in 1903 which specifically promoted Gregorian chant at the expense of other styles of church music. A chant introit is mentioned for a service notice in 1851, and Leicester's collection of Elgar-related manuscripts from St George's contains some fragments of chant.[7] Elgar possessed a Roman breviary and missal with the Psalms 'pointed for recitation or chanting' (given by his mother in 1871), and his clearly used copy of the *Missale Romanum*, dated January 1886 in his hand, contains a certain amount of chant.[8] While the Proper is not set musically here there are numerous versions of the Preface (including the 'Sursum corda') and particularly detailed music for Holy Saturday. This latter includes a chanted Litany (not unlike that in *Gerontius*), and it is clear that the Holy Week celebrations were a particularly strong memory for the composer; Elgar later enquired of Leicester as to whether the 'old' music was still performed in Holy Week.[9]

Most likely, Elgar's knowledge of the Gregorian repertory did not extend to the entire Proper before 1900, when he had to ask Leicester for a volume of Gregorian materials from which he wanted to derive themes for *Gerontius*.[10] Two years later he wrote to the publisher Schott asking for chants appropriate to the theme of 'Apostlehood' to provide leitmotivic material for his new oratorio.[11] He then wrote to Leicester again for a harmonised version of 'O sacrum convivium' and the Gradual 'Constitues eos'; the fact that Leicester was not fully able to oblige suggests that he still did not have access to the entire Proper.[12] Elgar's decision to use the 'Constitues eos' chant was reported by Basil Maine: on visiting a Catholic colleague in November 1902 he casually put his hand on a page in a book, and immediately found he had settled on the chant he needed to represent the Apostles, as if guided by divine inspiration.[13] His own copy of the *Graduale Romanum* is the 1902 edition, and he may well have believed this to be the most authentic source of the Latin Proper given his comment in a letter to Jaeger of 1903, namely that the later Solesmes version amplifies 'the original'.[14]

All this suggests that Elgar not only half-remembered the Gregorian fragments from his upbringing in later life, but went out of his way to flesh out (perhaps even invent?) this memory in the wake of the chant revival. This he seems to have summed up quite consciously in his personification of Gerontius:

> I imagined Gerontius to be a man like us, not a Priest or a Saint, but a *sinner* . . . now brought to book. Therefore I've not filled *his* part with Church tunes & rubbish but a good, healthy full-blooded romantic, remembered worldliness, so to speak . . . If he'd been a priest he wd. have sung or said [his prayer] as a climax but as he represents ME when ill he doesn't – he remembers his little Churchy prayey music in little snatches.[15]

Much of Elgar's mature output could be described in this way – full-blooded romanticism, tinged with 'Churchy prayey' elements, and particularly the modal inflections of Gregorian chant.

Indeed, the shape of Elgar's compositional career suggests that his attention to the implications of chant actually expanded after his years of active service in the church, as if he took on board the Pope's directives and integrated the refurbished Catholic heritage into his broader vocabulary. The two chants that Elgar adopted for *The Apostles* and *The Kingdom* possess melodic characteristics that are absolutely central to his style. The opening of 'Constitues eos' contains a conjunct interval followed by a downward leap of a third ($\hat{5}$–$\hat{4}$–$\hat{2}$–$\hat{3}$ – the $\hat{4}$ being diatonically flattened in the oratorio); 'O sacrum convivium', which dominates *The Kingdom*, begins with the pentatonic collection before introducing the remaining pitches of mode 5. Later lines contain progressions of thirds preceded or succeeded by conjunct motion, typical both of Gregorian chant and Elgar's own style (e.g. the theme dominating the first movement of the Cello Concerto, particularly when it appears in the violas, in the version that Elgar sketched first).[16]

The increasing Gregorian inflection of Elgar's music is remarkably – and no more simply – demonstrated than by comparing some of the many Litany chants he wrote for the Catholic liturgy in the last two or three decades of the nineteenth century and the four chants (1907) he provided for the overtly Anglican *New Cathedral Psalter* (eventually published in 1909).[17] In the

Litany chants, the harmony – if not always the melody – is conventionally tonal (in keeping with the settings of other Catholic composers, as is evident in Tozer's *Complete Benediction Manual* of 1898). John Allison has observed that the four chants published by Tozer in 1888 (and republished in the 1898 collection) preserve the harmonies of Elgar's original manuscripts and had thus not been modified by Tozer, as the composer was to complain in conversation with Leicester (1919).[18] Perhaps, then, Elgar was to become rather ashamed of the conventional 'non-Gregorian' framework of these early liturgical chants.

Elgar's Anglican chants of 1907, on the other hand, are markedly distinct from the majority of the other settings in the 1909 chant book. First, not one of them modulates to the dominant – or even reaches the dominant chord, at the midway point; this goal is virtually a norm in the remainder of the volume. Three of Elgar's four remain in the tonic at this point, the other modulates to the mediant. Secondly, not one of them presents the soprano part falling (or rising) to step $\hat{1}$ at the end: three end on $\hat{3}$, one on $\hat{5}$. Of the two single chants, one is entirely pentatonic melodically, the other is pentatonic for its first five pitches; and one of the double chants contains a ubiquitous Elgarian gesture (with a pentatonic flavour) of step $\hat{2}$ to steps $\hat{6}$–$\hat{5}$ below. The G major chant for the Venite (167 in the book – Ex. 8.1) is the most telling of the four: its melody is pentatonic, ending

Example 8.1 Elgar, *Venite* chant

VENITE

on B, step $\hat{3}$ (the avoidance of C natural might almost suggest a Phrygian melody beginning on B); both second and penultimate chords are the sub-mediant, E minor (thus loosening the tonal distinction between tonic and relative minor), and of the remaining six internal chords one is the first inversion of the mediant. Already, then, Elgar is using chords that tended to be marginalised in standard diatonic practice, in which mediant and submediant chords would seldom appear outside sequences (since the former tends to confuse the polarity between tonic and dominant, the latter tonic and relative minor). It is particularly instructive to compare this chant with a formula he repeatedly adopted for the Kyrie/Agnus Dei chants of his earlier Catholic Litany settings, for although the first half of the chant is identical melodically (and almost certainly the source for the later Anglican chant), the harmony is straightforwardly based on chords I and IV.[19] Most egregious of all, in the context of English harmonic practice, would have been the strange triple appoggiatura above E as the eighth chord, the three upper parts resolving by step on to the ninth chord (E minor). Not only is the submediant an odd chord on to which to place a strong dissonance, the internal augmented fourth is incorrectly resolved and the harmony seemingly limps up a third to the final chord of G major. Indeed, one could imagine an Anglican organist-academic condemning the second half of this chant for being aimless – and in a sense it is.

That Elgar gave particular attention to this ending is suggested by the fact that he modified it from his original sketched version in F major.[20] It may show the fruits of his experimentation with Gregorian chant, harmonising it with sequences of first inversions and occasional appoggiaturas, keeping the harmonic options open in the wake of a melody that lacks strong tonal direction. This is precisely the idiom he adopted in harmonising 'O Sacrum convivium' in *The Kingdom* (e.g. fig. 31, bars 3–5), a year before he wrote the chant. Yet, for all this, the chant simply 'works', with all the lines moving smoothly to local points of rest. There is not really the perception of a lack of harmonic direction, partly because no tonal goals are set up in the first place.

Another source for the development of Elgar's smooth, but apparently 'non-functional', harmonic progressions might well lie in his study of the figured-bass treatise attributed to Mozart; this, as he remarked to G. B. Shaw, he believed to be the only useful harmony textbook for a student composer.[21] The fact that other treatises in his possession (e.g. by Catel and Crotch) also contain references to the figured-bass approach, implies that Elgar took the name of the supposed author rather too seriously. Perhaps he even sensed that this practice (misread as something specifically 'Viennese') was part of his Catholic (and thus continental) heritage.

Chronological survey of the church and organ music

The canon of Elgar's music would not be seriously dented if the existing church and organ music were lost. There is much of quality, to be sure, but the quantity is slight and strongly biased towards the early years. Yet these facts tell us something about the nature of the composer and the way he developed. He wrote only a few, largely commissioned, pieces in the field of church music after 1897, at which point he expended considerable energy on sacred oratorios, as if to sublimate the religious impulse within the secular context of the concert hall or festival. After 1906 even this urge – which has remained essential to the public conception of Elgar – abated as he turned to symphony and concerto. This progression – church music to oratorio to orchestra – resonates with his well-known comments in favour of absolute music above all other forms. It was almost as if he were himself going through the development of German culture, a century or so before, by which music ceased to be merely a servant of religion and became a form of religion in its own right.

Elgar's neglect of solo organ music is even more striking after the publication of the G major sonata in 1895, since all his subsequent organ works were transcriptions. This does not necessarily signify a total contempt for the instrument, given that most organs of the time were designed with the practice of orchestral transcription in mind. Indeed, the instrument was thereby one of the most significant means of disseminating large-scale works to the provinces where orchestras seldom visited. An extraordinarily large number of organ transcriptions of Elgar's own works features on the list of pieces that Novello listed for royalty payments in 1921, a time when the composer's revenue was otherwise rather slim.[22] Given Elgar's own experience as organist of St George's Church, the instrument was clearly something on which he was accustomed to extemporise, and there is some evidence that he continued to do this in later life.[23] There is also the suggestion that he could use the instrument as a way of testing his orchestral and choral works when they were at the draft stage: parts of *The Apostles* were played to him by the Hereford Cathedral organist G. R. Sinclair over Easter 1903; and there is anecdotal evidence that Frank Percy Haines played drafts of at least one of the symphonies at King's College, Cambridge, whilst a student at Clare College, 1908–11.[24]

Most likely Elgar considered the organ an inferior sort of orchestra, ranked somewhat above the piano (which was certainly his main workbench, but never an instrument with which he was fully at home), but ultimately only capable of rendering 'three or four varieties of colour at once'.[25] He sometimes referred to his lack of skill at the organ, had contempt for the pedantic harmony rules of the 'village organist' and criticised Parry's orchestration: 'it's dead & is never more than an *organ part arranged*'.[26] Moreover, he stressed that the violin was 'his' instrument and clearly believed (undoubtedly rightly) that the orchestra was his most natural medium. Indeed, it was in this context – as a sonority within the orchestra – that he was to use the organ most extensively, from the early 'Sursum corda', through the 'Enigma' Variations, to the oratorios. Rainer Fanselau brings up the possibility that Elgar's introduction of the organ precisely at the point at which Jaeger suggested he extend the final (self-) portrait of the 'Enigma' Variations has some sort of autobiographical resonance.[27] But it is impossible to establish any certainty in this matter; possibly the new sonority alludes to the memory of Elgar's early career as an organist, perhaps also to the fact that the organ was at the root of his family's identity as Roman Catholic. But it is not impossible that the organ also had negative connotations: it was after all the instrument of the Anglican establishment, cross-fertilised with the stifling academic atmosphere of Stanford's Cambridge. Perhaps

Elgar felt himself an outsider from the culture that the organ inevitably invoked, despite its ubiquity as a secular concert instrument. Nevertheless, he remained on exceptionally close and fond terms with the organists of the three local cathedrals constituting the Three Choirs Festival: Hugh Blair (the first performer of the Sonata in G) and Ivor Atkins at Worcester, G. R. Sinclair (portrayed in the Variations) at Hereford, and Herbert Brewer of Gloucester. For Blair and Brewer Elgar did the extraordinary good turn of completing orchestrations.[28] It was as if Elgar considered the local cathedrals as part of his own heritage, places that he had conscientiously visited in order to assimilate the Anglican style as a crucial component of his compositional make-up. Even closer to home, though, there were frequent confessional problems surrounding the performance of the more overtly Catholic texts from his oratorios and he withdrew himself from consideration as future mayor of Hereford when the issue of his Catholic identity came to the fore.

While much of Elgar's (entirely Catholic) church music from the 1870s and 80s remains unpublished, it is attracting closer study. Most numerous are the settings of the Benediction hymn 'O salutaris hostia'. There are also several settings of various parts of the Mass Ordinary but, unfortunately, no complete Mass settings. Most interesting are those movements that he based on instrumental works by Mozart and Beethoven, namely the Gloria, modelled directly on the second movement of Mozart's Violin Sonata in F (K547), and the Credo based around themes from three Beethoven symphonies. This, his longest work from the 1870s, has often been noted for its bold approach to modulation and flatward tendencies.[29] A later example is the anthem, 'Ecce Sacerdos Magnus', written for the visit of the Bishop of Birmingham in 1888, and based around a melody from Haydn's *Harmoniemesse*. This was Elgar's first church piece to employ an instrumental accompaniment, one with its own motivic character. All this reflects his attitude as a composer, basing his own education on close study and imitation of respected precedents rather than following the dictates of textbooks and theory. In many ways, this links him with the culture of imitation that was so important to composition before the nineteenth century, giving him a practically based approach to arrangement and adaptation that was to become the mainstay of his income. In other words, his 'Romantic' inclination towards absolute music was balanced by a more traditional sense of invention as a form of arrangement and adaptation.

The best-known pieces from this era are the 'Ave verum corpus', 'Ave Maria' and 'Ave maris stella' from 1887 that Elgar published as Op. 2 (1902, 1907). These are characterised by their compact, lyrical style, typical of Catholic liturgical music of the time, with frequent repetition (often solo–tutti) and call-and-response phrasing. In this respect they could be aptly compared with Fauré's liturgical music, with which the latter two also share certain modal characteristics: e.g. the 'pentatonic' melodic progression from step $\hat{2}$, to the $\hat{6}$, $\hat{5}$ below ('Ave Maria' bb. 4–5, and much repeated subsequently), a fluidity between major tonic and its relative minor and modulation to the mediant (middle section of 'Ave Maria'), consecutive root-position chords and a general avoidance of perfect cadences and leading-notes proceeding to the tonic. Most strongly tonal is the well-known 'Ave verum', and in the manuscript of this (originally setting the 'Pie Jesu' text) Elgar noted its similarity to John Stainer's 'Love divine' (*Daughter of Jairus*). This then related to a more Anglican idiom, something that was to work very much to Elgar's advantage when the piece was published. Elgar's last Catholic liturgical piece was the F major 'O salutaris hostia' (printed in 1898, but possibly of earlier origins), a concise setting in which the repeated figuration in the organ accompaniment gradually pervades the vocal parts in close imitation. This latter section is also characterised by a sequence of modal cadences out of which F major effortlessly returns.

It was during his years as an organist that Elgar prepared his first collection of organ music. The *Vesper Voluntaries* appeared in print in 1890, just after the composer had ceased employment at St George's. These doubtlessly reflect something of the experimentation that service accompaniment fostered. He clearly followed continental models rather than the traditional Anglican organ style; the voluntaries display a degree of cyclic unity (with a matching Introduction, Intermezzo and Coda) and epigrammatic characterisation very much in the mode of Schumann (a composer whom he described as 'my ideal', in 1883). There is also something of Dvořák's rustic sentiment in the airy circle-of-fifths sequence of Voluntary 2, coupled with an occasional pentatonic accent (these Elgar could easily have assimilated from playing in the former's Sixth Symphony in 1884). The miniature format of the pieces enabled him to experiment with contrasting phrase-lengths and also some quite ambitious modulations (the seventh voluntary moves from F# minor to G major and back). These were among the features that soon rendered him the most ingenious English composer of his generation, accomplishing quite difficult compositional challenges in a manner that sounds deceptively simple.

Fanselau shows how the voluntaries originated as sketches based around improvisations, but progressively tied together through the linking of movements and transposition of some of the original pieces.[30] Most interesting is the sketch of tonalities for the overall collection, which shows Elgar consciously thinking in terms of the modal mixture of D minor and major and keys related by third to the tonic (i.e. mediant F major for voluntary III, F♯ minor, at least in the final version, for voluntary VII; and submediant B♭ major for voluntary IV).[31] The lack of any strong dominant area is striking and the D minor movements slip into F major with no modulatory ceremony. Again, all these features are plausible from a composer who had grown up with plainchant as a natural language that was assimilated side-by-side the 'modern' tonal idioms.

A similar approach to tonal planning is evident in Elgar's most substantial piece for organ, the Sonata in G of 1895. He began composition with the second, G minor movement, representing the tonic minor of the entire sonata and also introducing a typical ambiguity between B♭ major and the tonic at the outset. The two keys continue to alternate in the successive movements (B♭ for movement three, G minor for movement four), returning to G major only in the recapitulation of the second subject of the finale. The opening movement may indeed be rather orthodox and obvious in its sonata form, but it is full of colour and dramatic pacing (as Fanselau notes, it represents a surprisingly rare application of sonata form to organ, something not even attempted by Mendelssohn).[32] The Allegretto shows an extension of the small lyrical form earlier exploited in the *Vesper Voluntaries*, now developed with a highly contrapuntal texture that verges on the trio-sonata in the matching outer sections. This leads into the Andante espressivo, displaying Elgar in his idiosyncratically 'noble' mode where he exploited the instrument's limitless lung capacity in its long, sweeping phrases. The central section takes us to some distant memory (or is it a hope?) that is gradually integrated into the return of the opening melody. The work is rounded off by the brilliant Presto, which begins with an expectant scherzo-like texture leading to a march-like second theme. The central section returns us to the theme of the third movement, now transformed with motives from the finale and it is this theme that returns at the end in triumph ('full organ') together with a dazzling – and unexpected – combination of the first and second themes; it is also in the coda that we notice a family resemblance between the third movement theme, now in G major, and the very opening of the sonata. Only the second movement – the first to be written – seems to be exempt from any cyclic relationship, but even here, the opening figuration is based sequentially on steps $\hat{6}$–$\hat{5}$–$\hat{8}$, which are those relating the themes of movements one and three.

In all, the Organ Sonata is one of the most successful 'organ symphonies' of the late nineteenth century, easily rivalling the vast symphonic works from the Parisian organ school of Franck, Widor, and Vierne. It is not to be denied, though, that there is a certain degree of strain between Elgar's ambitions and the medium. Even Hugh Blair could not satisfactorily learn it in the four days between Elgar's completion of the work and the visit of American musicians, for whom the premiere was planned. The review in *The Musical Standard* noted that the work was 'much in the style of a chorus', and indeed the connection of the opening of the Sonata with that of *The Black Knight* (1893) has frequently been noted. This suggests that the work was very much coloured by the large-scale choral projects on which Elgar was working during the 1890s. The review also complained of the chordal repetitions, of which Elgar was clearly fond, 'but which is never good on the organ'.[33]

A similar sense of strain is evident in Elgar's next major liturgical work, his first specifically designed for Anglican use: the Te Deum and Benedictus of 1897 (dedicated to Sinclair, for the opening service of the Three Choirs Festival in Hereford that year). Superficially, the work is similar in length and scale to the grand settings of Stanford and his colleagues. But what is increasingly striking is the motivic and thematic density, largely in the accompaniment (orchestra, with organ as an alternative). This immediately suggests a Wagnerian conception of the orchestra as the main driving force, into which the vocal parts are inserted; the Wagnerian influence is also evidenced by several passages of almost gratuitous chromaticism.

Three themes predominate in the Te Deum: the opening gesture (typically sequenced on the flattened mediant in bar 5), the more lyrical theme for 'All the earth doth worship Thee' (featuring quasi-pentatonic steps), and a 12/8 theme (similar to that eventually opening the Second Symphony) at 'When Thou tookest upon Thee'. However, such is the structure of the text that Elgar has little opportunity for recapitulation, other than a short blast of the opening at 'Day by day we magnify Thee'. A recapitulation is stuffed into the final fourteen bars of postlude, where the chromatic remainder of the opening theme and the remaining two are squashed into a frantic medley (the ensuing Benedictus provides further development of these themes and a more leisurely reprise).

When Elgar was invited, over thirty years later by the Archbishop of Westminster, to compose a new, simple version of the Te Deum, he noted that 'the irregularity of the text stands in the way'.[34] Of course, back in 1897 he could have gone for the massive proportions of Bruckner's setting, whereby a similar motivic saturation is played out over a much larger timescale, but, in the context of liturgical practice, Elgar was clearly struggling with conflicting obligations. Sinclair's reaction ('It is *very very* modern, but I think it will do') sounds irredeemably provincial in the light of the sort of music being written in Europe around 1897, but his comment strikes a note that rings surprisingly true in retrospect.[35] For it is precisely the mismatches between technique, materials, function, and expectations that characterise the long story of modernity in music. Elgar never acknowledged the historical moment by which modernist artists showed the incompatibility between form and technique, on the one side, and communication and function, on the other. Yet he clearly came closer to this than any other British composer of his age and the fundamental tension in his music does at least chime with the contradictions in *fin de siècle* culture; like his friend and colleague, Richard Strauss, he was about as modern as a conservative could be.

The problems of the Te Deum were to some extent assuaged by Elgar's subsequent turn to the sacred oratorio, where the liturgical constraints of time, style, and forces no longer held. The Edwardian era – undoubtedly the peak of Elgar's career – is singularly lacking in church and organ music, marked only by a hymn tune, the four Anglican chants, one carol, and an anthem ('They are at Rest') for the anniversary of Victoria's death in 1909. However, it is in the short space between the death of Edward VII in 1910 and the outbreak of the Great War that Elgar produced some of his finest music for the Anglican church. First, the coronation offertory anthem 'O hearken thou', a highly skilled and intensely expressive miniature, typically based around A♭ and its mediant minor. Then, in 1912, after a delay of nearly two years, he sent Novello his setting of Psalm 48, 'Great is the Lord'; and two years later he provided a setting of Psalm 29, 'Give unto the Lord' and a simpler harvest anthem for parish choirs. Elgar described 'Great is the Lord' as 'very big stuff of Wesley length but alas! Not of Wesley grandeur'. Wesley seems an inapposite model for a composer who had just completed two symphonies, and the loose, short-breathed cantata format (perhaps a 'cantanthem', to use one of Elgar's apt neologisms) is unsuited to his skills of thematic development. The work is closely modelled on themes from the recent Violin Concerto, which only serves by comparison to emphasise a retrograde step taken by an Anglican *manqué*.

'Give unto the Lord' is a different matter: this work exploits the dramatic potential of the text (complete with barely disguised parallel fifths for 'and strippeth the forests bare') and its structural potential for the recapitulation of both opening themes. Then there is the interconnection between the thematic material: the opening theme shares much with that which opened both *The Black Knight* and the Organ Sonata: its first five pitches represent the pentatonic collection, with an octave emphasis on the submediant of E♭; it is precisely this pitch (C) which opens the second theme, 'worship the Lord in the beauty of holiness', creating the ubiquitous sequence of $\hat{6}$–$\hat{5}$–$\hat{2}$–$\hat{1}$ (or $\hat{3}$–$\hat{2}$–lower $\hat{6}$–$\hat{5}$, as it is momentarily heard in the subdominant, A♭). The remaining note from the pentatonic collection then appears, and the next two (non-pentatonic) notes are identical in both themes (E♭–D), the connection somewhat disguised by the syncopation of the second theme. This lyrical syncopation, in turn, becomes central to the entirely different mood of 'breaketh the cedars' (where it is triadic). The opening melodic emphasis on the submediant degree is matched by a harmonic emphasis on the submediant (the second chord, in first inversion, just as is the second chord of the Organ Sonata); this is flattened in a Neapolitan twist in the seventh bar (i.e. C♭ major in first inversion), which ultimately sets up the central tonality of the piece, B minor (i.e. the flattened, minor submediant). In sum, there is no other liturgical piece in which Elgar so managed to reconcile his late Romantic desire for thematic transformation coupled with dramatic contrast and balanced form, with the demands of the text and the function of the piece within the liturgy.

Although Elgar was to write virtually no more original organ music, a few significant pieces were to be arranged for organ. *Cantique* was developed in 1912 from an incomplete wind quintet in the 'Shed' music of 1879, in arrangements for orchestra, organ, and piano. After the war he was commissioned to write a piece for a War Memorial Carillon opened in 1923 in Loughborough. However, presumably given the extreme rarity of that instrument in England, Elgar retained the right to arrange it for organ.[36] Although this arrangement survives only in sketch form, there is enough material to make a convincing piece, one which combines chiming flourishes with a wistful cantilena that is quite beguiling in its constant effect of transitory melody; everything passes before we realise its significance.[37]

Elgar's association of the *Severn Suite* with the organ probably began with its fugue which he wrote in 1923 (in the wake of his recent study of Bach). This appears to have been sketched as a piano piece, but was first performed on the organ by Ivor Atkins in 1925, to celebrate the reopening of the organ in Worcester Cathedral.[38] The suite itself was commissioned for the national brass band championship at the Crystal Palace in 1930, at which its grateful dedicatee, George Bernard Shaw, heard the piece eight times in succession.[39] Apart from the fugue, most of the music derives from much earlier sources. It does not make sense to denigrate the piece in its guise as 'Organ Sonata 2' merely because most of the transcription was undertaken by Ivor Atkins. Although the work hardly represents the composer at his peak, Atkins's arrangement does have the virtue of an idiomatic organ style that Elgar himself found hard to achieve in the first sonata. There is also the fortuitous connection between the block-like chords of the opening, so suited to the wind idiom, with the type of attack offered by a large cathedral organ. The second movement, Toccata, clearly alludes to Bach and the keyboard tradition, although in Atkins's arrangement its rapid figurations seem very reminiscent of the toccata style of the recent French school. The fugue is nothing like the sort of piece that would traditionally accompany a Baroque toccata; indeed with its almost constant melodic line it seems purposely to avoid the sectional nature of a typical fugue, building to an emotional peak just before the end. Atkins's added cadenza (which Elgar seems to have approved) links the fugue to the Coda in which Elgar reworks the opening movement to produce a triumphal conclusion.

Fragments do survive for a new organ sonata in the very last years of Elgar's life, but this project was left incomplete. The late flowering of his interest in the organ suggests that he had managed to view the instrument apart from its church connotations, his interest in religion having all but receded. In all, though, the significance of Elgar's church and organ music lies almost more in what does not survive than in the small but striking oeuvre that remains. The lower part of the iceberg would include his early experiences as his father's assistant, the ongoing study of both tonal and modal idioms, and the experimentation with an instrument that offered a passable substitute for Elgar's 'true' instrument of the orchestra.

9 'A smiling with a sigh': the chamber music and works for strings

DANIEL M. GRIMLEY

Elgar's historical reputation has rested on his large-scale orchestral music. Through the success of the 'Enigma' Variations and the First Symphony in particular, he was seen as the first British composer to have created symphonic music of international scale and importance. Similarly, his last major orchestral work, the Cello Concerto, has often been heard as a retrospective farewell to the whole legacy of nineteenth-century Romantic music – in Michael Kennedy's evocative phrase, 'music of wood smoke and autumn bonfires, of the evening of life'.[1] While Elgar's choral works have likewise achieved canonic status in the modern repertoire, and the variations and the symphonies belong to the most elevated genre of Austro-German absolute music, Elgar's chamber music and works for strings occupy a more ambivalent historical position. Though the chamber music engages with a venerable tradition of serious instrumental works, Elgar's contribution has sometimes seemed conservative or backward-looking, especially alongside his dynamic work in the modern symphonic field. His works for string orchestra occupy a separate generic category, one that has tended to equate lightness of scoring with lack of musical depth (compare the rhetorical weight of a serenade as opposed to a symphony). But this view is not universally held. For many, Elgar's chamber works offer a vivid summing-up of his life's musical experience. Similarly, among Elgar's varied works for string ensemble, one outstanding masterpiece, the *Introduction and Allegro*, has had a catalysing influence on later English string music. In this sense, among others, Elgar's chamber music and works for strings are central to any assessment of his compositional output.

The Serenade for String Orchestra of 1892 is often assumed to be a revised form of an earlier set of *Three Sketches* for strings, entitled 'Spring Song' (Allegro), 'Elegy' (Adagio) and 'Finale' (Presto).[2] Elgar was enthusiastic about the music and wrote to Charles Buck: 'I *like 'em* (the first thing I ever did).'[3] The manuscript of the *Three Sketches* has been lost, however, and its association with the later Serenade remains unclear. Despite initial rejection, the Serenade has since become one of Elgar's most popular works, particularly with amateur groups, youth ensembles, and chamber orchestras. At the same time, the music's relaxed rhetoric and accessibility, characteristics of the genre as developed by composers such as Brahms,

Dvořák, Tchaikovsky, and Grieg, has perhaps precluded a deeper critical appreciation of its musical quality.

The Serenade is laid out in three separate movements, but the numerous motivic and harmonic connections across the work and the strong formal return at the end of the finale mean that it can also be heard as a single musical span. The rocking metre and direction, *piacevole* (peacefully), at the head of the first movement suggest a cradle song, an impression strengthened by the relative lack of harmonic tension. The movement begins with the viola's distinctive ostinato figure, a motto-like idea which Young suggests 'foreshadows the apprehensiveness that colours some part of the chamber music'.[4] The elliptical opening subject leads immediately towards the relative major, accompanied by a change of articulation at letter A. In the middle section, the tonic major functions as the contrasting key area, providing a change of harmonic colour without threatening the movement's underlying stability. Once again, Elgar uses a change of texture to support a moment of formal articulation. The music returns to the minor mode at a climax (bar 86) that corresponds to the earlier change of articulation in bar 14. For a moment the middle section's arching melodic idea is transferred to the bass as the upper strings shift from light staccato to agitated heavy accents (Ex. 9.1). The coda unfolds a new melodic development based on the opening subject, which returns to bring the movement to a hushed conclusion.

The second movement alludes to the serenade's alternative generic function as a musical greeting (a nocturne or evening-song) addressed to a waiting beloved, but any hint of eroticism remains coolly restrained. The linear chromaticism of the extended sixteen-bar introduction, for example, reinforces rather than destabilises the music's prevailing diatonic propriety. The contrasting 'B' section is characterised by a Griegian antiphonal dialogue between different instrumental groups that contrasts with the homophonic texture of the surrounding melodic paragraphs. The return of the opening melody is transformed by a rustling accompaniment figure and octave doubling (the first violins reunite only at the climactic high point of the melody in bar 59). The musical moment of consummation, however, is sustained only momentarily, and the movement closes with a return of the introduction, whose chromaticism sounds especially poignant in its new context.

Unlike the preceding movements, the finale is an asymmetrical through-composed design: a compressed ternary-form structure that leads directly into an extended reprise of the middle (rather than the opening) section of the first movement. The return of the first-movement material is heralded by the viola's ostinato figure, all trace of apprehensiveness gone. Moore hears an echo of *Parsifal* in the interlocking descending cadential fourths

Example 9.1 Elgar, Serenade for Strings, Op. 20, first movement, bb. 82–90

of the final page, but the mood and tonality of the final bars surely allude to another of Wagner's pastoral heroes, Siegfried. Wagner composed the *Siegfried Idyll* as a birthday serenade for his wife, Cosima, and Elgar offered his own serenade to his partner in turn, noting on the score, 'Braut helped a great deal to make these little tunes.'[5] Appropriately, the final bars of the Serenade sound Arcadian rather than anxious. Cadential accidentals (F×) resolve the structural minor–major ambiguity of the first movement, and the lower strings liquidate the viola's motto figure, so that the Serenade finishes with none of the darker undertones that colour Elgar's later work.

The pastoral discourse of the Serenade for string orchestra is unlike the kind of neo-Baroque pastiche that can be found in comparable examples of contemporary string writing such as Parry's amiable *Lady Radnor's Suite* (1894). The *Introduction and Allegro*, however, is closer to a specific Baroque source. The music was written in response to a suggestion from Jaeger, for a work intended to showcase the virtuoso ensemble playing of the newly formed London Symphony Orchestra. In a letter dated 28 October 1904, Jaeger recalled an outstanding performance of Bach's Brandenburg Concerto No. 3 conducted by Fritz Steinbach that he and Elgar had heard at the Lower Rhine Festival in May:

> I'll hope you can write the [London] Symphony orchestra a short new work. Why not a *brilliant* quick *String* Scherzo, or something for those fine strings *only*? a real bring down the House *torrent* of a thing such as Bach could write (remember that *Cologne* Brandenburger Concerto!) a five minutes work would do it! It wouldn't take you away from your *big* work for long. You might even write a *modern Fugue* for Strings, or *Strings & Organ*! That would sell like Cakes.[6]

Echoes of baroque musical syntax can be heard in the intense seriousness of the opening gesture with its falling arpeggio figuration (recalling the beginning of a large-scale keyboard toccata or fantasia), and the interplay of solo concertante and ripieno groups which is such a striking feature of the work's texture. The programme note for the premiere, conducted by Elgar at the Queen's Hall on 8 March 1905, drew attention to this unusual textural quality and commented that:

> The employment in this piece of a solo quartet in addition to the orchestral strings (themselves really a quintet as regards 'parts') is a return to the practices of a bygone day, and therefore comes to us as something of a novelty. The combination gives the composer exceptional opportunities for variety of 'values' (to employ the painter's term), and is therefore of more than usual interest.[7]

If the effect ultimately sounds remote from the sound-world that we currently associate with Baroque music, it is worth recalling that 'big-band' performances of eighteenth-century music reflected an early twentieth-century performance practice and were not merely anachronistic. Elgar's own orchestral arrangement of Bach's Fantasia and Fugue in C minor, BWV 537 offers a thrilling illustration of the stylistic context in which Baroque music was then heard and imagined. Indeed, a suitable musical translation of the term 'value' cited in the programme note might be 'Klangfarben', a concept more readily associated with music from the early twentieth century and particularly relevant to Elgar's musical practice. The *Introduction and Allegro* takes baroque music simply as a point of departure for developing its own individual sense of tone colour and musical space. It is this quality, especially the spatial effect of the constant interplay between individual instrumental groups and the whole ensemble, that was to have the greatest impact on subsequent English works for string orchestra, such as Vaughan Williams's *Fantasia on a Theme of Thomas Tallis* and Frank Bridge's eloquent Suite for strings.

The compositional origins of the *Introduction and Allegro* can be traced to a sketchbook that contains material for *The Apostles* and *The Kingdom*.[8] The sketchbook also contains an extended draft for the melody that first appears six bars after fig. 2 in the *Introduction and Allegro*, popularly known as the 'Welsh tune'. Elgar later provided an account of the inspiration for this idea in the programme note for the work's premiere, prefacing his remarks with a quotation from Shakespeare's *Cymbeline*, Act 4, scene 2, 'A smiling with a sigh':

> . . . in Cardiganshire, I thought of writing a brilliant piece for string orchestra. On the cliff, between blue sea and blue sky, thinking out my theme, there came up to me the sound of singing. The songs were too far away to reach me distinctly, but one point common to all was impressed upon me, and led me to think, perhaps wrongly, that it was a real Welsh idiom – I mean the fall of a third –

> Fitting the need of the moment, I made the tune which appears in the Introduction (as a link) and in the *Coda* of this work; and so my gaudery became touched with romance. The tune may therefore be called, as is the melody in the overture 'In the South', a canto popolare, but the suggesting country is in this case Wales, and not Italy.
>
> The sketch was forgotten until a short time ago, when it was brought to mind by hearing, far down our valley of the Wye, a song similar to that so pleasantly heard on Ynys Lochtyn. The singer of the Wye unknowingly reminded me of my sketch. This I have now completed, and, although there

may be (and I hope there is) a Welsh feeling in the one theme – to quote Shakespeare again: 'All the water in the Wye cannot wash the Welsh blood out of its body' – the work is really a tribute to that sweet borderland where I have made my home.[9]

Many writers have since speculated upon the identity of the Welsh theme: Ian Parrott and others, for example, suggest *Mae hen wlad fy nhadau* ('The Land of my Fathers'), the second half of the Welsh national anthem.[10] The precise identity of the melody is arguably of lesser importance than its function in the finished work, in particular the sense of otherness or difference that it evokes from the surrounding music. Ironically, the melody was not even originally intended for use in a piece for strings, since the sketch includes three instrumental indications, including 'cor ang' written over the tune (the tessitura is ideally suited to cor anglais).[11] Elgar then wrote the word 'Apsoltes' [sic] over a continuation of the sketch, before identifying it at a later date with the printed stamp 'Op. 47'. It seems likely, given the context of the sketchbook, that the idea was originally intended for use in *The Apostles*, possibly to illustrate Christ in the wilderness at the start of the first scene where Elgar provided a brief orchestral interlude for distantly heard reed instruments (two oboes and cor anglais).

As James Hepokoski has recently argued, the 'Welsh tune' forms a crucial element in the structural argument of the *Introduction and Allegro*, where it functions as a musical symbol of loss, yearning, and absence.[12] Significantly, as Hepokoski has observed, Elgar's *rehearing* of the melody in the Wye valley apparently takes place in a historic borderland region between England and Wales that could be understood as emblematic of a particular state of musical mind hovering between active thought and passive remembrance. (Moore writes of 'the dialogue of experience above and below the level of consciousness – the dialogue of reality and the dream through memory'.)[13] The music begins, however, very much in the present tense: in spite of its Baroque origins, the craggy opening gesture sounds strikingly modern. After this bold cadential statement, the quartet muses on material that foreshadows the opening of the following *Allegro*, establishing its presence as an independent textural element in the music's discourse. The material is passed to the ripieno group, and interspersed with echoes of the opening four bars and magical hushed nature sounds. The violinist W. H. Reed compared the effect of the tremolo accompaniment beneath one of the fragmentary statements of the Welsh tune later in the piece (six bars after fig. 15) to the sound of the wind passing through an Aeolian harp.[14] Reed's description could equally well apply to the two luminous interjections (six and eight bars after fig. 1) which augur the very first announcement of the Welsh tune. Matthew Riley identifies this kind of device as a prototypical gesture in Elgar's music, and concludes:

> Especially common is a sense that 'reality' – determined by the conventional
> frame and form of a movement – gives way, in a sudden moment of
> transformation, to a magical inner world of pastoral simplicity, childlike
> innocence, or imaginative vision. Such transformative moments –
> 'thresholds' (the word used by the guardian angel in *Gerontius*) – are usually
> the places where the imitation of natural sounds is heard.[15]

The Welsh tune emerges on the solo viola from within the quartet. Significantly, the viola's delicate inner timbre is only gradually joined by other
members of the ensemble until a second tutti statement begins five bars after
fig. 3, but the melody fails to reach its expected point of cadential arrival.
Instead, the tune evaporates on the mysterious sustained D♭ chord four bars
before fig. 5, so that the reprise of the opening introductory gesture sounds
very much like a brutal return to reality and the musical 'present tense' of
the home key. The introduction closes with a brief epilogue that mourns
the passing of the Welsh tune with a descending chromatic bass line.

Hans Keller has drawn attention to the synthesised 'folky' character of
the *Allegro*'s first subject, with its pentatonic colouring.[16] The music's tight
motivic integrity and 'open string' character emphasise the fresh start after
the wistful ending of the introduction. The *Allegro* again exploits the dialogue between solo quartet and full ensemble, but the expected arrival of
the Welsh tune as lyrical second subject, Hepokoski observes, is replaced by
a new block of music, beginning with the busy semiquaver passage at fig. 10.
This is one of the most noteworthy passages in Elgar's music: a Sibelius-like
episode of gestational activity, a creative flux out of which a figure of structural importance seems destined to emerge. Despite the energetic knees-up
from fig. 12 and virtuoso brilliance of the following scale figuration, however, the sense of arrival is delayed until the heroic apotheosis of the Welsh
tune in the reprise, where the music gathers itself together in a radiant tutti.
For the time being, the music is left with merely a glimpse of the tune that
signals closure, similar to the end of the introduction, which sounds all the
more poignant for its formal absence.

The contrapuntal middle section, which Elgar described to Jaeger as 'no
working-out part but a devil of a fugue instead',[17] returns to the austere
present tense of the opening bars, foregrounding the neo-Baroque idiom
which underpins the work. Julian Rushton has persuasively discussed the
form and historical context of the fugue.[18] As with the introduction, the
passage is not intended to recreate a Baroque fugue in a literal stylistic sense.
Its intervallic angularity suggests rather an attempt to write an objective
modern fugue and to create a new kind of modernist contrapuntal syntax.
Structurally, Elgar's fugue can be compared with the two fugal passages
in the finale of Carl Nielsen's Fifth Symphony (1920–2), which similarly
serve as 'substitutes' for the expected development or 'working-out' section.
Significantly, given the textural dialogue that motivates the work, the solo

quartet does not actively partake in the fugal argument by playing the subject until a relatively late stage, at the rugged climax at fig. 19. Their first entry is a statement of the bass line from three bars after fig. 1, which forms an increasingly prominent countermelody as the fugue develops (Ex. 9.2). The main body of the fugue is intended principally to showcase the orchestra's ensemble ability, simultaneously striking a serious, forward-looking tone. Only after the climax does the music relax, in a dream-like transition where fragments of the fugue subject are interspersed with semiquaver flurries from fig. 10 until the reprise begins the whole cycle once again.

As its title in fact suggests, the *Introduction and Allegro* is defined by a series of binary oppositions. The textural dialogue between solo quartet and orchestral ensemble is the most striking and form-defining element of the work's discourse. Equally important is the stylistic dialogue between modernist neo-Baroque elements and the retrospective Romantic quality of the Welsh tune with its magical nature associations. This dualism is reinforced by the work's tonal argument, which hinges on the tension between minor and major modes. The closing bars bring the work to a characteristically energetic and rousing conclusion. One of the cadential flourishes even includes a passing reference to the wistful E♭ tonal domain in which the Welsh tune was first heard in the introduction (six bars after fig. 32), breezily swept up in the excitement of closure. Given the ambiguous qualities of the endings in many of Elgar's later works however, such as the First and Second Symphonies, the Violin Concerto and *Falstaff*, it is difficult to hear the *Introduction and Allegro*'s attempt to synthesise and resolve its basic structural oppositions as anything other than contingent. It is this sense of balance, precariously maintained, that makes the final bars seem so precipitate: the musical expression of a 'smiling with a sigh' that Elgar had alluded to by placing his Shakespeare quotation at the head of the programme note for the work's premiere.

Though the 1901 sketchbook contains a few fragments for string quartet,[19] Elgar's interest in chamber music and works for strings after the *Introduction and Allegro* seems to have taken second place to his desire, or perceived need, to achieve success in the symphonic field. Parts of the First Symphony were originally intended for a quartet,[20] before finding their way into the finished orchestral work. The Elegy for strings of 1909, written for the Musicians' Company and commissioned by Alfred Littleton (chairman of Novello), is marked by the sense of restrained nobility that Elgar had sought to develop ever since the funeral march from his incidental music for *Grania and Diarmid* (1901). The score is dated 'Mordiford Bridge', and Moore makes much of its possible links with Elgar's attachment to the Herefordshire landscape.[21] The mood of the work, however, is remote from the magical nature music of parts of the *Introduction and Allegro*, and the effect is of emotionally distanced remembrance rather than enchantment.

Example 9.2 Elgar, *Introduction and Allegro*, fig. 17

Sospiri, from early 1914, was originally composed as one of two new pieces for the publisher W. W. Elkin to accompany an earlier hit for violin and piano, *Salut d'Amour*. The first piece was 'Carissima', and the second was originally titled 'Soupir d'amour'. Elgar himself Italianised the title, and offered it for publication instead to Breitkopf & Härtel. By comparison with the *Introduction and Allegro*, *Sospiri* is a small-scale piece. In Barbirolli's famous 1966 recording of the orchestral version for strings and harp, however, the music gains a Mahlerian poignancy: the sustained diatonic dissonance of the music's appoggiaturas even resembles elements of Mahler's harmonic syntax.[22] The return of the principal theme in the reprise, accompanied by shivering tremolando strings, generates an impressive intensity as though the emotion which had threatened to break through in the slow movement of the Second Symphony were once again near the music's surface.

The chamber music

Elgar returned to chamber-music composition only in 1918–19, at the end of the First World War, when he completed three major works: the Violin Sonata, the String Quartet, and the Piano Quintet, at Brinkwells near Petworth in West Sussex. Situated on a heavily wooded ridge above the River Arun with views to the South Downs escarpment, Brinkwells remains a secluded and atmospheric location even today, encouraging many commentators to perceive a special relationship between the music and its local environment.[23] The impetus for Elgar's decision to embark on a series of chamber works towards the end of the war is worth contemplating. Brian Trowell suggests that the idea may have been prompted by W. W. Cobbett's proposal, supported by the Worshipful Company of Musicians, 'to provide a corpus of works to head an English tradition of non-Teutonic chamber music'.[24] As with earlier works such as *The Spirit of England*, however, Elgar adopted an essentially Germanic musical syntax as one of the starting points for his new chamber-music style, challenging the notion of a purely 'English' musical idiom. Elgar's chamber music is characterised by a post-Brahmsian developing variation, a thematic technique normally associated, in Brahms's work, with a process of phrase compression, resulting in a sense of either intensification (winding up towards some climactic point of arrival), or of liquidation and release.[25] In Elgar's music, thematic development is also associated with processes of expansion, often on a large scale at the level of formal periods rather than individual phrases, such as the transition from the bridge passage to the second subject in the first movement of the Piano Quintet. Elgar's music also looks to non-German models. As Trowell notes, Elgar's opinion of Fauré's chamber music reveals 'not only sincere admiration, but also a resentment that the German hegemony in London concerts, symbolized in the figure of Joachim, had deprived Fauré's very different works of a fair hearing'.[26] Similarly, Franck's Violin Sonata and Piano Quintet offered powerful models of cyclical thematic design, texture, and harmonic syntax that were relevant for Elgar's work, especially the Piano Quintet. In spite of its apparent localism, Elgar's chamber music demands to be heard in a broader European context and not simply within a narrow nationalist domain.

Elgar's chamber works are also motivated by a prevailing sense of hollowness and loss that is seemingly at odds with much of the music's surface articulation. Contemporary reviews of the premiere of the Sonata dwelt on the outer movements' vigorous physical character. *The Globe*, for example, praised Elgar's 'vigorous, healthy music', and in a letter to the *Daily Telegraph* before the actual premiere, W. H. Reed wrote of the first movement's 'strong masculine theme, full of dignity and breathing of open-air life'.[27] Qualities of vigour and physicality were central to the cultural construction of masculinity in the early twentieth century.[28] In Victorian and Edwardian England in particular, these qualities were associated with social values and a moral order, the ideal of a 'muscular Christianity' advanced by writers such as Charles Kingsley with which the chivalric *nobilmente* mode of much of Elgar's music can be readily aligned. The outwardly energetic character of the chamber works can therefore be heard as an attempt to portray an idealised masculine subjectivity, a male heroic musical subject that had appeared earlier in Elgar's symphonic work.[29] What makes the chamber music unusual is that this heroic musical subject often seems heavily compromised or absent: in spite of their busy surface activity, the works do not articulate the kind of heroic gestures common in Elgar's earlier works. Rather they are marked, as Trowell notes, by 'a tendency towards harmonic stasis within a section, towards statement and repetition rather than development'.[30] Similarly, crucial structural landmarks often seem strained or effortful rather than expansive or grandiloquent, as though the music were trying to break out of its boundaries rather than comfortably filling them. Such characteristics are not unique to Elgar's chamber works: indeed, they are common to modernist musical practice. But, in the context of Elgar's music they assume special significance that transcends a purely local musical identity.

The Violin Sonata is prototypical in its expression of loss and melancholia. The finished draft of the work bears an epitaph 'M./ob. Sep 1918', to which Elgar added 'that is Marie Joshua'.[31] Trowell argues that the Franckian return of the second movement in the sonata's finale was intended as a tribute to Marie Joshua, and simultaneously also a reference to his 'Windflower', Alice Stuart-Wortley.[32] But the work can also be heard as tragic in a broader, less autobiographical sense. The first movement is a compact Allegro that opens with a stern auxiliary cadence, a subdominant gesture that veers towards the tonic without achieving any real harmonic stability. A counter-statement at fig. 1 marks a fresh start, but the opening's tendency to wander towards the flat side of the tonic has long-term structural implications and highlights the absence of dynamic tonal polarisation, one of the prerequisites of a sonata structure. The troubled first-subject group is succeeded by a mysterious contrasting episode that Reed again compared to the 'elfin' sounds of an Aeolian harp.[33] The reprise, beginning at fig. 11, is harmonically altered (the second subject is stated on D rather than G), a Schubertian formal gesture that allows Elgar to regain the tonic from the flat side while simultaneously reinforcing the harmonic pattern of the opening bars. The coda, beginning at fig. 19, opens with a third restatement of the opening material but, despite an increasingly urgent dialogue between violin and piano, is unable to generate any sustained sense of melodic or harmonic momentum. The terse final bars suggest stern defiance as opposed to heroic inevitability and the last-minute shift to the tonic major is achieved without peroration, enforced through sheer dynamic weight alone.

The 'Romance' attracted most favourable critical comment following the sonata's premiere. Critics were struck by the eloquence of the middle section, which anticipates the third movement of the Cello Concerto, but the contrasting outer sections caused some confusion. Reed, for example, described the movement as 'utterly unlike anything I have ever heard in chamber or any other music: it is most fantastic, and full of subtle touches of great beauty', and perceptively summarised the form as 'the slow movement and a somewhat dignified scherzo combined'.[34] Trowell comments on the exotic quality of the rhythm, which he hears as 'a kind of triple-time bolero', but Reed's description perhaps captures better the music's eerie *commedia*-like quality.[35] Several of the movement's gestures, such as the violin's brief cadenzas and the *grazioso a tempo* bars, recall the second movement of Debussy's Violin Sonata, likewise haunted by images from a *Petrushka*-like imagination. The middle section emerges like the Welsh tune in the *Introduction and Allegro*: a mediant harmonic shift underpinned by a sudden dynamic drop to suggest a heightened state of emotional awareness or *Innigkeit*. The melody consists of a remarkable chain of descending appoggiaturas that characteristically evades harmonic resolution, even at the *Largamente* climax at fig. 32. The end of the episode begins to lead towards even remoter harmonic domains (A♭ major), but is deflected before the return of the opening section, the piano's B triad (fig. 34) in angular contrast to the preceding harmony so that the middle section's yearning sounds all the more unresolved.

Elgar described the finale as 'very broad & *soothing* like the last movement of the IInd Symphony',[36] and the movement opens with a sense of pastoral calm hitherto unheard. Formally, the movement is strophic, alternating the flowing opening group with a clipped martial theme (fig. 40) that recalls the opening movement and a chromatic closing group (fig. 43) that Trowell suggests is an allusion to the 'bliss' motive from Wagner's *Ring*.[37] The second appearance of this closing group ushers in the return of the middle section of the 'Romance', which Elgar initially marked 'l'istesso tempo/keep in this tempo: *not* as in Andante',[38] in order to deny the music's sense of nostalgic retrospection. The expectation generated by this formal and expressive return is the attainment of harmonic or thematic resolution, especially given the unresolved status of the passage in the centre of the second movement. Significantly for the music's heroic narrative, however, the return remains unresolved, the longed-for apotheosis of the melody denied after fig. 54, and the music turns instead to the tonic minor. The coda is similar in effect to that of the first movement: brisk, energetic music whose vigour cannot conceal an inner emptiness. Reed described the final bars as 'a very lofty conception, gradually rising to a climax, the work ending in a blaze', but it is difficult to avoid the impression of music struggling to achieve a state of fulfilment that it can no longer sustain.

The crisis in the Sonata's heroic male subject is precipitated both by the hollow rhetoric of the outer movements, and also by the ultimate withholding of a transfigured return of the second movement, the emotional core of the work. This denial is key to understanding the music's underlying melancholy. As Judith Butler has written, 'where melancholy is the refusal of grief, it is also always the incorporation of loss, *the miming of a death it cannot mourn*' (my emphasis).[39] The String Quartet and Piano Quintet trace similar expressive trajectories. Elgar advised Harriet Cohen not to open a concert with the Quartet because 'it starts in rather a phantom-like way',[40] and according to Trowell 'it is easy to hear the hoarse whisper of some gaunt visitant in the depressed modal harmony and strangely-spaced homophony of its opening bars'.[41] Whether or not the music is motivated by a sense of the supernatural, the opening two-bar sentence acts as a curiously formal and archaic threshold. Moore argues that the movement is powerfully affected by Elgar's war-time experience, hence the first subject's rhythmic and harmonic instability accentuated by the stringendo at fig. 2. Only the wistful second subject, announced at fig. 4, offers a glimpse of a more contemplative state of mind, but in the development it becomes transformed into a wild ride, an intensely driven fortissimo that culminates in a return of the stringendo at fig. 11. In the reprise the second subject is marked *più lento*, held back by an intensified nostalgia so that the movement sounds increasingly retrospective. The coda attempts a final burst of energetic activity at fig. 17, but swiftly returns to the archaism of the opening gesture. The 'last whisper of the primary question', Moore suggests, is uttered in a 'new and barren harmonic world', an uncomfortably inconclusive point of rest despite the earnestness of the closing bars.

By comparison with other contemporary European quartets, such as the Second Quartets of Bartók and Schoenberg, or Vaughan Williams's remarkable Phantasy Quartet, Elgar's approach to the medium easily seems conservative or backward-looking. But such an interpretation is to misunderstand both the quartet's sound-world and its historical context. The textural austerity of Elgar's work, and its delicate interplay with modal and diatonic harmonic elements, is close to the music of other composers such as Fauré and Sibelius who sought to move decisively away from a direct engagement with the European avant-garde in order to pursue their own individual musical pathways. Sibelius's quartet, subtitled *Voces Intimae* (intimate voices) and composed in London and Paris in 1910–11, is particularly comparable with much of Elgar's later work. Together, these quartets offer a more diverse and pluralistic view of musical progress, in which Elgar's chamber works present their own compelling narrative. As the critic L. Dutton Green, writing of the Sonata, suggested, Elgar's work 'seems like a protest against the far-fetched devices of the ultra-moderns – it seems to say: See what can be done yet with the old forms, the old methods of composing, the old scales: if you only know how to do it your work may yet be new, yet original, yet beautiful.'[42]

The striking diatonicism of the Quartet's second movement can therefore be heard as a deliberate attempt to define a new musical language that steers away from post-Romantic chromaticism rather than merely an anachronistic or reactionary return to an outmoded tonal syntax. This, surely, is the meaning of Elgar's oft-quoted suggestion to Troyte Griffith that 'there is something in it which has never been done before'.[43] The direction 'Piacevole' which stands at the head of the movement is not so much a tempo indication as emblematic of the movement's quiet, interiorised discourse. The first violin sits and listens as the music unwinds through the first twenty-two bars, and much of the movement is characterised by a sense of patient anticipation. As Trowell notes, it is remarkable how here and in the first movement Elgar creates the impression of diatonic harmonic space without sounding strong root-position tonic triads. Brian Newbould has observed how Elgar recomposes the opening tune in the coda, omitting a bar (four bars after fig. 35) so that the texture fragments in almost Mahlerian fashion.[44] But the heart of the movement is the moment of magical intensity, first heard at fig. 25 and then echoed at fig. 33 in the recapitulation, a *valse triste* where Elgar dwells on the enharmonic variance of specific chromatic pitch elements (e♭/d♯ and a♭/g♯). It is the final resolution of this latter pitch, A♭, with its reference to the outer movement's modal instability, that eventually brings the movement to a close.

By contrast, the emphasis in the finale is squarely upon physical activity. As Moore suggests, 'it was as if this music faced a time when all must go faster – when every cinder of melodic expression from the old world would be consumed in the energy which had fired it, now the war was over'.[45] After the taut opening, the first violin unfurls an expansive *brillante* motto that swiftly propels the ensemble forwards. Though the second subject slackens slightly, the dialogue at fig. 45 is the closest Elgar comes in his chamber works to the gestational flux of the *Introduction and Allegro*. The sudden expansiveness of fig. 56 appears to herald a broader, nobler apotheosis, but as in the finale of Sibelius's quartet the finale is swept along by its own terrifying forward momentum. In a gesture remarkably similar to that at the end of the Violin Sonata, the concluding bars of the Quartet attempt to achieve resolution through sheer force of musical motion alone, the chromatic pitch elements patiently resolved at the end of the preceding movement now hastily gathered together in an urgent final attempt to impose cadential order upon a texture that threatens to break apart.

Many of the stories and myths that surround the Piano Quintet point to Algernon Blackwood, the author of *A Prisoner in Fairyland*, later adapted as *The Starlight Express*, whom Elgar first met in December 1915. Blackwood was the most likely source of the spurious tale of the 'impious Spanish monks' which appears to have attracted Alice Elgar and Billy Reed in particular.[46] The mood and colour of Blackwood's novels, with their tales of enchanted escape to a pastoral childhood fairyland, might seem strangely aligned with certain aspects of Elgar's chamber music, but both the Quartet and the Quintet ultimately suggest a darker, less restful musical imagination. The Quintet opens with a strikingly empty gesture: the texture of the introduction sounds as though it were written *against* the ensemble rather than trying to bring them together. The opposition of 'shuddering' string accompaniment and the piano's cold melodic line sounds bleaker than the comparable opening of Brahms's Piano Quintet in F minor, Op. 34, for example, and provides a structural dissonance between instrumental groups that motivates the subsequent form of the movement. The introduction also announces a number of chromatic pitch elements that figure prominently in later sections, notably the modulatory episode four bars after fig. 4. The introduction's second gesture, the unstable string phrase at fig. 1, is triggered by a diminution of the chromatic descent (e-d♯/e♭-d♮) from the tail of the piano's opening melody, and is filled with nostalgia and regret (Ex. 9.3). In Trowell's hermeneutic account, the opening of the Allegro is 'an entirely justified call to arms', a furious response to the ruinous textural disjunction of the opening.[47] The bridge passage four bars after fig. 4 has often been described as Spanish or 'oriental' in character on account of its modal mixture (in fact derived from the shifting chromaticism of the opening),

Example 9.3 Elgar, Piano Quintet, first movement, fig. 1

but the music simultaneously marks a new stage in the movement's textural discourse. Here, for the first time, piano and strings begin to operate in a co-operative rather than antagonistic and aggressive manner, a bringing together of instrumental forces into a single unified ensemble. The texturally inverted return of the opening at the start of the development suggests that such communal action is ultimately in vain, an impression reinforced by the onset of the fugue at fig. 11. As in the *Introduction and Allegro*, the music conveys a vivid seriousness of purpose, but its forward momentum is almost brought to a complete halt by the violent antiphonal exchanges of piano and strings between figs. 12 and 13, before being swept into the reprise at fig. 14. Elgar brings the second subject back in the secondary dominant, delaying the return of the tonic until the final bars so that it assumes the character of exhausted defeat. Though it provides tonal closure, the coda merely serves to reinforce, rather than resolve, the timbral hollowness of the opening bars.

In the context of this war-torn opening movement, the Adagio that follows could be heard as a hymn of remembrance. The music opens with rich four-part string writing, with viola on top, the kind of stable diatonic gesture absent from much of the preceding Allegro. The opening eight-bar phrase is expanded into a forty-two-bar sentence that continually seems oriented towards cadential closure until finally achieving rest at fig. 30. The secondary group signals a shift to a more discursive discourse (piano/string antiphony followed by accompanied solo statements for first violin and cello), but the passage is initiated by a variation of the unstable string figure from the introduction (compare figs. 1 and 30). Though the development opens with a restatement of the viola's first subject (on the flattened supertonic), the return of unstable material from the Allegro unsettles the music's harmonic stability, so that the climax (fig. 35) sounds anxious and turbulent rather than affirmatory. The reprise becomes the real apotheosis of the movement, raised to a higher register and dynamic level (fig. 37), but the sense of unease that pervades the development is not entirely resolved, even by the restful cadences of the coda.

Significantly, given the shadows that hover over the end of the Adagio, the finale begins with the unstable string figure from the opening Allegro (fig. 1) before attempting what initially seems a straightforwardly heroic solution to the work's problems. The confident *con dignità* theme with which the main body of the movement opens suggests diatonic security but swiftly leads in less stable chromatic directions. The music that follows is built from a series of increasingly urgent exchanges between this new heroic material and its contrasting polonaise-like secondary group (fig. 49), interrupted by a ghostly return of the first movement (fig. 55). It is the secondary group that ultimately determines the finale's outcome. The polonaise's chromatic

Example 9.4 Elgar, Piano Quintet, finale: chromatic descent into fig. 73

tail (five bars after fig. 49) generates much of the movement's energetic sequential passagework. After the reprise at fig. 60, however, following the return of the opening Allegro, the chromatic tail increasingly begins to dominate the musical discourse so that it assumes a vertiginous, rather than merely propulsive, quality. The grandioso apotheosis of the polonaise at fig. 72, which initiates the coda, sounds grotesque and overblown, an impression reinforced by the nightmarish chromatic descent into fig. 73 (Ex. 9.4). By comparison, the return of the heroic first subject that attempts to achieve closure inevitably sounds underplayed, its desire to clinch the Quintet's prevailing major–minor tension compromised by the chromatic saturation of the preceding bars. There is no retrospective of previously heard material whose wistful nostalgia is denied, as in the Sonata, but a deliberate unbalancing of the conclusion.

The heroic masculine subject of Elgar's chamber music whose authority is continually denied, refused, or undermined may be understood as Elgar himself. Commentators have drawn attention to the composer's emotional breakdown in 1917, and interpret the chamber music as a form of creative therapy, works whose outward physicality suggests health and renewed bodily vigour even as they allude to a broken inner voice or spirit. The chamber works might equally well be understood as a powerfully internalised response to the experience of war. Though Elgar wrote to Laurence Binyon on 5 November 1918 that 'I do not feel drawn to peace music somehow',[48] the chamber music could be heard as an attempt to achieve a creative reconciliation, through a re-engagement with a European musical culture that had been ruined by the conflict. Chamber music's conventional (pre-war) associations of seriousness, intimacy, and conversational dialogue lend themselves particularly well to an expression of optimistic faith, though Elgar's works constantly threaten to collapse under the burden of such expectation. In this context, the chamber works could be heard as Elgar's most eloquent epitaph for the war dead. But the chamber works can also be heard on a higher level as the expression of Elgar's confrontation with a new modernist subjectivity. The sense of alienation that pervades the chamber music is not a technical or aesthetic deficiency, but a vivid and compelling composing-out of a fractured musical identity.

10 In search of the symphony: orchestral music to 1908

JULIAN RUSHTON

If any work by Elgar belongs to the internationally recognised canon of orchestral masterpieces, it is the *Variations on an Original Theme*, Op. 36; yet this was only his second large-scale orchestral work to reach performance. Elgar's growing skill and imagination in deploying large orchestral forces were already evident, and his claim that *The Black Knight* was a kind of choral symphony[1] suggests a conscious direction of his career towards that form, 'the highest development of art'.[2] The Variations accomplished his first breakthrough to international success. The concert overture *Froissart* (Op. 19), composed for the Three Choirs Festival at Worcester (1890), is scarcely less remarkable, as the earliest of Elgar's larger orchestral conceptions to survive his self-criticism, or his unwillingness to finish large-scale compositions for which no performance could be anticipated; earlier works inspired by the Lake District and Scotland were abandoned, as was an early attempt at a violin concerto. By the time he composed *Froissart* Elgar was already well into his thirties, and its orchestral mastery derives from practical experience, as well as intense study of orchestral scores and alert listening when the opportunity arose. Elgar's break with what, in his intermittently tactless inaugural lecture at Birmingham, he identified as the 'whiteness', the 'false rhapsody', of English music is nowhere more apparent than in the brilliance of his orchestral inventions.[3]

Shorter works

The earliest orchestral pieces belong to the modest genre of 'characteristic' music. Elgar began his career as a miniaturist for practical reasons, but he had a natural gift for succinct sound-pictures and the mature composer continued to develop this side of his musical personality. Several groupings of characteristic pieces, some originally theatre music or Bavarian dances, were published as suites, and this category served as late as the *Severn Suite*, Op. 87 (1932), composed for orchestra as well as brass band. But Elgar was not to be satisfied with an output mainly of shorter pieces, for within himself he felt the urge to attempt, and the ability to achieve, 'something great'; and for all that the thought came to him in rural peace, by the river, that something had eventually to be a symphony.[4]

The modest requirements of local music-making are illustrated by two orchestral pieces from 1878. *Intonation No. 2* (a title curiously suggestive of the 1950s avant-garde) is for six woodwind and strings, and *Introductory Overture for the Christy Minstrels* (performed in the Worcester Music Hall) is for flute, cornet, percussion, and strings. Elgar was soon producing quadrilles and polkas, some for the Powick Lunatic Asylum; in 1881, a Worcester audience heard his *Air de ballet*; in 1883 his music reached Birmingham with *Intermezzo moresque*; and in May 1884, shortly before his twenty-seventh birthday, the second performance of *Sevillana* actually took place in London. But this expansion of his geographical range led nowhere, and four years elapsed before the orchestral version of *Salut d'amour*, a suite, and some (lost) string pieces were performed.[5] It was not much preparation for *The Black Knight* and *Froissart*.

Elgar's shorter pieces, serendipitously, usually last under five minutes, fitting one side of a '78' record.[6] Many titles remind us of the foreign domination of English music; *Salut d'amour* was originally *Liebesgrüss*, rather than 'Love's greeting'. Exoticism is based on conventional evocative signs rather than fieldwork, and much of *Sevillana* is frankly a Viennese waltz; in Spanish vein, Elgar was worsted by the French, such as Bizet (*Carmen*, 1875) and Chabrier (*España*, 1883). The *Intermezzo*, adapted as *Sérénade Mauresque*, succeeds not because of any accuracy in its evocation but because Elgar hit the right note of unpretentious, faintly scented charm. It became the second of *Three Characteristic Pieces* published in 1899 as Op. 10, where it is preceded by a brisk Mazurka, and followed by a double Gavotte, an ancient style of pomp and counterpoint brilliantly subverted by a modern counterpart.[7] The *Three Characteristic Pieces* use a full orchestra, and when they were published Elgar had already composed the Variations, the apogee (with the *Falstaff* interludes) of his command of the miniature. But he did not abandon smaller ensembles. The same year he presented *Sérénade lyrique*, a 'Mélodie' in slow-waltz style originally written for violin and piano, to Ivan Caryll's small orchestra, and he continued to orchestrate earlier pieces, such as *Rosemary*, for appropriately delicate ensembles. *Sérénade* makes adroit use of harp, as does *Dream Children* (1902), a miniature suite inspired by some lines of Charles Lamb; its first movement is an example, well ahead of the Elegy and *Sospiri*, of Elgar's texture becoming evanescent to the point of inaudibility. Christopher Grogan calls *Dream Children* 'perhaps the earliest manifestation of a vein of nostalgia which was to become an essential part of his idiom'.[8] A more substantial pair of suites, *The Wand of Youth*, was completed in 1907–8, and contains music of such originality, especially in the handling of rhythm, that the origin of some movements in very early sketches has been doubted in spite of Elgar's own testimony.[9] Nostalgia can still impinge upon music of inventive high spirits; as always, with Elgar, brilliance is sharpened in profile by moments of wistfulness, although these are eventually trampled upon by the last movements of each suite, which evoke giants and wild bears.

Stylised composition in short forms was an invaluable training, even for the writing of symphonies. The symphonic tradition is packed with allusions to simple forms and 'characteristic' music, particularly in middle movements. Slow movements evoke songs or arias; some are variations; some suggest funeral marches; others are not even slow (Beethoven's Seventh). Innumerable minuets begat the 'scherzo and trio'; Berlioz and Tchaikovsky substituted waltzes, Dvořák the furiant, Brahms the intermezzo. Elgar's marches stretch the functional expectations of the genre with their orchestral, harmonic, and contrapuntal daring, and contributed directly to his developing symphonic capabilities. The typical march schema determines the approximate length, the alternation of the main section with a sustained melody ('trio') triumphantly recalled towards the end – a pattern which defines *Colonel Bogey* as much as *Pomp and Circumstance*. Following the successful Imperial March (Op. 32, 1897), commissioned by Novello and first played in the Crystal Palace on massed bands, Elgar began his famous five (Op. 39) in 1901.[10] The first March is relatively over-exposed. It follows the traditional schema, despite an off-key beginning, but like the other marches it is not intended for military use, being rather an elaborate 'portrait' of the march designed for a large concert hall (it uses two harps and organ), such as the Royal Albert Hall where it is annually deployed at the Last Night of the Proms. No. 4 (1907) replicates No. 1 with a trio melody hardly inferior to 'Land of Hope and Glory' (to which No. 1 owes its fame). More subversively, Nos. 2 and 3 are in minor keys, with a modal tendency (flattened sevenths), and No. 2 offers hints of tonal ambiguity. With their true orchestral writing, the symphonic development of rhythmically driving ideas, and the perhaps ironic delicacy of the 'trio' in No. 3 (anticipating *Falstaff*), the whole or sole point of these pieces is not pomp and circumstance, at least if that implies jingo and Empire. With the overtures, the marches completed Elgar's preparation for his first trial of strength with the symphony; but we should not overlook the role of miniatures as episodes, variations, even as developments, within his ripest symphonic works.

Concert overtures

In overtures, Elgar could expand characteristic music into large forms without feeling burdened by generic expectations, other than those implied by the use of evocative titles or programmes. He might have agreed with a contemporary who opined that 'overtures are allowed greater laxity of rule' than symphony movements.[11] In all his three overtures, following the lead of Berlioz and Mendelssohn, Elgar distends sonata form to the point where, unaided, it can no longer guarantee coherence. *In the South* (subtitled *Alassio*, Op. 50, 1904) takes on the dimensions of a symphonic poem.[12] None of the overtures, however, is programmatic in the sense of following a linear narrative, as does *Falstaff*.

The title *Froissart* alludes to the *Chroniques* of the fourteenth-century author Jean Froissart, unreliable historically but 'instinct with the spirit of chivalry'.[13] The brilliant opening attacks us, as if in the present tense, but later, more expansive passages reflect upon a topic as if from a past time better than our own. Elgar prefaced his overture with the line 'When chivalry lifted up its lance on high', but nostalgia is only possible if one forgets that such lances were also lowered to inflict injury and death.[14] The music evades stern realities and engages with an idealised world in which honour governed behaviour between friend and foe alike. Most Elgarian about this first essay in music for a large-scale concert, and compensating for a certain diffuseness, are the plethora of thematic ideas and the confidence of the scoring.

The successors to *Froissart* are not the next overture, *Cockaigne*, so much as the never-to-be-written symphony in tribute to General Gordon, *In the South*, and *Falstaff* where chivalric values are viewed more harshly. The advantage of a 'topic' like an Italian journey is that the music can glory in being episodic.[15] The tremendous driving main theme was registered in the Hereford visitors' book as 'Dan triumphant (after a fight)'.[16] Comparison to Strauss is inevitable, though the original notation was in the E of *Don Juan*, not the eventual E♭ of *Ein Heldenleben*. Energy is quickly expended into lyricism, with the first idea developing beneath (Ex. 10.1). These and other ideas are duly developed and concisely recapitulated before the opening idea forms the basis for the *grandioso* coda (fig. 58). But where a symphonic sonata form would normally engage in development, Elgar introduces a new idea, inspired by remains of the military might of the Roman Empire (fig. 20). Development does follow, and the exuberance of the main ideas takes on a more anguished form; then energy is again dispersed for the gentle interlude of the 'canto popolare' (fig. 34), first heard on the most reticent of orchestral soloists, the viola. The effect is that 'development' seems less an issue than 'transition' – of tonality, as in sonatas, but more importantly of mood – in shaping music for which the sonata dynamic is only a shell; the essential form is something more epic than dramatic. The nature of the themes, their ordering, and the level of contrast make *In the South* feel like a rondo, but also, thanks to the correspondence

Example 10.1 Elgar, *In the South*

of opening and closing phases in theme and energy as well as key, a kind of gigantic arch.

Elgar's review of Italy and its past is comparable to Byron's *Childe Harold* and its musical embodiment by Berlioz (*Harold en Italie*). The opening surge is redolent of joy on arriving in 'das Land wo die Zitronen blühn'.[17] In sober fact the Elgars visited Italy in winter, as is perhaps reflected in turbulent transitions or the colder textures within the secondary theme-group; this passage (fig. 13, in 2/4), Elgar called 'musing', but its chromaticism aches more than that word implies. It is surrounded by more genial material (fig. 10, resumed at fig. 17), still in 3/4, incorporating a shape based on the word 'Moglio', a village-name that appealed to Elgar. Deprived of sunshine, the musical persona turns to historical tourism and is moved by the grandeur that was Rome. The contrast with the less glorious present possibly causes the storm and stress of the next transition, leading to the pastoral, escapist interlude. Thus Elgar can return refreshed to his main material, and the exuberance and beauty of the music overcome impertinent doubts about 'unity'. Such willingness to admit parenthetical material was anticipated by *Froissart*; a similar willingness obtains in *Cockaigne*.

Cockaigne (*In London Town*, Op. 40, 1901) engages with the vernacular more openly than Elgar's other major works, and is consequently one of his most endearing. 'Cockaigne' originally meant an imaginary land of plenty, but perhaps because of a fortuitous resemblance to 'cockney' it became associated with an idealised view of London. Elgar, with characteristic generosity of thematic invention, evokes aspects busy, cheerful, sentimental, and plain vulgar, the latter subtly inflected, of course, towards idealisation through nostalgia. *Cockaigne* is every bit as patriotic as *Pomp and Circumstance* and more ingenious, for instance in adapting a single musical shape in contrasting, even contradictory, moods. While anticipating the First Symphony, this procedure more obviously echoes Wagner's *Die Meistersinger*, where the grandiose tread of the Masters is adapted for the impudent cavorting of the apprentices. However, though both overtures use busy counterpoint within a loose sonata pattern, Elgar's rhetoric is entirely different; his London is not only the hub of an Empire but the city of music-hall and Covent Garden (market, not opera). The overture begins skittishly, to discover grandeur in the course of its peregrinations. The first theme-group is again ternary. Its middle part (see Ex. 10.2) is a fine example of making much of a simple idea; it is at first marked *nobilmente* (fig. 3), then presented in cheeky diminution (fig. 7), and later *dolcissimo*, as a pastoral (fig. 11). The tender sequel is interrupted by a deliberately commonplace march, first only on clarinets, eventually on full brass, resplendently vulgar. Elgar's energetic build-up from this point deceives, premature apotheosis being avoided (fig. 20) in a bubble of woodwind, breaking over tritone-unrelated chords

Example 10.2 Elgar, *Cockaigne*, fig. 3

Fig.7: Clarinet Solo, *scherzando*

Fig.11: Strings, *dolcissimo*

(F, with prominent sixth, and B with a seventh, the bass throughout being A). We overhear a distant out-of-tune marching band and perhaps a short *scène d'amour* before the powerful recapitulation of the main themes. This time the build-up duly reaches its *nobilmente* apotheosis with a glowing entry of the organ; this is in E♭ although the overture ends a few bars later in C. Such tonal sleight of hand proved vital in the complex design of the First Symphony.

The Variations

Elgar's *Variations on an Original Theme*, Op. 36 (1899) is known by the misleading title 'Enigma' Variations: Elgar must have directed that this word should be written over the theme, but the conundrum is not the subject of musical treatment. Attempts to find a definitive 'solution' abound, although it is unclear that anything needs to be solved.[18] Many attempts, denying the originality of the theme, seek a solution by discovering a source; others follow Elgar's 'through and over the whole set another and larger theme "goes"', although it is highly unlikely that at the time of composition he can have had in mind any musical theme which *combined* with the original.[19] The 'enigma' entered the historical record after the work was already planned as orchestral variations designed to 'picture' members of the Elgar circle (although several equally, perhaps more, eligible are not included).[20] Philosophic interpretations of Elgar's 'larger theme' include 'friendship' (hardly an enigma, given the dedication 'To my friends pictured within') or 'patriotism' (despite the absence of the tub-thumping recently featured in *Caractacus*).

This network of potential significations has given rise to a substantial literature, mostly unconcerned with musical values. Yet Elgar's priorities were surely to engage with issues of diversity, unity, and coherence which are first and foremost musical. As a set of variations, Op. 36 is striking in its freedom, yet almost every melodic shape derives from the two parts of the delicately conceived and orchestrated theme. In variation sets, thematic beauty is not always an advantage, and in some Elgar might have taken as a model (Brahms's 'Haydn' Variations, or Parry's *Symphonic Variations* of 1897), the melody is of less concern than the proportions of the theme and the underlying harmonic progressions. Elgar never loses touch with the contour and rhythmic character of the theme while he devises new characters by changing (the word seems more apt than 'varying') metre, instrumentation, harmony, and even form, for the ternary design of the theme is not always reproduced in the variations. Only two sections bear out his remark that 'the connexion between the Variations and the Theme is often of the slightest texture': 'Dorabella', marked 'intermezzo' and partly based on an earlier sketch, and the thirteenth variation, headed ('***'), which quotes Mendelssohn's *Calm Sea and Prosperous Voyage* and imitates the drear sound of an ocean-liner's engine.[21]

Variations is an inspired collection of character-pieces related by the theme, and another sub-literature has developed, based on Elgar's remarks, exploring the personalities of those 'pictured'.[22] But as Elgar observed almost at the point of conception, these should not matter to the audience member who 'nose nuffin'.[23] The variation closest to the theme (No. 1, 'C.A.E.') is dedicated to Alice Elgar and the finale ('E.D.U.') is a self-portrait, and more importantly his principal exercise in symphonic development between *Froissart* and *Cockaigne*. It begins with an explosive crescendo, and introduces a completely new melody in counterpoint with the middle section of the theme, as well as reprises of the 'Nimrod' and 'C.A.E.' variations; the organ

Example 10.3 Elgar, First Symphony

Variations Op.36, Finale, fig.82-83

Symphony No.1, first movement from bar 3

Third movement (Adagio), from fig.96

enters in an accelerating orgy of sound whose inevitable-seeming flow makes it the more surprising that at the first performance the piece was shorter by nearly a hundred bars (or about ninety seconds). The last grand lunge towards the minor mode closes the work with a chance anticipation of the opening of the First Symphony, still nearly a decade away (Ex. 10.3).

The First Symphony

The extension of the Op. 36 finale might remind us that programmes, for Elgar, were secondary to the desire to make music. Nevertheless, most early literature on his First Symphony is concerned with underlying meanings rather than musical substance.[24] A symphony was probably Elgar's most persistent compositional ambition for at least ten years before he completed one, but when he proposed one to Leeds in 1898, it may have been intended as a symphonic tribute to General Gordon, killed in the Sudan in 1885.[25] A programme symphony was a natural ambition at this time; writing before the eventual First Symphony, Frederick Niecks remarked of Elgar: 'Earnest and intense, and ultra-modern as he is, he could not but be a composer of programme music.'[26] But in his Birmingham lecture of 13 December 1905, Elgar was reported as having claimed the 'absolute' symphony, without programme, as the summit of musical art, a view which echoed that of Parry among others.[27] Reporting the lecture in the *Manchester Guardian*, Ernest Newman remarked that Elgar's past practice diverged from his own ideal.[28] Appropriately, it was to Newman that the programme-note for the first symphony was entrusted, and to him that Elgar wrote his most revealing comments. It now appears that he was already working towards the symphony in 1904; further work in June 1907, when Alice reported him 'playing great beautiful tune', was again interrupted, and the elements were gathered together and completed between June and September 1908.[29]

Elgar took longer to achieve his symphonic ambition even than Brahms, who was in his early forties when his first symphony was performed. Like Brahms, Elgar felt the weight of expectation engendered by a concert canon revolving round Beethoven. Both entered the symphonic arena with works of the utmost seriousness and formal complexity. Their most obvious similarity is that the finales as well as the first movements have a slow introduction. Nothing, however, could be more different than the beginnings of the symphonies, and one of Elgar's formal devices, relating the outer and inner pairs of movements thematically and even adapting the same notes for his scherzo and slow movement, which are not even in the same key, was anticipated by Bruckner in his Fifth Symphony; however, Elgar originally intended this music for a string quartet, begun late in 1907 (Ex. 10.4; the bracket marks the only pitch differences until the end of the extract).[30] Aesthetically, Elgar's work is remote from Bruckner's, which he is unlikely to have known; at least subconsciously, Elgar was continuing to work on a project to reconcile Brahms and Wagner.

If nothing else in this astonishing masterpiece were original, the opening would be: for symphonic introductions are seldom self-contained melodies, completely cadenced. This is the so-called motto, Alice's 'great beautiful tune', marked *Nobilmente* (see Ex. 10.3, above). It has been associated with the beginning, in the same key, of Wagner's *Parsifal*; the four-note ascent from Ab to D flat forms identical second phrases, though Elgar doubles the note-values.[31] The implication of a sacred character is strengthened by a connection with the Good Friday music of *Parsifal*, through the Angel's Farewell in *Gerontius*, to the slow movement of the symphony – which itself embeds a reference to the 'motto' in its richest, predominantly string, texture at fig. 96 (Ex. 10.3).[32] Were the *Gerontius* connection conscious – unlikely – it would imply that Elgar composed the slow movement and then speeded it up to form the scherzo; but the scherzo is heard first.[33] Polarity between the unrelated keys of Ab and D can also be connected with *Parsifal*, but Wagner does not bring these keys into direct conflict, and the Good Friday music

Example 10.4 Elgar, First Symphony, thematic correspondence between second and third movements

Symphony No.1, Scherzo

Slow movement

is in D major (like Elgar's slow movement), whereas the conflicts in Elgar's first movement and finale involve D minor.

Elgar's First Symphony is held to be 'in' A♭ major, but much of it adheres to minor modes. The tonality of the first-movement Allegro is clearly not major (see below); the Scherzo is in F♯ minor, and the finale sets out in D minor, to reach its most emphatic climax in F minor. The slow movement is in D major; the first movement begins and ends in A♭, and there, of course, the finale also ends. Few symphonies spend so little time expressing the

tonic, and in the finale forces almost beyond the composer's control strive
to define a work in D minor.[34] This issue is, however, complicated in the
first movement. Following the closed musical period in A♭ (the 'motto'), it
breaks without ceremony into an Allegro theme, often said to be in D minor,
with its one-flat key signature, its forceful upward D minor arpeggio, and
the subsequent move to its relative, F major. But writing to Newman, who
was preparing the 'analysis' (programme notes), Elgar referred to a 'feeling
of A minor'.[35] A minor disturbs the overt tranquillity of the A♭ ending to the
movement by taking advantage of the pitch common to both key-chords,
C♮. But at the start, and even allowing for Elgar's predilection (as in *Pomp and
Circumstance* No. 2) for the flattened seventh degree, A minor is undermined
by the persistence of G♮ in the bass, emphasised by its upper neighbour A♭
(a pitch that also does nothing to help the case for D minor).[36] And the G
is reinforced by the flow into the recapitulation when the theme recurs at
its original pitch, combined with a motive that re-emerges in the preceding
bars to produce a clash of implied tonal centres which Elgar identified as
A minor and G major: 'I have a nice *sub-acid* feeling when they come
together.'[37]

A more realistic interpretation of the main theme, which embodies rest-
lessness and uncertain striving, is that while not exactly atonal, it belongs
to no single key. Its entry is perhaps the most strikingly modernist passage
in Elgar, a mark of the Zeitgeist, for it was also in 1908 that Schoenberg, in
the vocal finale to his Second Quartet, represented the 'air of other plan-
ets' by passages untranslatable into tonality.[38] The question of which key
Elgar is proposing matters less than recognition that the jump from the
'nobilmente' motto into the Allegro, with no hint of Wagnerian transition,
makes a rent in the musical fabric which it takes a whole symphony to
repair.

The motto is remarkable not only for its self-contained nature, but also
for the sparseness of its support, a bass which combines solidity of pulse
with a certain indeterminacy of harmonic implication, the latter not much
solidified by the intermittent counterpoint of the horns. 'I have no tangible
poetic or other basis', Elgar told Newman, while relating music without
a programme to 'experience of life' incommunicable in any other way. 'It
is, perhaps[,] obvious that the opening theme is intended to be simple &,
in intention, noble and elevating (I do hate to attempt to describe what
I feel): the sort of *ideal* call – in the sense of persuasion, not coercion or
command – & something above the everyday and sordid things.'[39] The
problem posed by a consciously post-Wagnerian symphony is that conflicts
and their resolution, or at least an achieved conclusion, form a drama of ideas
which verbal articulation will almost certainly oversimplify, if not actually

cheapen; as Aidan Thomson observes, the motto and its expression of an ideal are 'less a symphonic ideal than an ideal in a symphonic context. Yet ironically, the "musical ideal" (or, as Elgar put it, "the highest development of art") of transcendent absolute music was exactly the same as that which had been dramatically reified in *Parsifal*.'[40]

Besides linking the outer and inner movements thematically in pairs, Elgar drew the slow movement into the argument by recycling the descending shape of the 'motto' within its glorious melodic flowering (Ex. 10.3). This shape also affects the finale, a theme that appears first staccato, then legato (like the paired scherzo and slow movement). The extent of thematic integration and tonal argument in this symphony, however, would take a book to expound, even if one did not enter into the trickier area of 'meaning'. For the present a few comments must suffice to show Elgar's application of the lessons of his earlier music within the form which he respected most highly, and whose conventions, despite the extreme daring of his key-scheme, he observes even as he defies them. Elgar falls somewhat between the claims of Sibelius, that a symphony should develop from the smallest amount of material, and Mahler, that it embraces a whole world. His thematic connections do not preclude his usual abundance of invention, though he keeps at bay the robust popular styles used in *Cockaigne*. The exposition of the first movement strives upward to reach a mainly falling group of themes (fig. 11, fig. 12, with delicate flute tracery); eventually F major is left behind and the key of its ending (supporting the idea of the first theme being in D after all) is A minor (before fig. 18). Wisps of the motto begin the development (muted horns) and new material keeps breaking in, notably the motive alluded to, which shades development into recapitulation. There is also a markedly sinister rise and fall which recurs balefully in the finale. Much of the middle of the movement is quiet, almost tentative in its syncopations and halting of the tempo, and while the recovery and pacing of the recapitulation are exemplary, the coda seems drained of energy.

If thematically the middle movements form a unit, they also mark an extreme contrast. The F♯ minor scherzo is in Elgar's finest perpetual motion vein, but incorporates a crisp march before veering off, in what one reads as a 'trio' in B♭, to a wistful tune Elgar instructed his players to perform 'like something you hear by the river' – a country river, the Teme, not the Thames. It is a moment of wistful nostalgia for the reeds among which the boy dreamed of the 'something great' which was now in full flood, and a miniature which is not allowed to remain small. The lyric continuation brings the music to D minor, then continues as, with a switch to F♯ (fig. 71), the scherzo re-enters underneath – not the only, or the least, of many contrapuntal 'japes' which here serve a serious enough purpose. For this scherzo is filled with diablerie; even the 'river' theme is mocked, served up in the crudest fortissimo (fig. 77) before resuming its true character amid a flicker of harps. The slowing down at the end, and the merge into the third movement, show high spirits to have been a mask; and the theme now emerging from a rich bed of string tone takes us into a more adult world of feeling and loss, nostalgia and love bleeding from the haunting duet of violin and clarinet, tenderness from the harp, sensitivity even from the brass, muted in a cavernous cadence.

Where the tonal jump from the first movement to the scherzo tempted Elgar into a bogus theoretical justification,[41] the finale takes off in the slow movement's D, but in a chromatically inflected minor mode. One might expect a transition to an Ab finale, as in Debussy's string quartet where the slow movement, lying third, is likewise a tritone away from home.[42] The sinister theme of the first movement reappears, and a significant new theme makes a quiet entrance on the bassoons. The back desks of violins twice attempt the motto, greeted by a hysterical flurry from flute and harp, and twice melting into chromatic uncertainty. Then the real finale gets underway with a Brahmsian surge. Most of the movement carries on as if the key of Ab need not exist, and when another attempt at the motto (fig. 129) enters too far on the flat side the music is taken over by the staccato theme, now in a broad legato, its textural lushness flirting dangerously with complacency. The resumption of the surging main theme is a call to order and brings the staccato theme back in the course of things, in F minor and double fortissimo – the tonal region now permitting Elgar to revive the motto in the home key. But – except in the obvious sense that it begins the peroration to the whole symphony – how final really *is* this 'grandioso' (fig. 146)? When an eruption of trombones seems to attack the increasingly triumphant 'motto', the outcome seems to be imposed by Elgar rather than, as one might piously if misguidedly hope, one that emerges organically. Indeed, the very act of completing the symphony by returning it to its beginning, while ostensibly conclusive, contains through its very circularity the possibility that mighty striving can never reach an end.

Traditional interpretations may be affronted by this overriding of Elgar's own words, replacing his 'great charity (love) and a *massive* hope in the future' with uncertainty;[43] and one should not overlook his retrospective association of the 'ideal call' with 'Out of the infinite morning/Intrepid you hear us cry' in *The Music Makers* (a surge from choral *p* to *fff* tutti in two bars).[44] In that the interpretation suggested here replaces a modernistic, teleological narrative with post-modern ambiguity, it will no doubt be superseded in its turn but, it is to be hoped, without losing a sense of significant complexity and without reversion to hearing the symphony as blandly harmonious and superficially grand. For ambiguity of this kind is a compositional strength; as with (say) Mahler, uncertainties become part of the composer's truthfulness. Elgar's symphony is an enigma, not in the trivial sense of a hermeneutic game (as usually with 'solutions' to Op. 36) but in the Pauline sense of a dark reflecting glass,[45] from which each succeeding age receives back some partial truth about itself.

11 The later orchestral music (1910–34)

CHRISTOPHER MARK

Whatever Elgar actually said concerning 'absolute music' in his Birmingham lecture on Brahms's Symphony No. 3, and whatever he actually *meant* to say, to view his own symphonies and concertos as 'purely tonal pattern-weaving', to use Ernest Newman's phrase, would be to deny an essential – perhaps *the* essential – aspect of one's experience of them.[1] A more productive approach is to see these works as 'fixing' by means of a highly sophisticated compositional technique a series of emotional states or attitudes, these being bound up to a large extent with aspects of the composer's own life. Various comments by Elgar confirm – or, at the very least, suggest – that this is the case. Indeed, both the Violin Concerto and Symphony No. 2 have prefatory inscriptions that point to extra-musical impulses, their enigmatic nature increasing the listener's desire to search for 'meaning'. Meanwhile it could be said that *Falstaff*, described by the composer as a 'symphonic study', differs chiefly to the extent that the subject-matter is precisely identified and specific events illustrated. What follows is an interpretation of Elgar's later orchestral music (the works already mentioned, plus the Cello Concerto and Anthony Payne's elaboration of the sketches for Symphony No. 3) that pivots around what this particular author perceives to be its emotional meaning, but argued from observations about technique intended to provide snapshots of Elgar's symphonic approach.

Violin Concerto in B minor, Op. 61 (1910)

With the remarkable success of his Symphony No. 1, Elgar gained the confidence to attempt in the Violin Concerto one of his most ambitious structures. It is one of the longest examples of the genre, lasting fifty minutes in the composer's famous recording with Yehudi Menuhin and closer to fifty-five in Nigel Kennedy's 1997 recording.[2] It is not simply the length that marks Elgar's ambition, however. Rather, it is the musical language – gauged not in terms of style (clearly, Elgar's approach can only be regarded as conservative when measured against contemporary works by Debussy and the emerging modernism of Schoenberg and Stravinsky) but in terms of the music's relationship to the generic and formal conventions with which it engages, and the way in which these conventions are manipulated to produce a highly individual mode of utterance.

A central feature of Symphony No. 1 is the opposition between those parts exhibiting a 'public' manner, and those concerned with 'private' feeling.[3] This is seen at the outset in the contrast between the opening Ab processional (the 'motto theme') and the deeply restless Allegro first-subject group. The 'heart' of the work is the introspective third movement (Adagio), confessional in tone, while the symphony ends with a massive tutti, apparently affirmative and celebratory – a public ceremonial.[4] It is clear from the Violin Concerto's inscription that it, too, will revolve around the public/private dichotomy: '*AQUÍ ESTÁ ENCERRADA EL ALMA DE* ...' ('Here is enshrined the soul of...') is a public declaration, but the dedication, to Alice Stuart-Wortley (who is 'enshrined' by the 'Windflower' themes), is private, as is the reason for the Spanish.[5] The genre of the concerto has particularly strong opportunities for exploring the public/private dichotomy, through the contrast between the soloist as individual and the orchestra as collective, and – in the case of the Violin Concerto – the contrast between virtuosic display (a defining aspect of the concerto as a public event) and the inward-looking lyricism for which the instrument is so well suited. Elgar exploits these opportunities to the full. But he also turns expectation of what is to be 'public', what 'private', on its head, to remarkable effect.

Central to the character of the Violin Concerto – to the image of it that one carries away after a performance – is the nature of the cadenza, which is placed towards the end of the final movement. Cadenzas are traditionally highly public, and are signalled as such by the entire orchestra and conductor stopping to admire the soloist as he or she goes through various virtuosic contortions and bold (originally unscripted) thematic developments. Elgar, however, constructs his cadenza as a very private space. As Ernest Newman observes in an essay on the concerto published just before its first performance, 'The Cadenza . . . is an interlude of serious and profound contemplation, as it were the soul retiring into itself and seeking its strength inwardly, in the midst of the swirling life all around it.'[6] Far from standing back and allowing the soloist full rein, the orchestra accompanies, however lightly, as an extension of the ruminations. Another aspect of the public/private dichotomy in the work as a whole is the contrast between 'the idyllic' and representations of reality, and this too forms a vital aspect of the cadenza. For while, as the cadenza begins, 'it sadly *thinks over* the 1st movement',[7] it also contains long stretches of warm, optimistic B major – an idyll glimpsed, or even inhabited, before the shift to B minor at fig. 104 leads to the impassioned shift flatward at fig. 105. The end of the cadenza sees the possibility of recapturing the idyllic, only for the anticipated close in a serene D major to be sidestepped at the last moment by the return of the soloist's very first B minor utterance. This leads to the return of the bustling main material of the finale, which is the most public movement of all in its almost relentless display. One should guard against being overly reductive with respect to a work replete with 'key moments', but it seems appropriate to describe this as *the* key moment of the work. For it to be appreciated fully, however, we need to know something of its context within the work as a whole.

Ernest Newman got to the heart of the Violin Concerto (and Elgar's music in general) with these comments:

> As in the Symphony, we always get the feeling that we are not listening to mere music-making, not witnessing a mere attempt to fill a conventional form, but following up a long and always interesting trail of human experience; all this music has been lived before it was put on paper. It all has the same highly-strung, nervous quality as the Symphony; and in the naturalness of the sequence of its moods, the ebb and flow of passion in it, it gives us the same impression as its predecessor of the thinking controlling the form, instead of the form controlling the thinking.[8]

The first movement is a fine demonstration of 'the thinking controlling the form', and of the way in which the soloist is constituted as the experiencing subject. The orchestral exposition comprises a succession of six themes, the first four of which make up the first-subject group.[9] This is a good example of Elgar's 'mosaic technique': short-breathed two-bar themes, usually treated immediately in sequence, are bound together by a fluid (and remarkably rich) harmonic continuum in which tonal centres are suggested rather than confirmed, in the manner of Wagner's roving tonality.[10] The opening itself is ambiguous: bar 1 suggests D major, but the latter part of bar 2 and bar 3 suggest B minor; neither key – nor any other – is confirmed during the course of the section. The arrival of the second-subject group four bars after fig. 4 is marked simply by the character of its first theme, the second of the two 'Windflower' themes, adumbrated from fig. 4 (the first is at fig. 3), and by the initial relaxation in harmonic rhythm. The music here is not particularly stable, tonally speaking, either: the third bar after fig. 4 points towards a cadence in C♯ minor, so that when an A major triad ensues the section begins with an interrupted cadence. For two bars it seems as if A is going to establish itself (it is an odd choice of key for a work in B minor, until one remembers the D major slant of the opening), but again there is no firm cadence to confirm it, and from one bar after fig. 5 sequential treatment takes the harmonic flow to distant territory. Only with the strong F♯ pedal (V of B minor) from fig. 6 does a clear indication of the tonic emerge. It is the soloist's first phrase that finally leads the way to the work's first perfect cadence (at three bars after fig. 9).

In exerting control, the soloist is marked as the central character – not merely as 'the master', as Tovey suggests,[11] but as the subject whose experiences are laid bare. Throughout the rest of the work there is little doubt that we are 'seeing' things from the point of view of the solo instrument. Rarely is it silent. The later part of the development section (from fig. 23) is the only passage in the first movement (apart from the orchestral exposition) where the soloist does not play, but even here the persona is not absent: the orchestra is an extension of the soloist's world, projecting an inner turmoil. The transformation of the second-subject theme at fig. 24 is an excellent example of Michael Kennedy's point about themes being 'inflated after their first appearances to a size where they threaten to burst'.[12] And this notion of 'extension' is perhaps supported by there being little sense of the conflict between orchestra and soloist that is often seen as characteristic of the Romantic concerto; indeed, there is remarkably little dialogue as such. As is usually the case with Elgar, the recapitulation is substantially reworked, and becomes increasingly concerned with a public face, the coda (from two bars after fig. 42) involving itself with fairly conventional virtuoso gestures. It begins with the 'Windflower' second-subject theme, underpinned by a B *major* 6/3 chord in a glimpse of the cadenza's idyll.

That the slow movement, like the cadenza, inhabits a much more private space is signalled not only by its material, but also its key: B♭ major is as far removed from the bustling B minor at the end of the first movement and the beginning of the third as can be imagined.[13] Newman described the music as inhabiting a 'dream-world'; Michael Kennedy writes of it as being 'unequalled in Elgar's work as an expression of passionate regret'.[14] One would not want to argue against either of these views, though it is worth noting that, in a later publication, Kennedy relays Elgar's own comment to Vera Hockman (a young violinist present at a gathering to hear the test pressing of the Elgar/Menuhin recording on 2 September 1932) that, in the coda, 'two souls merge and melt into one'; this suggests that the ending, at least, has little to do with regret.[15] The Andante is certainly not an untroubled movement, but it is within its boundaries that the idyllic is most sustained, especially in the opening section (up to fig. 47), with its echoes of the dreamy opening of Part II of *The Dream of Gerontius* and a serene cadence on to G major at one bar before fig. 47.[16]

The Violin Concerto is no less rich in thematic interconnections than Elgar's other large-scale orchestral works, and the second movement has clear links with the first, as Ex. 1. shows. The last movement, too, employs a variety of reworkings of the initial shape (Ex. 1. e, f and g). Significantly, the most literal recollections are reserved for the cadenza – not only of the very opening, but also of fig. 35 at fig. 105, and of five bars after fig. 53

Example 11.1 Elgar, thematic transformation in the Violin Concerto

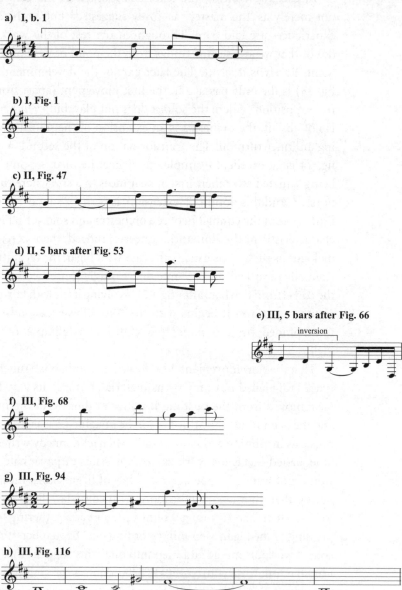

a) I, b. 1

b) I, Fig. 1

c) II, Fig. 47

d) II, 5 bars after Fig. 53

e) III, 5 bars after Fig. 66

inversion

f) III, Fig. 68

g) III, Fig. 94

h) III, Fig. 116

(Ex. 1.d) at fig. 106, both recalled at pitch. It would be an exaggeration to say that the sideslipping to B minor at the end of the cadenza – the readjustment, as it were, for re-entry into the public world – is a betrayal of the cadenza's interior landscape. But in the midst of the closing rhetorical flourishes – which include a grand final transformation of the opening shape in the key most associated with the idyllic, B major (see Ex. 1.h) – it is difficult not to feel regret for the loss of the intimate.

Symphony No. 2 in E♭, Op. 63 (1911)

'Loss' has been one of the central topics in commentaries on Symphony No. 2, prompted by the subdued ending, the dedication 'to the Memory of His late Majesty King Edward VII', and the inscription from Shelley, 'Rarely, rarely comest thou,/Spirit of Delight!' Hepokoski speculates that the 'Spirit of Delight' might be

> Not just one thing, we may suppose, but many. Some of the likeliest candidates, none of which excludes the others, are the innocence, faith, and purity of the 'clean' world of youth; the only partially sublimated erotic fantasy of his love for Alice Stuart-Wortley; the once-healthy tradition of the genre of the symphony and the culture for which it had bracingly stood; the exuberant, unproblematic joy that music had brought to the composer in his 'learning days' before its enchantments had been subjected to the processes of rationalization and marketplace competition.[17]

However, while some of the symphony is clearly concerned with mourning, Elgar himself referred to 'the whole of the sorrow [being] smoothed out & ennobled in the last movement'.[18] This suggests a cathartic process, and there is much to support this interpretation. For instance, the augmented version of the so-called 'Spirit of Delight' theme (beginning at one bar before fig. 168; cf. the last two quavers of bar 2 and bar 3 of the first movement) has a breadth and harmonic poise that suggests acceptance. And while the main melodic lines descend, adopting the conventional attitude of mourning, they are counterbalanced by the upward-moving scales and arpeggios of fig. 168ff. and (crucially) the ascent in the first violins at fig. 171. The scoring is among Elgar's most luminous, nowhere more so than in the final progression (from two bars after fig. 171); and the final chord's dignified fade to pianissimo epitomises the ennoblement that Elgar refers to.

There is little of the 'private' here, despite an approach towards a more intimate tone between figs. 170 and 171: if the sorrowful aspects of the slow movement were prompted by Elgar's feelings at the death of his friend Alfred Rodewald, the symphony ends as a public commemoration of the composer's much-revered monarch.[19] Indeed, the movement has a civic air from the very start, established by the character of the material and by the relatively conventional form.[20] Robert Meikle goes so far as to say of the opening theme that 'There is something about its placid, unruffled, even slightly self-satisfied air, that imparts the unmistakable atmosphere of a Sunday bandstand in the park.'[21] The second theme, meanwhile, at fig. 139, overflows with pomp, and was labelled 'Hans himself' when first sketched in 1903 with reference to the first conductor of Symphony No. 1 (and a champion of Elgar's music in general), Hans Richter.[22] Equally grand is the third theme: marked *nobilmente*, it too is supported by a walking bass and is marked to be played 'sul G'. The form, meanwhile, though not as stiff as Meikle suggests,[23] pays rather more obeisance to convention than Elgar is generally wont to do: the three themes articulate a straightforward progression from the tonic to the dominant via the subdominant; the beginning of the development is heavily signposted, by a French sixth (one bar before fig. 145); and themes two and three are transposed to the tonic in the recapitulation (the final 'triumph' of the tonic is celebrated by peals of horn notes at four bars after fig. 164, an addition to the equivalent passage in the exposition at fig. 143).

But if Elgar's 'passionate pilgrimage of a soul' (as the composer also described the symphony)[24] is conveyed here via conventional tonal signposts, the journey in the first movement is rather less orthodox. As Tovey points out, 'The tonic, E♭, stands firm at the outset and the drift towards another key is sudden and decisive. But when that other key appears it proves an iridescent mixture of several keys, remote enough for the home tonic itself to appear in its new surroundings as one of the chords of the main theme in the second group.'[25] Ex. 11.2 (the music between figs. 8 and 9) gives some idea of this iridescence. The first phrase is cast in an expanded G major, ending on V/V, but the second veers more decisively away. Indeed, at figs. 9 and 10 the music is back in E♭, however fleetingly. It is only at the big climax at fig. 20 that a clear secondary tonal centre emerges, with V/V setting up the close of the exposition in B♭ at two bars before fig. 22. In the recapitulation the climax returns transposed to the tonic, in traditional fashion, but little else about the tonal relationships between the exposition and recapitulation conforms to expectations. Meikle charts these relationships, and regards them as 'haphazard':[26] 'The effect is that we lose all sense of the tonal pressure, of the exploitation of tension between the tonic and other keys – whether the traditional "related" keys or not – that had hitherto been fundamental to the symphony as manifested through sonata-form structures.'[27]

But to say this is to fail to recognise the significance of the element of fantasy in Elgar, in which movement from point to point no less logical in itself often takes precedence over large-scale patterning. The truer picture, though, lies in an interaction of both approaches, and some evidence for this may be found in Elgar's comment on the genesis of Symphony No. 2 as reported by Charles Sanford Terry:

In every movement its form and above all its climax were clearly in his mind. Indeed, as he has often told me, it is the *climax* which he invariably settles first. But withal there is a great mass of fluctuating material which *might* fit into the work as it developed in his mind to finality – for it had

Example 11.2 Elgar, Second Symphony, first movement, figs. 8–9

been created in the same 'oven' which had cast them all. Nothing satisfied him until itself and its context seemed, as he said, inevitable. In that particular I remember how he satisfied himself as to the sequence of the second upon the first subject in the first movement.[28]

Elgar's sketch outline of the third movement, reproduced by Kent (who describes it as 'a kind of musico-literary précis'), further supports this view.[29]

While there is little in this outline to suggest that sonority was uppermost in Elgar's mind when conceiving his 'great mass of fluctuating material', it is clear from his lecture on orchestration that it must have been.[30] In a symphony that is particularly impressive in terms of sonorous imagination, the dreamy first span of the first-movement development section (figs. 24–35) stands out. This is the only part of the first movement to explore an interior world to any degree (a world that is nightmarishly transformed in the third movement: compare figs. 28 and 119). It is impossible to divorce sonority and harmony here: the initial shift from a B♭ triad to the A♭–C–E♮ augmented triad is not merely coloured by the spacing of strings and horns – rather, the harmonic character depends upon it. The melodic figure seems new, but in typical Elgarian half-light fashion it is linked with the 'Spirit of Delight' theme via the descending semitone (here F–E, in bar 3 E♭–D).

Equally striking in sonority are the string chords that frame the second movement (see Ex. 11.3, which reproduces the opening). Comprising two strands of parallel 6/3 chords circling in inversion, the modal (C Aeolian) harmony foreshadows a Vaughan Williams trait, but such investment in the expressive power of diatonicism already occupied a central position in English practice: as Jeremy Dibble has shown, the broad, surging tune beginning at fig. 68 has strong parallels with the (harmonically more orthodox) slow movement from Parry's Symphony No. 4 (which Elgar heard under Richter in 1889), and beyond that with the music of such figures as S. S. Wesley.[31]

Falstaff: Symphonic Study in C minor, Op. 68 (1913)

Jerrold Northrop Moore has described Elgar's study of one of the largest (in several senses) characters in English literature as one of the composer's most chromatic works, in which diatonicism has a very specialised role: '*Falstaff* was the story of disintegration to a point where there was nothing left to emerge out of any personal past. In writing it Edward upset the diatonic basis of his own expression. Here for the first time his themes were predominantly chromatic and short-breathed; the "old-world state"

Example 11.3 Elgar, Second Symphony, second movement (opening)

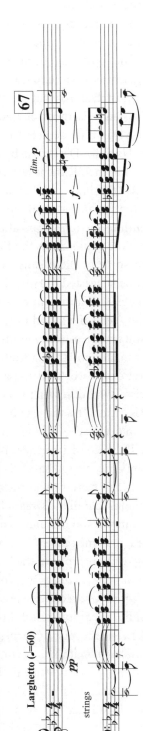

of diatonic melody was reserved for "what might have been".'[32] One might wish to interrogate aspects of this statement (we have already seen that the themes of the Violin Concerto are relatively short-breathed, for instance, and a distinction should be made in *Falstaff*, as in all Elgar's works, between chromaticism as ornamentation and chromaticism as organising principle), but the nostalgic role of diatonicism is certainly of central importance. Nostalgia is most obviously to the fore in the Dream Interlude (figs. 76–81), which depicts Falstaff reflecting on his time as page to the Duke of Norfolk. Described by Elgar as 'simple in form and somewhat antiquated in mood', the Interlude is cast entirely in A minor with Aeolian inflections (the final cadence at three bars after fig. 80 employs the flattened seventh, for instance), apart, that is, from a brief excursion to F in the seventh to the tenth bars after fig. 79. Nostalgia in music is a slippery concept, little explored in the literature. It cannot be discussed in depth here, but some of the means by which it is created in the Dream Interlude can be suggested. Firstly, the Interlude's self-contained nature lifts it out of the narrative stream of the rest of the work: time stops, or at least, a different (reflective) kind of time is entered into. Reinforcing this sense of removal is the simplicity of utterance within the context of the generally more chromatic, and thematically and contrapuntally more 'artful', textures of the rest of the work. As in parts of the Violin Concerto, the *fact* of the diatonicism symbolises that which is yearned for, 'the idyllic'; the sense of longing is created by the way in which the diatonicism is *used* – the wide melodic intervals, the sighing appoggiaturas, the arching inner parts (as at fig. 79). The second interlude, the pastoral scene at Shallow's orchard in Gloucestershire, also A-based, is more diversified in its material and tonal excursions, but has a similar melancholic effect.

The violin solo in the Dream Interlude inevitably conjures up the figure of Elgar himself, and it is indeed difficult to resist seeing the work as autobiographical in some sense.[33] Certainly there are parallels between Falstaff's changing relationship with the King and Elgar's changing relationship with his musical public: *Falstaff* was composed only two years after the premiere of Symphony No. 2 received a less than rousing response from a small audience, sending Elgar into one of his periods of despair.[34] The later work, too, had a lukewarm reception.[35] Ernest Newman suggested why: 'The style of the score shows us in many places quite a new Elgar, and one that the public used to the older Elgar will not assimilate very easily.'[36] One aspect of this new style was a leaner, less expansive manner, with fewer of the big *nobilmente* tunes for which Elgar was (and still is) popularly known. A near-exception is Prince Hal's theme, first heard at fig. 4 and reprised at fig. 127 to form the work's apotheosis at his coronation: at first the theme appears to have all the hallmarks of Elgar's *nobilmente* mode, but it is soon unsettled by

Example 11.4 Elgar, *Falstaff*, fig. 4

the rather awkward restart in the minor in the fifth bar (Ex. 11.4) – a premonition, perhaps, of the tragedy to come.[37] It is the final playing-out of that tragedy – Falstaff's dissolution and death after being banished by the King – that is most likely to have bemused Elgar's listeners, and which still shocks today. As Daniel Grimley observes, 'The function of the final bars [from the eleventh bar after fig. 146] . . . is to undermine the retrospective effect of the preceding passage',[38] a passage that ends with a warm, affectionate cadence into C major after recalling a theme identified by Elgar in a letter to Ernest Newman as representing 'the undercurrent of our failings & sorrows'.[39] The final bars deny 'any sense of transfiguration, or of Falstaff's narrative presence. Rather, the coda turns towards an objective, hard-sounding E minor, and the impersonal military rhythm of the King's theme. The effect of the final pizzicato string chord is deadening, in sharp contrast to the warm glow of Falstaff's death.'[40] The subdued final reprise of Prince Hal's theme that leads up to these events (figs. 144–5) is sad, but not bitter: there is no trace of irony, suggesting that, in Elgar's eyes, Falstaff nobly accepts his fate. Falstaff is thus a victim of the public/private dichotomy, his private, carefree relationship with the Prince being rejected of necessity on the latter's ascent to the throne.

If Elgar could not himself quite avoid all sense of bitterness at the public's reaction to *Falstaff*, we should not underestimate the difficulties and potential confusions confronting the listener trying to 'assimilate' it. It is not just a question of the disorientating ending: there are also problems surrounding the work's programme and form. Elgar baulked at describing the work as 'programme music'. In an interview with Gerald Cumberland published in *The Daily Citizen* of 18 July 1913 he had this to say on the matter:

> it must not be imagined that my orchestral poem is programme music –
> that it provides a series of incidents with connecting links such as we have,
> for example, in Strauss's 'Ein Heldenleben' or in the same composer's
> 'Domestic' Symphony. Nothing has been farther from my intention. All I
> have striven to do is to paint a musical portrait – or, rather, a sketch
> portrait.[41]

However, his own published description of the work goes some way towards encouraging the listener to treat it as such,[42] leading to some of the problems outlined by Kennedy.[43] The form, meanwhile, is highly complex, mixing, as Grimley suggests, 'elements of sonata, rondo and variation forms'.[44] None of this detracts, however, from the irresistible sweep of the work, much of which is due to an impressive and (*pace* Kennedy)[45] striking variety of thematic invention, manipulated with considerable virtuosity.

Cello Concerto in E minor, Op. 85 (1919)

The thematic invention in the Cello Concerto is less open-handed, and if *Falstaff* represents something of a retreat from the orchestral opulence of Symphonies Nos. 1 and 2 and the Violin Concerto, the Cello Concerto is even more pared down. This partly serves the need to ensure that the soloist will be heard in the middle of the texture, but it also reflects the deeply melancholic nature of the work.

A good deal of Elgar's music is melancholic. This seems to reflect his personality. He was frequently disillusioned, as letters to friends show, and the diminishing of his output in the latter part of his life (the Cello Concerto was the last major work completed) suggests he was gradually taken over by despondency. A number of reasons have been put forward for this, including the collapse with the onset of the First World War of the society he had idealised and within which he had struggled to gain recognition; the death of friends; and increasingly poor health. A letter to Alice Stuart-Wortley indicating the latter also describes his feelings about the war:

> Terrible gun-firing, raid, etc. etc. . . . I am not well and the place is so noisy
> & I do not sleep. The guns are the quietest things here. I long for the
> country & Stoke. I think all the time of it – and you. I have been thinking
> also so much of our lost festivals – no more music . . . Everything good &
> nice & clean & fresh & sweet is far away – never to return.[46]

	To [1]	[1] – [7]	[7] – [8]	[8] – [13]	[13] – [14]	[14] – [18]
Section		**A**	**B**	**C**	**B¹**	**A¹**
No. of bars	8	38	8	21	5	26
Key	E minor/Aeolian			E major	E minor/Aeolian	
Notes		Archshape. 6 statements of thematic shape. Arch defined by starting notes (E or F sharp)		G sharp minor 'parenthesis' within 1ˢᵗ statement. Shift to G major, various harmonic 'excursions'	Compressed version of B	Compressed version of A: now four statements
Metre	4/4	9/8	12/8	12/8 (6/8)	12/8	9/8

Figure 1. Elgar Cello Concerto, first movement, form scheme

The melancholic vein of the Cello Concerto has hardly been a bone of contention. Here, for example, are a few statements from Kennedy:

- 'The Cello Concerto, of all Elgar's orchestral works, is the most elusive and withdrawn, the most subdued in its orchestral dress.'
- [regarding the main 9/8 theme:] 'This is overpoweringly the music of wood smoke and autumn bonfires, of the evening of life; sadness and disillusion are dominant and the music comes perilously close to what Jaeger would have called a 'whine' of self-pity.'
- [regarding the music towards the end of the work]: 'Elgar recalls a theme from the slow movement, and the music assumes a nihilist note that is unequalled in intensity elsewhere in his output, surpassing even the note of agony and ruin in *Gerontius*.'[47]

The most immediate expressions of melancholy in the Cello Concerto lie in Elgar's use of the minor key, relatively slow tempi, yearning suspensions and appoggiaturas, chromatic inflections, and wide melodic leaps. But since melancholy is a phenomenon that is sustained in time – which might be said to feed on the passing of time – it is likely to arise most powerfully from formal organisation, and this can be seen clearly in the first movement, which is obsessed with return on several levels.

The movement as a whole is an arch shape (Figure 1). So too is the A section. This peaks with a tutti version of the melody initially played by the violas, only to fade to a quieter version; it is significant that, of the six statements of the melody, the climactic fourth and fifth are the only ones to begin on the tonic E, the others beginning more tentatively on the supertonic.[48] There is nothing tentative about the end of the A section, however, despite the low dynamic level: indeed, there is a grim finality about the E at one bar before fig. 7, with the augmentation of the final part of the long descent, G–F♯–E, giving particular weight to the tonic's arrival (as does the articulation: two pizzicato attacks leading up to the bowed E). After this, much of the rest of the movement is characterised by attempts to break away from the atmosphere of brooding. Section C, which lifts the spirits a little with its shift to the major mode, comes closest to achieving this through its more mobile harmony. But a good deal of it is ruminative (musical daydreaming, almost) rather than purposefully directed, and the final outcome, after the melodic peak (two bars after fig. 10, repeated at two bars after fig. 12), is a listless collapse onto the dominant, presaging the seemingly inevitable return of section B.

In B^1 and A^1 attempts to inject greater impetus are made through the addition of several new gestures. Thus in B^1 there is a more ardent delivery of the melodic peak (compare the second and third bars after fig. 13 with the fourth bar after fig. 7); while in A^1 the bar before the scalar run-up to the climactic e''' is lent greater impetus by a series of appoggiaturas (compare two bars before fig. 16 with two bars before fig. 5), and in the second bar after fig. 16 there is a new rhetorical statement from the soloist, *ff, molto sostenuto* and accented. In interpreting these, it seems appropriate to bear in mind the following comments by Hepokoski on the symphonies:

> the two Elgar symphonies survey the composer's general world vision. That vision ranges widely, from the expansive or boisterous to the desperately conflicted and, further, to the fully interior, intimate, and private. But it is touched throughout by a melancholy awareness of the dreamlike quality and transitoriness of things: ghosts of unsustainability, regret, and loss of innocence lurk everywhere. In this valedictory world the magnificent, *fortissimo* moments of attainment and affirmation seem simultaneously to be melting away, and Elgar often shores up such moments with rises and underswells in unexpected places, as if he were trying to sustain an illusion forever slipping away from his grasp. In such an environment of dissolution, diminuendos and simple descending sequences can take on enormous expressive significance.[49]

The additions to B^1 and A^1 all attempt, not so much to shore up *ff* moments (though the rhetorical statement from two bars after fig. 16 might come into this category), as to recover the more affirmative outlook of section C, while the scalar ascents to e''' seem like desperate attempts to *create* affirmative moments in the first place.

The most significant 'return' in the work – that which seals its fundamentally melancholic nature – is that of the four bars of recitative that open the work just before the end of the fourth movement (at fig. 72). This comes after the most highly charged section of the work, the Poco più lento from fig. 66 that emerges from the sonata form that constitutes most of the movement (in terms of bar numbers, at any rate). The intensity is born of chromatic, roving harmony, coupled with liberal use of appoggiaturas and the generally high tessitura of the soloist. The material initially evokes the idiolect, rather than the substance, of the languorous slow movement: it is not until four bars after fig. 71 that the slow-movement theme itself emerges, following a passage of liquidation draining the music of the will to move forward. Supported by a texture that lacks the rhythmic impetus of its original context, the theme is transformed into a wistful reminiscence – of music which itself has been described as nostalgic. Although the bass line moves steadily downwards by step from five bars after fig. 71, there is little sense of goal-directedness: the final step to the orchestral E that supports the return of the work's opening seems inevitable enough, but the preceding V^7 in 6/4 position is only just sufficient to fulfil conventional cadential requirements. The unforced acceptance of the return of the work's initial state is a graphic symbol – an enactment, almost – of melancholy. It is followed by what I can only describe as the musical equivalent of a 'stiff upper lip' – the self-consciously energetic music of the final fifteen bars. Whether or not one agrees with Hepokoski's interpretation of the closing passage of Elgar's Symphony No. 1,[50] the ending of the Cello Concerto cannot be taken at face value.

Coda: The Sketches for Symphony No. 3, elaborated by Anthony Payne (1998)

It will not have escaped the reader's notice that a good deal of attention has been accorded in this chapter to the way in which works end, and that these have all been regarded as having a fundamental effect on what they are ultimately 'about'. One of the biggest tasks facing Anthony Payne in his famous elaboration of Elgar's sketches for a Third Symphony was to invent the ending, about which the composer left no clue.[51] It is a testament to the stature of his achievement that he has created one of the great Elgarian perorations, inspired by one of Elgar's finest miniatures, 'The Wagon Passes' from the Nursery Suite (1931): a processional based on the off-beat accompaniment pattern of the movement's first theme (bars 17ff.) builds from bar 303 to a climax at bars 311–13 before subsiding to what Payne describes as a tying-up of 'one or two loose thematic ends to strengthen the web of the work's symphonic dialectic'. This 'tying-up' Payne describes as follows:

> The allusion to the first movement's open fourths in the scherzo's uncanny cadence is picked up with a further reference, given to the first violins over the final C minor chord. At the same time, the basses and bassoons quietly resolve the cadence which the solo viola had left hanging in mid-air at the end of the Adagio.[52]

All the works discussed in this chapter recall thematic material from earlier in the work. The effect here may seem less dramatic, but it is no less powerful, the resolution of the viola theme and the final tam-tam stroke bringing a profound sense of rest after 'the blaze of a consuming vision' of which Payne writes.[53]

Payne's own estimation of his achievement was 'the building of a frame, or perhaps rather a context, to display the exceptionally rich expressive qualities and the symphonic potential in Elgar's material'.[54] The result is indeed a persuasive demonstration that, contrary to the opinion of some commentators, Elgar's powers of invention had not left him. Like the Cello Concerto and *Falstaff*, Symphony No. 3 was clearly going to be pared down in comparison with the earlier orchestral works: there is less thematic material, more economical working-out, and less opulent textures, while the first-movement exposition is placed within repeat marks. However, as Payne points out, Elgar's vision as he (Payne) translates it is 'different in its sheer breadth of emotion from any of his other symphonic works'. Thus the second movement employs a 'lighter manner' that goes 'far beyond his established symphonic practice', while the slow movement is of 'searing intensity . . . tragic in its import', with the sketches containing some of Elgar's most elliptical harmony.[55] One can only speculate how Symphony No. 3 might have been received had Elgar finished it. Beside Webern's Concerto, Op. 24, Berg's *Lulu* Suite, or Bartók's Fifth String Quartet, all written in the year of Elgar's death, it would obviously have seemed deeply conservative in technique and aesthetic outlook to a disinterested observer. And to a British public suspicious of such 'progressive' works but willing to accept the milder modernisms of native works such as Vaughan Williams's Fourth Symphony (the harsh dissonances of which serve to reinforce the conservative framework) or Britten's *A Boy was Born*, both also completed in 1934, it would hardly have seemed less so. By the standards of much twentieth-century composition, Elgar's style advanced little. He was a conservative all his life. But his final, partial vision demonstrates no less than the early ones the dangers of valuation according to a progressivist yardstick.

12 Elgar's unwumbling: the theatre music

J. P. E. HARPER-SCOTT

In the nineteenth and early twentieth centuries (before the advent of film) it was not unusual for theatrical productions to be accompanied by elaborate musical scores. Although it accounts for only a small part of Elgar's output, his contribution to the tradition was nevertheless creatively significant. Any study of Elgar's theatre music should focus principally on *The Starlight Express*, his finest theatre piece, and by far the longest. He said it was the kind of piece he had waited a generation to set.[1] But it must more generally be a study of his musical concerns *c.*1914–18, the period in which he wrote six of the ten theatre pieces, and the end of his modernist period of composition from *In the South* to *Falstaff*. Yet one cannot account for it all along those lines.

Peacetime potboilers

Initially, Elgar hoped his theatre music would provide a captive audience on which to try ideas for more serious works, as well as to raise money. His first commission (in 1901) was for incidental music for the play *Diarmuid and Grania*, a collaboration between George Moore and W. B. Yeats. (Elgar modernised the title to *Grania and Diarmid*). After the play's run, Moore pestered Elgar with grander projects: 'The sooner you begin writing the [Grania] opera the better[:] the subject evidently suits you.'[2] But Elgar did not bite, nor did he care whether the play was revived. He was interested only in profit and convenience, writing to Jaeger that the noble *Grania* Funeral March (a fine early essay in the craft of his mature marches) would 'be *useful* for commemorations – it's not difficult & will arrange & the existing Funeral marches are hackneyed'.[3] In fact apart from the march, he wrote very little for the play: only a few minutes of instrumental music and a short spinning song for a Druidess.

Yet even if Elgar had been interested in a bigger project, it would have been risky. The Yeats–Moore–Elgar version of *Tóraigheacht Diarmuid agus Gráinne* (The Pursuit of Diarmait and Gráinne) was not the only reinterpretation of the ancient prose romance before the public in 1901. It had come only four years after the production at Covent Garden of *Diarmid*, a vast Wagnerian opera in four acts by the Scottish composer Hamish MacCunn, to a libretto by the Marquis of Lorne (by 1901, the ninth Duke of Argyll).[4] There is no record that Elgar heard or was even aware of MacCunn's *Diarmid*,[5] yet it remained in the repertory till the First World War, and the editor of the first revision of *Grove's Dictionary* thought the work the first of a projected trilogy.[6] It was, then, perhaps wise of Elgar not to make more of his *Grania* music. The purses of London audiences might not have opened twice in five years for a post-Wagnerian Ossianic opera, and rejection could have turned the highly strung composer off composition for good (compare the aftermath of the *Gerontius* premiere).

The Crown of India, Elgar's next theatre piece, has irked some commentators (Diana McVeagh says that 'it is pompous and it is trivial'[7]). He wrote it in 1912 as part of an artistic bid (the biggest part played by the New Delhi architecture of Herbert Baker and Edwin Lutyens) to provide a respectable façade for Britain's hubristic imperialism.[8] Modern Elgarians informed by postcolonial thinking may now wince at it, but the commission was no more disturbing than the one Benjamin Britten accepted from the Japanese government in 1940 for his *Sinfonia da Requiem*, and Elgar may deserve the same forgiveness.[9] It was the height of 'the Tory-ental era',[10] and it seemed that Henry Hamilton – whose masque it was – could have picked no more suitable English composer. Elgar might have been predestined to write the piece: born exactly a month into the Indian Mutiny, which forced the Crown to take control of India, he married the only daughter of a major-general who 'kill[ed] about a thousand men' in it.[11] But alongside a basic political sympathy, there was for Elgar also a pressing financial motivation. The Coliseum commission came a week after Elgar's costly move to Hampstead, and he snapped it up eagerly. 'When I write a big serious work e.g. *Gerontius* we have had to starve & go without fires for twelve months as a reward: this small effort allows me to buy scientific works I have yearned for & I spend my time between the Coliseum & the old bookshops . . . God bless the Music Halls!'[12]

In the first tableau of the tendentious pageant, a chorus and orchestra accompany a pair of soloists depicting Agra and St George (contralto and bass respectively). A stream of Mogul Emperors and 'John Company' – a symbolic nabob who anthropomorphises the British East India Company – further populate the picture. In every movement Elgar used a crudely over-elaborate oriental 'topic',[13] essentially *Pomp and Circumstance* in a minor key with trills, plus on-stage snake charmers and tom-toms. This stereotypical 'Oriental' music is typical of nineteenth-century Orientalisms.[14]

It is possible to regard Elgar's Oriental 'topic' as an 'otherisation' of India, a deliberate ridiculing of an ancient culture for nakedly imperialistic ends. Although it is intellectually irresponsible to judge an Edwardian's politics by the political standards of the early twenty-first century, Edward Said's diatribe on the West's comportment towards the East –'a systematic discipline of *accumulation* . . . of human beings and territories'[15] – is still persuasive, however hyperbolic. But it should not be applied uncritically in every case: it is reasonable also to imagine a composer failing to slip into an entirely unfamiliar musical vernacular and compounding his failure by the addition of very awkward but 'right-feeling' embellishments – the opposite effect of the *babu* trying to speak English. And musical babuism-in-reverse is different from gratuitous cultural imperialism. Elgar was a man of his time, but not a particularly wicked man. His Orientalism is nowadays more likely to offend than delight, but he cannot be blamed for the historical accident of his birth.[16]

The masque's opening, an imperious limning of imperial India, was originally sketched to exalt a canine;[17] it establishes the 'topic'. The second number, a lilting 3/8 movement in A minor, accompanies a group of nautch girls. This was a sketch originally intended for *Falstaff*,[18] and its key, mood, and mostly airy instrumentation call to mind the later work's interludes. Elgar's Tory-entalism (as thoroughly inauthentic but as evocative as Rimsky-Korsakov's in *Sheherazade*) has its giddy apogee in the March of the Mogul Emperors, where cymbals and military bass and side-drum accompany raucous trilling brass and strings before four mighty tam-tam strokes end their case (in support of Delhi). Having set the scene in the first tableau, the second ('Ave Imperator!') suggests that continued British rule is both necessary and desirable – and, moreover, that the whole of Indian history has been building to it.

Elgar initially found the masque's tone troubling – 'there is far too much of the political business'[19] – but after minor alterations he said 'it was an inoffensive thing & some of the music is good'.[20] He was right about the music, but if its composition was an instance of political myopia, it was typical of the man.[21] As with the *Grania* music, Elgar arranged a suite, published by Novello, to turn the work to profitable use (and make it possible for posterity to enjoy it).

He produced a second mythical theatre piece five years after the war: half an hour of incidental music for Laurence Binyon's play *King Arthur*. Lady Elgar had died on 7 April 1920, and Elgar seemed artistically spent. In January 1923 he wrote to Binyon: 'I *want* to do it but since my dear wife's death I have *done nothing* & fear my music has vanished.'[22] This request from a former collaborator offered a gentle way out of his morbid semi-retirement, and the attempt at revitalisation worked. In total he wrote 120 pages of music for the play, and added still more (to the battle scene) when the play was in performance.[23]

Binyon's play, based on Thomas Malory's *Le Morte d'Arthur*, had nine scenes. He required of Elgar an overture and short pieces of music between scenes, which should introduce the main character of the next section. The music is very good, and Elgar reused several promising themes when he came to sketch his Third Symphony in 1932–3; others spilled into *The Spanish Lady*. Arthur's 'chivalry' theme made its way into the finale of the symphony, and two ideas from the banquet in scene 4 appear in the second movement. Guenevere's theme was incorporated into *The Spanish Lady*'s overture and Act 2 scene 2; some of the battle music was also carried over.

The music for scene 8 is especially well judged. The final stage direction called for 'a wide distance of moonlit water, over which glides a barge, bearing King Arthur, and the three queens sorrowing over him, to the island of Avalon'. Elgar produces a Dorian rumination on the space within a perfect fourth, often repeated, with solemn tolling from the convent bells at Amesbury. Arthur's 'chivalry' theme returns finally in augmentation, all life sapped from it. The stage direction asks too much of the theatre, but Elgar's understated closing number conjures the exact right mood.

Elgar's last and slightest theatre piece, the 1928 incidental music for Bertram P. Matthews's play *Beau Brummel* [sic], was probably written only out of a sense of duty to a friend (he knew the play's producer, Gerald Lawrence). If he took any inspiration from the script, it was possibly its air of ruin and decay, here centred on the decline of the quondam royal favourite and dandy. Elgar now suited neither the musical nor political world, and could not fail to empathise with Brummell. The Act 1 Minuet, a pretty piece, was published by Elkin in 1929.

War work (1): settings of nationalistic poetry

In September 1914 Elgar finalised a new poem for 'Land of Hope and Glory' with Arthur Benson, the author of its two earlier incarnations.[24] Then on 10 November he telephoned Mme Cammaerts to discuss a proposed setting of her husband Émile's poem 'Après Anvers', thereby initiating an association with the royalist Belgian poet that would result in three wartime theatre pieces.

'Après Anvers', which Elgar set as his *Carillon*, Op. 75, contained bellicose invocations to reclaim various Belgian cities, and at last to enter triumphantly into Berlin. A friend advised Elgar to 'provide an illustrative prelude and entr'actes as background music for a recitation of the poem'.[25] He acted on her advice, and retained this basic formula for the two later Cammaerts settings. The poet implores the beleaguered Belgians to dance on the ruins of their cities and towns:

Au son du tambour, au son du clairon
Sur les ruines d'Aerschot, de Dinant, de Termonde,
Dansons, Belges, dansons
Et chantons notre gloire.

[To the sound of the drum, to the sound of the bugle,
On the ruins of Aerschot, Dinant, and Termonde,
Dance, Belgians, let us dance
And sing our glory.]

The mood of the poem perhaps calls for music to inspire the frenzied gyrations of *Le sacre du printemps*, yet Elgar provided a dainty waltz, almost as surprising in its context as the Viennese waltz of the Overman in Strauss's *Also sprach Zarathustra*. It suggests the unrealistic bourgeois insouciance of the (English) ballroom more than the grittily realistic defiance of devastated Belgium. But over this waltz, and slicing through it in duple time, goes the carillon itself, foregrounding the ruined bell towers and churches of Flanders. One might hear in this juxtaposition a suggestion that the rejoicing called for in the recitations which come between snatches of music, and the only ground for hope in the work, is *religious* – not military.

In the second Cammaerts setting, *Une voix dans le désert*, Op. 77 (composed in 1915), the spiritual emphasis is clearer. The voice in the man-made desert belongs to a peasant girl, whose sole comfort is the thought that flowers might spring from the graves of the victims of war. The mixture of complacency and defiance in the first setting becomes in the second a dreadful reflection on the blind destructiveness of war. Human voices here are frail and rather hopeless, their petitions humble. (The orchestra is smaller and less powerful than in *Carillon*, too.) Flanking the beautiful central soprano solo, 'Quand nos bourgeons se rouvriront', is bleak orchestral writing. Voiceless side-drum and muted strings vividly communicate the hoarseness of the little girl's appeal: accepting the inevitability of disaster, her only hope is for resurrection. Elgar wrote the final Cammaerts setting, *Le drapeau belge* ('The Belgian Flag'), Op. 79, merely to fulfil Elkin's contract. The verse, set in simple strophes, draws out apposite symbolism from the flag's colours. Although completed early in 1916, it did not receive its premiere till April 1917, at a birthday concert for the Belgian King Albert.[26]

A year after completing *Le drapeau belge*, Elgar set four sea songs by Rudyard Kipling as *The Fringes of the Fleet*.[27] The shared jaunty jingoism of Elgar and Kipling ought to have ensured a comfortable artistic match – Elgar had been called 'the Rudyard Kipling of the musicians' as early as 1898[28] – but Kipling was recalcitrant and for a year refused to countenance the setting of his (poetically unremarkable) verses as musical entertainment. Eventually he relented, and the poems were set for four baritones (dressed as sailors) and orchestra. The music is lightweight, but it proved immensely popular, and seemed certain to enjoy a long run – until Kipling inexplicably returned to his earlier obdurateness apropos of his poetry. Chagrined, Elgar was forced to withdraw the piece. 'Most of what I do is not worth much from a financial point of view, and if I do happen to write something that "goes" with the public and by which I look like benefiting financially, some perverse fate always intervenes and stops it immediately.'[29] It was his last great public success.

Elgarian diatonicism

By 1912 the King for whom Elgar wrote the *Coronation Ode* was two years in the grave, and England's Liberal politics under Asquith were inimical to Elgar. The Second Symphony had been received coolly – the audience 'sat there like a lot of stuffed pigs'[30] – and *The Music Makers* fared no better. Elgar's last modernist work, *Falstaff*, was premiered in 1913, the same year as *Gurrelieder* (in Vienna), and its reception was as cool as Schoenberg's was warm. In retrospect we can identify an ominous augury: the public was abandoning the *echt*-Edwardian composer.

It was a crucial period in musical history, and its significance for the generation of early modernists born around 1860 (which includes Elgar) is summarised usefully by James Hepokoski:

> The premiere in Dresden of Strauss's *Der Rosenkavalier* on 26 January 1911 and the death of Gustav Mahler on 18 May 1911 . . . ceded the Austro-Germanic sphere of *avant-garde* authority to expressionism and the Schoenbergians. A parallel story could be told of Paris on 13 June 1911, where as part of the Summer Ballets Russes offerings Stravinsky's *Petrushka* would take command of the musically new, decisively overtaking the Debussy style, not to mention that of the more orthodox D'Indy and Dukas (Ravel's glitteringly hedonistic – and coolly mechanistic – *Daphnis et Chloë* would follow in 1912; Stravinsky's *Le sacre du printemps* in 1913.)[31]

He also calls attention to Henry Wood's premiere of Schoenberg's *Five Orchestral Pieces* on 3 September 1912. If, then, we are to identify a creative 'turn' in Elgar's music, it should be with the death of Edward VII and the first performances in England of avant-garde music, and not with the death of his wife in 1920. He reacted to his change in fortune by turning to a different audience, in the theatre, and paid little further attention to the concert hall till his last years. (He only felt the sea change slowly over four or five years, but that is the English way.)[32]

Perhaps the most immediately striking fact about Elgar's theatre music is the 'untroubled"simplicity' of its diatonicism. Although one would be surprised to hear complex modernist chromaticism in his lightweight Kipling settings there is no immediately obvious reason why some of the more substantial works like *The Starlight Express* should be composed of such 'antiquated' musical materials.[33]

But Elgar had always reserved a 'pure', monotonal diatonicism – of the sort Beethoven might have written in 1820 – for crucial moments, and it becomes more meaningful as a result. One thinks of contexts like the symphonic slow movements, the First Symphony's 'motto', and *Falstaff*'s first interlude. Even in Elgar's largely accessible language such moments stand out, and they are among the most significant in his music. This meaningful opposition of diatonicism and chromaticism was learned from Wagner, but Elgar makes the technique distinctively his own. In the language of *The Starlight Express*, it represents his idea of 'unwumbling'. Diatonicism, for Elgar, may point to security, to the past, even to a prelapsarian Eden, but it points with the knowledge that there is no real hope in dreams or idealisations; and we should bear this slightly cynical view in mind when approaching *The Starlight Express*.

War work (2): whimsy and fantasy

But there is one more theatre piece to discuss first. In 1917 Elgar was asked to score a ballet based on a fan design by Charles Conder, to raise money for war charities. The scene of *The Sanguine Fan* is set in a mythical woodland glade in Louis XV's France. A young man and two young girls meet before a shrine to Eros. The boy wishes to woo one of them, and supplicates before the god of love. Pan and Echo, already in love, are at hand; Pan is sleepy, Echo flirtatious. The humans quarrel, and the young man curses Eros, who revenges himself with a lethal bolt of lightning. The pleasantly vicious little story ends with Pan watching the devastation with some amusement.

A distinctly English eighteenth-century France is connoted by a graceful and very Elgarian minuet whose contour is occasionally reminiscent of the 'Enigma' theme and the Violin Concerto, and there are also echoes of the 'flashback' introduction to *Falstaff*'s Dream Interlude in Pan's clarinet as the god falls asleep.[34] The music grows steadily more lively, as Echo's flirtation with the young man leads through premonitions of a thunderstorm to Eros's murderous tantrum. But Elgar's musical storms never become venomous, and the ballet ends quietly, as it began, with the English-seeming French minuet.[35]

Youth's precious and fantastic insouciance was celebrated in much Victorian and Edwardian art, and Elgar's not least: *Dream Children, The*

Wand of Youth, and (later) the *Nursery Suite* spring from the same seed as Lewis Carroll's *Alice* stories and J. M. Barrie's *Peter Pan*.[36] During the war Elgar wrote his lengthiest and most interesting work on such a theme, incidental music and songs for *The Starlight Express* – an unassuming but intelligent reflection on humankind's possibilities in a world which was, like its apparently unwanted Edwardian composer, growing increasingly 'wumbled' (i.e., confused, disillusioned, blind to revelation). It was a piece close to his heart.

The story is a theatrical adaptation by Violet Pearn of Algernon Blackwood's novel *A Prisoner in Fairyland*,[37] part whimsical tale of childhood, part adult love story with Classical allusions. On the face of it, the story is about a 'wumbled' businessman, Henry Rogers, and his 'unwumbling', namely his personal journey to self-realisation, love, and happiness. His cousin, 'Daddy', is a father of three and an author who has lost his Muse. (In Pearn's adaptation, Daddy becomes the central adult character; Elgar doubtless identified with him as a troubled artist.) Efficacious revelation must 'stick', and in this story the unwumbling adhesive is starlight, which is used as a symbol for sympathy. The children and Henry 'unwumble' the village and their parents by 'coming out' of their bodies in dreams and gathering the starlight. Essential to their 'unwumbling' is, then, a return to childhood.

Elgar had demonstrated with the *Wand of Youth* suites in 1907 and 1908 that a return to his childhood appealed as a means of escaping unpleasant realities – in that case, his fiftieth birthday. (It was no accident that several movements from the *Wand of Youth* suites were reused in the music for *The Starlight Express*.)[38] But he was interested in escape only insofar as it was a universal existential possibility. And the existential point of the *Wand of Youth* is quite clear: through a return to one's own childhood, not just childhood itself, one may find the answers to present problems and use them to work towards a more satisfactory future.

Elgar's childhood imaginings are only subtly different from Blackwood's. Sleep creates a bridge between Daddy's wumbled and unwumbled realities, while for the boyish Elgar an actual bridge crossed a stream dividing the mundane world of the Old Folk from the Fairyland of Youth. But unlike *The Wand of Youth*, *The Starlight Express* does not convince us that a return to childhood can affect the adult's reality. Return is not a remedy but a palliation; there is no transcendent adult state waiting at the end of the play's adventure, only a Self-negating resurrected pre-pubescence.

The nocturnal scenes in Act 2 are the heart of the play, and Elgar saved the best music for them. As various characters fall asleep and are coaxed out of their bodies by the children and their friends the sprites, Elgar provides brief solo string cadenzas, each a variation of that which opens Ex. 12.1. The

Example 12.1 *Elgar: Starlight Express*, violin cadenza and 'They'll listen to my song'

Ex. 12.1: Violin cadenza and 'They'll listen to my song' (wind doublings omitted).
BL Add. MS 52530B ff. 131-6.

Example 12.1 (*cont.*)

Example 12.1 (*cont.*)

music in the example accompanies a significant moment in the play, the first attempt to unwumble Daddy.[39] Its atmosphere is a familiar one: the world of the Dream Interlude from *Falstaff*, with its simple diatonic (minor) key, solo violin, and gentle string and harp accompaniment. The exact form of the materials is different, but the mood is unmistakable: it is an Elgarian dream 'topic'.[40] As the Laugher – the sprite trying to unwumble Daddy – resumes her song (now much less nonchalantly than before the solo during which she makes the attempt), a pathetic ostinato of harp harmonics begins, recalling another moment from *Falstaff*, and a more unnerving one: Falstaff's death (starting at fig. 141). Although she can make time stand still – for her beautiful cadenza on 'laughter' – the Laugher is ultimately unsuccessful, and the reason for her failure is critical. Daddy (i.e. his spirit) begins to 'come OUT' (of his body), but his progress is halted when his head 'sticks'. He will literally have to take leave of his senses – *lose his mind* – before he can be unwumbled. This he does at the climax of Act 3, and although he has now completed the children's story he was struggling to write when the play begins, we might wonder whether his journey has been an entirely worthwhile one.

Elgar's music confirms the play's disquieting point that adulthood's problems cannot be defeated by individual action, only repudiated by individual surrender. Pearn's substitution of the Star of Bethlehem for Blackwood's original Pleiades points to the world's only hope: according to the stage directions, Elgar's arrangement of 'The First Nowell', which ends his setting, should proclaim 'whose Star has arisen again for the sake of the wumbled world'. The finale is big-boned but perhaps not quite certain of itself, its bell-ringing more bombastic than celebratory. Notwithstanding its obvious charm, *The Starlight Express* is essentially a rather disturbing work. Its significance for Elgar was not limited to the time of its writing and performance, but reached both forwards and backwards in his work.

Conclusion

If there is hope for and in this world, it is out of our hands: the sentiment is understandable in time of war. *The Starlight Express* avers that humankind's nature seems incapable of proper goodness: it wumbles beauty on the way from inspiration to explanation. Writers in the second half of the twentieth century went further, suggesting that humankind's nature seemed capable of unspeakable evil, and in fact tended inevitably towards it. William Golding wrote: 'Before the second world war I believed in the perfectibility of social man; . . . but I must say that anyone who moved through those years without understanding that man produces evil as a bee produces honey must have been blind or wrong in the head.'[41] The lesson is always pertinent, especially when the myth of the Anglophone Capitalist as World's Hero defeating the 'axis of evil' has resurfaced, and the twenty-first century seems destined to forget the most painful lesson of the twentieth, namely that accusing fingers must always be pointed back up the arm. Elgar's music always seems aware of humankind's inbuilt capacity for self-destruction, and does not write heroic narratives. He consistently stresses human impotence, yet even in his blinding realisation in *Gerontius*, The Soul confines himself only to Purgatory, not Hell: humankind cannot achieve, but can still hope.

Notwithstanding its frequent and moving tenderness, the old lie *dulce et decorum est pro patria mori* coruscates from the surface of Elgar's war music; but there is more to it than that. The laureate's job in wartime is to speak of a nation's duty as much as its grief, even if his view of duty appears purblind. Elgar took his role as laureate seriously, but one needs little imagination to see beyond it. European man tore himself apart from 1914 to 1918 in a way that had never been seen before, and there was no place for heroic daydreaming in Elgar's war music. Humanity had lost. Could God triumph?

The spiritual undercurrent of the Cammaerts settings and the Christian conclusion of *The Starlight Express* suggest that Elgar thought so. His immediate answer to harsh reality is denial, a retreat into the brittle but tempting shell of youth or innocence. There is no suggestion of a solution, no surety of victory on the battlefield, only encouragement to hope.

Elgar had to leave the concert hall when post-Edwardian England lost interest in his music. Catalysed by the war, his retreat granted him a new audience for his music and his concerns; and after Lady Elgar's death it gave him a way back into composition. By nourishing his creative preoccupations when his popularity was low, Elgar cultivated an environment for personal artistic renewal. When his *Arthur* music lent itself to larger-scale re-treatment, the possibilities of a Third Symphony and an opera were opened up: only his death could stop what his restorative sojourn in the theatre had enabled him to begin. Elgar's theatre music, then, is both the cause of his own unwumbling and – in several cases – propounds his idea of unwumbling: what humankind's unwumbling might be and how it could be achieved. Although his *Weltanschauung* grew increasingly pessimistic, he could still posit grounds for hope unlimited by the capabilities of humankind. Without a God humanity cannot redeem its situation – but Elgar had 'a *massive* hope in the future'.[42]

13 Elgar and recording

TIMOTHY DAY

The size and nature of Elgar's recorded legacy

Elgar first went into a recording studio in January 1914 at the age of fifty-six. In the next twenty years he was to take part in more than fifty recording sessions and leave behind him a recorded legacy of more than fifteen hours as an orchestral conductor.[1]

His earlier recordings, those up to 1925, about a third of the total, were made by means of the acoustic process. In an orchestral acoustic recording session you would have seen thirty or forty men huddled together in front of one or two or occasionally three recording 'horns' sticking out from the wall, capturing the sounds. There would be only a handful of violinists, perhaps six in all, and probably only a single cellist, who would be mounted on a platform which could be moved back and forth, nearer or further away from the recording device. The flutes and clarinets and oboes would be sitting immediately behind the small body of strings, but if the first flute or the first clarinet had a solo, he – invariably he – would stand up and gingerly but quickly make his way through the strings and lean forward within a few inches of the mouth of the horn. Bassoonists would often be seated opposite the violinists with the horn players mounted on platforms high behind them with their backs to the conductor so that the bells of their instruments were directed at the recording horns. Other brass instruments and any other 'extras' required hovered 'on the outskirts', as one producer described it. Various mirrors were placed around the studio so that the conductor could have contact with the bassoons and horns. There might be no double-bass at all but instead a contrabassoon or tuba playing the double-bass part, and there might be other bass instruments lurking about – though not to be found in the score – performing a similar function, a couple of euphoniums maybe and a bass clarinet, to make audible lines which otherwise would never be captured. The producer, the recording expert as he was called in these early days, would frequently have to remind players to moderate their tone, not to play so forcibly, but also not to play so quietly either. The recording horns simply couldn't capture quiet sounds and loud sounds would cause the recording needle to jump. In the earliest days, the sounds of a double-bass couldn't be captured at all. And in addition the acoustic process was able to reproduce only a very limited frequency range; this did not mean that notes outside this range were inaudible but it did mean that the particular tone qualities and timbres of all sounds were distorted to different extents.

In other words, in Elgar's recordings up to 1925, we're not hearing the same symphony orchestra he would conduct in live concerts in the Queen's Hall, but an abbreviated ensemble, and a forlorn, unhappy and very warm body of men they always were too, one record man remembered.[2] Neither is the sound quality very close to what we would have actually experienced, even in that rather dead, dry, and stuffy recording studio. And of the longer pieces recorded acoustically we generally hear only abridgements and abbreviated versions. We hear *Carissima* complete, which easily fits on one side of a twelve-inch shellac disc. But within the same four- or four-and-a-half-minute compass was also fitted, for example, *Cockaigne*, which actually lasts about a quarter-of-an-hour. The reason for this truncating was essentially economic. You could indeed cut a symphony or a concerto, or *Die Walküre* for that matter, into four-and-a-half-minute minute chunks – later on that is precisely what did happen. But after just two decades of commercial recording in England nobody would have bought the discs. Not enough copies would be sold to generate any profits.

That Elgar's Second Symphony was recorded in 1924 uncut – the only acoustic recording of a major work of his which was not truncated – was indicative not of great improvements in sound quality but of a growing interest in gramophone records of classical music, evidence of expanding markets. In 1923 in England *The Gramophone* had been launched, a serious magazine reviewing records and attempting to encourage, or to shame, the record companies into issuing more and more of a wider repertory. That the same work was recorded again only three years later, however, was indeed the result of a major technological advance. In 1925 the electrical process was introduced, recording with a microphone. The human ear can encompass frequencies between twenty and 20,000 Hz; the acoustic process was linked to a range between 168 and 2,000 Hz. One great advantage of electrical recording was that it made possible the reproduction of a much wider frequency range; at the end of Elgar's recording career a range of up to 8,000 Hz could consistently be recorded. So the quality of sound could be captured with much greater fidelity. The microphone allowed the full complement of the symphony orchestra to be recorded, and not in the cramped conditions of a stuffy recording studio but in its normal layout and arrangement on the stage of the Queen's Hall. So in the electrical recording of the Second Symphony there were both tuba parts instead of just one player, three percussionists instead of two, both harp parts, and strings 16/14/10/10/4 instead of, in the earlier version, 4/3/2/2/1; there was just one adjustment, an extra reinforcing contrabassoon on the double-bass part.

There did remain though – and would remain until Elgar's recording career was completed – the noisy shellac surfaces of records on playback and the four-and-a-half minute chunks into which works had to be chopped.

Why did Elgar record?

Why was Elgar prepared to make records when most musicians and music-lovers before the First War were hostile, contemptuous, or patronising? In 1925 the scholar and choral conductor, Sir Richard Terry, thought that musicians should apologise for so long having abused the gramophone as a mere toy, an instrument without any soul.[3] But most of them didn't and many continued to treat it with indifference. Elgar's public pronouncements on recording were invariably positive and encouraging: as early as 1917 he could declare in *The Voice*, the house magazine of the Gramophone Company, that 'the records of my own compositions conducted by me are remarkably faithful reproductions of the originals'. But he was under no illusions. He told Troyte Griffith in 1921: 'You are extravagant over the gramophone', and went on to point to some of its limitations. The 'vagaries' of recording though he at least found 'interesting'. He was an amateur scientist himself after all. He loved doing experiments in his hut in the garden; in November 1908 he was writing to his friends of 'Elgar's Sulphuretted Hydrogen Machine' which he hoped to patent.[4] In old age he would spend hours examining fossilised algae under his microscope.[5] He liked the very idea of recording. He would play over and over again passages from *The Dream of Gerontius* issued on the Velvet Face label in 1924, with a complement of nine strings, an eight-voiced chorus, and instead of an organ a bass concertina, much to the annoyance of his friend Sir Ivor Atkins, who complained that it was a travesty of the music. But Elgar was delighted and astonished that it had been done at all.[6] He loved playing records, and would spend whole afternoons listening. He was always gleeful about the latest technical advances: 'Let's have the full power on', he would say. 'Listen to this big crescendo.' And he would pile the discs one on top of another, without their sleeves, and keep jabbing the needle down until he found the passage he was after.

He thought recording a tremendous boon and was sure it would advance technically quite quickly and become more and more useful. The ability it gave musicians, both executants and composers, to listen to whole works and also to tiny details over and over again he thought invaluable. But the gramophone was of even greater importance for music-lovers, in the 'humanising sphere' of music, in fostering the appreciation of great music. He wanted gramophones and records in every school, so that a love and appreciation of music should be fostered early, something much more important in his opinion – he spoke as a one-time peripatetic music teacher at girls' schools – than 'old fashioned and worse than useless trifling with the keyboard'. The possibilities were probably brought home to him forcibly during the war. A soldier at the Front wrote to him to tell him how the gramophone was the only thing that kept him and his fellows sane, that they kept on playing the record of *Starlight Express*, and that everyone loved it, 'even those who only go for Ragtime revues'. Not that Elgar was one to despise records of popular music. At a demonstration of new equipment at a reception in 1927 he assured his audience that he had 'much sympathy with some of the music which is not quite correctly called "Jazz"'. After all, he reminded them, had he not considered introducing four saxophones thirty years before in *Caractacus*?[7]

He was lured into the recording studio by a man who already in the first decade of the century was acknowledged as a leading Elgar conductor. This was Landon Ronald, who was retained by the Company as a multi-talented 'musical adviser', conductor, accompanist, arranger, and friend and colleague and astute assessor of a great number of London musicians. And when Elgar had been enticed into the studio, the man with whom he had closest dealings, who became in effect his producer, was little 'Freddy' Gaisberg, an American, a gifted musician himself, knowledgeable, enthusiastic, respectful, yet fun, who soon became a close friend and a guest of the composer at his home in Hampstead, where, he said, he unfailingly felt 'comfortable and at perfect ease'.

And the Company treated Elgar very well. He was certainly valuable to them: 'The name of Sir Edward Elgar in connection with a record imparts volumes', as the *Talking Machine News* put it in April 1914 in their review of his first disc. The association of the first English composer of the day with recording was invaluable at a time when the industry was battling to demonstrate its value, or its potential value, to serious musicians and music-lovers, and gave the Gramophone Company itself an immense advantage over its competitors. A four-year contract signed in December 1925 for sessions 'as required by the Company' gave Elgar an annual payment of £500 with £500 on signing the contract; in 1927 he was offered £500 per annum for life, which sum represented rather more than the annual salary of most professional men. From the very beginning of his association the Company was very generous in giving him gramophones and records. 'Can't I have one of the new gramophones like my friend Walford Davies has – a later pattern than my more-than-two-year-old one?' he wrote to them in 1929. The latest model was dispatched immediately.

Elgar seems never to have been in the least intimidated in front of the horn or the microphone. Many musicians were irritated, even exasperated by the conditions, the cutting and the rescoring, these 'monstrous concessions [which] were wrung from composers', as a later commentator described them;[8] 'this absurd gramophone business' Busoni called it.[9] Elgar accepted the cutting, and he was quite willing to write a special harp part to replace passages of the original accompaniment for the 1916 recording of the Violin Concerto – there was no harp part in the original. Occasionally he could be completely withdrawn: at a recording session in November 1929, he conducted 'with the barest movement of the stick', and he made little attempt at any discussion with the orchestra. Generally though he enjoyed sessions and this enjoyment certainly communicated itself to the players and has often been detected in the recorded performances: 'the entire performance has about it the atmosphere of tremendous good fun', said one commentator of the disc of his arrangements of Handel and Bach recorded in October 1923.[10]

Elgar's reputation as a conductor

The composer's daughter was probably giving a just assessment in reporting that 'the popular view' was that Elgar 'was not a great conductor except perhaps of his own works'.[11] He was self-taught, and certainly did not possess the technical or the kind of personal skills that are usually found in highly competent professional conductors. He couldn't get the difficult rhythm right in the final bars of the slow movement of the Cello Concerto and so left Beatrice Harrison, his soloist on many occasions, to lead the orchestra herself.[12] He became an economical and practical rehearser but in his forties could still exasperate the players by talking too much and worrying them and repeating passages without it being clear what the repetition was aiming to achieve.[13] He was often nervous and agitated and his beat could appear unsteady. When things were going well he might begin to relive the music, to become so engrossed and caught up in the sounds and the emotion of the moment that he failed to keep a cool head and direct his players with the required scrupulous clarity. He always clouded the climax of the first movement of the Second Symphony, a viola player remembered, because he became too involved in the music.[14] His stick technique and his ability to make clear his intentions certainly improved over the years. Sir Dan Godfrey, himself a highly professional conductor, thought it was 'interesting to note his increasing efficiency in purely technical matters' in 1924.[15] But in the end the power and beauty of his admired interpretations were not achieved through purely technical expertise.

Of course players were on their mettle whenever he conducted them. After all, if you knew that a conductor as eminent as Hans Richter had begun a rehearsal with the words: 'Gentlemen, let us now rehearse the greatest symphony of modern times, written by the greatest modern composer', you were not likely to treat a session with Elgar as an ordinary, run-of-the-mill encounter.[16] Elgar's nervous energy was always likely to have a catalytic effect on experienced professional orchestral players even if it might fail to bring out the best in the members of amateur choral societies. He was physically striking and looked more 'distinguished', people would say, as he grew older. He often appeared distant, with what was sometimes described as an 'aristocratic' aloofness, a country squire with the clothes of formal cut and the moustache and the military bearing. But you looked again and saw something else, an artist, a man who dreamed dreams and saw visions, lofty, dignified, resolute, but also strange and apart and mystical. You watched his delicate hands. Even more you watched his arrestingly alive face and the earnest eyes, and waited for his features to light up with a smile full of emotion and gratitude and thankfulness when the music went well. He did not command orchestral players, one of them felt, he implored them 'to give all the fire and energy and poetry that was in them'.[17]

The characteristics of Elgar's recorded performances

How do these performances strike us today? Many quick movements are faster than we are accustomed to. Tempos are generally much less steady than we expect and even where an opening speed follows the metronome mark indicated on the score there are likely to be a great many fluctuations within a designated tempo. Vibrato, especially in the strings, is much less pronounced than we are used to, and continuous string vibrato is not a feature. On the other hand, portamento is common. There is much less attention to detail, particularly to rhythmic detail, than we expect, and ensemble is a good deal less meticulous than it is today.

Many of the characteristic qualities demonstrated in these performances directed by Elgar are features of period style. The use of portamento as an expressive device was decreasing in the two decades that Elgar recorded, which also saw the beginning of the introduction of continuous vibrato in string playing. In the finale of the Violin Concerto, completed in 1910, he marks the second theme, at fig. 73, *cantabile e vibrato*, instructing the soloist here to draw on vibrato as a particular expressive resource; in his lifetime non-vibrato string tone would have been the norm.

But what were the particular qualities in performances directed by Elgar that struck his contemporaries? Flexibility of tempo was certainly a characteristic of the performing styles of all musicians throughout Elgar's life, in orchestral and chamber music, in songs and in organ music, even in works as austere and untheatrical as the unaccompanied liturgical music of composers like Byrd and Gibbons. Yet Elgar's idiosyncratic way of phrasing, his constant accelerandos and ritenutos, and the subtlety with which he employed tenutos and agogic accentuation were frequently commented upon, as was his 'uneasy, wilful beat', his 'very personal *rubato*'.[18] He himself explained that performances which were square or wooden were caricatures of his thought; his music, he said, should be played 'elastically and mystically'[19] and he recognised the authentic accents of his expression when it 'throbbed and seethed' as he intended that it should.[20]

At the same time, his contemporaries noted, there was a characteristic sweep to his own interpretations. A *Musical Times* reviewer in 1926 thought that 'things which other conductors carefully foster, he seems to leave to take their chance ... At the end we realise that details and rhetorical niceties have been put in their right place, and that the essential tale has been vividly told.' George Bernard Shaw once told Elgar that in conducting his own works a composer can strike an admirer as callous. Detail, however beautiful, was firmly kept in its place, and as a result, the large-scale structure of the music emerged and conveyed a sense of awe-inspiring strength and power. Perhaps the comparative lack of sophistication in Elgar's stick technique – his rather stiff and graceless movements seemed like 'the long straight beat of the British bandmaster' to a Chicago journalist in 1907[21] – was no disadvantage in obtaining the momentum and forward thrust that seems to have been so often experienced by listeners; there was less temptation to lavish too much care and linger lovingly over incidental beauties. Most of his contemporaries thought his performances unsentimental and lacking any trace of self-indulgence. Yet under his direction they did undeniably 'throb and seethe' as he wanted them to. The score and individual parts of any work by Elgar are always thick with expressive directions; it is impossible not to discern the intensity and fervour behind the marks on the page. And if you lifted your eyes from the music and watched the 'nervous, electric beat',[22] the expressive gestures of the left hand, and the hands – sometimes the whole body – quivering with excitement, you were unlikely to fail to infuse your part with a degree of tension and excitement.

A note of disappointment can perhaps be felt in some of the comments on Elgar's recorded performances which were reissued in the centenary year. Their quality and value were recognised but they sometimes did seem 'very brusque'. One critic thought that by the time Elgar came to make his last recordings he had 'grown more casual about details than memory of earlier performances suggests he was before his virtual retirement early in the 1920s'.[23] There seems to be no evidence that would support this thesis and in fact the recorded evidence contradicts it: the later recordings are neater and cleaner in articulation and not so cavalier with note values.[24]

The likeliest explanation of such a remark is simply that a quarter of a century on, the reviewer has become accustomed to steadier and cleaner and neater performances which are much more literal realisations of the text, the result to a considerable degree of more and more recording and broadcasting.

Elgar's fast speeds seem to have been no faster than his contemporaries, and it has been established pretty conclusively that the requirements of making records – the four-and-a-half-minute side-length of discs – did not result in Elgar rushing his players. In his lifetime he was never repeatedly criticised for fast speeds in concert performances. Yet there were certainly comments on his speeds on the recordings when they were first released: 'I suggest that you keep your speed on the slow side. The tendency is to take some of the Variations at a break-neck pace.'[25] The explanation for this must surely be a phenomenon that has been frequently and increasingly commented upon in more recent decades, that we listen to and interpret the same musical gestures in live performances in concert-halls and in recorded ones in domestic settings in different ways.

The authority and historical value of the recordings

The renowned Elgarians of the generation after Henry Wood and Hamilton Harty, conductors like Boult and Barbirolli, certainly knew his recordings and loved them, but it seems unlikely they studied them: they had after all taken independent possession of the music's style and idea from the composer's live performances. No doubt many conductors who directed Elgar's works in the second half of the twentieth century did not think of consulting them. Others perhaps were like the American Leonard Slatkin in the 1980s, who deliberately avoided listening to them until his own interpretations were 'committed', until he had evolved his own way through the score and in performances. Georg Solti did study Elgar's 1930 recording of the First Symphony in arriving at his 'view' of that work, which he himself recorded in 1972. The Elgar scholar, Jerrold Northrop Moore, considered this 'a clear case of a recorded performance generating as much attention as the score itself', and thought that this would be 'disquieting' to 'conventional musicology'.[26] Solti himself said he was 'overjoyed' at 'how straightforward was [the composer's] own approach, without any sentimentality. It was a classical interpretation – marvellous. I realised that my view must then be right.'[27] Moore considered that Solti had 'studied well' and commended his interpretation for combining flexibility and structural cohesion, a crucial distinguishing mark of the composer's own accounts of his works, he thought: 'the varied metronomic pulses called for in the score must be drawn together through an expression of some terseness – the indulgences will take care of themselves.'[28]

Does such admiration, though, derive simply from the effects of minute inflections in performing style? In 1929 H. C. Colles seemed to imply a transhistorical significance for such expressive details. After listening to the composer direct *The Kingdom* he pleaded for more recordings by Elgar because 'his mind . . . moves in a region for which notation offers no precise record . . . [such] things as the pauses and accents, directions for *rubato* . . . and such indeterminate suggestions of mood as his favourite *Nobilmente*, acquire their authoritative interpretation only from him'.[29] But Jerrold Northrop Moore admitted that even Solti didn't follow Elgar's interpretation 'slavishly'; in fact it would be easy, he said, to indicate 'dozens of divergent points'.[30] And the impact created on Moore clearly derived from many other details than particular objective facts concerning tempos, speed fluctuations, vibrato, and phrasing. He is after all an American who came to England and spent twenty years researching the life of the composer, towards whom he clearly feels reverence and an almost mystical attachment: he considers that Elgar's own recorded performance of his First Symphony 'speaks . . . with an eloquence that it would be presumptuous to attempt to characterise'. Moore accounts for Solti's deviations from Elgar's own interpretation of the First Symphony with great ingenuity: Solti's is a 'cosmopolitan' voice 'that discourses Bartók, Beethoven, Wagner, Mahler, Strauss to the world', and the authenticity and authority of his own interpretation, he feels, may be explained by reference to the 'cosmopolitan' interpretation the work might well have received at its premiere under that other Hungarian musician, Hans Richter.[31]

The recorded evidence does show clearly that an Elgar interpretation was never a carbon copy. He made two electrical recordings of the *Falstaff* interludes, of *Cockaigne*, and of the first, second, and fourth *Pomp and Circumstance* Marches. They are quite different, in phrasing, in tempo fluctuation, even in the basic speeds. To what extent the differences in orchestral balance and timbre are the result of technology, or of Elgar's preferences, or arose by chance is difficult to determine. He certainly expected others' interpretations to have their own individuality. He listened to John Barbirolli's 1928 recording of the *Introduction and Allegro* and noticed differences from the way he himself did things. But he knew, he said, that 'Mr Barbirolli is an extremely able youth and, very properly, has ideas of his own.'

He expressed delight in changes in the characteristic performing styles he had known all his life. Leon Goossens was the first to apply vibrato to the oboe, and when his playing began to be widely known in the 1920s other woodwind players were not immediately impressed. But Elgar, at the age of seventy-five, was won over; he listened to the test pressings of his recordings of *Froissart* and exclaimed: 'Leon G's oboe passages . . . are divine – what an artist!' There has been much debate about his recording with Yehudi Menuhin of his Violin Concerto. Elgar often performed the work with Albert Sammons, who was certainly for many years regarded as its greatest exponent. Sammons's performance is quite unlike Menuhin's, more direct and vigorous, and much more volatile. In Sammons's recording, made with Sir Henry Wood, the fast movements are much quicker, quite near in fact to the version Elgar made in 1916 with Marie Hall. Menuhin luxuriates over very beautiful passages in a way that was certainly not usually characteristic of Elgar. It has been suggested that the seventy-five-year-old composer considered that perhaps more could not be asked of this boy than the astonishing amount that he was giving, or that he was overawed by this assured and prodigiously gifted youth, and so – against his better judgement and artistic convictions – gave way and allowed the soloist more freedom than he really would have wished. Maybe. But he did after all prepare himself by studying Menuhin's recording of Max Bruch's First Violin Concerto and noting the player's idiosyncrasies to try and create something fresh. And he did describe Menuhin as 'the most wonderful artist I have ever heard'.[32] Not a word of criticism of Menuhin seems to have passed Elgar's lips. Perhaps he just liked the boy's playing as much as he said he did. He loved Casals's playing of the Cello Concerto, which was also by some considered '*too* beautiful, *too* intimate' without the 'austerity' and the 'gruffness' that were considered essential qualities of Elgar's own interpretations of his music. He loved Toscanini's performances of the 'Enigma' Variations which some criticised for their lack of 'Englishness'.[33]

So Elgar himself seems not to have regarded his own performances as having any particular prescriptive value for other performers. Moore can account for Elgar's unique authority as displayed in two different interpretations by explaining that he 'seems to have known so precisely the range of possibilities inherent in any given work of his, that both versions of each sound valid, authoritative, and truly Elgarian'.[34] But while many later commentators recognised these recordings as possessing compelling interest and beauty for music-lovers and conductors – 'the sense of witnessing historic events is irresistible, with Elgar consistently hypnotic as a conductor'[35] – most acknowledged that they were not performances for 'our' day. Critics though often failed to try and understand them as historical documents or to distinguish between competence and the characteristics of a performing style: Elgar's performances were 'flawed', this soloist 'adopts' an 'exaggeratedly portamento style',[36] that soloist 'overdoes' portamento and rubato.[37]

As the 'early music' movement gained momentum in the 1960s and 1970s, and great efforts were made to cultivate historically informed styles in Ockeghem, Purcell, Bach, Handel, and Mozart, some musicians began to

wonder: if we devote so much care and attention to establishing the historic
details concerning timbre, phrasing, articulation, tempi and so on in Bach,
why do we continue to ignore the evidence presented to us so blatantly
by the composers themselves on recordings? In 1971 a record critic saw
the way the wind was blowing. Heaven preserve us, he said, from those
scholars who may want us to introduce portamenti and other characteristic
features of performance style in Elgar in the name of period authenticity.[38]
Clearly the implications were disturbing and they were faced squarely by a
distinguished scholar of recording and performance studies in an article in
1984 in *Early Music*, a journal whose readers by and large were probably still
chiefly concerned with historical performance in Machaut or Monteverdi
or Bach:

> The best of Elgar's performances are still extraordinarily moving, and they
> can, and should, influence our own performances. They can guide us, not
> towards the sterile reconstruction of a dead style, but towards the creation
> of performances of his music which speak as forcefully to us as Elgar's own
> performances spoke to his contemporaries.[39]

Elgar's own performances have stimulated the thoughts and imagina-
tions of succeeding generations of performers, enabled conductors and
orchestral players to rethink this music in startlingly new ways, and allowed
musicians to avoid being provincial in time. They might also assist the cultural historian to examine the changing contexts of music in performance
and to understand why the same chords and rhythms, timbres and expressive gestures evoked in one listener 'boastful self-confidence, emotional
vulgarity, material extravagance, a ruthless philistinism',[40] and in another,
belonging to another epoch, 'human feeling so nervous and subtle as . . . had
never before spoken' in English music.[41]

14 Broadcasting's ally: Elgar and the BBC

JENNY DOCTOR

> The composer has an ally in Broadcasting. Radio needs all the music it can get. If the composer can write the kind that is wanted he need not wait for a performance. Music with attractive melodies, used and harmonised with distinction of thought and fancy, is nowadays hard to find ... Generally speaking, when a man gets home tired and 'fed up', he wants to be cheered by a good, lilting tune and harmony that is distinctive without being so 'modernish' as to disturb the increasing tranquillity of his mental state.[1]

Thus the first *BBC Handbook* characterised the relationship between 'broadcasting and the composer' in 1928 – the sixth year of the BBC's existence – burbling on to specify that music by 'thoroughly "English" composers is always welcomed'. The challenge for the young BBC was to discover the *right* music with which to define its image, with which to broadcast, quite literally, its musical identity. And as part of that, the BBC sought a specific ally, a sort of composer-mentor who could adorn and distinguish the music programmes: a 'thoroughly English' composer with the right demeanour and a broadly recognised reputation, who wrote music with 'a good, lilting tune' and just the right kind of appeal – 'distinctive without being modernish'. That was the challenge indeed.

The fledgling British Broadcasting Company was hugely ambitious, using its ever-increasing powers and financial base to negotiate ways to make a name and establish a reputation of national and international importance and influence. When founded in 1922 and placed in the hands of John Reith, it was a tiny organisation[2] bounded by the current state of technology, with few employees, a small audience base consisting of amateur radio enthusiasts, no identity, and no direct remit with respect to output. But there was huge potential for this new mass-market medium – and, interestingly from a musical point of view, there were no expectations, conventions or traditions about how music on air might be shaped or what it might consist of. In those early days, everything was new and had creative potential; there were few rules beyond the technological limitations. But the idealistic vision, marketing strategies, eagerness to create, willingness to seize propitious opportunities, and pure, core ambition – all of which propelled the BBC rapidly and decisively to prominence and unforeseen power – had enormous impact on the development of programme policies that served its, as well as the public's, needs.[3]

Reith's BBC assumed the role of a benevolent dictator, carrying on Victorian aspirations for social improvement; his oft-quoted policies aimed 'to entertain, to interest, to enlighten, in all these ways to bring the very best of everything and to spare no effort to do it, to the greatest possible number'.[4] In the 1920s, the BBC devoted nearly two thirds of broadcast time to music, almost a fifth of that art music. Given that inter-war listeners often received only one or two BBC wavelengths, this significant percentage led to much grumbling against 'high-brow' programmes. But in Reith's view, such tactics would eventually lead to a national appreciation of art music – not least British art music.

Who were the men who so quickly attained and retained such power within this new, vital force in the British music industry? What were the musical goals of these BBC decision-makers and how did they go about creating policies, programmes, and promotional choices that would so profoundly affect the musical tastes and attitudes of the British public, not to mention the lives and careers of British musicians? It is important to remember that British broadcasting evolved from technological experiments developed by the military and shipping industry during and just after the First World War, that many early radio pioneers were demobilised military men. The structure of the organisation they built certainly reflected that fact, as did less evident aesthetic decisions involving the construction of the BBC's image.

For instance, Percy Pitt, the man who headed BBC music in the 1920s, was not recognised as a high-powered player in the British music establishment when appointed in 1923. But his 'outsider' status was not surprising in the context of Reith's BBC, which favoured pragmatism over academic standing. A composer and accomplished conductor with continental training, Pitt had an unusual outlook: he brought an interest in opera and new European developments to the BBC; moreover, at a time when many established concert organisers believed broadcasting was detrimental to box-office takings and refused transmissions from their concert halls, Pitt's close association with the British National Opera Company allowed the BBC to tap into its performances from the earliest days of broadcasting.[5] This enabled performances of large-scale works to find a place in BBC programmes from the start – an important component of the early BBC music profile.

But though highly prized on the continent, grand opera was not yet significant in the general profile of British music-making. The emphasis there fell into two main categories. On the popular side, there was the realm of lighter music and operetta. Song and light music played a huge part in BBC output from the beginning, as attested by the formation of a separate Variety Department devoted to producing programmes of such fare – interesting as an early manifestation of twentieth-century genre discrimination. Opposing this was the powerful BBC objective – highly significant in those latter years of the so-called English musical renaissance – to establish a national reputation for serious music-making that would be appreciated both at home and abroad. At that time in Britain that meant, quite simply, excellence in composition and performance in the realm of *symphonic repertory*. And here with this new technology, for the first time since it was deemed desirable, was a way for the British to break into the continental art-music monopoly: a way to bring British music-making, British musical decisions, and even British music to national and international attention. The British music establishment and the BBC were in agreement on this, if on no other question.

For the BBC, it is significant to note, the path to this goal lay in transmitting not merely studio performances, but full-scale public symphony concerts. Both to raise profile and to provide opportunities for audiences to experience orchestral sounds live – particularly important given the distortion levels resulting from early microphones, transmitters, and radio receivers – the BBC sought the means to broadcast public concerts. But there were immediate practical problems: as was mentioned above, prominent concert managements initially refused the BBC permission to relay their concerts. Hence, the BBC launched public concert series of its own, amidst huge amounts of self-generated hype and publicity. The first took place in 1924, when six symphony concerts were transmitted from Central Hall, Westminster, followed the next year by four concerts presented from Covent Garden. During the 1926–7 season, the BBC launched its highly prestigious series of National Symphony Concerts, presented by an orchestra of 150 players. Of course during that season, the BBC pounced on the opportunity to take over the prestigious Queen's Hall Promenade Concerts, and in conjunction with that, negotiated a contract with conductor Henry Wood and cleared the right to broadcast from the highly desirable Queen's Hall. With that coup, the tide turned, and the BBC encountered no further impediments to relaying public symphony concerts. With the establishment in 1930 of the BBC Symphony Orchestra and the appointment of its resident conductor, Adrian Boult, the BBC not only controlled and had the permanent benefit for its broadcasts of one of the best orchestras in the country, but the orchestra toured at home and abroad, flaunting the BBC brand for music excellence on traditional platforms, as well as across the ether.[6]

Within a period of less than ten years, then, the BBC went a long way towards achieving the ambitious goals of establishing its reputation, image, and power-base as the foremost music impresario in the country, with international reach. But there is one highly significant part of the story that is yet to be mentioned: what did the BBC do to further the standing of national music, both within the country's borders and without? How did it shape this part of the branding construct and why? The answers are of course complex, involving a variety of policies, projects, programmes, and series, too numerous to mention here. However, to glimpse one significant strategy by which the early BBC chose to promote national music identity, we return to the idea of that thoroughly English composer-mentor, who wrote music – both popular and symphonic would be best – with just the right kind of appeal. There was only one man then who could embody that image and all the BBC hoped it stood for: Edward Elgar.

By the early 1920s, it is well established, Elgar had become a figure of paradox. While Europe emerged from the shock of war, Elgar went through a period of intense creativity, producing the String Quartet, the Piano Quintet and ultimately the Cello Concerto; following the death of his wife Alice in April 1920, as a new social and economic order began to build around him, Elgar submerged into depression, his creative powers stultified, his sense of self-worth withdrawn. Thus, at the start of the BBC's existence in 1922, Elgar had assumed a patina of age, expressing feelings of outmodedness and neglect.

> Some could discern neither the poet nor the dreamer in this courtly man, his hair and moustache now white, his high nose more pronounced – a Master of the King's Music (1924) who brushed aside talk of music, affecting ignorance of it. Others, recognizing that the musical and moral values of his world had given way to newer, sharper attitudes, understood his reluctance to commit himself to compositions, and his haunting fear that the day of his music was done.[7]

How did this disillusioned self-image compare to the way Elgar was viewed by others? Specifically what did this composer represent to the youthful, ambitious, image-seeking BBC? A slightly different description provides valuable clues:

> His 'image' to many of the public is still as the embodiment of certain aspects of the period from 1900 to 1914. He even looked like a soldier or a squire. It was very reassuring to English philistines to have a composer who did not look much like one. Besides, to those who did know of Elgar the musician, he fitted the image they had devised for him: 'Pomp and Circumstance'; 'Imperial March'; 'The Banner of St George'. So we have Elgar the Edwardian or Elgar the Imperialist and for a long time he obscured the real Elgar, who was someone very different.[8]

A composer who did not look like one, a squire, an Edwardian. A soldier, associated equally with rousing marching music, with *Land of Hope and*

Glory – popularly recognised as the second national anthem – as with symphonic music and oratorio. In short, Elgar represented nationalism, imperialism, a time of English glory that preceded the horror-filled legacies of the Great War. His music was of a past age, out of step with current fashion, and, in some respects, evoked a spirit and time that seemed inappropriately opulent following the war's carnage, destruction, and pain. Nevertheless, in the 1920s, that decade of regrouping, rebuilding, industrial and technological upheaval, and social transformation, it was useful at times to pull out and exploit stability gained by evoking a sense of 'tradition'. To the demobilised soldiers who constructed and ran the early BBC, Elgar – the composer who did not look like one,[9] who loved racehorses and dogs, a music establishment 'outsider', who could not bear to talk about music, who in fact feared he was creatively finished – could not have been more appropriate as the epitome of a national icon.[10]

Elgar's presence in BBC programmes, both as conductor and composer, has been avidly investigated and described in the past, this being the fourth article written under the rubric 'Elgar and the BBC' – the first issued more than seventy years ago, the second a quarter of a century ago, and the third a decade ago.[11] In particular, Ronald Taylor's essay traces and lists many programmes that defined the rich intersection of Elgar and broadcasting over the last twelve years of the composer's life, while Humphrey Burton's rediscovery of the fascinating paper-trail surrounding the BBC's commissioning of the Third Symphony was one of several catalysts resulting in Anthony Payne's 'elaboration from the sketches'. With so many details concerning Elgar's interactions with the BBC already in print, there is room for this essay to take a broader view. What were the benefits of this symbiotic association? How did it play out over time?

The primary virtue of Elgar as a national broadcasting icon lay in the fact that his musical output was so varied and appealed to so many tastes. This was a constant preoccupation for the early BBC, and in fact has been a continuing concern guiding BBC policies to the present day: how does an organisation charged with serving the public at large best use limited time and resources to satisfy the preferences and desires of millions of individuals? Various policies and approaches have been tried, implemented, and continue to be adapted, but a first response remains the same: it is impossible. And a second: find and exploit those rare figures who appeal across social, cultural, and economic divides. Elgar and his music did exactly that: his compositional achievements in the years before the war coupled with his war efforts and wartime output meant that here was a musician with appeal for both the Ordinary Listener and the music connoisseur. A plain-speaking article published for the BBC Elgar Celebrations in 1932 encapsulates that connection in a particularly inter-war manner:

Rarely has there existed a great composer whose mind and outlook more closely conformed to that of his audience and who was less concerned with all the great man, great meddler, great consoler business which underlies so much German music. His utter aloofness from musical 'shop', his complete identification with the outward life of a matchlessly tailored and tonsored English gentleman, who hunts, shoots, fishes and bets – this, allied to a supreme mastery of almost every phase of musical technique, combine to present us with a new and most refreshing figure in musical history, the modern English master musician. His music expresses no emotion which is beyond the reach of the middle classes. Is it a stirring march you want, a jolly good shindy to work off some excess energy, a quiet field-path stroll, a tramp up Painswick Beacon to see the Severn, a devotional hour in some cathedral, the morbid thrill of a State funeral procession, a laze in a punt with a volume of Bridges? – Elgar is the man to crystallise all this for you in music, the splendour and quietude of which, as the occasion requires, seem to strike an absolutely new note in music.[12]

Thus Elgar's name is sprinkled liberally throughout early broadcast records, his songs, marches and lighter works, like those of compatriots such as Liza Lehmann, Ivor Novello, Roger Quilter, Arthur Sullivan, Edward German, and Maude Valérie White, arranged for all sorts of combinations suiting the primitive microphones, studio conditions, broadcasting budgets, and preferences of performers in those initial years.[13] Following the BBC's 'First Symphony Concert' on 21 June 1923,[14] Elgar's larger-scale works also begin to appear in programme records, though one must keep in mind when reading them that 'orchestra' in early BBC parlance often comprised a small ensemble of players, the number dependent on microphone capability, studio size, and budget. The first orchestral broadcast of Elgar took place as early as 8 July 1923, when 'Mr Drysdale Kilburn's Orchestra' aired the overture *Cockaigne* from the London Station (2LO) alongside the Prelude to *Lohengrin* and a suite from Grieg's *Peer Gynt*.[15]

When Elgar himself first partook in a broadcast on St George's Day, 23 April 1924, he was in good company: he was somewhat upstaged by King George V opening the British Empire Exhibition at Wembley, in what was *his* first broadcast. Heard by at least ten million people – many in mass crowds gathered in city centres – this event established a new practice of 'royal broadcasting', giving the infant BBC a huge boost.[16] Not only was the speech aired, but the accompanying pageant was too, with Elgar, soon to be appointed Master of the King's Music, conducting massed bands and choirs in works the nation loved and knew: *Land of Hope and Glory* (at the King's request), the *Imperial March*, Parry's *Jerusalem* and the National Anthem.

Elgar's depressed account of rehearsing the musical contributions is oft-quoted, but nevertheless gives insight into his projected take on this modern, mass-media extravaganza:

> I was standing alone (criticising) in the middle of the enormous stadium in the sun: all the ridiculous court programme, soldiers, awnings etc: 17,000 men hammering, loud speakers, amplifiers – four aeroplanes circling over etc etc – all mechanical & horrible – no soul & no romance & no imagination.[17]

His words conjure a vision of a lonely figure illuminated at the centre of a football pitch, surrounded by, but isolated from, tiers of crowds, soldiers and workmen, with planes zooming overhead, and buffeted by noise, noise, indiscriminate, modern noise. He seems to reject this soulless, ructious world in the next lines, in which he rather affectedly writes of discovering and being moved by simple daisies below him, symbols of the unsullied, natural world where he belongs. However, as others have pointed out, this construction of Elgar as a has-been longing to bury himself in his beloved countryside does not do justice to the fascination the composer clearly had with modern developments. His home had a telephone as early as 1904, he owned motor cars – though he rather failed as a driver, he was an enthusiastic passenger – and, as has long been documented, he had ardent interest in gramophone technology, as a consumer, a recording artist, and a spokesman.[18] Thus, although the pageant itself may have depressed Elgar's sensibilities, the potential of radio did not elude him, not only as a hugely effective means of raising his public profile and disseminating his music at a time when he felt particularly neglected, but also as a way of bringing in ever-needed income. As a musician, Elgar was pragmatic, his early earnings derived from teaching and playing, his initial opportunities as a composer gained by writing works for which there was a recognised market. Despite his negative take on the Wembley experience, that performance to millions effectively launched Elgar in the last decade of his life on a new branch of his career, in partnership with the most up-and-coming, most technologically driven, perhaps the noisiest, most mass-oriented British organisation of the day.

In effect, from 1924 Elgar was implicated in a plethora of BBC events of note, reflecting not only his status with respect to broadcasting policies, but also his friendships with three BBC men of influence who greatly admired his music: Percy Pitt, the Music Director of the 1920s who had known Elgar since the turn of the century; Landon Ronald, a conductor, principal of the Guildhall School of Music and member of the BBC Music Advisory Committee from its founding in 1925; and Adrian Boult, when he succeeded as BBC Music Director in 1930. These conductors, in addition to countless other performers, ensured that nearly all Elgar's oeuvre was broadcast in his lifetime, some works many times – and a few, such as the *Pomp and Circumstance* March No. 1 and *Salut d'amour*, aired so often that it is impractical to take count.[19]

With respect to his own broadcasting appearances, which numbered twenty-eight in all, Elgar – following a practice that had begun in British concert halls before the war – inaugurated the BBC's convention of featuring composer-conductors in broadcasts of public concerts.[20] It is important to recognise, given the BBC's primary remit to broadcast, that these were in fact Elgar *appearances*, live before audiences, the BBC missing no opportunity to attract valuable, image-building attention and interest.[21] For this reason, no doubt, Elgar was well represented as a sure draw in the first season of BBC public concerts (noted earlier) in February and March 1924, relayed from Central Hall, Westminster. Landon Ronald conducted the 7 March concert, finishing with the Second Symphony 'by special request of a large number of Broadcasting Listeners'.[22] And Elgar himself had the honour of presenting the season finale – the only composer to conduct a programme devoted to his own works.[23] In fact, Elgar became a fixture of BBC public concerts during his lifetime, the only composer-conductor to appear annually, or even more frequently, often conducting all-Elgar programmes.

By the time that Elgar's contribution to British music – and the BBC – was marked in the Elgar Celebration concerts in November and December 1932, the composer was too frail to conduct complete programmes. But the celebrations – sadly commencing just as news of Pitt's death was announced – comprised three symphony concerts devoted entirely to Elgar (30 November, conducted by Ronald; 7 December, conducted by Elgar and Boult; and 14 December, conducted by Boult), as well as a studio broadcast of Elgar part-songs presented by the Wireless Singers (4 December) and a performance of *Falstaff* conducted by Boult in the Sunday Orchestral Concert series (11 December). As the programme recalled, 'many of the events which mark red-letter days in the ten years' history of the BBC, have been Elgar Concerts – many more than any other composer could claim'.[24]

In addition to public concerts, Elgar served as a national icon in the annual broadcasts commemorating Armistice Day. Each year from 1923, on 11 November, Elgar and his music were featured, as necessary a symbol of the occasion as the Cenotaph remains today. Initially the various BBC stations broadcast their own programmes, but Elgar was usually present on each in some way, often with performances of *For the Fallen*, or the entire *Spirit of England*, and ending with one of the marches. As the BBC grew, so did the elaborateness of its Armistice Day programming. By 1932, in the centre of a page devoted to the day's special events, a prominent box simply announced the closing item: '10.15pm, "For the Fallen", A poem by Laurence Binyon, set to music by Sir Edward Elgar, O.M., conducted by the composer'.

Between 1922 and 1934, Elgar and the BBC developed a mutually beneficial association. Elgar provided the BBC with a sense of stability, with an image of national popularity and music tradition, with a solid, sensible, popular, quintessentially English music figurehead. The BBC provided Elgar with publicity, attention, an audience of millions, and generous conducting fees. In the final years, of course, the BBC's commissioning of a new Elgar symphony aroused huge publicity and excitement; if completed, it would undoubtedly have added an entirely new dimension to this symbiotic and mutually satisfying relationship. The BBC so wished to be seen as the glorious patron, as the benevolent force that permitted the creation of a major, new Elgar work (without having to pay too much for it, of course). But owing to the composer's illness and death, this remained a commission unfulfilled, like so many BBC commissioning projects of the inter-war years.[25] It is unfortunate that in the shadow of this enormous disappointment, the true significance of Elgar's substantial relationship with British broadcasting has been overlooked. The elderly composer, through his frequent appearances and, even more fundamentally, through the general appeal and popularity of his music, proved a vital ally to the young BBC, an essential element in the formation of its musical identity.

15 Elgar in German criticism

AIDAN J. THOMSON

'If we had nothing but Elgars, then there might be an end to conservatories, and our theory teachers might lose their entire earnings.'[1] Thus wrote not an irate member of Britain's musical establishment but an admiring German critic, Max Hehemann, one of several early twentieth-century German musicians to write articles about Elgar in musical periodicals. The period of German interest in Elgar in the years immediately following the successful Düsseldorf performances of *The Dream of Gerontius* in 1901 and 1902 was relatively brief: as Michael Kennedy has observed, Elgar came 'at the end of an epoch in European music, at the dawn of a renaissance in England', with the result that he soon 'ceased to exercise the European musician's curiosity'.[2] But soon is not immediately: in this short period Elgar's works received an acclaim outside Britain they have not known since. The criticism that exists therefore offers us valuable insights into Elgar at a time when the composer was at his creative peak, but from outside British musical society, and thus from outside the cultural-political battleground of the British musical renaissance within which the critical discourse on Elgar's music took place.[3] Consequently, we can examine afresh the commonly held idea of Elgar as a musical embodiment of 'Englishness', not least the extent to which the composer's Englishness was perceived as compatible with his Catholicism. Before doing so, however, we must first become acquainted with the critics themselves.

The critics

The first German periodical article about Elgar to make a lasting impression was Otto Lessmann's 1900 piece in the *Allgemeine Musik-Zeitung*, of which Lessmann was then the editor.[4] In this article Lessmann (1844–1918), who had attended the Birmingham premiere of *Gerontius*, described Elgar as the 'coming man' [*kommende Mann*] of English music, a phrase that he was to use again two years later in a piece about the 1902 Sheffield music festival, in which he compared Elgar favourably with Parry and other British composers.[5] He continued to promote Elgar in the pages of the *Zeitung*, going so far as to claim that the 'Enigma' Variations, which he heard Felix Weingartner conduct in Berlin on 15 November 1901, equalled 'the best which has been produced anywhere – in the way of orchestral variations – since Beethoven'.[6]

This performance of the Variations occurred towards the beginning of a period of increased exposure in Germany for Elgar's music, most notably in the successful performances of *Gerontius* in Düsseldorf in December 1901 and, at the Lower Rhine Music Festival, in May 1902. This period provides the background to the first of two articles about the composer written by Max Hehemann (1873–1933), which appeared in the leading German music periodical *Die Musik*.[7] Hehemann was an enthusiastic promoter of Elgar's choral music, preparing a guide to *The Apostles* for German audiences in 1904, but in a second article about the composer in 1905, this time for the *Neue Zeitschrift für Musik*, he also expressed his wish that Elgar might finish the symphony 'which his friends have long expected from him' as it would be 'crucial [*entscheidend*] for his position as an instrumental composer'.[8] This was a matter of particular concern for Hehemann as he had hoped Elgar would complete the symphony in time for a projected all-Elgar concert in Essen on 29 October 1904; in the end, this concert did not take place.[9]

December 1903 saw the appearance of another article about Elgar, this time by Hugo Conrat in the *Neue Musik-Zeitung*.[10] Its author, Hugo Conrat, is almost certainly the same Conrat (d. *c.* 1910) who befriended Brahms, whose *Zigeunerlieder* used eleven of his German translations of Hungarian 'national poems'. A wealthy Viennese businessman of Jewish-Hungarian extraction, Conrat regularly came into close contact with Viennese artists, musicians, and critics without actually being one himself. He was, for a time, the honorary treasurer of the Vienna Tonkünstlerverein; his wife held a weekly salon for intellectuals and artists on the Walfischgasse in Vienna; and his youngest daughter befriended Alma Mahler.[11] Conrat may not have come into contact with Elgar's music until March 1903, when the Variations received their Vienna premiere; although *Cockaigne* was played there in October 1903, *Gerontius* was not performed in Austria until 1905.[12] It is perhaps significant that Conrat's article was written from London rather than Vienna. According to Ronald Taylor, it was based on an interview Elgar had had with Conrat, although Taylor provides no evidence to support this assertion.[13]

Whereas Elgar appears not to have maintained contact with Conrat, we know that he met, and corresponded with, Fritz Volbach (1861–1940), the author of articles about him in the *Allgemeine Musik-Zeitung* (1904) and in the Roman Catholic periodical, *Hochland* (1907).[14] Born in Wipperfürth, Volbach studied composition in Cologne under Ferdinand Hiller, but made his name primarily as the conductor of the Mainz oratorio society (the Liedertafel und Damengesangverein). He was introduced to Elgar in 1900 by Ludwig Strecker, the head of Schott's Edition, and met him again at the

Sheffield Festival in 1902, where Volbach's symphonic poem *Easter* was performed. By this time, he and Elgar were regular correspondents, although they were not to meet again after 1908, when Volbach conducted *The Kingdom* in Mainz.[15] From their letters, we learn that Elgar not only appreciated the articles Volbach wrote to publicise his work, but that in the case of the *Allgemeine Musik-Zeitung* article he had read it prior to publication.[16] According to Volbach's son, Walther, the two men were drawn together by their mystical Catholicism, and Volbach senior makes much of this aspect of Elgar's personality in both articles, especially in his piece for *Hochland*.

Another Rhenish-based composer-critic writing about Elgar was Otto Neitzel (1852–1920), from 1887 onwards the music critic of the *Kölnische Zeitung*. Neitzel contributed articles to the weekly Breitkopf and Härtel periodical, *Signale für die musikalische Welt*, about *Gerontius* (1902) and *The Apostles* (1904).[17] In his review of the 1904 Lower Rhine Music Festival in Cologne for the *Zeitschrift der internationalen Musikgesellschaft*, he described *The Apostles* as the 'principal work' [*Hauptwerk*] of the festival: praise indeed from a relatively progressive critic who greatly admired Richard Strauss.[18] Unlike Volbach, Neitzel's religious background was almost certainly Protestant (he was born in Falkenburg, Pomerania); consequently, perhaps, he focuses less on any didactic religious message in the works, and more on the musical colours evoked by mystical Catholicism.

By no means are these the only critics writing about Elgar in Germany in the years immediately following the Düsseldorf performances of *Gerontius*. However, they are probably the most important: Volbach, Conrat, and Hehemann each provide a brief biography of the composer whilst they, along with Neitzel and Lessmann, examine his works in detail that goes beyond mere description. Moreover, all of them, to a greater or lesser extent, examine both what they perceived to be Elgar's English qualities, and the role Catholicism played in his music. It is to their critical writings that we now turn.

Elgar as an 'English' composer

More than his compatriots, Hehemann was inclined to see Elgar not only as England's leading composer but also at the forefront of a burgeoning national school.[19] Unfortunately, quite whom this school comprised, and how it was specifically English, remains a mystery. On the one hand, in his later article Hehemann claimed that

> In contrast to the followers of Mendelssohn, Elgar remembered his national character [*Volkstum*] and founded his art on what lived in the people as an ancient possession [*als uraltes Gut*]. He set his goal to be a truly English composer and, as such, to speak the language of his land.[20]

On the other hand, in his earlier article he criticised Elgar for displaying 'the typical Mendelssohnian characteristic of inner coolness [that] marks out even the greatest piece of English music':[21]

> Even Elgar, little though he usually has to do with the German master [i.e. Mendelssohn], is not a man of over-flowing feeling, and he is at his least effective when he sings of love. One seeks in vain for warm-blooded melodies from him; the sensuality of a Richard Strauss, for example, is completely foreign to him.[22]

One can infer from this that Hehemann saw an Elgar-inspired English national school as falling stylistically somewhere between Mendelssohnian aridity and post-Wagnerian sumptuousness. The difficulty with this, however, is in clarifying whether Hehemann envisaged future English composers sincerely speaking the 'language of their land' in an accent that was anything other than Elgarian. Indeed, at one point, Hehemann seemed to imply that this was impossible: in asserting that 'Elgar's music is rooted in his national character, whose soul in turn is sometimes quite astonishingly reflected in his music', he presented Elgar not just as *a* leading English composer, but as *the* exemplar of Englishness in music.[23] Particularly in his later article, Hehemann appeared to be drawing on remarks recently made by the composer himself. In the first of his professorial lectures in Birmingham, Elgar had claimed that English music had a future 'if the younger generation are true to themselves [. . .] and draw inspiration from their own land'; this inspiration was 'something broad, noble, chivalrous, healthy and above all, an out-of-door sort of spirit'. But this vision, as Jerrold Northrop Moore has observed, was essentially Elgar's private one; Hehemann's 'national school' was therefore less an established fact than it was an aspiration.[24] Moreover, in neither article did Hehemann refer to any English composer other than Elgar, and one is left wondering if the 'national school' had a membership of more than one.

Other writers were more sceptical of the idea of a national school based around Elgar. Writing in 1902, Otto Lessmann commented that English music was largely characterised by composers who knew 'an impressive amount about the arts of counterpoint', but the conceptual material of whose works was of poor quality.[25] As the 'coming man' for English music, Elgar was the one composer capable of 'rescu[ing] the compositional spirit of his countrymen from the retarding fetters [*hemmenden Banden*] of a tradition that has been cultivated for far too long'. In particular, Elgar offered an originality that even the best of his English rivals, Parry, lacked. Lessmann praised Parry for his skilful writing in *Blest Pair of Sirens*, but complained that 'an individual personality [did] not speak in this music'. By contrast, Elgar, in 'draw[ing] from his own depth of feeling [*Gemütstiefe*]', was the 'only one' in English music who 'recently has had the courage to be and remain himself'. Parry, Lessmann claimed, could only be at best the 'link' [*Bindgelied*] between Elgar and lesser English composers. To be cast as the intermediary implicitly linked Parry to what Lessmann described as the 'scholasticism' of post-Mendelssohnian nineteenth-century English music. Elgar had freed himself from this school of composition; he had not yet, however, created any alternative school.

Quite what Elgar's originality consisted of remains a moot point when we consider that Lessmann praised the English composer for 'throw[ing] open mind and heart, to the achievements which the mighty tone masters of the century now ebbed away, have left us as a heritage for the one to come'.[26] The implication is that Elgar had joined the European mainstream in writing in a post-Wagnerian, post-Brahmsian, implicitly German idiom. Other critics made this point explicitly. In commenting that Elgar's teachers 'were and remain the works of our great [German] masters', Fritz Volbach noted that Elgar was aware of the dramatic potential of post-Wagnerian chromaticism, citing a particular example from *Lohengrin* with which Elgar was familiar.[27] Hugo Conrat, too, noted that, as a modern composer, Elgar 'naturally follows the path which Wagner has shown the world'.[28] Hehemann, meanwhile, observed that Elgar was a 'child of his time' in lacking the 'plasticity of invention of a Beethoven or a Wagner', but this did not stop him from claiming, after the German-language premiere of *Gerontius* at Düsseldorf in December 1901, that 'Elgar is entitled to live as one of us' [*hat Elgar Heimatreich bei uns*].[29] Elgar's work found itself incorporated into broader German cultural discourse: in claiming that Judas's suicide in *The Apostles* was a 'companion piece' [*Seitenstück*] to the scene in Goethe's *Faust* when the remorseful Gretchen kneels at the altar, Volbach linked Elgar's oratorio with a work at the centre of the German literary canon.[30] Even the personality of the composer could be 'teutonified': Conrat felt that Elgar lacked characteristic English reserve, and could easily be mistaken 'for a captain in the Austrian army'.[31]

Yet, perhaps paradoxically, all these critics could view Elgar as a recognisably English composer as well as part of pan-German culture. Conrat began his article with a description of the rolling hills and valleys of rural England in which Elgar had grown up; Volbach emphasised that Elgar 'came from a family of purely Anglo-Saxon blood'; and although Hehemann acknowledged that in *Gerontius* 'Elgar's nationality has [. . .] left the least mark', he added that this is the case only 'superficially' [*äusserlich*].[32] Such apparent inconsistencies merely illustrate the widespread belief of the period that the artists who most merited *international* attention by implication also epitomised their own nation. Since a composer's work was underpinned by the strength of his sincerity, a truly sincere composer would necessarily evince his own national traditions in his work. Thus Elgar was admired in Germany for being, apparently, the deus ex machina of English music, but this construction was partly a result of his international appeal, which, in turn, was 'proof' of his '*echt*-Englishness'. Paradoxically, however, that international appeal, particularly in a period when German was the lingua franca of European music, meant Elgar could be appropriated quite easily into German culture, thus 'denationalising' him.

Catholicism

Matters of nationality and national culture are somewhat complicated when we consider Elgar's Catholicism, a matter which some English critics felt to be at odds with the very idea of Englishness.[33] For critics such as Hehemann, however, Catholicism provided Elgar with his individual muse: 'The more stimulating the Catholic ritual [*Kultus*] is than another for the fantasy of the artist, the richer the artistic material it gives him, and the more vivid the ideas.' Indeed, it was in *Gerontius* that 'Elgar's style managed to achieve its fullest independence, with a romantic-mystical atmosphere of the sort we feel in old churches, which a delicate waft of incense [*ein zarter Hauch von Weihrauchduft*] has never left'.[34] Yet this stylistic independence meant that it was in *Gerontius* that Elgar's nationality 'superficially, left the least mark': here the composer 'found generally human subject-matter, and its strange Catholic mysticism allows the national colouring of the music naturally to take second place, even if it never denies itself in any bar'.[35] Hehemann thus tries to get the best of both worlds: Elgar's national qualities were not overtly apparent in *Gerontius*, but they were still present, as they would have had to be for Hehemann's theory about Elgar being at the centre of a national school of composition to carry any credibility.

Otto Neitzel preferred to see in Elgar the conjoining of the separate cultures of the composer's nationality and his faith. 'It seems', Neitzel observed, 'as if England's atmosphere, which encourages the strengthening of the individual, may have aroused a protestantising desire for exploration [*eine protestantisierende Erforschungslust*] in the Catholic.' Elgar thus appears to be a Catholic exponent of a Protestant English cultural tradition that was underpinned by ideas of critical enquiry and progress. Significantly, perhaps, Neitzel's comments were directed not at *Gerontius*, but at *The Apostles*, a denominational hybrid within whose Protestant-like evangelising he could still discern – and criticise – a Catholic devoutness that appeared to obscure the musical argument:

A further characteristic feature of *The Apostles* is the preference for mystical Catholic contemplation, on which Elgar likes to dwell, and of which he has already given so much evidence in the second part of *The Dream of Gerontius* . . . Now those parts of the work devoted to mysticism, however much it lies in the nature of the subject, for the most part get somewhat spineless, and the outlines of the musical form run the frequent risk of becoming blurred through the solemnity and grandeur of expression.[36]

More intriguingly, however, in an earlier article Neitzel claimed that *Gerontius* was 'called into life directly or indirectly by the example of Richard Strauss', specifically *Tod und Verklärung*, despite the fact that Elgar had not heard the tone poem when he wrote *Gerontius*.[37] Admittedly, the resultant links between Strauss and Cardinal Newman were only a consequence of their sharing 'the same airborne spores [*der gleichen Keime, welche zuweilen in der Luft fliegen*], creating what we call a meeting of "Great Minds" [*"Schöner Geister"*]'.[38] But the significance of this is that Elgar, once again, is simultaneously linked to two cultural traditions: that of English Catholicism and, more importantly for Neitzel, that of Strauss's post-*Parsifal*-ian transfiguration.[39] *Gerontius* is viewed as part of contemporary secular discourse on dying, a procession from earthly life to eternal paradise in which Newman's decision to 'guide only his hero's last moments completely into the influence of the Catholic faith' was as valid as Strauss's 'solemn but short entry into Elysium'.[40] Like the agnostic British critic Ernest Newman, who declared that *Gerontius* was 'alive with that humanity that is above and beyond theology', Neitzel plays down the creative input of the composer's faith in his most avowedly Catholic work: because it addressed contemporary concerns about the hereafter in general, *Gerontius* was deemed to have transcended its theological origins.[41] Elgar and his work are effectively de-Catholicised, once more recontextualised as part of German (and by implication international) musical discourse.

Volbach

For Hehemann and Neitzel, Elgar's Catholicism and Elgar's English qualities coexisted in an uneasy creative dialectic. For Fritz Volbach, however, Catholicism provided the key to understanding Elgar, his works, and his relationship to English art in general. Nowhere was this more apparent than in Elgar's relationship to Turner. In a visit to the National Gallery with the composer in 1902, Volbach, referring to a seascape by Turner before which he 'had a similar sense as when hearing *Gerontius*', had said 'That is Elgar'; Elgar's reply to this was 'Yes, I like it best of all.' Recalling this episode, Volbach's son Walther argued that this reflected a mystical manner of thought on Elgar's part that was Catholic-inspired, and that it was the 'common sense of mysticism, usual with Catholics' that had drawn Elgar and his father together.[42]

It is tempting to agree with Walther Volbach's conclusion, particularly when one remembers that the second of his father's articles about Elgar appeared in a Catholic periodical, *Hochland*. In that article, Volbach senior strongly emphasised the Catholic mysticism of *Gerontius*, writing that '[t]he entire magic of the deepest, innermost mysticism . . . and a blessedness and depth of being, which we experience best in the transfigured representations of visionary experience by the likes of Suso, express themselves in this poem'.[43] There is more to this than meets the eye. Heinrich Suso (*c.* 1295–1366) was a pupil of Meister Eckhart (*c.* 1260–1328), the greatest of the Rhenish mystics of the fourteenth century. These mystics were Dominican friars, who provided religious instruction for pious, non-monastic women, known as beguines, most of whom knew no Latin. Consequently, the friars had to deliver their sermons in German, a task made harder by the fact that there *was* no single German language then, merely a number of spoken dialects, none of which possessed the technical vocabulary to express abstract theological terms. The friars therefore had to 'improvise' these terms. These improvisations were the first attempt to express abstract concepts in German, with the result that Eckhart can be (and, during the nineteenth century, often was) seen as one of the founding fathers of German philosophy.[44] Indeed, insofar as a formalisation of language fosters national identity, Eckhart can even be considered an important precursor of German national consciousness.[45]

It is somewhat ironic, then, that the popularity Eckhart and Suso enjoyed in the early years of the Second Reich, the ultimate realisation of that consciousness, was because their mystical writings represented an anti-modernist challenge to the scepticism and rationalism that had emerged from the German Protestant cultural tradition of which they were among the progenitors.[46] But it perhaps emphasises the extent to which 'mysticism' had acquired a somewhat broader definition by the beginning of the twentieth century. Volbach's own writing provides good examples of this. In his *Hochland* article, Elgar and Turner are presented as capable of penetrating the phenomenal world and reaching an ideal, mystical reality: their relationship was 'striking [*in die Augen springend*] as far as the objectives and the manner of expression of their art are concerned'. However, the nature of their mysticism differed: whereas Elgar 'express[ed] the inexpressible' in *Gerontius* through his 'deepest religious feeling', Turner's paintings displayed the 'deepened, pantheistic conception of the mystery of nature' [*vertieften pantheistischen Naturauffassung*].[47] Here, 'mysticism' has simply become synonymous with 'spiritual'. It has this meaning, too, in Volbach's *Allgemeine Musik-Zeitung* article, when the author writes that '[t]he representation of mystical, incomprehensible moods is Elgar's domain. His work is pervaded by an atmosphere of half-light, as it reigns in Gothic cathedrals, an atmosphere of mysterious premonition.'[48] The reference to Gothic cathedrals means that 'mysticism' now involves a sense of spiritual union with a particular place and/or the distant past. It was this sense that underpinned Volbach's conception both of Elgar and of Englishness.

For Volbach, Elgar was the musical heir to a particular tradition of great English poets and artists that included not only Turner, but also Robert Browning ('a favourite of Elgar's and a relative in feeling and form'), Constable, Gainsborough, and Reynolds.[49] This tradition was hardly 'mystical' in the Catholic sense, but it was certainly mystical in spirit, whether via Turner's pantheism or via the landscapes of Constable and Gainsborough. In particular, the mystical relationship of English creative artists to their native countryside (a matter of interest for German critics for some years, particularly in literary genres) is here implicitly extended into music.[50] Consequently, long before there was any talk of an English pastoral school in music, an English composer was named heir to an artistic tradition that is characterised by its representation of the English land. However, by implicitly comparing Elgar with Constable and Gainsborough, and thus linking him to a non-urban England of yesteryear, Volbach appears to be promoting a vision of Englishness, and English art, that reacts against modernity, rather than embraces it. In apparently embodying this vision, Elgar and his works therefore become politicised as anti-modernist paradigms in exactly the same way that Suso's works had become politicised in contemporary German sociocultural debate.

We can see this in the way that Volbach demonstrates how his mystical image of Englishness can operate in music, even in that most English of genres, the oratorio. Unlike Lessmann or, implicitly, Hehemann, he does not tie Elgar to a particular English musical tradition. Instead, Volbach considers Elgar to be the third great member of a sublime, epic tradition of oratorio-writing that had begun with Handel, was revitalised by Liszt in such works as *Christus* (1856–66) and *St Elizabeth* (1858–62), but which consciously excluded Mendelssohn. The idea that oratorio should be a sublime epic genre, rather than a more earthbound dramatic one, was, Volbach claimed, one that none of Handel's successors, 'least of all Mendelssohn', was capable of grasping. By contrast, with Liszt, 'as with Handel, we feel the nearness of God'; Elgar's works too 'were held together by the idea of the invisible Divine and Sublime'.[51] Elgar therefore represented a fusion of the 'true' mystical values of Handelian oratorio with the mysticism inherent in English art.

But this raises some uncomfortable conclusions. The kernel of Volbach's mystical English artistic tradition was its nature imagery and, in Elgar's case,

Catholicism: a conservative vision, which implicitly excluded any diversity of cultures and faiths. Volbach was writing in a country which often defined its essential Germanness in explicitly rural terms, as a reaction to the perceived evils and injustices of modern cities. In particular, given the widespread association of urban capitalism with Jewishness, we can argue that a national culture founded on rural imagery, exemplified by a Roman Catholic composer, and as dismissive of a Jewish composer as Volbach was of Mendelssohn, was, at the very least, couched in terms similar to those used by anti-Semitic cultural commentators of the period.[52] This construction of Elgar would have made him highly palatable to Volbach's more reactionary Catholic readers, but, for that reason, it can be seen as a projection of Englishness that mirrored certain current constructions of 'Deutschtum' rather than as an explanation of Elgar's place within English culture.

Volbach's writing underlines the extent to which German perceptions of Elgar and English music depended on how they were constructed by individual critics. There was no fixed opinion about what constituted 'Englishness' in music, merely that it was inherent in Elgar's individuality of style; this, in turn, reflected standards of taste in German music of the period. Consequently, Elgar was viewed not only as the man to revitalise English music, but as an English response to the nineteenth-century Germanic canon, and thus as a subject for critical enquiry within the multifarious discourses on that canon. These discourses were not ideologically neutral, but reflected partisan political positions within contemporary cultural debate. Thus rather than striving to find one overarching German view of Elgar, we should be aiming instead to contextualise the various discourses within which criticism of his works took place. By doing so, we can refine our understanding of how Elgar and his music were received by German audiences of the early twentieth century.

16 Functional music: imperialism, the Great War, and Elgar as popular composer

CHARLES EDWARD McGUIRE

As Edward Elgar's compositions for imperial ceremonies and the First World War have specific functions (royal celebrations, marching music, rallying cries, and charitable offerings), they can be considered together within an analysis.[1] The compositions share a number of characteristics: none is abstract in nature, Elgar composed many of them to sound specifically 'popular', and none can claim 'secret' or 'hidden' meanings, like the 'Enigma' Variations or the Violin Concerto. In the period before the war, these compositions solidified Elgar's reputation as an important national figure. During the war, they aptly represented the complex difficulties individual Britons faced from the violence and carnage of battle. After the war, they placed Elgar in the forefront of society as an official ceremonial figure. They allowed him to represent a musical tradition rapidly declining throughout elite Great Britain, but prominent in middle-class quarters. These works were inspirational in their own time, and many are still rousing today. As important examples of period pieces, they show Elgar transcending the limits of concert music to successfully negotiate popular forms.

Throughout this chapter, 'popular' describes music that might be easily disseminated, might be performed in non-elite contexts and venues (bandstands, rallies, music-halls, the London Coliseum, etc.), or might have been written by Elgar to garner a broad audience. A close analogy to this type of composition would be Beethoven's *Wellingtons Sieg* (or 'Battle Symphony'), a potboiler meant to capture timely sentiment. Elgar often designed his 'functional' music to be popular through concentrating on broad styles of composition, including singable melody as opposed to motivic transformation.[2] But while Elgar hoped his popular compositions would find their way into multiple venues (as the *Pomp and Circumstance* Marches did), he composed his functional works with a specific purpose or commission in mind (including *The Banner of St George*, composed to celebrate Queen Victoria's jubilee year).

It is important to note that in no essential way does Elgar's popular and functional music for Empire and the First World War differ from the rest of his output. There is no great divide between the serious, abstract Elgar of the symphonies, concertos, and chamber music; the dramatic Elgar of the programme music and choral pieces; and the jubilant Elgar of the marches, war music, and imperial compositions. These compositions include some uninspired moments, to be sure. But they also contain some of his best melodies and his most poignant drama. As such they deserve a great deal of further enquiry and further hearings.

Yet an analysis of this group of compositions must surmount two potential pitfalls. First, Elgar composed a number of works in the First World War or immediately thereafter which are neither popular nor functional, such as the escapist incidental music for *The Starlight Express* and the ballet *The Sanguine Fan*, and must therefore be excluded from this discussion.[3] While *The Sanguine Fan* was used within a charity concert, each is related to the larger issue of wartime and imperial composition only by its place in Elgar's biography. Similarly, while the late chamber music and the Cello Concerto have their roots within Elgar's own wartime experiences, direct relation to the functional work of the group of compositions is slight.[4] To avoid an unwieldy sample of material, the present study will not consider these works, focusing instead on those works written for imperial and wartime functions.

Second, this group of compositions, more than any other within Elgar's oeuvre, frequently engenders great controversy, and has always done so. August Jaeger, Elgar's friend and agent for his publisher Novello, famously complained about the ending chorus of *Caractacus*, noting that it was too overbearingly patriotic.[5] Such criticism often took shape from its context. The pejorative view of Elgar as popular and jingoistic in the 1920s and 1930s and again in the late 1980s epitomised the backlash against the damage and loss of the First World War and the advent of post-colonial studies.[6] One reaction to this hyper-patriotic Elgar was a vision of him rejecting imperialism as seen in such works as Michael Kennedy's 1968 *Portrait of Elgar*, which ahistorically attempted to divorce Elgar from anything as authoritarian and paternalistic as Empire.[7] The equally problematic stance of the 'Good Empire' and Elgar as supporting and incorporating all of the seemingly chivalric, 'good' qualities of Empire ('Truth and Right and Freedom', in the recent words of James Day)[8] was similarly a blanket statement, which grew only in the peace and Western prosperity of the late 1990s.[9] It remains to be seen in the increasingly balkanised critical world following 11 September 2001 which vision of empire – and of Elgar – will win out.

Accepting Elgar's complex and often contradictory character transcends the binary oppositions (jingoistic versus rationally imperial; abstract versus functional music; and elite versus popular music) of most criticism of his work. All sides selectively present evidence of Elgar embracing or dismissing the army, imperialism, and the propaganda of the Great War. We are so used to the final images of Elgar – the overstuffed, philistine Colonel

Bogey[10] – that an adequate understanding of the composer's challenging rise to fame is nearly impossible within current discourse. We look to certain aspects of Elgar's character, such as his struggle against religious and class prejudice, his hypochondria, his sensitivity, and his profound mood-swings; and we use them to fashion a nineteenth-century narrative of the artist-hero, which Elgar certainly was not. He did struggle throughout his life, but many of those struggles were of his own making, especially after 1910. These contradictions, unstable as they made him, were part of the great power behind his compositions. It is thus easy to forget that Elgar achieved one of his own most basic goals – international recognition within his own time – before he was fifty. This accomplishment was possible because of Elgar's own proclivities, namely his enthusiastic, almost boyish love of technology and ceremony, and the historical chance of the explosive growth of native English music when elite artistic culture was still widely reported within the press and consumed by the middle classes.

Processional: before the Great War

Seeking national recognition throughout his career, Elgar took advantage of a number of directives and commissions for ceremonial music when they came his way. Just before the onset of his fame, Elgar completed two at the request of Novello for Queen Victoria's jubilee year: the *Imperial March* and *The Banner of St George*, the former a tuneful march and the latter a semi-narrative ballad. These compositions were premiered in the spring of 1897. Of the two, the *Imperial March* was more successful and was swiftly performed throughout London. Immediately after its Crystal Palace premiere (19 April), it was heard at the Queen's Hall, an official Jubilee royal garden party, the Albert Hall, a state concert, and the Three Choirs Festival. This minor sensation was enough to keep Elgar's name both in the press and in the minds of both the palace and the middle class.

Within the next few years, Elgar had real compositional triumphs with the 'Enigma' Variations and the first two *Pomp and Circumstance* Marches. *The Dream of Gerontius* was also well on its way to becoming a great success. This popular acclaim led to 'state' functional compositions. He completed the *Coronation Ode* (text by A. C. Benson) for the coronation of Edward VII, including within it the tune from the *Pomp and Circumstance* march in D major set to words, as *Land of Hope and Glory*. At the London premiere on 26 October 1902, the audience became so enthusiastic at hearing this tune that it was encored.[11] The first strain as cast by Benson celebrated an expanding British Empire in no uncertain terms:

> Land of Hope and Glory, Mother of the Free,
> How shall we extol thee, who are born of thee?
> Truth and right and freedom, each a holy gem,
> Stars of solemn brightness, weave thy diadem![12]

The celebratory text had an immediate appeal, and fed Elgar's growing fame.

Elgar's recognition soon went beyond such commissions. He received many official honours, beginning with the award of a doctorate by Cambridge University in 1900, continuing with his knighthood and appointment as Peyton Professor at the University of Birmingham in 1904, the award of the Freedom of the City of Worcester as well as doctorates from Oxford and Yale in 1905, and a doctorate from the University of Aberdeen in 1906. While Elgar was certainly not the first composer to be given such commissions and honours in Great Britain, the speed of his accession to fame thrust him into an international spotlight and gave him power to promote various political and musical causes.[13]

Thus it was only natural that Elgar, whose popular and political stance reflected the great optimism of the Edwardian era, should be the composer chosen to commemorate the 1911 Delhi Durbar. This high point of the British monarch's tour of India adapted a Mogul ceremony in order to consolidate and legitimise his authority. The masque was premiered at the London Coliseum in March 1912. The text, by Henry Hamilton, justifies George V's rule over India by dramatising his choice between Delhi and Calcutta as India's capital, and re-enacting the Durbar, a fealty ceremony. Elgar's music – close to an hour's worth – became immediately popular because of its tuneful celebratory nature.[14] It remained so long after its Coliseum run: Elgar conducted a small suite drawn from the Masque at the Three Choirs Festival at Hereford in 1912; the BBC broadcast parts of the work over a hundred times between 1923 and 1934; and Boosey & Co. published numerous scores and arrangements from it. Elgar also recorded part of the work with the London Symphony Orchestra in 1930. As Corissa Gould notes, '*The Crown of India* not only gave [Elgar] the kind of commercial success he had been striving for, it also provided definite proof of the popularity of his music and his status as a composer.'[15] *The Crown of India* is an excellent statement of Elgar's own paternalistic beliefs about the British Empire in the pre-war era – for instance, Elgar opposes the Indian princes' clumsy 3/2 march to the 'tuneful diatonicism and stately pomp' of the British administrators; music for Britain is also largely diatonic, and music for the colony is chromatic.[16] Elgar used such methods throughout his career to oppose antagonists to protagonists in his dramatic works.

With these larger compositions, plus a small handful of others (including a few part-songs such as 'Follow the Colours' and 'Reveille'), Elgar steadily rose in popular and cultural appeal. If his compositions were sometimes seen as vulgar, they were also increasingly populist, and worked well to represent the ideals of a nation at the peak of its world power.[17] As we shall see, the Great War and its aftermath would drastically change both this power and Elgar's role as its symbol and promoter.

Sir Edward sees it through: charity music of the First World War

Elgar's music during the war is often seen as necessary for the time, but insignificant in comparison to the rest of his work.[18] Others have remarked that despite the will, 'nothing great' issued from Elgar's pen in this period. According to these critics, at a time when the nation most needed him to offer inspiration, Elgar failed utterly.[19] Such assessments are fair neither to Elgar nor to history, for the First World War was not a musical war, but the last great literary one.[20] With the explosion of printing technology in the nineteenth century, near-instantaneous newspaper production meant that news from the front took less time than ever before to reach the eyes of those at home. As a literate nation, Great Britain responded with a flood of amateur and professional poetry and novels. Music was hard-pressed to compete. Those works capturing the public's attention were either popular pieces like 'A Long Way to Tipperary', 'Land of Hope and Glory', or well-loved Germanic music.[21]

While such trends are easily seen in hindsight, Elgar the public figure reacted in a visceral manner at the beginning of the war, using his public position to aid the national effort. Tempering his initial disappointment at being too old to serve,[22] he immediately threw himself into the role of home guard soldier, becoming first a Special Constable in Hampstead, and later a member of the Hampstead Volunteer Reserve.[23] As the war continued, he lent his fame to other public projects, including membership of the General Committee for Formation of Recruiting Bands, and accepting honorary offices of soldiers' institutions, such as the Cologne YMCA.[24] Publicised German atrocities in Belgium and Poland engendered easy musical responses, with works such as the frequently-performed *Carillon* (1914) and *Polonia* (1915). Elgar completed the former, a melodrama with orchestral accompaniment, at the end of 1914, to place in an anthology of poetry, art, and music titled *King Albert's Book*.[25] At the behest of Emil Mlynarsky, Elgar composed *Polonia*, a small symphonic prelude that uses folk- and art-music quotations from Polish national themes, to raise money for the Polish Victims Relief Committee.

Such charity compositions display Elgar's engagement with national culture, but increasingly Elgar's war music competed with his earlier compositions. As Ernest Newman presciently stated, Elgar's *Pomp and Circumstance* March in D was 'a vigorous, bracing piece of music, full of the animal spirits that one would expect to be of irresistible appeal to the soldier'.[26] A popular composition, it only became more popular as the war continued, from its presentation at the Queen's Hall billed with the premiere of *Sospiri* on 15 August 1914 to its impromptu crowd performance during an air-raid as *Land of Hope and Glory* on 27 September 1917. But Elgar was unable to sustain such success. Caught between the initial world-cleansing rhetoric of the war's leaders, and young Britain's anger at the 'Old Lie' of selfless nobility and sacrifice, Elgar could please neither. With the exception of *The Starlight Express*, he could not embrace the pastoral identity of the popular war poets and home-front novelists. Nor could he join the march into abstract art of Lord Beaverbrook's Ministry of Information.[27] Instead, he presented a number of polished compositions that were patronised especially by the older generation. This generation included both Newman, whose contemporary positioning of Elgar far above the German avant-garde would fuel the younger generation's rejection of Elgar in the 1920s; and the Lords of the Admiralty, who supported *The Fringes of the Fleet* in its initial public performances at the London Coliseum. And while his recordings made it to the trenches in France, soldiers praised not his current military or charity works, but escapist ones like *The Starlight Express*.[28]

Elgar best gauged national mood in *The Spirit of England*. This composition is a setting of three poems from *The Winnowing Fan* by Laurence Binyon, a poet, dramatist, and art historian. These poems typify popular early-war poetry: they juxtapose the war in terms of 'the grandeur' of England's 'fate', its heritage, and the righteousness of the cause with natural images of the countryside. The subjects of two of the poems, 'For the Fallen' and 'To Women', focus on the plight of those on the home front. 'The Fourth of August' glorifies the present soldiers through invoking the 'glorious dead' who 'battled that we might be free', mapping traditional tropes of England as a land of 'Truth and Right and Freedom' on to the conflict.

In completing the setting, Elgar faced two major difficulties. As Binyon's poems were popular, other composers strove to set them. Early in 1915, the Cambridge composer Cyril Bradley Rootham forwarded a setting of 'For the Fallen' to Novello, causing Elgar to delay completing his own setting of this poem. Nevertheless it was performed, together with 'To Women', on 3 May 1916. At the urging of friends, and perhaps bolstered by the critical success of his two completed settings, Elgar turned to completing 'The Fourth of August' during 1916.[29] While some of his earlier war works came out in a white heat, completing this setting occupied Elgar until April 1917.

Part of Elgar's difficulty completing the composition stemmed from the poem's sixth verse:

> She fights the fraud that feeds desire on
> Lies, in a lust to enslave or kill,
> The barren creed of blood and iron,
> Vampire of Europe's wasted will . . .

Out of the seven verses Elgar set, this is the only one that does not discuss either the grandeur of nature or the nobility of the British forces. In his mind, it was aimed at Germany. Possibly Elgar's great disappointment with German behaviour during the war or his knowledge of his own professional debt to German musicians inhibited him from creating new music to represent Binyon's threat to British civilisation.[30] Instead, Elgar used part of the Demon music from *The Dream of Gerontius*. But this use illustrates the great pity Elgar felt for the destruction of his pre-war world and the banality into which he assumed German culture had descended. He noted that

> the Hun is branded as less than a beast for many generations . . . A lunatic asylum is, after the first shock, not entirely sad; so few patients are aware of the strangeness of their situation; most of them are placid & foolishly calm; but the horror of the fallen intellect – *knowing* what it once was & *knowing* what it has become – is beyond words frightful.[31]

In this way Elgar could salvage his continuing respect for the Germany he once knew as a beacon of musical culture.

Novello and others promoted *The Spirit of England* as the grand response to the war by Great Britain's greatest living composer. Newman wrote long analyses about it for the *Musical Times*.[32] Novello undertook a massive advertisement campaign and a review of the premiere of the last two numbers as part of a charity concert organised by frequent Elgarian singer, Clara Butt; early announcements characterise it as 'A Remarkable Scheme'.[33] Following Newman's lengthy analysis, an enthusiastic, almost fawning review testified to the great power of the last movement:

> It was heard by many with tears and emotion born of the poignancy of the words and the wonderful appeal of the music. Surely this solemn inspiration of poet and composer is the nearest approach we have by way of a British Requiem for our fallen soldiers and sailors![34]

Notices of the 'complete' work (with the first movement intact) were given similar treatment; the *Musical Times* excerpted a long, laudatory review by Newman in the *Birmingham Daily Post*.[35] After the war it became a regular feature of Armistice Day celebrations throughout Great Britain, and was broadcast by the BBC at least six times during Elgar's life.[36]

If *The Spirit of England* was a serious 'British Requiem', capable of moving many in a concert hall to tears through its potency, *The Fringes of the Fleet*, a setting of four poems by Elgar's great contemporary Rudyard Kipling, was an entr'acte 'in broad saltwater style'.[37] The first two largely syllabic songs are infectiously jaunty. They offer typical examples of the public face of the war, with references to sport and male camaraderie – which Elgar makes explicit through frequent call-and-response figures between the male soloist and mostly unison male trio response. 'Submarines', the third of the four songs, is an exquisite example of minimal means and maximum effect. Elgar set much of the song to an ostinato, over which the baritone sings a simple minor triad (Ex. 16.1). Such seriousness might have become maudlin or even melodramatic, but in Elgar's hands, the poem is a matter-of-fact presentation of the daily risk of death that submariners faced ('The ships destroy us above/And ensnare us beneath'). Even the climax for the submarine's successful strike, a sustained D on the word 'dies', remains relentlessly realistic – the orchestra slips down a fifth with a mixture of diatonic and chromatic steps, evoking the sinking of the submarine's target. The fourth song, 'The Sweepers', returns to the call-and-response style of the first two songs, but does so in a serious G minor, echoed by an almost recitation-tone quality for 'Mines located in the fairway,/Boats now working up the chain' and analogous places (Ex. 16.2). As popular songs – their execution, small tessituras, and limited chromaticism make them so – they are effective. Occasional flashes of shanty-like sounds (especially in the first and last pieces) give them a sense of nostalgia. *Fringes* was premiered on 11 June 1917 at the London Coliseum, with Elgar conducting, and was presented with the four voices in costume as 'brawny and weatherworn mariners . . . before a rural rustic pub'; the composition was so successful that at the end of its Coliseum performances, it toured the provinces, and was quickly recorded.[38] Elgar even added a fifth song to the cycle, 'Inside the Bar' (to a text by Sir Gilbert Parker), to capitalise on this success.

Contemporary critics recognised the composition's popularity. Unlike *The Spirit of England*, which tapped official emotions and grieving, *Fringes* gave practical licence to the stoical sailors pictured within. It was a quiet celebration, and some reviewers posited a new sort of 'improving' popularity from it – music that reached beyond the words it set:

> The little cycle cannot of course be said to show the greater gifts of the Elgar we know. But it shows him in a vein familiar yet distinguished: alert, vigorous, and at times finely imaginative. It is popular, but popular in the good sense of the word. Further, we were of course prepared to find the composer entering fully into the patriotic spirit of one who has long stood for a new Imperialism in poetry. Elgar, to some degree, has stood for the same in music. But here he has done more; he has grappled successfully with the strange and glamorous Kipling spirit, which can draw strong lurid poetry out of a soldier's and sailor's slang, out of the very mechanism and technicalities of war. Best of all, where Kipling sometimes fails, through jerky mannerism or mere mechanical neatness, Elgar's music upholds him with its manly austerity and its breadth and dignity of conception.[39]

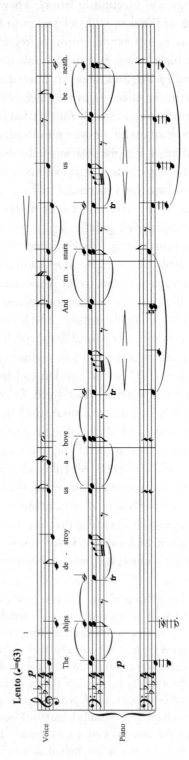

Example 16.1 Elgar (Kipling), *The Fringes of the Fleet*, 'Submarines', bb. 2–5

Example 16.2 Elgar (Kipling), *The Fringes of the Fleet*, 'The Sweepers', bb. 19–20

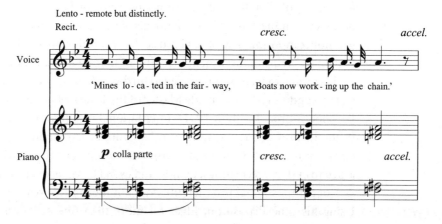

Even within a wartime hierarchy critics strove to find a higher purpose in contemplating Elgar's popular works. In this case, that higher purpose was to improve Kipling's imperial, patriotic words. Even if the people would no longer need the same sort of comfort in the new world beyond the confines of the Great War, they would desire Elgar's music to help them understand that world.

Recessional: after the First World War

An ageing composer, increasingly identified with the old men the Great War left behind, Elgar could easily have receded in importance in the celebrations and official functions of the post-war period. In terms of compositional output alone, this might at first seem to be the case. Within this period, there are only two new major works to consider: the memorial *With Proud Thanksgiving*, redacted from *The Spirit of England* and originally composed for the unveiling of the memorial Cenotaph in 1920, and *The Pageant of Empire*, songs and incidental music for a massed public demonstration of imperial unity at Wembley. As Robert Anderson notes, Elgar was featured prominently within this exhibition; out of eighty compositions performed, Elgar had written twenty. These works spanned his functional career from the distant past (the *Imperial March* and *Land of Hope and Glory*) to the present, including some music written specifically for the occasion.[40] Elgar's fame offered him a sure place in these proceedings. With the growth of recording and broadcasting technology, Elgar's imperial and war compositions found their way further into the British consciousness; multiple broadcasts of *The Banner of St George*, the *Imperial March*, the *Pomp and Circumstance* Marches, the *Crown of India* suite, *Carillon*, *The Spirit of England*, and the

Pageant of Empire filled the airwaves in the 1920s and early 1930s.[41] Performances of 'For the Fallen' from *The Spirit of England* were a regular occurrence at the Three Choirs Festivals of the same period.[42] Even if Elgar was not composing new official music, he was still the official face of Great Britain – a living embodiment of a kind of nostalgic English identity.

Becoming that embodiment led to further official recognition, including state recognition (he was made Master of the King's Music in 1924 and first Baronet of Broadheath in 1931), international recognition (he was elected to the Institut de France and given La Croix de Commandeur de l'Ordre de la Couronne of Belgium in 1920), and commercial recognition (he was asked to endorse recordings, pianos, and even Du Maurier cigarettes).[43] His lack of compositional productivity does not mean these years were wasted. Using his official position, Elgar on more than one occasion advocated increased public funding of music and sought opportunities to use emerging technology to promote music.[44] Technology responded through lavish recording contracts. Even though Elgar's recordings posted a loss in 1921, His Master's Voice renewed Elgar's contract, paying him £500 per annum for three years, because '[Elgar's] name would be of inestimable value to any other Company'.[45] To the insecure individual who yearns always for notice, this public acceptance must have been ambrosia. Such honours were reserved for the privileged few of Elgar's time, and should not compromise his legacy today. Elgar *was* a man of his time. He composed music for its functioning political institutions, he paid homage to its politics, and he believed in its ideals. Even if we question those ideals today, the music he wrote to encompass them is still an important part of his development and our common history.

Notes

Chapter 1

1. For a detailed account of the elaboration, see Anthony Payne, *Elgar's Third Symphony: The Story of the Reconstruction* (London: Faber, 1998). When the symphony was first broadcast, the present writer (JR), with no score to hand, found he could follow most of it from the sketches published in W. H. Reed's memoir, *Elgar as I Knew Him* (London: Gollancz, 1936). The elaboration was intended as a pre-emptive strike, since from the expiry of copyright in 2005 the published sketches (there are others) would enter the public domain; Payne's work, it was hoped, might inhibit anyone else minded, in Elgar's word, to 'tinker' with the symphony. Only time will tell if this strategy was successful.

2. Among memoirs the most indispensable include Basil Maine's biography (vol. I of *Elgar. His Life and Works* (London: G. Bell, 1933)); W. H. Reed, *Elgar as I Knew Him*; Mrs Richard Powell, *Edward Elgar: Memories of a Variation* (London: Oxford University Press, 1937); Rosa Burley (with Frank Carruthers), *Edward Elgar: The Record of a Friendship* (London: Barrie and Jenkins, 1972); the less formally organised recollections of many other friends including Hubert Leicester and Troyte Griffith; and the narrative interwoven round letters by Elgar's godson, E. Wulstan Atkins, in *The Elgar–Atkins Friendship* (London: David and Charles, 1984).

3. See the bibliography and table of bibliographical abbreviations.

4. This Companion normally refers to the collections edited by Jerrold Northrop Moore, *Publishers*, *Lifetime*, and *Windflower*.

5. Letter to August Jaeger, 9 October 1900. *Publishers*, 244.

6. Letter to Sir Sidney Colvin, 13 December 1921. *Lifetime*, 359.

7. Titles were then by no means common for artists, and it was another half-century before honours were regularly offered to sportsmen; popular musicians had to wait still longer. Several twentieth-century British composers were knighted, but not made baronet; only one (Benjamin Britten) became a lord, in his last months of life. Britten and Vaughan Williams are believed to have refused knighthoods; but they, Walton, and Tippett were appointed OM.

8. Bertrand Russell, *Freedom and Organization 1814–1914* (London: G. Allen & Unwin, 1934).

9. Guido Heldt, 'Elgar', in Ludwig Finscher (ed.), *Die Musik in Geschichte und Gegenwart, Personenteil*, vol. VI (Kassel: Bärenreiter, 2001), 227–43; see pp. 238 and 242 (cited). 'Zu den Desideraten der Elgar-Forschung zum gegenwärtigen Zeitpunkt am ehesten Arbeiten zählen, die nicht den Mann oder den nationalen Komponisten in den Blick nehmen, sondern die Musik: Bis auf vereinzelte Versuche sind seine autodidaktischen Lernerfahrungen, ist das Mosaik aus Einflüssen und Modellen nicht kaum angegangen.'

10. Maine, *Elgar*, vol. I, 18. Maine presumably got his information from Elgar and earlier 'authorised' biographies such as that by R. J. Buckley.

11. Diana McVeagh, *Edward Elgar: His Life and Music* (London: J. M. Dent, 1955), 189.

12. Maine, *Elgar*, vol. I, 17. See also Peter Dennison, 'Elgar's Musical Apprenticeship', in Monk, *Studies*, 1–34.

13. Maine, *Elgar*, vol. I, 33–5.

14. *Future*, 237–9.

15. See for instance the third edition of Kennedy, *Portrait*, 31–3; Brian Trowell, 'Elgar's Use of Literature' in Monk, *Literature*, 217–19; Trowell, 'The Road to Brinkwells: The Late Chamber Music', in Foreman (ed.), '*Oh My Horses*': *Elgar and the Great War* (Rickmansworth: Elgar Editions, 2001), 353–62.

16. 20 July 1884; *Lifetime*, 11. Byron Adams is surely mistaken in interpreting this reticence as indifference; it is rather the opposite. 'The "Dark Saying" of the Enigma: Homoeroticism and the Elgarian Paradox', *19th-Century Music* 23/3 (2000), 219.

17. Alice Elgar is one of a select company of composer's wives (including Harriet Smithson Berlioz and Cosima Wagner) who have received independent study. See Percy M. Young, *Alice Elgar: Enigma of a Victorian Lady* (London: Dennis Dobson, 1978).

18. See chapter 3, and *Publishers*.

19. G. B. Shaw, from his semi-detached position as an Irishman, advocated a return to the values of 'absolute music' in older English masters. See for instance Dan H. Laurence (ed.), *Shaw's Music: The Complete Musical Criticism of Bernard Shaw* (London: The Bodley Head, 1981), vol. III, 177–9. On Newman see *Future*, 105–6, and chapters 8 and 11.

20. Jurgen Schaarwächter lists eighty-seven British symphonies from Elgar's birth to 1907, and 332 from 1908 (the year of Elgar's first) to 1957. *Die britische Sinfonie 1914–1945* (Cologne: Dohr, 1995), 434–43.

21. See Michael Kennedy, *The Works of Ralph Vaughan Williams* (London: Oxford University Press, 1964), 129; Ursula Vaughan Williams and Imogen Holst (eds.), *Heirs and Rebels* (London: Oxford University Press, 1959), 50.

22. Reed, *Elgar as I Knew Him*, 109–19; see also chapter 8.

23. Jeremy Crump, 'The Identity of English Music: the Reception of Elgar, 1898–1935', in Robert Colls and Philip Dodd (eds.), *Englishness: Politics and Culture 1880–1920* (London: Croom Helm, 1986), 164–90.

24. Hepokoski: *Sibelius: Symphony No. 5* (Cambridge: Cambridge University Press, 1993), 2–3.

25. See Henri-Louis de la Grange, 'Music about Music in Mahler: Reminiscences, Allusions or Quotations?', in Stephen Hefling (ed.), *Mahler Studies* (Cambridge: Cambridge University Press, 1997), 122–68.

26. Eric Hobsbawm, *The Age of Empire: 1875–1914* (London: Abacus, 1987), 59.

27. Philip Dodd, 'Englishness and National Culture', in Colls and Dodd (eds.), *Englishness: Politics and Culture*, 1.

28. David Cannadine, 'The Context, Performance and Meaning of Ritual: The British Monarchy and the "Invention of Tradition", *c.*1820–1977', in Eric Hobsbawm and Terence Ranger (eds.), *The Invention of Tradition* (Cambridge: Cambridge University Press, 1983), 101–64.

29. Jeffrey Richards, 'Elgar's Empire', in *Music and Empire: Britain 1876–1953* (Manchester: Manchester University Press, 2001), 44–87.

30. A monograph by Matthew Riley, forthcoming, will deal comprehensively with this question.

31. Crump, 'The Identity of English Music', 179–86.

32. Moore, *Elgar*, 34.

33. Ibid., 151.

34. Matthew Riley, 'Rustling Reeds and Lofty Pines: Elgar and the Music of Nature', *19th-Century Music* 26/2 (2002), 155–64. See also Robert Stradling's discussion of the significance of the Severn valley in English music, 'England's Glory: Sensibilities of Place in English Music, 1900–1950', in Andrew Leyshon, David Matless and George Revill (eds.), *The Place of Music* (London: Guilford Press, 1998), 176–96.

35. *Future*, 57.

36. 25 May 1911, quoted in Moore, *Elgar*, 616.

Chapter 2

1. G. Bernard Shaw, 'Sir Edward Elgar', *Music & Letters*, 1 (January 1920), 10.

2. Ernest Walker, *A History of English Music* (Oxford: Oxford University Press, 1907), 299, 306–7.

3. See *Music & Letters* 16/1 (January 1935).

4. Thomas Dunhill, *Sir Edward Elgar* (London: Blackie & Son, 1938).

5. *The Strand Magazine* (May 1904), 541–2.

6. Elgar played in the first violin section when Cowen conducted this symphony at the Three Choirs Festival (Worcester, 1887).

7. *Future*, 33–35, original emphasis.

8. After Elgar returned from London in 1891, his involvement with music and music-making in Worcester increased, at first principally through his friendship with Hugh Blair, then assistant organist at the Cathedral. Blair was conductor of the Worcester Festival Choral Society and Elgar led the orchestra. This collaboration not only involved public concerts but also orchestral services in the cathedral. Blair was the dedicatee of *The Black Knight*, the first executant of the Organ Sonata, and had much to do with the commissioning of *The Light of Life*. Two dedications to Swinnerton Heap – the Organ Sonata and *The Light of Life* – indicate a similar musical interaction. It is also not without significance that the organ works of both Blair and Heap show a marked stylistic deference to the music composed by Elgar in the 1890s.

9. Elgar, 'The College Hall' [3 June 1931], *The Three Pears Magazine* (Worcester, 1931).

10. Mackenzie joined the ducal orchestra in Sondershausen in 1857 at the age of ten and participated in performances of Liszt, Wagner, and Berlioz. He returned to Britain in 1862, studying with Prosper Sainton at the Royal Academy of Music. Much of his orchestral experience at this time was gained by playing in London theatre orchestras.

11. Elgar, 'The College Hall' [3 June 1931], *The Three Pears Magazine* (Worcester, 1931).

12. A measure of Elgar's admiration of Parry at this time is revealed by an account he later related to *The Musical Times* (1 October 1900, 647) in which he replaced Parry's baton with his own before a performance of *Judith* with the Worcester Choral Society on 14 April 1891: 'I played first fiddle then and put my stick on his desk. I wanted to make it immortal.'

13. Kennedy, *Portrait*, 55.

14. Ibid. 47.

15. Letter from Jaeger to Parry, 25 September 1896, Shulbrede Priory.
16. Diary of Sir Hubert Parry, 10 December 1906, Shulbrede Priory. (He may have been affected by Jaeger's description of 'a mosaic of abstract musical ideas'. *The Apostles: Book of Words and Analytical and Descriptive Notes* (London: Novello, 1903), second edition).
17. Ibid., 7 December 1908.
18. Ibid. 13 September 1911.
19. See *The Strand Magazine* (May 1904), 539.
20. See *Lbm* 47902 f. 99; Elgar is also known to have considered including Parry in his scheme for the 'Enigma' Variations (along with Sullivan), though he abandoned the idea after admitting that the variation would have been an exercise in stylistic imitation rather than a 'character' sketch. See Maine, *Elgar*, 101.
21. Letter from Elgar to Parry, [1904], quoted in C. L. Graves, *Hubert Parry* (London, Macmillan, 1926), vol. II, 35.
22. Letter from Elgar to Parry, 30 January 1905, *Lcm.*
23. Elgar, *Future*, 48–9.
24. See A. C. Mackenzie, *A Musician's Narrative* (London: Cassell, 1927), 205.
25. On one occasion only, Stanford conducted *Gerontius*, at Leeds on 22 March 1905, after Elgar had telegraphed to say that he was too ill to conduct. As a Dublin Protestant, Stanford had an inbuilt antipathy to *Gerontius*'s overt Catholic sentiment – one affirmed by his famous verbal outburst 'it stinks of incense' – yet he is also known to have deeply admired the closing section of Part 1.
26. See Jeremy Dibble, *Charles Villiers Stanford: Man and Musician* (Oxford: Oxford University Press, 2002), 313.
27. Ibid., 328.
28. Kennedy, *Portrait*, 156.
29. See Ursula Vaughan Williams and Imogen Holst, *Heirs and Rebels* (London: Oxford University Press, 1959), 11.
30. *Publishers*, 51–2.
31. *Lifetime*, 106.
32. *Publishers*, 492.
33. The role of Bantock and Delius (who became vice-president) is evident from surviving correspondence; see Lionel Carley, *Delius: A Life in Letters 1862–1908* (London: Scolar Press, 1983), 310–13.
34. The works performed at Gloucester in 1922 were Bliss's *Colour Symphony* and Goossens's *Silence* for chorus and orchestra. In later years, Elgar softened in his attitude to Bliss and declared that the latter had been 'one of the very few artists in whom I took an interest' (Arthur Bliss, *As I Remember* (London: Faber & Faber,

1970; revised & enlarged, London: Thames Publishing, 1989), 94. Elgar wrote appreciatively to Bliss to accept the dedication of *Pastorale* (9 May 1929; *Lifetime*, 418).
35. Bax, however, maintained in his autobiography, *Farewell My Youth* (London: Longmans, Green and Co., 1943) 32, that Elgar 'was totally uninterested in, and probably ignorant of, the work of any of his contemporaries or juniors'.
36. *Lifetime*, 382–4.
37. See Vaughan Williams, 'A Musical Autobiography', in Michael Kennedy (ed.), *National Music and Other Essays* (Oxford: Oxford University Press, 1987), 182.
38. H. Hughes, 'Sir E. Elgar on the Music Crisis', *Daily Telegraph* (5 November 1931); *Publishers*, 442.
39. G. Hughes, *Sidelights on a Century of Music (1825–1924)* (London: MacDonald, 1969), 180.

Chapter 3

1. Moore, *Publishers*, 239.
2. Percy A. Scholes, *The Mirror of Music 1844–1944* (London and Oxford: Oxford University Press, 1947), 3.
3. *Publishers*, 6.
4. Ibid., 10.
5. Ibid., 11, 13.
6. Ibid., 32.
7. Ibid., 42.
8. Ibid., 51.
9. Ibid., 595.
10. Jaeger's guides, each entitled 'book of words', were published by Novello in the years of performance, 1900, 1903, and 1906, following guides to *King Olaf* by Joseph Bennett, and *Caractacus* by Herbert Thompson. German versions by Max Hehemann follow Jaeger faithfully; they were also published by Novello.
11. *Publishers*, 272.
12. Ibid., 563–4.
13. Ibid., 582.
14. Ibid., 744.
15. Ibid., 776.
16. Moore, *Elgar on Record: The Composer and the Gramophone* (Oxford: Oxford University Press, 1974), 31, 34.
17. *Publishers*, 830, 831.
18. Ibid., 832–3.
19. Ibid., 873.
20. Ibid., 897.

Chapter 4

1. Anderson, *Elgar*, 149.
2. Maine, *Elgar*, vol. I, 7.
3. Vyvyan Holland, *Time Remembered* (London: Thames and Hudson, 1966), 20.

4. 13 December 1921. *Lifetime*, 359.
5. Young, *Elgar*, 32.
6. *Yorkshire Weekly Post*, July 1912, cited in Young, *Elgar*, 14.
7. The source of Ex. 4.1 is the Jesuit Archive, Mayfair, London, MS 839/2/1.
8. W. R. Mitchell, *The Giggleswick Scores of Edward Elgar* (Settle: Castleberg, 1990), 5–8.
9. *Publishers*, 212.
10. Reed, *Elgar as I Knew Him*, 99.
11. Nancy Price, *Into an Hour Glass* (London: Museum Press, 1953), 212, 216.
12. The instrument is illustrated in Alec Cobbe, *Composer Instruments. A Catalogue of the Cobbe Collection of Keyboard Instruments with Composer Associations* (Hatchlands, 2000), 54–55.
13. Robert J. Buckley, *Sir Edward Elgar*, (London: John Lane, The Bodley Head, 1904) 31.
14. Moore, *Elgar*, 738.
15. Moore, *Elgar on Record*, 208.
16. Maine, *Elgar*, vol. I, 77.
17. Young, *Elgar*, 258.
18. Reed, *Elgar as I Knew Him*, 98.
19. London, British Library (henceforth Lbl) Add. MS 58003, f.2*v*.
20. See Elgar, *My Friends Pictured Within. The subjects of the Enigma Variations as portrayed in contemporary photographs and Elgar's manuscript* (Sevenoaks: Novello, n.d. [1946], republication of notes for Aeolian Company's piano rolls, 1929); see also Julian Rushton, *Elgar: Enigma Variations*, 10–12.
21. Anderson, *Elgar*, 8.
22. The shed books are Lbl Add. MSS. 60516 A–E.
23. Lbl Add. MS 49774D f.34*v*.
24. Lbl Add. MS 63150 f.17.
25. Lbl Add. MS 49974D f.33.
26. McVeagh, *Elgar*, 206. See also chapter 2, note 16.
27. See Anderson, *Manuscript*, plate 35; Trowell, 'Elgar's Use of Literature', in Monk, *Literature*, 257.
28. See Christopher Kent, '*Falstaff*: Elgar's Symphonic Study', in Monk, *Literature*, 85–7.
29. Christopher Kent, 'A View of Elgar's Methods of Composition through the Sketches of the Symphony No. 2 in E♭ (Op. 63)', *Proceedings of the Royal Musical Association* 103 (1976–7), 41–60.
30. Lbl Add. MS 47902.
31. *Publishers*, 312.
32. See Anderson, *Manuscript*, plate 22; E. Wulstan Atkins, *The Elgar–Atkins Friendship*, 194.
33. Lbl Add. MS 47904 ff.169–169*v*.

34. See Christopher Kent, 'Edward Elgar: A Composer at Work. A study of his creative processes as seen through his sketches and proof corrections', Ph.D. thesis, University of London, King's College, 1978, vol. I, 184–5; vol. II, 110.
35. See ECE Vol. 27, xiii.
36. Lbl Add. MS 58003 f.20*v*.
37. Lbl Add. MS 47904A f.151. Kent, 'Edward Elgar', vol. I, 168; vol. II, 95.
38. Kent, 'Edward Elgar', vol. 1, 185–6 and 194; vol. II, 112 and 118.

Chapter 5
1. Burley and Carruthers, *Edward Elgar: The Record of a friendship*, 31.

Chapter 6
1. Letter to A. J. Jaeger, 1 March 1898. He added the claim that it is 'different to anything, in structure, ever done before'. Moore, *Publishers*, 67.
2. Elgar's original title, *Lux Christi*, was presumably considered too Roman Catholic a title by Novello: see chapter 3.
3. See Charles Edward McGuire, *Elgar's Oratorios: The Creation of an Epic Narrative* (Aldershot: Ashgate, 2002).
4. Moore, *Elgar*, 183–4.
5. See Elgar's letter of November 1908, *Lifetime*, 205.
6. On its genesis, see Moore, *Elgar*, 225–6; Anderson, *Manuscript*, 36–43.
7. It's piquant to discover that he at one time mooted parts for a quartet of saxophones, for which actual sketches exist. Anderson, *Manuscript*, 41.
8. 'Loose your locks, your bosoms bare/Breathe the godhead brooding there/Hov'ring round your floating hair' – what did they think of this in Leeds in 1898? But then, recalling the flock of cast-iron floozies flaunting their untrammelled charms in City Square (erected two years before and adjacent to the Queen's Hotel where Elgar stayed), the folk of that proud city were unshockable in artistic matters.
9. *Publishers*, 79.

Chapter 7
1. Eric Fenby, *Delius as I Knew Him* (Cambridge: Cambridge University Press, 1981), 124.
2. Ibid., 178.
3. Although Elgar did not himself so designate *Gerontius*, it is invariably referred to as an oratorio and was so consistently during his lifetime.
4. Michael De-la-Noy, *Elgar the Man* (London: Allen Lane, 1983), 230.

5. As Michael Kennedy notes, Elgar 'had for many years avoided going to church, and while dying refused to see a priest'. *Portrait*, 268/328.

6. Given Carice Elgar Blake's disrespect of her father's explicit directions concerning the fate of his Third Symphony, as well as other matters, Moore's report, presumably from Mrs Blake herself, that she 'persuaded her father that burial must be beside Alice at Little Malvern' must be regarded with at least a dollop of scepticism. Moore, *Elgar*, 823.

7. Reed, *Elgar as I Knew Him*, 115.

8. Ibid., 115.

9. Kennedy, *Portrait*, 269/330.

10. Moore, *Elgar*, 823.

11. Kennedy, *Portrait*, 225/269.

12. 9 October 1900. *Publishers*, 244.

13. 5 November 1918. *Lifetime*, 320.

14. Merlin Holland and Rupert Hart-Davis (eds.) *The Complete Letters of Oscar Wilde* (New York: Henry Holt and Company, 2000), 665, n. 2.

15. Richard Ellman, *Oscar Wilde* (New York: Alfred A. Knopf, 1988), 57.

16. Oscar Wilde, *Complete Poetry*, ed. Isobel Kirby (Oxford: Oxford University Press, 1997), 4.

17. Richard Ellman (ed.), *The Artist as Critic: Critical Writings of Oscar Wilde* (Chicago: University of Chicago Press, 1982), 341–2.

18. Ibid., 234.

19. Ellis Hanson, *Decadence and Catholicism* (Cambridge, MA: Harvard University Press, 1997), 2–5.

20. Ibid., 7.

21. Two years later Elgar arranged the Good Friday Music from *Parsifal* for the Worcester High School Orchestra. Anderson, *Elgar*, 421.

22. Hanson, *Decadence*, 36.

23. Edward Algernon Baughan, *Music and Musicians* (London: John Lane, The Bodley Head, 1906), 63. Elgar disparaged Baughan's writings severely on occasion; see Gerald Cumberland [pseudonym of Charles F. Kenyon], *Set Down in Malice: A Book of Reminiscences* (London: Grant Richards, 1919), 80.

24. Aidan Thomson, 'Re-reading Elgar: Hermeneutics, Criticism and Reception in England and Germany, 1900–1914' (D.Phil dissertation., Oxford University, 2003), 60.

25. Anderson, *Elgar*, 212.

26. Neville Cardus, 'Genius, Original and Final', reprinted from the *Manchester Guardian* in Geoffrey Hodgkins (ed.), *The Best of Me: A Gerontius Centenary Companion* (Rickmansworth: Elgar Editions, 1999), 261.

27. McGuire, *Elgar's Oratorios*, 175.

28. Ibid., 139ff.

29. See Moore, *Elgar*, 332–3.

30. W. J. Turner, 'Elgar and Handel', in Redwood, *Companion*, 176–7.

31. Ralph Vaughan Williams, *National Music and Other Essays*, second edition (Oxford: Oxford University Press, 1987), 182.

32. Quoted in Jeremy Dibble, *C. Hubert H. Parry: His Life and Music* (Oxford: Clarendon Press, 1992), 391.

33. Baughan, *Music and Musicians*, 202–3.

34. Neither its Roman Catholicism nor its Wagnerism enhanced the reception of *The Dream of Gerontius* among die-hard members of the Anglican clergy. For the first performance of *Gerontius* at a Three Choirs Festival in 1902, the Dean of Worcester insisted that Newman's poem be censored to remove any language suggestive of Catholic doctrine. Clerical suspicion of *Gerontius* may well have extended beyond the text to the music itself, for the Anglican clergy of Worcester frowned upon the music of Wagner. As late as 1926, T. A. Lacey, a Canon of Worcester, protested at the inclusion of the *Parsifal* Prelude in the programme of the Three Choirs Festival, noting that Wagner was a 'sensualist', the sensuality of whose pietism was matched only by 'the sensuality of his erotics'. Elgar replied to Lacey's objections with withering contempt; *Lifetime*, 394, 396.

35. Frances Kingsley (ed.), *Charles Kingsley: His Letters and Memories of his Life*, vol. I (London: C. Kegan Paul and Co., 1881), 201.

36. Peter Gay, *The Tender Passion* (Oxford: Oxford University Press, 1986), 236.

37. John Henry Newman, *Apologia pro Vita Sua: Being a History of His Religious Opinions*, ed. Martin J. Svaglic (Oxford: Oxford University Press, 1967), 252.

38. 31 May 1875 in Wilfrid Ward, *The Life of John Henry Newman*, vol. II (London: Longmans, Green and Co., 1912), 410.

39. The initial impetus for *The Dream of Gerontius* came from a serious illness of Newman's own, as well as his memories of the exemplary death in 1853 of Father John Joseph Gordon, the 'fratri desideratissimo' to whose memory the poem is dedicated.

40. Elgar may well have been aware of Newman's devotion to St John; see Byron Adams, 'The "Dark Saying" of the Enigma: Homoeroticism and the Elgarian Paradox', in Sophie Fuller and Lloyd Whitesell (eds.), *Queer Episodes in Music and Modern Identity* (Urbana and Chicago: University of Illinois Press, 2002), 233–4.

41. Mosse, *Nationalism and Sexuality* (New York: Howard Fertig, 1985), 10–11.

42. McGuire points out that Elgar had to manipulate the text in order to create a pretext

for this duet. Charles McGuire, 'One Story, Two Visions', in Hodgkins, *The Best of Me*, 96.

43. Paul Verlaine, 'Parsifal', *Oeuvres poétiques complètes*, ed. Jacques Borel (Paris: Gallimard, 1962), 427.

44. Hanson, *Decadence*, 37.

45. Concerning a passage in *Gerontius*, Jaeger wrote to Elgar on 29 May 1900 that 'I have not seen or heard *anything* since "Parsifal" that has stirred me, & stirred me, & spoken to me with the trumpet tongue of genius as has this part of your latest & *by far* greatest work . . . I feel as if I wanted to kiss the hand that penned these marvellous pages'. *Publishers*, 183 (Jaeger's emphases).

46. Ibid., 205. Elgar's first draft of the climax, which is subdued and ineffective, can be found between pages 192 and 197 of this volume.

47. Arnold Bax, *Farewell, My Youth and Other Writings*, ed. Lewis Foreman (Aldershot: Ashgate Press, 1992), 26.

48. *Lifetime*, 248.

49. Elgar first developed this paradoxical creative strategy of portraying himself through other's eyes in 1899: the 'Enigma' Variations, Op. 36. See Adams, 'The "Dark Saying" of the Enigma', 230–3. During the composition of *Gerontius*, Elgar wrote to Jaeger on 28 August 1900 that its protagonist 'represents ME when ill'. *Publishers*, 228.

50. Hanson, *Decadence*, 94.

51. Ibid., 95.

52. Oscar Wilde, *The Soul of Man and Prison Writings* (Oxford: Oxford University Press, 1990), 123.

53. Baughan, *Music and Musicians*, 201.

54. Anderson, *Manuscript*, 57.

55. Moore, *Elgar*, 371.

56. Ibid., 421.

57. *Lifetime*, 114. Some Elgar Scholars have transcribed this exclamation as 'GIGANTIC WORX'.

58. See both Moore, *Elgar*, 386 and Anderson, *Elgar*, 58.

59. McGuire, *Elgar's Oratorios*, 191–3.

60. 'Impressions at Bayreuth', *The Times*, 21 August 1909.

61. 3 March 1957 in Michael Kennedy, *The Works of Ralph Vaughan Williams*, (London: Oxford University Press, 1964), 388.

62. For an investigation of elements of Roman Catholic dogma found in *The Apostles*, see McGuire, 'Elgar, Judas and the Theology of Betrayal', *19th-Century Music* 23/3 (2000), 244–5.

63. The full title of Dowson's poem is 'Non sum qualis eram bonæ sub regno Cynarae', in Phyllis M. Jones (ed.), *Modern Verse 1900–1940* (Oxford: Oxford University Press, 1940), 48–9.

64. McGuire, 'Elgar, Judas', 248–9.

65. Moore, *Elgar*, 403.

66. McGuire, 'Elgar, Judas', 241. The following paragraphs on Judas have as their foundation McGuire's exploration of how Elgar moulded that character in *The Apostles*.

67. Judas' extended scene, with choral interjections like those that pervade Mary Magdalene's earlier solo, is cast in large part in the dark and 'demonic' key of D minor, associated of course with Mozart's *Don Giovanni* and Requiem but also with Kundry in her aspect as temptress.

68. Just before the composition of *Gerontius*, Elgar had considered the calling of the apostles as a subject and had approached Capel-Cure, who viewed the idea with dismay, given the tight time constraints attendant upon that first Birmingham commission. As Jerrold Northrop Moore suggests, one of the compelling reasons for Elgar's attraction to the subject of the apostles in the first place was his fascination with Judas. See Moore, *Elgar*, 294–5.

69. 17 July 1903. *Lifetime*, 131.

70. Kennedy, *Portrait*, 94.

71. 26 October 1900. Moore, *Elgar*, 335.

72. 9 October 1900. *Publishers*, 244.

73. See Adams, 'The "Dark Saying" of the Enigma', 222.

74. Consider Jaeger's pointed cry to Parry, who had generously sent money to defray medical expenses: see Dibble, *C. Hubert Parry*, 417. Around this time, Jaeger confided to Rosa Burley – 'almost with tears in his eyes' – how much he disliked Elgar's 'undesirable' new society friends. She observed that Jaeger 'whether justly or not, undoubtedly felt neglected by Edward in the later years of success'; see Burley and Carruthers, *Elgar: The Record of a Friendship*, 178.

75. For an example of such a public renunciation of music, carried out, as was his remark to Delius, in the guise of a bit of 'clever' repartee, see Arnold Bax, *Farewell, My Youth and Other Writings*, 26–27.

76. Oscar Wilde, 'The Ballad of Reading Gaol', in *The Soul of Man*, 189, lines 649–54.

77. Elgar places quotation marks around this verse in the score in order to underscore its import.

78. *Daily Telegraph*, 3 October 1906. Moore, *Elgar*, 505.

79. Ibid., 505.

80. *The Times*, 4 October 1906.

81. Newman summarises these reservations in *Elgar* (London: John Lane, 1906), 114.

82. *Birmingham Post*, 22 March 1907, cited in Moore, *Elgar*, 507. On Newman and the First Symphony, see chapter 11.

83. 3 March 1957. Kennedy, *Ralph Vaughan Williams*, 388.

84. Anderson, *Manuscript*, 81.

85. See Moore, *Elgar*, 493. For chilling eye-witness testimony to the composer's swiftly changing moods while he was composing *The Kingdom*, see Mrs Richard Powell (née Dora Penny), *Edward Elgar: Memories of a Variation*, second edition (Oxford: Oxford University Press, 1947, 69–74; 3rd edition, Aldershot: Scolar Press, 1994, 89–94). Mrs Powell's recollections are particularly unsettling due to her complete lack of psychological penetration.

86. *Publishers*, 228 (Elgar's emphases).

87. In a controversial entry on the composer published in the 1924 edition of Guido Adler's *Handbuch der Musikgeschichte*, E. J. Dent asserted that 'to English ears Elgar is over-emotional and not entirely free of vulgarity'. See Brian Trowell, 'Elgar's Use of Literature', in Monk, *Literature*, 286.

88. In an obituary tribute to Elgar, Vaughan Williams mischievously opined that '[w]e must, I believe, look for the germs of the Elgarian idiom to the little group of organists who were writing small but rather charming music when Elgar was a young man, such as Henry Smart and John Goss'. Vaughan Williams, *National Music and Other Essays* (Oxford: Oxford University Press, 1987), 253.

89. See William Gaunt, *The Aesthetic Adventure* (New York: Harcourt, Brace, 1945), 214–15.

90. Quoted in Anderson, *Manuscript*, 77.

91. For a thorough investigation of Elgar's intermittent interest in *The Last Judgement*, see Anderson, *Manuscript*, 81–90.

92. Kennedy, *Ralph Vaughan Williams*, 195–6.

93. Moore, *Elgar*, 779.

94. *The Complete Poetical Works of Percy Bysshe Shelley*, ed. Thomas Hutchinson (Oxford: Oxford University Press, 1905), 443.

95. Kennedy, *Portrait*, 268. Anderson identifies the music that Elgar wrote out as a theme originally intended for a projected sombre *Cockaigne* Overture No. 2, which itself was initially suggested by James Thomson's poem 'The City of Dreadful Night', and then transferred to *The Last Judgement*. See Anderson, *Manuscript*, 88. See also Thomson, 'Re-reading Elgar', 250–2.

Chapter 8

1. Sir Frederick Ponsonby, writing to the Keeper of the Privy Purse, the Earl of Shaftesbury, 8 April 1924; *Lifetime*, 383.

2. Ibid., 478.

3. Moore, *Elgar*, 57.

4. Leicester, Elgar's old friend and choirmaster at St George's, wrote a pamphlet in celebration of the centenary of the church in 1929 (Alderman Leicester, *Notes on Catholic Worcester* (Worcester, 1928 – Worcester County Record Office L.282.0942448), 33).

5. Moore, *Elgar*, 21, 78.

6. For example, Allison, *Edward Elgar: Sacred Music* (Bridgend: Seren, 1994).

7. Elgar Birthplace Museum, Gradual in E minor, MSS 199, 200.

8. Both now situated in the Elgar Birthplace Museum.

9. 17 February 1913; Moore, *Elgar*, 642.

10. *Lifetime*, 84.

11. Moore's note, *Publishers*, 384–5.

12. *Lifetime*, 123–4.

13. Maine, *Elgar, his Life and Works*, vol. I, 116.

14. *Publishers*, 486–7. His only known copy of a Solesmes-derived collection is the *Manuale Missae et Officiorum* of 1903 (in five-line, modern notation, and clearly used, given the number of pencil annotations), now in the Elgar Birthplace Museum.

15. *Publishers*, 228.

16. Moore, *Elgar*, 715.

17. A full catalogue of the Litany chants is provided by John Allison, 'A Study of Edward Elgar's Sacred Music with Reference to his Life and Works' (Ph.D. thesis, University of Cape Town, 1989), 201–7.

18. Allison, *Edward Elgar: Sacred Music*, 47; see *Lifetime*, 329.

19. See Elgar Birthplace Museum, MS 182, where various versions of this formula appear nine times.

20. Allison, 'A Study of Elgar's Sacred Music', 216.

21. Peter Dennison, 'Elgar's Musical Apprenticeship', in Monk, *Studies*, 4.

22. *Publishers*, 815–16.

23. Moore, *Elgar*, 56; *Lifetime*, 475.

24. Sinclair (*Publishers*, 430) identifies the introduction to scene IV of *The Apostles*; see also *Lifetime* 127. Haines: information from his sister (Mrs Nellie Haines Roberts), c.1975, communicated by John Rutter.

25. Birmingham lecture on orchestration, 1 November 1906 (*Future*, 251). See also Christopher Kent, 'The Organ of St George's Church, Worcester in the Early Life of Edward Elgar', *Journal of the British Institute of Organ Studies* 18 (1995), 92–107; 94.

26. Respectively *Publishers*, 45, 186, 69.

27. Rainer Fanselau, *Die Orgel im Werk Edward Elgars* (Göttingen: Andreas Funke, 1973), 289–91.

28. Blair, Advent Cantata, 'Blessed are they who watch' (1894); Brewer, part of the oratorio *Emmaus* (1901).

29. Moore, *Elgar*, 61–2; Allison, *Edward Elgar. Sacred Music*, 22.

30. Fanselau, *Die Orgel*, 76–80.

31. See ECE XV (Organ Music).

32. Fanselau, *Die Orgel*, 153.

33. See Ibid., 165, 173.

34. *Lifetime*, 415.

35. Moore, *Elgar*, 223.

36. *Lifetime*, 373–7.

37. ECE XV (Organ Music), 98–101.

38. Ibid., vii–viii.

39. *Lifetime*, 429–31.

Chapter 9

1. Kennedy, *Portrait*, 237/282.

2. The *Sketches* were played at the Worcestershire Musical Union Concert conducted by the Reverend Vine Hall on 7 May 1888.

3. Moore, *Elgar*, 124.

4. Young, *Elgar*, 291.

5. Moore, *Elgar*, 160.

6. Moore, *Elgar*, 451.

7. A copy of the programme note is held at the Elgar Birthplace Museum. The title page reads: 'Programme/ Historical and Analytical Notes/ by Edgar F. Jacques and F. Gilbert Webb'. Elgar evidently read and approved the programme note before it went to print.

8. British Library Add. MS 63153, titled 'Sketchbook I/Edward Elgar Nov 19, 1901/Falstaff'. It also contains drafts of the *Concert Allegro* for solo piano and a piano version of 'The Tame Bears' from the *Wand of Youth* Suite No. 2. The library also holds the complete autograph full score of the *Introduction and Allegro*, which was used as the *Stichvorlage*, Add. MS 58015. Here, the score is laid out differently to the final published version, so that each instrument is grouped together rather than being divided between quartet and orchestral groups.

9. Programme note, 18. The piece is described as 'Introduction and Allegro in G minor and major (Op. 47) / for Strings (Orchestra and Quartet)', and was dedicated to Professor S. S. Sanford of Yale University.

10. Parrott, *Elgar*, 59.

11. The other indications are 'Wind' and 'corno?' at the end of the second system.

12. James Hepokoski, 'Reflections on a "Welsh tune": Elgar's *Introduction and Allegro*, Op. 47', paper read at the Elgar Conference, University of Surrey, 13 April 2002.

13. Moore, *Elgar*, 454.

14. Reed, *Elgar*, 147–8. The basis for Reed's observation is an Aeolian harp that belonged to Elgar, and which he suspended outside his study in Hereford.

15. Matthew Riley: 'Rustling Reeds and Lofty Pines: Elgar and the Music of Nature', *19th-Century Music* 26/2 (2002), 177.

16. Hans Keller, 'Elgar the Progressive', *Essays on Music*, ed. Christopher Wintle (Cambridge: Cambridge University Press, 1994), 63–7.

17. 26 January 1905, *Publishers*, 607–8.

18. Julian Rushton, 'The Devil of a Fugue. Berlioz, Elgar, and *Introduction and Allegro*', *Elgar Society Journal* 11/5 (2000), 276–87.

19. British Library Add. MS 63153, f.29 recto.

20. Reproduced in Anderson, *Manuscript*, 98.

21. Moore, *Elgar*, 555. Moore quoted a letter from Elgar to G. H. Jack of 1931 where Elgar mentions Mordiford bridge. Mordiford is on the River Lugg just outside Hereford on the eastern side of the city.

22. Reissued on EMI CD 7243 5 67240 2 0 (2000). Barbirolli's tempo is exceptionally slow, which emphasises the resemblance with the 'Adagietto' from Mahler's Fifth Symphony (1902).

23. See Michael Pope's preface to the Eulenburg miniature score of the Quintet (1971) for a useful summary.

24. 'The Road to Brinkwells: The Late Chamber Music', in Foreman (ed.), *'Oh My Horses!'*, 367.

25. See Walter Frisch, *Brahms and the Principle of Developing Variation* (Berkeley: University of California Press, 1984).

26. Trowell, 'The Road to Brinkwells', 367.

27. *The Globe*, 22 March 1919; *The Daily Telegraph*, 11 March 1919.

28. See, for example, *Manliness and Morality: Middle-class Morality in Britain and America 1800–1940*, ed. J. A. Mangan and James Walvin (Manchester: Manchester University Press, 1987); J. Rutherford, *Forever England: Reflections on Masculinity and Empire* (London: Lawrence and Wishart, 1997), and Peter Middleton, *The Inward Gaze: Masculinity and Subjectivity in Modern Culture* (London: Routledge, 1992).

29. See Byron Adams, 'The "Dark Saying" of the Enigma'. For provocative readings of gendered musical identity in absolute music, see Robert Fink, 'Desire, Repression and Brahms's First Symphony', *Repercussions* 2/1 (1993), 75–103; Susan McClary, 'Narrative Agendas in "Absolute Music": Identity and Difference in Brahms' Third Symphony', in Ruth A. Solie (ed.), *Music and Difference: Gender and Sexuality in Music Scholarship* (Berkeley: University of California Press, 1993), 326–44.

30. Trowell, 'The Road to Brinkwells', note 62, 384.

31. Elgar Birthplace MS 27, 1. Elgar first met Marie Joshua at a New Year party in 1910, and she became a strong admirer of his music: he wrote to offer her the dedication of the Sonata (which she intended to refuse), but she died before she could reply.

32. Trowell, 'The Road to Brinkwells', 371–2.

33. Reed, letter to the *Daily Telegraph*, 11 March 1919.

34. Ibid.

35. Interestingly, the violin's characteristic triplet upbeat, which presumably lends the music its 'bolero' or waltz-like character, was originally written as a quaver and straight semiquavers. An early draft violin part (Elgar birthplace MS 30a) also includes a dal segno repeat and a number of differences in the violin's cadenzas.

36. Letter to Alice Stuart-Wortley, 11 September 1918. *Windflower*, 212.

37. Trowell, 'The Road to Brinkwells', 372.

38. Elgar Birthplace MS 28. The point is noted by Trowell, 372.

39. Judith Butler, 'Melancholy gender/refused identification', in Maurice Berger, Brian Wallis, Simon Watson (eds.), *Constructing Masculinity* (London: Routledge, 1995), 30.

40. *Lifetime*, 457.

41. Trowell, 'The Road to Brinkwells', 372–3.

42. *The Arts Gazette*, 29 March 1919.

43. Moore, *Elgar*, 731.

44. Brian Newbould, '"Never done before": Elgar's Other Enigma', *Music and Letters* 77/2 (1996), 228–41.

45. Moore, *Elgar*, 734.

46. I am grateful to Byron Adams for this suggestion. See also Trowell, 'The Road to Brinkwells', 368.

47. Trowell, 'The Road to Brinkwells', 370.

48. *Lifetime*, 320.

Chapter 10

1. *Lifetime*, 67; see also chapter 6.

2. 'Retrospect', Elgar's Birmingham lecture of 13 December 1905, *Future*, 207; reports of the lecture, ibid., 98: 'the height of music', 105: 'by far the highest form of musical art'.

3. *Future*, 49 and 53.

4. See his letter of 13 December 1921 to Sidney Colvin. *Lifetime*, 359; cited chapter 4, note 4.

5. The Suite in D and Three Sketches for Strings, probably not identical with the Serenade in E.

6. That Elgar recorded early works late in his life indicates continuing regard for them. The *Pomp and Circumstance* marches required judicious cutting to fit onto a 78 recording.

7. Op. 10 is dedicated to Lady Mary Lygon, who is also associated with Variation XIII of Op. 36.

8. Christopher Grogan, Foreword to ESE 25 (*Dream Children, The Wand of Youth*), vii.

9. Grogan, op. cit., xi.

10. March No. 5 was completed and performed as late as 1930, but is still included within Op. 39.

11. Sir Henry Hadow (1859–1937), *Studies in Modern Music* (1893), cited from the 11th impression (London: Seeley, Service & Co., 1926), 141.

12. The distinction between concert overture and symphonic poem is not precise, and other labels, such as Tchaikovsky's 'Fantasy-overture', blur it further.

13. Sir Paul Harvey, *The Oxford Companion to English Literature*, fourth edition (Oxford: Oxford University Press, 1967), 316.

14. See Anderson, *Elgar and Chivalry* (Rickmansworth: Elgar Editions, 2002), 74–96.

15. Elgar's own performances, which are usually among the fastest, take twelve and half minutes for *Froissart* and twenty for *In the South*.

16. This fragment in the 'Moods of Dan' is dated 8–10 July 1899. See Young, *Elgar*, 400.

17. 'The land where lemons (and oranges) grow': Mignon's song from Goethe's *Wilhelm Meister*.

18. For a sceptical view of this see Julian Rushton, *Elgar: 'Enigma' Variations*, 64–78, 84–8.

19. The Elgar circle was confident a tune was involved, and for a time 'Auld Lang Syne' made most of the running; recently 'Rule, Britannia' has become a more accepted 'solution', but it replicates, rather than combining with, part of the theme and therefore does not 'go with' it.

20. See Rushton, *Elgar: Enigma Variations*, 7–10, where I suggest that Mrs Elgar's social circle was disproportionately involved, the only significant musical figures being Dr George Sinclair (Variation 12, more inspired by Sinclair's bulldog, Dan), A. J. Jaeger ('Nimrod'), and Elgar himself. Others were amateur musicians or simply friends; planned variations on major composers (Parry, Sullivan) and on Ivor Atkins and Nicholas Kilburn were not composed, although sketches suggest that Variation 3 may have been conceived in connection with Atkins (see Rushton, 15).

21. On the controversy over the true dedication of '***' see ibid., 52–3 and 74–6; Kennedy, *Portrait* (1987 edition only), 96–8; Trowell, 'Elgar's Use of Literature', in Monk, *Literature*, 217–24 .

22. Elgar, *My Friends Pictured Within*, written for the Aeolian Company's piano rolls in 1929 and published by Novello in 1946; see also Percy

M. Young, 'Friends Pictured Within', in Monk, *Studies*, 81–106.

23. Letter to Jaeger, 24 October 1898. *Publishers*, 95.

24. Striking exceptions are Robert Meikle ('"The True Foundation": The Symphonies', in Monk, *Literature*; James Hepokoski, 'Elgar', in D. Kern Holoman (ed.), *The Nineteenth-Century Symphony* (New York: Schirmer, 1997); and recent unpublished work by Aidan Thomson, J. P. E. Harper-Scott, and Timothy Jackson.

25. On 20 October Elgar wrote to Jaeger that he liked the 'idee' of a Gordon symphony, 'but my dear man *why* should I try??', since there would be no financial return; the next day he wrote to F. G. Edwards that it 'simmereth mighty pleasantly in my brain-pan'. He then became absorbed in the Variations. *Publishers*, 93–4. Leeds demanded a choral work instead (this became *Caractacus*).

26. Frederick Niecks, *Programme Music in the Last Four Centuries. A Contribution to the History of Musical Expression* (London: Novello, *c.*1906), 389.

27. This, at least, is the tenor of the argument through Parry's article 'Symphony', in *Grove's Dictionary of Music and Musicians*, London 1879–89, reprinted 1898 (vol. IV, 10–43).

28. Newman's article is reproduced in *Future*, 105–6. Elgar was careful to tell Newman that, in the First Symphony, 'I have no tangible poetic or other basis' (*Lifetime*, 199).

29. Anderson, *Manuscript*, 97; Kent, *Guide*, 240.

30. A symphony was already in Elgar's mind, but the music, a draft of the end of the Scherzo and twenty-two bars of slow movement, is laid out for quartet (although earlier notations for the latter go back to 1904). Robert Anderson observes that it was not Elgar's practice to draft orchestral works on four staves (ECE, vol. 38 (Chamber Music), vi; see also ibid., xxiv, and *Manuscript*, 99).

31. Aidan Thomson, 'Re-Reading Elgar: Hermeneutics, Criticism and Reception in England and Germany, 1900–1914', D.Phil. thesis, Oxford University, 2002, 135. Comparison is also made with the opening of *The Apostles*. The *Parsifal* connection was made by A. J. Sheldon in *Edward Elgar* (London: Musical Opinion, 1932), 48, and by Ian Parrott in *Elgar* (London: Dent, 1971), 69.

32. *Parsifal* connections were made by A. J. Sheldon in 1932 (*Edward Elgar* (London: [Musical Opinion, 1932, 48]) and Parrott (*Elgar*, 69), and developed by Thomson, 'Re-Reading Elgar'.

33. The scherzo as second movement was no longer exceptional, but Bruckner's Fifth has the scherzo third, after the slow movement.

34. Kent lists the 1907 drafts as 'String quartet in D (fragments)' (*Guide*, 228). Besides the passages which became part of the first symphony, there is a 12/8 allegro in D minor headed 'acrobatic – music becoming', some of which later entered *The Music Makers*.

35. 23 November 1908, to Newman. *Lifetime*, 203.

36. Although Elgar dismissed the key-signature as merely 'convenient for the players' (*Publishers*, 710), the passage is usually referred to D minor in the literature including McVeagh, *Elgar*, 164, Hepokoski ('Elgar', 330–1), and Timothy Jackson. Meikle ('The True Foundation', 48ff.) and Harper-Scott, proceeding from different premises, refer to A minor. I am grateful to Paul Harper-Scott for the chance to read his unpublished paper on the symphony, and to Professor Jackson for a view of his unpublished graphic analysis.

37. *Lifetime*, 203.

38. Schoenberg's resolution to F♯ major incidentally involves strong adjacent references to C major, the tritone non-relationship also exploited by Elgar.

39. 4 November 1908, to Newman. *Lifetime*, 199–200.

40. Thomson, 'Re-Reading Elgar', 140.

41. Elgar suggested to Jaeger that F♯ was the subdominant of the subdominant of A♭, surely a tenuous connection, and tendentious theory. *Publishers*, 710.

42. Debussy's 'Premier Quatuor' is in G minor, the slow movement in D flat. Introductions to both slow movement and finale avoid any juxtaposition of these keys.

43. *Lifetime*, 205.

44. *The Music Makers*, fig. 79.

45. I Corinthians 13:12: 'For now we see in a mirror darkly: but then face to face'; the Greek employs the word 'Enigma'.

Chapter 11

1. Elgar's lecture was delivered on 8 November 1905, and his reported view that 'music, as a simple art was at its best when it was simple, without description' created a number of responses in the press, including a counterblast from Newman. See *Future*, 94–110 (quoted from 106), and chapter 10 above.

2. EMI 7243 5 66979 2 8 (re-mastered 1999) and EMI 7243 4 56413 2 8 (1997) respectively.

3. This was not, of course, a new feature of Elgar's music. As Julian Rushton points out, 'Enigma' Variations is 'both public, in its broader musical gestures and its strongly marked characterisations, and private, in its internal cross-references and its gallery of portraits'. *Elgar: Enigma Variations*, 85.

4. James Hepokoski sees this as false: 'The sheer stress and trembling of the A♭ "resolution" can leave us with lingering questions about how affirmative this symphony actually is' ('Elgar', 336). See also chapter 10 above.

5. See Kennedy, *Portrait*, 129/160; Moore, *Elgar*, 569, 575–6.

6. Ernest Newman, 'Elgar's Violin Concerto', *MT* 51 (1910), 634.

7. *Lifetime*, 221.

8. Newman, 'Elgar's Violin Concerto', 632.

9. Tovey, *Essays in Musical Analysis III: Concertos* (London: Oxford University Press, 1936), 153–4.

10. The phrase 'mosaic technique' has been used by recent commentators, but it was applied contemporaneously too. Parry commented on *The Kingdom* in his diary (10 December 1906): 'To the London performance of The Kingdom. Impressive bits. But I do not follow his strange libretto – and the mosaic-like juxtaposition of thematic bits jars and bewilders' (Jeremy Dibble, 'Parry and Elgar: A New Perspective', *MT* 125 (1984), 641). In describing his construction of the development section of the first movement of the third symphony, Anthony Payne refers to fitting together various scraps of sketches 'as if they were jigsaw pieces, a method I am sure Elgar himself used in constructing his broad paragraphs' (Payne, *Elgar's Third Symphony*, 50).

11. 'The master who is to hold this large orchestra spell-bound, and set all these themes out on their various different planes, has not yet spoken. We have now reached the moment when the orchestra is eagerly awaiting him. The strings speak of him wistfully, as in the two bars represented by [the first two bars of the work – though now re-harmonised to be clearly in B minor]. Their sentence is finished for them by the master himself.' Tovey, *Concertos*, 154.

12. Kennedy, *Portrait*, 70 (1968 edition only. In 1987 Kennedy rewrites the passage without withdrawing the implied criticism of the end of the Variations).

13. B minor and B♭ major share a common mediant, D, but this is not a relationship that Elgar 'draws out'. The key relationship parallels that in Saint-Saëns's Violin Concerto No. 3, as Tovey points out (*Concertos*, 156).

14. Newman, 'Elgar's Violin Concerto', 633; Kennedy, *Portrait of Elgar*, 210/251.

15. Michael Kennedy, notes for EMI Great Recordings of the Century re-issue of Elgar/Menuhin, EMI 7243 5 66979 2 8, 1999, p. 4.

16. As in the *Gerontius* context, there is a fixed modal field but a variable final (in the Concerto, B♭, D, or F).

17. Hepokoski, 'Elgar', 336.

18. *Publishers*, 741–2.

19. See Christopher Kent, 'A View of Elgar's Methods of Composition through the Sketches of the Symphony No. 2 in E♭ (Op. 63)', *Proceedings of the Royal Musical Association* 103 (1976), 50.

20. Hepokoski might be indulging the fanciful when he says that 'the Second Symphony drives toward and finally achieves the "resolving", arm-swinging image of itself being conducted on the podium in the institutional ceremony of the public concert' (Hepokoski, 'Elgar', 340), but his identification of the type of utterance seems true enough.

21. See Monk, *Literature*, 55.

22. See Moore, *Elgar*, 609–10 and Kent, 'A View of Elgar's Methods of Composition', 57. It is this labelling that prompted Hepokoski's statement in note 20.

23. See Monk, *Literature*, 56.

24. Kennedy, *Portrait*, 203/243.

25. Tovey, *Essays in Musical Analysis: Symphonies and Other Orchestral Works*, second edition (London: Oxford University Press, 1981), 299.

26. Monk, *Literature*, 52–3.

27. Ibid., 52.

28. Terry's MS notes, quoted in Moore, *Elgar*, 601.

29. Kent, 'A view of Elgar's methods of composition', 53.

30. See *Future*, 232–59.

31. Dibble, 'Parry and Elgar', 642.

32. Moore, *Elgar*, 652.

33. Elgar asked Eric Fenby to tell Delius that he was growing 'more like Falstaff every day'. Fenby, *Delius as I Knew Him* (London: G. Bell, 1936), 113.

34. See Moore, *Elgar*, 615.

35. Ibid., 654–7.

36. *Birmingham Daily Post*, 3 October 1913, cited in ibid., 654.

37. As Kennedy points out (Kennedy, *Portrait of Elgar*, 216.), the theme is not actually marked *nobilmente*, though the apotheosis is marked *Grandioso*.

38. Daniel Grimley, '"*Falstaff (Tragedy)*": Narrative and Retrospection in Elgar's Symphonic Study', unpublished paper delivered at the Elgar Conference, University of Surrey, 13–14 April 2002.

39. See Moore, *Elgar*, 643. In the letter Elgar quotes the cello line between the sixth and ninth bars of fig. 64.

40. Grimley, '"*Falstaff* (Tragedy)"'.

41. Quoted in Moore, *Elgar*, 649.

42. *Falstaff: An Analytical Note* (London: Novello, 1913).

43. See Kennedy, *Portrait*, 216/257

44. "*Falstaff* (Tragedy)".
45. Kennedy, *Portrait*, 215 (1968 edition only: the specific critique of thematic invention was removed in 1987).
46. *Windflower*, 190.
47. Kennedy, *Portrait*, 236–7/282–3.
48. This is not to say that the F♯ versions are transposed in the normal sense: they still employ the E minor/Aeolian scale, but with the tune shifted a step up.
49. Hepokoski, 'Elgar', 329.
50. See note 4.
51. For the story of Payne's completion, including some of the most penetrating insights into Elgar's style and emotional world in print, see Payne, *Elgar's Third Symphony*, and his documentary on NMCD052.
52. Payne, *Elgar's Third Symphony*, 108–9.
53. Ibid., 108.
54. NMCD052.
55. Payne, introduction to the score (London: Boosey and Hawkes, 1998).

Chapter 12
1. Letter to the *Daily Telegraph*, 30 December 1915.
2. *Lifetime*, 102. Percy M. Young documents in detail the operatic negotiations between Moore and Elgar in 'Elgar and the Irish Dramatists', in Monk, *Literature*, 121–39.
3. *Publishers*, 329.
4. Argyll, who succeeded to the dukedom in April 1900, later had some dealings with Elgar. See Robert Anderson, *Elgar*, 106, and Moore, *Elgar*, 442. According to one legend, the hero Diarmuid O'Duibhne was the progenitor of the duke's clan (Campbell), although the Deeny family of Ireland also claims him.
5. Peter Dennison's list of the works Elgar heard or performed in 'up to about 1902' – the year after *Grania and Diarmid* – includes four early works by MacCunn, his Opp. 2–5, but *Diarmid* (Op. 34) is not among them. See Dennison, 'Elgar's Musical Apprenticeship', in Monk, *Studies*, 1–34 (at p. 17).
6. 'MacCunn, Hamish', in J. A. Fuller-Maitland (ed.), *Grove's Dictionary of Music and Musicians* (London: Macmillan & Co., 1907).
7. McVeagh, *Elgar*, 186–7.
8. The specific cause was the King-Emperor's visit to India for the reunification of Bengal and the shift of the capital from Calcutta to New Delhi.
9. Britten was commissioned to write the piece as a tribute to the ancient Japanese dynasty and its modern Emperor. In the event he decided that a tribute to the memory of his parents would be more appropriate, hence the work's dark tone.
10. Niall Ferguson, *Empire: How Britain Made the Modern World* (London: Penguin, 2003), 213.
11. 'Roberts, Sir Henry Gee', in Sidney Lee (ed.), *Dictionary of National Biography* (London: Smith, Elder & Co., 1896).
12. *Lifetime*, 244.
13. On the 'topic' as a semiotic musical construct, see V. Kofi Agawu, *Playing with Signs: A Semiotic Interpretation of Classic Music* (Princeton: Princeton University Press, 1991), especially chapter 2.
14. The stereotypical nature may be gauged by the fact that Elgar used his 'Turkish' piano piece, *In Smyrna*, as the basis for sections of *The Crown of India*.
15. Edward W. Said, *Orientalism* (London: Routledge and Kegan Paul, 1978), 123.
16. It may be added that the orientalisms of early twenty-first-century pop music are little more culturally sensitive than Elgar's. See Corissa Gould, 'Edward Elgar, *The Crown of India*, and the image of Empire', *Elgar Society Journal* 13 (2003), 25–35, for 'a reading of [the work] as a social text of the early twentieth century' (33), which draws on and goes beyond some of Said's ideas.
17. The tune was originally 'the sinful youth of Dan'; see Anderson, *Elgar*, 264. (Dan was the bulldog of George Robertson Sinclair, the 'G.R.S.' of the Variations, Op. 36.)
18. Anderson, *Manuscript*, 127.
19. Anderson, *Elgar*, 264.
20. *Lifetime*, 244.
21. See Moore, *Elgar*, 664, for another political misjudgement.
22. *Lifetime*, 370.
23. Anderson gives a comprehensive account of the *Arthur* music in 'fyrst the noble Arthur', in Monk, *Literature*, 164–81. See also Anderson, *Elgar and Chivalry* for an extensive treatment of Elgar's chivalric interests and influences.
24. For their interesting correspondence see *Lifetime*, 277–83.
25. Burley and Carruthers, *Edward Elgar: The Record of a Friendship*, 198.
26. The first two poems had been translated by the poet's wife, Tita Brands Cammaerts – daughter of the first Angel in *Gerontius* – but the third was translated by Lord Curzon of Kedleston, a former Viceroy of India, the undoing of whose partition of Bengal led to the commission for *The Crown of India*. (Moreover, Hardinge's 1911 durbar was modelled on Curzon's spectacular one in 1903.)
27. A fortnight into the run, Elgar added a fifth song, set to words by Gilbert Parker.
28. *The Court Journal* of 8 October 1898, quoted in Moore, *Elgar*, 244.

29. W. H. Reed, *Elgar*, 121. See Chapter 16 for a more extended discussion of *The Friuges of the Fleet.*

30. Anderson, *Elgar*, 102.

31. James Hepokoski, *Sibelius: Symphony No. 5*, 15.

32. The arrival of mature musical modernism in England was delayed, ironically enough, by Edward VII's death, which led to the cancellation of London performances of Stravinsky's *Firebird* (see Richard Buckle, *Diaghilev* (London: Weidenfeld and Nicolson, 1979), 167).

33. 'Antiquated' is Elgar's own word, used in connection with *Falstaff*'s first interlude (Elgar, 'Falstaff', *MT* 54 (1913), 575–9; 578).

34. Compare *Falstaff*, fig. 76, and *The Sanguine Fan*, BL Add. MS 52533 f.6.

35. Matthew Riley has fascinating things to say on Elgar's nature imagery – in which Pan plays an important part – in this work and in others, in 'Rustling Reeds and Lofty Pines: Elgar and the Music of Nature', *19th-Century Music* 16 (2002), 155–77.

36. Michael Allis undertakes a valuable exploration of Elgar's nostalgic child-centred works in 'Elgar and the Art of Retrospective Narrative', *Journal of Musicological Research* 19 (2000), 289–328.

37. Pearn and Blackwood collaborated also on *Karma: A Reincarnation Play in Prologue* (London: Macmillan, 1918) and *Through the Crack: a Play in Five Scenes* (London: S. French, 1925). The gestation of the play and Elgar's incidental music is given in detail by K. E. L. Simmons in 'Elgar and the Wonderful Stranger: music for *The Starlight Express*', in Monk, *Studies*, 142–213. Basil Dean was behind the production, which ran for only a few weeks; twenty years later he persuaded Benjamin Britten to produce a substantial score for J. B. Priestley's *Johnson Over Jordan* (1939), which also ended its run after only a few weeks.

38. The most important borrowing was from 'The Little Bells' from the second suite, whose second strain became the ubiquitous 'star music', used prominently in the songs 'To the Children', 'Curfew Song', and the finale, as well as in the short instrumental pieces in the score. He also borrowed 'Sun Dance' and 'Fairy Pipers' from the first suite (the former played complete as an interlude before Act 2 scene 2) and 'Moths and Butterflies' and 'Fountains Dance' from the second.

39. In George Hurst's fine Chandos recording of songs from *The Starlight Express* (CHAN 6582), a simple misreading of Elgar's handwriting has been elevated to the level of composer's intention in the lines before Ex. 12.1 begins. The

intended 'O sprites come swiftly/Unwumble deftly' becomes, through a confusion of Elgar's 'u's and 'n's, the bizarre 'O sprites come swiftly/Nu wumble deftly'.

40. The solo instrument's reinforcement of the vocal line is also distantly redolent of the rising violin figuration after figure 10 in *The Dream of Gerontius*, Part II, a dream of a different kind.

41. William Golding, 'Fable', in *The Hot Gates, and other Occasional Pieces* (London: Faber, 1965), 86–7.

42. From a letter about his First Symphony to Walford Davies (13 November 1908): *Lifetime*, 205.

Chapter 13

1. A full and detailed account of Elgar's career in the studio and of his relationship with the Gramophone Company is given in Jerrold Northrop Moore, *Elgar on Record* (London: EMI Records in association with Oxford University Press, 1974), from which all unsourced information in this account is taken. See also John Knowles, *Elgar's Interpreters on Record: An Elgar Discography* (Watford: The Elgar Society, 1977). Pavilion Records issued on five CDs *The Elgar Edition – Acoustic Recordings 1914–25* (Pearl, CD GEMM CDS 9951/5, 1992). EMI issued volumes 1 and 2 and, in 1993, volume 3, as box-sets of CDs, *The Elgar Edition: The Complete Electrical Recordings of Sir Edward Elgar* (EMI Classics CDS 7 54560 2; CDS 7 54564 2; CDS 7 54568 2, 1992). Volume 3 includes Elgar's 'Five Piano Improvisations'.

2. Stanley Chapple, 'In the Recording Studio', *Gramophone* 6/67 (1928), 289–91; for a fuller outline of early recording conditions see Timothy Day, *A Century of Recorded Music: Listening to Musical History* (New Haven: Yale University Press, 2000), 6–12 and 16–18.

3. Richard Terry, *Daily Telegraph*, 10 July 1925.

4. Moore, *Elgar*, 544.

5. Compton Mackenzie, 'Editorial', *Gramophone* 35/409 (1957), 1.

6. Jerrold Northrop Moore, 'An Elgar Discography', *Recorded Sound* 2/9 (1963), 7.

7. Elgar contemplated using four saxophones, but he was advised against this because of the extra difficulty there would be in finding players. So he wrote extra trumpet parts instead. Moore, *Publishers*, 80.

8. Lionel Salter, *Gramophone* 47/563 (1970), 1656.

9. Ferruccio Busoni, *Letters to his Wife*, trans. by Rosamond Ley (London: E. Arnold & Co., 1938), 305.

10. Moore, 'An Elgar Discography', 25.

11. Ibid., 1.

12. Ibid., 6.
13. Moore, *Elgar*, 243.
14. Kennedy, *Portrait*, 304.
15. Sir Dan Godfrey, *Memories and Music: Thirty-five Years of Conducting* (London: Hutchinson, 1924), 124–5.
16. Reed, *Elgar* (London, 1939), 97.
17. Moore, *Elgar*, 793.
18. From contemporary reviews quoted in Robert Philip, 'The Recordings of Edward Elgar (1857–1934): Authenticity and Performance Practice', *Early Music* 12/4 (1984), 487.
19. Kennedy, *Portrait*, 178–9.
20. Reed, *Elgar*, 50–51.
21. Quoted in Moore, *Elgar*, 511.
22. Sir Adrian Boult, 'Composer as Conductor', in H. A. Chambers, *Edward Elgar Centenary Sketches* (London: Novello, 1957), 9.
23. Dyneley Hussey, *MT* 98/1374 (1957), 429.
24. Philip, 'The Recordings of Edward Elgar', 484.
25. 'K. K.' *The Gramophone* 4/4 (1927), 416.
26. Moore, *Gramophone* 50/591 (1972), 334.
27. Alan Blyth, 'Sir Georg Solti', *Gramophone* 50/593 (1972), 659.
28. Moore, *Gramophone* 50/591 (1972), 334.
29. H. C. Colles, *The Times*, 4 March 1929; reproduced in Moore, *Elgar*, 779.
30. Ibid.
31. Ibid.
32. Kennedy, *Portrait*, 321.
33. Ibid., 322–3.
34. Moore, 'An Elgar Discography', 6.
35. Ivan March (ed.), *The Penguin Guide to Compact Discs and Cassettes*, new edition (London, 1996), 424.
36. Edward Greenfield, Robert Layton, and Ivan March, *The Penguin Guide to Compact Discs and Cassettes* (London, 1992), 359.
37. *The Monthly Letter* (July 1957), 7.
38. Trevor Harvey, *Gramophone* 49/580 (1971), 520.
39. Philip, 'The Recordings of Edward Elgar', 489.
40. Edward Sackville-West and Desmond Shawe-Taylor, *The Record Guide* (London: Collins, 1951), 220.
41. Ernest Newman, *The Nation*, 16 November 1910, quoted in Diana McVeagh, Preface to the Eulenburg miniature score of the Violin Concerto (London, 1989), vi.

Chapter 14
1. 'Broadcasting and the Composer', *BBC Handbook 1928* (London: BBC, 1928), 83.
2. The Company's Board represented the six most important British manufacturers of radio equipment, and significantly, it was granted sole right to broadcast in the UK. On 1 January 1927, the Company became a new independent, public body, the British Broadcasting Corporation, set up by a royal charter valid for ten years.
3. For detail about early BBC music policies and programmes, see Jennifer Doctor, *The BBC and Ultra-Modern Music, 1922–1936: Shaping a Nation's Tastes* (Cambridge: Cambridge University Press, 1999).
4. J. C. W. Reith, 'What is Our Policy?', *Radio Times* (14 March 1924), 442.
5. Pitt was artistic director of the BNOC from its founding in 1920 to 1924. The first BBC outside broadcast, from Covent Garden on 8 January 1923, relayed an act of Mozart's *Die Zauberflöte*, performed by the BNOC with Pitt conducting.
6. See Nicholas Kenyon, *The BBC Symphony Orchestra: The First Fifty Years 1930–1980* (London: British Broadcasting Corporation, 1981).
7. Diana McVeagh, 'Elgar, Edward', in Stanley Sadie (ed.), *The New Grove Dictionary of Music and Musicians*, second edition (London: Macmillan, 2001), vol. VIII, 121.
8. Michael Kennedy, 'Elgar the Edwardian', in Monk, *Studies*, 107.
9. This description is fortified by photographs of Elgar issued in BBC publications in his lifetime, depicting a serious elderly, soldier-like gentleman with thick moustache, usually in profile facing to the left; in images of the composer as conductor, he is awkwardly posed, holding an extremely long, commanding baton (see, for example, the programme for the Elgar Celebration Concert, BBC Symphony Concerts, Queen's Hall, London, 30 November 1932, cover and 22).
10. For a brilliant discussion of Elgar and nationalism, see Jeremy Crump, 'The Identity of English Music'.
11. The previous articles are: 'Elgar and the BBC', in Elgar Celebration Concert (concert programme), 23–4; Humphrey Burton, 'Elgar and the BBC: with particular reference to the unfinished Third Symphony', *Journal of The Royal Society of Arts* 127 (March 1979), 224–36; Ronald Taylor, 'Music in the Air: Elgar and the BBC', in Monk, *Literature*, 327–55.
12. Robert Lorenz, 'Elgar, Composer of English Music', in Elgar Celebration Concert (concert programme), 21.
13. The first BBC broadcast of Elgar took place within its first week of operation: at 8 p.m. on 17 November 1922, a Duo Art Pianola performance of *Pomp and Circumstance* March No. 1 was aired. For chronologies of BBC broadcasts that Elgar conducted and BBC relays of public

concerts given in his lifetime that included his works, see Taylor, 'Music in the Air', 327–55.

14. Programmes as Broadcast record (PasB), London, 2LO, 23 June 1923 (BBC Written Archives Centre (BBC WAC)). Pitt conducted a programme of Mozart, Wagner, Saint-Saëns and Schubert.

15. PasB, London, 2LO, 8 July 1923 (BBC WAC).

16. Asa Briggs, *The History of Broadcasting in the United Kingdom*, vol. I: *The Birth of Broadcasting* (London: Oxford University Press, 1961), 290.

17. Letter to Alice Stuart-Wortley, 16 April 1924. *Windflower*, 290.

18. Jerrold Northrop Moore, *Elgar on Record: The Composer and the Gramophone*; see also chapter 14.

19. Taylor, 'Music in the Air', 336–7, 351–5.

20. For more information about programmes Elgar conducted for the BBC, see Taylor, 330–35.

21. Much space was given to these Elgar appearances in BBC publicity, as well as in the concert programmes: photographs, articles and extensive programme notes were printed in *Radio Times* – and articles in *The Listener* too, once it was issued – tangibly substantiating the importance of the occasions, as well as promoting and encouraging listeners' interest.

22. 'The Central Hall Concert', Friday 7 March, *Radio Times* (29 February 1924), 377.

23. '6th Symphony Concert', Friday 2 May, *Radio Times* (25 April 1924), 189. Elgar conducted *Cockaigne*, the Cello Concerto (Beatrice Harrison, cello), the 'Enigma' Variations, *Wand of Youth* Suite No. 1, and *Pomp and Circumstance* Marches Nos. 2 and 3.

24. 'Elgar and the BBC', in *Elgar Celebration Concert*, 23.

25. For details of the early BBC's commissioning activities, see Doctor, *The BBC and Ultra-Modern Music*.

Chapter 15

1. Max Hehemann, 'Edward Elgar', *Die Musik* 2/7 (1903), 15.

2. Kennedy, *Portrait*, 131.

3. On this 'renaissance', see Robert Stradling and Meirion Hughes, *The English Musical Renaissance 1860–1940: Construction and Deconstruction* (London: Routledge, 1993).

4. This article appears in translation in 'Occasional Notes', *MT* 42 (1901), 20.

5. 'Occasional Notes', *MT* 42 (1901), 20; Otto Lessmann, 'Das dritte Musikfest in Sheffield am 1.–3. Oktober', *Zeitschrift der internationalen Musikgesellschaft* (*ZIMG*) 4 (1902–3), 50.

6. 'Occasional Notes', *MT* 42 (1901), 805.

7. 'Edward Elgar', *Die Musik* 2/7 (1903), 15–25.

8. Edward Elgar, *Die Apostel*, erläutert von Max Hehemann (London: Novello, 1904); Max Hehemann, 'Edward Elgar', *Neue Zeitschrift für Musik* 72 (1905), 760–2, 761.

9. *Publishers*, 554.

10. Hugo Conrat, 'Edward Elgar', *Neue Musik-Zeitung* 24 (1903–4), 33–4, 51–2.

11. Alma Mahler-Werfel, *Diaries 1898–1902*, selected and translated by Anthony Beaumont (London: Faber, 1998), 256, n.25; Henry-Louis De La Grange, *Gustav Mahler*, vol. II: *Vienna: The Years of Challenge (1897–1904)* (Oxford University Press, 1995), 715–16.

12. On Viennese critical reaction to *Gerontius*, see Sandra McColl, '*Gerontius* in the City of Dreams: Newman, Elgar, and the Viennese Critics', *International Review of the Aesthetics and Sociology of Music* 32 (2001), 47–64.

13. Ronald Taylor, 'Essay on Edward Elgar by H. Conrat', *Elgar Society Newsletter*, 9 (1976), 26.

14. 'Die "Apostel" von Edward Elgar', *Allgemeine Musik-Zeitung* 31 (1904), 849–50, 869–70; 'Edward Elgar', *Hochland* 5 (1907), 316–21.

15. Volbach also conducted both *Gerontius* and *The Apostles* in Mainz in 1903 and 1904 (Kennedy, *Portrait*, 130).

16. Elgar thanked Volbach for the 'beautiful article on "The Apostles"' (letter, 26 July 1904), presumably a copy of the article that would appear later that year in the *Allgemeine Musik-Zeitung*; in another letter, dated 16 January 1908, Elgar refers again to the 'beautiful articles you have written', presumably alluding to the piece Volbach had recently written for *Hochland*. See Walther Volbach, 'Edward Elgar and Fritz Volbach', *Musical Opinion* 60 (1937), 871.

17. 'Zwei "Urneuheiten": Elgar's "Traum des Gerontius" und Reznicek's "Till Eulenspiegel"', *Signale für die musikalische Welt* 60 (1902), 145–8; 'Die Apostel. Oratorium von Edward Elgar, op. 49. Erstaufführung in Deutschland beim Niederrheinischen Musikfest in Köln im Mai 1904', *Signale für die musikalische Welt* 62 (1904), 676–8.

18. Otto Neitzel, 'Köln', 'Musikberichte', *ZIMG* 5 (1903–4), 456–7.

19. Hehemann, 'Edward Elgar' (1903), 16: 'recently [. . .] a national school has been flowering forth [*blüht empor*]'.

20. Hehemann, 'Edward Elgar' (1905), 761.

21. Hehemann, 'Edward Elgar' (1903), 16.

22. Ibid.

23. Ibid.

24. Moore, *Elgar*, 459; *Future*, 57.

25. Henry Coward and Frederic Cowen were cited as particular examples of such composers. Lessmann, 'Das dritte Musikfest'; this and following quotations are from 50–1.

26. 'Occasional Notes', *MT* 42 (1901), 20.
27. Volbach, 'Edward Elgar', 317, 319.
28. Conrat, 'Edward Elgar', 51.
29. Hehemann, 'Edward Elgar' (1905), 761.
30. Volbach, 'Die "Apostel"', 870.
31. Conrat, 'Edward Elgar', 34.
32. Volbach, 'Die "Apostel"', 849; Hehemann 'Edward Elgar' (1903), 17.
33. See, for example, Charles Maclean, 'Worcester', 'Notizien', *ZIMG* 4 (1902–3), 31–2. On Catholicism, see also Chapters 8 and 9.
34. Hehemann, 'Edward Elgar' (1905), 761.
35. Hehemann 'Edward Elgar' (1903), 17.
36. Neitzel, '"Die Apostel"', 677.
37. Peter Dennison, 'Elgar's Musical Apprenticeship', in Monk, *Studies*, 13.
38. Neitzel, 'Zwei "Urneuheiten"', 145.
39. Neitzel explicitly described Part II of *Gerontius*, after the Demons' chorus, as being 'in the manner of the third act of *Parsifal*, only that Gerontius is spared the snake-bite of remorse and the neglected good deeds' (ibid., 146).
40. Ibid., 145.
41. Ernest Newman, *Elgar* (London: John Lane, 1906), 56.
42. Walther Volbach, 'Edward Elgar and Fritz Volbach', 870.
43. Fritz Volbach, 'Edward Elgar', 317.
44. James M. Clark, *The Great German Mystics* (Oxford: Blackwell, 1949), 26–35.
45. Ernest Gellner, *Nationalism* (London: Weidenfeld and Nicolson, 1997), 28.
46. Roy Pascal, *From Naturalism to Expressionism: German Literature and Society 1880–1918* (London: Weidenfeld and Nicolson, 1973), 171.
47. Fritz Volbach, 'Edward Elgar', 317, 316.
48. Volbach, 'Die "Apostel"', 849. Elgar's English biographer, R. J. Buckley, uses similar imagery – and, in the process, misquotes Longfellow's poem *The Singers* – when claiming that, at the chord succession at the words 'Rescue him' in *Gerontius*, 'imagination is carried back to the middle ages, to "cathedrals dim and vast, where [*sic*] the majestic organ rolled Contrition from its mouths of gold"'. *Sir Edward Elgar* (London: John Lane, 1905), 69.
49. Volbach, 'Edward Elgar', 318, 316.
50. See, for instance, B. Prilipp, 'Heimatkunst im modernen englischen Roman', in *Die Grenzboten* 63/3 (1904), 89–98.
51. Volbach, 'Edward Elgar', 318.
52. On the association of urban capitalism and Jewishness, see, for instance, Eric Hobsbawm, *The Age of Empire* (London: Weidenfeld and Nicolson, 1987), 89, 158.

Chapter 16
1. Many recent publications follow a similar strategy. See, for instance, Lewis Foreman (ed.), '*Oh My Horses!*', which includes discussions of Elgar's music and empire, and chapter 3 of Jeffrey Richards' *Imperialism and Music: Britain 1876–1953* (Manchester: Manchester University Press, 2001), which concentrates on imputing an imperial strain throughout Elgar's entire career.
2. Gerald Cumberland described Elgar's music in precisely this way in 'The Present in the Eyes of the Future: A Chapter in Musical History', *Musical Opinion and Music Trade Review* (hereafter *MOMTR*), March 1914, 451: 'it is not altogether difficult to account for [Elgar's] popularity. He could write recognisable melodies, and it must be remembered that he wrote them at a time when the art of inventing melodies was fast dying out . . .'
3. For a somewhat different view of *The Starlight Express*, see chapter 13.
4. Such difficulties notwithstanding, many biographies and imperial studies use the late chamber works and the Cello Concerto as a partial endpoint for their discussions of the period; see, for instance, Brian Trowell, 'The Road to Brinkwells' – the capstone article in Foreman, '*Oh My Horses!*', 347–85.
5. *Publishers*, 76–9.
6. Examples include Frank Howes' 1935 essay from *Music and Letters*, 'The Two Elgars', reprinted in Redwood, *Companion*, 238–62; Jeremy Crump's 'The Identity of English Music' and Meirion Hughes's 'The Duc d'Elgar: Making a Composer Gentleman', in Christopher Norris (ed.), *Music and the Politics of Culture* (London: Lawrence and Wishart, 1989), 41–68.
7. See the comments regarding the final scene of *Caractacus* in Kennedy, *Portrait*, 74; Richards (op. cit., 44–50) discusses this passage in detail.
8. James Day, *Englishness in Music from Elizabethan Times to Elgar, Tippett and Britten* (London: Thames Publishing, 1999), 152. The words come from A. C. Benson's lyrics to 'Land of Hope and Glory'.
9. Generally positive approaches to 'Elgar and Empire' include Richards, *Imperialism and Music*, chapter 3, and Bernard Potter's 'Elgar and Empire: Music, Nationalism and the War' in Foreman, '*Oh My Horses!*', 133–173, as well as Robert Anderson's *Elgar and Chivalry*.
10. Osbert Sitwell, *Laughter in the Next Room* (Boston: Little, Brown, 1948, 22; London: Macmillan, 1949, 195–7).
11. Anderson, *Elgar*, 56.
12. The first strain, as recorded by Clara Butt in 1912 and Edward Hamilton in 1914, later

became a popular stand-alone item for proms, and similar concerts. This better-known version is even more explicit in its celebration of Empire, as the last lines were altered to: 'Wider still and wider, shall thy bounds be set; / God, who made thee mighty, make thee mightier yet!'

13. Elgar used this power frequently, by appending his name to public letters and petitions that supported his own political views, such as signing a letter against Irish Home Rule on 2 March 1914, thus directly supporting a facet of Empire.

14. For further details regarding the context of the production, see Corissa Gould, 'Edward Elgar, *The Crown of India*, and the Image of Empire', *Elgar Society Journal* 13/1 (2003), 25–35, and the discussion of the masque in Deborah Heckert's 'Contemplating History: National Identity and Uses of the Past in the English Masque, 1860–1940' (Ph.D. dissertation, SUNY Stonybrook, 2003); see also chapter 13 above.

15. Gould, 'Edward Elgar, *The Crown of India*', 29.

16. Ibid., 30–1. On this kind of musical exoticism, see Edward Said, *Orientalism* (Harmondsworth: Penguin, 1985; New York, Vintage Books, 1978).

17. Accusations of Elgar's 'vulgarity' are legion. See for instance the unsigned review of Elgar's Symphony No. 1 in A♭, *MOMTR*, January 1915, 244.

18. Michael Kennedy places the war years in his influential *Portrait of Elgar* as the first unit in a third section entitled 'Decline 1914–1934' (Kennedy, *Portrait*, 265–87).

19. See Anderson's *Elgar and Chivalry*, 339.

20. Numerous explorations of British culture and music during the First World War have been published in recent years. Besides the ones specifically devoted to Elgar mentioned above, some of the material for this section is drawn from James DeGroot, *Blighty! British Society in the Era of the Great War* (London and New York: Longman, 1996); George Robb, *British Culture and the First World War* (Basingstoke: Palgrave, 2002); Stuart Sillar, *Art and Survival in the First World War* (New York, Basingstoke: Macmillan, 1987); Richard Cork, *The Bitter Truth: the Avant-Garde and the First World War* (New Haven: Yale University Press, 1994); and Glenn Watkins' *Proof Through the Night: Music and the Great War* (Berkeley: University of California Press, 2003). Of course, there was a great musical flowering of British response to the war after the fact, through compositions such as Ralph Vaughan Williams' 'Pastoral' Symphony and *Shepherds of the Delectable Mountains*; Gustav Holst's *Ode to Death*; Herbert Howells' Elegy for

viola and strings; Arthur Bliss's *Morning Heroes*, John Foulds' Requiem; and Frederick Delius's Requiem.

21. For instance, a long description in *The Musical Times* of 1 December 1917, 549, regarding the power of music to heal shattered nerves on the front includes a description of an amateur concert given to the soldiers in the trenches. Most of the compositions performed were by Germans or Austrians, with no British composers represented at all. Amateur choral societies formed on the front lines were more likely to sing Handel's *Messiah* than the work of contemporary British composers (see for instance *MT*, 1 June 1918, 260).

22. In the early days of the war, Elgar wrote to Alice Stuart-Wortley 'I *wish* I could go to the front but they may find some menial occupation for a worthless person' (*Windflower*, 136). In a sort of chivalric bravado he wrote to Lady Colvin on 25 August 1914 that 'I am going to die a Man if not a musician' (Moore, *Elgar*, 668).

23. Andrew Neill, 'Elgar's War: From the Diaries of Lady Elgar, 1914–1918', in Foreman, '*Oh My Horses!*', 24–25.

24. See *MOMTR*, March 1915, 377 and *The Times*, 11 April 1919, 9.

25. See Lewis Foreman's 'A Voice in the Desert' in Foreman, '*Oh My Horses!*', esp. 267–73.

26. Ernest Newman, 'The Artist and the People', *MT*, 1 October 1914, 605.

27. Robb, *British Culture*, 130–52.

28. See the letter from J. Lawrence Fry to Elgar, 5 October 1917, quoted in Moore, *Elgar*, 695.

29. Newman noted that 'To Women' and 'For the Fallen' 'provided a beauty that is by turns touching, thrilling, and consoling . . . it takes a lifetime of incessant practice to attain a touch at once so light and sure as this.' Newman, review of *The Spirit of England*, published in *Birmingham Post*, 9 May 1916. Excerpted in *Windflower*, 298.

30. Elgar's obligation extends to Jaeger, whose constructive criticism aided Elgar's early compositions; the conductor Hans Richter, whose patronage advanced Elgar to national fame; and the composer Richard Strauss, whose public comments garnered Elgar an international reputation.

31. *Lifetime*, 307.

32. Newman, '"The Spirit of England": Edward Elgar's New Choral Work', *MT*, 1 May 1916, 235–9, and 'Elgar's "'Fourth of August"', *MT*, 1 July 1917, 295–7. Both articles are generously littered with musical examples. Recent detailed analyses of the music include those by John Norris ('The Spirit of Elgar: Crucible of Remembrance', in Foreman, '*Oh My Horses!*',

237–61) and Watkins, *Proof Through the Night*, 52–6.

33. *MT*, 1 April 1916, 201.
34. *MT*, 1 June 1916, 296.
35. *MT*, 1 November 1917, 506.
36. Ronald Taylor, 'Music in the Air: Elgar and the BBC', in Monk, *Literature*, 336 and 352.
37. The characterisation is Elgar's own, see Moore, *Elgar*, 706. At the time of *Fringes'* publication, Kipling had lost his only son to the war, and he subsequently protested at Elgar's treatment of his texts. Consequently, the works were performed, published, and well liked, but Elgar did not assign them an opus number.
38. Charles A. Hooey, 'An Elgarian Tragedy: Remembering Charles Mott' in Foreman, *Oh My Horses!*, 319.
39. W. Wright Roberts, 'Elgar's "Fringes of the Fleet"' in *MOMTR*, February 1918, 278.

40. Anderson, *Elgar*, 151.
41. Taylor, 'Music in the Air', 351–5.
42. Anthony Boden, *Three Choirs: A History of the Festival* (Phoenix Mill: Alan Sutton, 1992), 268.
43. Maurice Devereux solicited Elgar's endorsement for Du Maurier Cigarettes in October 1931; Elgar put an emphatic '*Yes*' and 'Up jumps two legs!' on the bottom of one letter. For his endorsement, Elgar received 200 cigarettes each month. HWCRO 970.5:445, parcel 5/xvi.
44. See for instance, Elgar's remarks reported at the opening of the Dudley Opera House in the *MT*, 1 December 1919, 674, as well as his speech given at the opening of the His Master's Voice's Oxford Road building on 20 July 1921 (Moore, *Elgar on Record*, 37–41).
45. Moore, *Elgar on Record*, 44.

Select bibliography

Adams, Byron. 'The "Dark Saying" of the Enigma: Homoeroticism and the Elgarian
    Paradox', in Sophie Fuller and Lloyd Whitesell (eds.), *Queer Episodes in Music
    and Modern Identity* (Urbana and Chicago: University of Illinois Press, 2002),
    216–44, previously in *19th-Century Music* 23/3(2000), 218–35
Allis, Michael. 'Elgar and the Art of Retrospective Narrative', *Journal of
    Musicological Research* 19 (2000), 298–328
Allison, John. 'A Study of Edward Elgar's Sacred Music with Reference to his Life
    and Works' (Ph.D. thesis, University of Cape Town, 1989)
    Edward Elgar: Sacred Music (Bridgend: Seren, 1994)
Anderson, Robert. *Elgar in Manuscript* (London: The British Library, 1990)
    Elgar (The Master Musicians) (London: J. M. Dent, 1993)
    Elgar and Chivalry (Rickmansworth: Elgar Editions, 2002)
Atkins, E. Wulstan. *The Elgar–Atkins Friendship* (London: David and Charles, 1984)
Buckley, Robert J. *Sir Edward Elgar* (London: John Lane, The Bodley Head, 1904)
Burley, Rosa, and Carruthers, Frank. *Edward Elgar: The Record of a Friendship*
    (London: Barrie and Jenkins, 1972)
Craggs, Stewart R. *Edward Elgar: A Source Book* (Aldershot: Scolar Press, 1995)
Crump, Jeremy. 'The Identity of English Music: the Reception of Elgar 1898–1935',
    in Robert Colls and Philip Dodd (eds.), *Englishness: Politics and Culture,
    1880–1920* (London: Croom-Helm, 1986), 164–90
Del Mar, Norman. *Conducting Elgar* (Oxford: Oxford University Press, 1998)
Dunhill, Thomas. *Sir Edward Elgar* (London: Blackie & Son, 1938)
Elgar, Sir Edward. 'Falstaff', *The Musical Times* 54 (1913), 575–9
    (ed. Percy M. Young). *A Future for English Music* (London: Dennis Dobson, 1968)
    (ed. Jerrold Northrop Moore). *Elgar and his Publishers: Letters of a Creative Life*,
    2 vols. (Oxford: Clarendon Press, 1987)
    (ed. Jerrold Northrop Moore). *Elgar: The Windflower Letters* (Oxford: Clarendon
    Press, 1989)
    (ed. Jerrold Northrop Moore). *Edward Elgar: Letters of a Lifetime* (Oxford:
    Clarendon Press, 1990)
Fanselau, Rainer. *Die Orgel im Werk Edward Elgars* (Göttinger
    Musikwissenschaftliche Arbeiten 5. Göttingen: Andreas Funke, 1973)
Foreman, Lewis (ed.). *'Oh My Horses!': Elgar and the Great War* (Rickmansworth:
    Elgar Editions, 2001)
Gassmann, Michael. *Edward Elgar und die deutsche symphonische tradition: Studien
    zu Einfluß und Eigenständigkeit* (Hildesheim: OLMS, 2002)
Hepokoski, James. 'Elgar', in D. Kern Holoman (ed.), *The Nineteenth-Century
    Symphony* (New York: Schirmer, 1997), 327–44
Hodgkins, Geoffrey. *Providence and Art: A Study in Elgar's Religious Beliefs*
    (Rickmansworth: The Elgar Society, 1979)

(ed.). *The Best of Me: A Gerontius Centenary Companion* (Rickmansworth: Elgar Editions, 1999)

Hughes, Meirion. 'The Duc d'Elgar: Making a Composer Gentleman', in Christopher Norris (ed.), *Music and the Politics of Culture* (London: Lawrence and Wishart, 1989), 41–68

Kennedy, Michael. *Portrait of Elgar* (Oxford: Clarendon Press, 1968; third revised edition, 1987)

Elgar Orchestral Music (London: BBC Publications, 1970)

Kent, Christopher. *Elgar: A Guide to Research* (New York: Garland, 1993)

McGuire, Charles Edward. 'Elgar, Judas, and the Theology of Betrayal', *19th-Century Music* 13/3 (2000), 236–72

Elgar's Oratorios: The Creation of an Epic Narrative (Aldershot: Ashgate, 2002)

McVeagh, Diana. *Edward Elgar: His Life and Music* (London: J. M. Dent, 1955)

'Elgar', in Stanley Sadie (ed.), *The New Grove Dictionary of Music and Musicians*, second edition (London: Macmillan, 2001), vol. VIII, 115–37

Maine, Basil. *Elgar: His Life and Works*, 2 vols. (London: G. Bell, 1933)

Monk, Raymond (ed.). *Elgar Studies* (Aldershot: Scolar Press, 1990)

(ed.). *Edward Elgar, Music and Literature* (Aldershot: Scolar Press, 1993)

Moore, Jerrold Northrop. *Elgar on Record: The Composer and the Gramophone* (Oxford: Oxford University Press, 1974)

Edward Elgar, a Creative Life (London: Oxford University Press, 1984)

Newman, Ernest. *Elgar* (Music of the Masters) (London: John Lane, 1906)

Parrott, Ian. *Elgar* (The Master Musicians) (London: J. M. Dent, 1971)

Payne, Anthony. *Elgar's Third Symphony: The Story of the Reconstruction* (London: Faber, 1998)

Powell, Mrs Richard (Dorabella). *Edward Elgar: Memories of a Variation* (London: Oxford University Press, 1937; revised edition, Aldershot: Scolar Press, 1994)

Redwood, Christopher (ed.). *An Elgar Companion* (Ashbourne: Moorland, 1982)

Reed, William H. *Elgar as I Knew Him* (London: Gollancz, 1936, reprinted 1973)

Elgar (The Master Musicians) (London: J. M. Dent, 1939)

Richards, Jeffrey. 'Elgar's Empire', in *Music and Imperialism: Britain 1876–1953* (Manchester: Manchester University Press, 2001), 44–87

Riley, Matthew. 'Rustling Reeds and Lofty Pines: Elgar and the Music of Nature', *19th-Century Music* 26/2 (2002), 155–77

Rushton, Julian. *Elgar: Enigma Variations* (Cambridge: Cambridge University Press, 1999)

Shera, F. H. *Elgar: Instrumental Works (The Musical Pilgrim)* (London: Oxford University Press, 1931)

Thomson, Aidan. 'Re-Reading Elgar: Hermeneutics, Criticism and Reception in England and Germany, 1900–1914' (D.Phil. thesis, Oxford University, 2002)

Tovey, Donald F. *Essays in Musical Analysis (Symphonies, Concertos, Illustrative Music)* (London: Oxford University Press, 1935–9)

Turner, Patrick. *Elgar's 'Enigma' Variations – A Centenary Celebration* (London: Thames Publishing, 1999)

Young, Percy M. *Elgar OM: A Study of a Musician* (London: Collins, 1955)

Alice Elgar: Enigma of a Victorian Lady (London: Dennis Dobson, 1978)

Index

Acworth, H. A., 26, 64, 70, 72, 75, 76, 77, 78
Alexandra, Queen, 28, 30, 60
Allen, Sir Hugh, 23
Allgemeine Musik-Zeitung, 204, 205–6, 211
Anderson, Robert, 1, 86, 101, 223
Argyll, 9th Duke of, *see* Campbell, John
    Douglas Sutherland
Armes, Philip, 17
Arnold, Matthew, 61
Ashton, Sir Frederick, 56, 57
Asquith, Herbert Henry, 176
Associated Board of the Royal Schools of
    Music, 12
Atkins, Sir Ivor, 17, 95, 104, 113, 118,
    186
Augustine, St
    Civitas Dei, 104

Bach, Carl Philip Emmanuel, 4
Bach, Johann Sebastian, 27, 118, 193–4
    Bach Gesellschaft, 28
    Brandenburg Concerto No. 3, 27, 123
    St Matthew Passion, 100
Baker, Sir Herbert, 172
Bantock, Sir Granville, 21–2, 23
    Dante and Beatrice, 22
    Russian Scenes, 22
Barbirolli, Sir John, 1, 129, 191, 192
Barrie, Sir James M., 60
    Peter Pan, 58, 178
Bartók, Béla, 192
    String Quartet No. 2, 133
    String Quartet No. 5, 170
Baudelaire, Charles, 85, 91, 96
Baughan, E. A., 86, 89, 94
Bax, Sir Arnold, 22
BBC (British Broadcasting Company
    [/Corporation]), 9, 30, 195–203,
    217
BBC Symphony Orchestra, 197
Beethoven, Ludwig van, 5, 51, 107, 113, 148,
    177, 192, 205, 208
    Symphony No. 7, 141
    Wellingtons Sieg, 214
Bennett, Joseph, 87, 100
Benson, A. C., 28, 104, 174, 216
Berg, Alban
    Lulu Suite, 170
Berlioz, Hector, 141, 142
    Harold en Italie, 144
    Treatise on Orchestration, 5

Binge, Ronald, 77
Binyon, Laurence, 83, 138, 173, 203, 219–20
    Winnowing Fan, The, 219
Birmingham, 6, 8, 17, 18, 20, 52, 82, 87, 90, 95,
    113, 140, 147, 204
    Birmingham and Midland Institute, 22
    Birmingham Festival, 18, 20, 94, 100,
        101
    Birmingham Oratory, 91
    Birmingham Popular Concerts, 17
    Peyton Chair, University, *see* Elgar, Sir
        Edward William
Birmingham Daily Post, 220
Bizet, Georges, 4
    Carmen, 140
    Jeux d'enfants, 65
Blackwood, Algernon, 134, 178, 182
    A Prisoner in Fairyland, 134, 178
Blair, Hugh, 17, 113, 115
Blake, Carice Elgar, 7, 25, 32, 57, 58, 82,
    188
Bliss, Sir Arthur, 22
Boosey & Co., publisher, 28, 30, 68,
    217
Boosey and Hawkes, publisher, 30, 43
Boughton, Edgar, 22
Boult, Sir Adrian, 101, 102, 191, 197, 201,
    202
Bournemouth Municipal Orchestra, 22
Brahms, Johannes, 4, 89, 120, 141, 148, 205;
    developing variation, 129; influence
    on Elgar, 53, 54, 56, 64, 67, 75, 208
    Piano Quintet in F minor, 134
    Requiem, 66, 89
    Serenade No. 1, 67
    Symphony No. 1, 148
    Symphony No. 3, 154
    Variations on a theme by Haydn
        ('St Antony'), 69, 146
    Zigeunerlieder, 205
Breitkopf & Härtel, publisher, 24, 26, 28, 129,
    206
Brewer, Sir Herbert, 17, 113
Brian, Havergal, 22
Bridge, Frank
    Suite for strings, 124
Bridges, Robert, 200
British Empire Exhibition, 200, 223–4
British Library, 31
British National Opera Company, 196
British Shakespeare Society, 24

Cambridge Companions to Music